LEADING CASES IN THE LAW OF BANKING

Fourth Edition

By

LORD CHORLEY, Q.C., LL.D., M.A.
of the Inner Temple, Barrister,
formerly Sir Ernest Cassel Professor
of Commercial Law in the University of London,
Gilbart Lecturer 1938–39, 1953–54, 1964, 1966–68

and

P. E. SMART, LL.B., A.I.B.

LONDON
SWEET & MAXWELL
1977

First Edition 1953
Second Edition 1966
Third Edition 1973
Fourth Edition 1977

Published in 1977 *by*
Sweet & Maxwell Limited of
11 *New Fetter Lane, London,*
in association with
The Institute of Bankers, and
printed in Great Britain by
The Eastern Press Limited
of London and Reading

ISBN Hardback 0 421 23160 2
Paperback 0 421 23170 X

PREFACE TO FOURTH EDITION

THE Council of The Institute of Bankers, having decided with regret that it was no longer practicable to continue publication of their detailed *Legal Decisions affecting Bankers*, have associated themselves with the publication of this new edition of *Leading Cases in the Law of Banking*, which may now be regarded in part as successor to the Legal Decisions series, in digesting the cases that are of interest and concern to bankers. The eight volumes of the Legal Decisions series, covering cases up to 1966, will of course still be of use to bankers and others seeking full reports of cases that may not be otherwise easily accessible to them. The Table of Cases in this book includes the LDB reference for every case referred to which is to be found there.

In view of the transfer of the first author's *Law of Banking* from Pitmans to Sweet and Maxwell, it was obviously appropriate for the Case Book, which has from the first been based upon it, to follow. The text of this edition has again been kept in step with the *Law of Banking*.

In preparing this edition we have been able to consider more than 40 cases heard since the third edition was prepared in 1973. Perhaps the most important are *Lloyds Bank Ltd.* v. *Bundy*, which has extended the significance of the banker-customer relationship; *Metropolitan Police Commissioner* v. *Charles*, in which the Theft Act cases on the issuing of cheques reached their climax in the House of Lords; and *Aluminium Industrie BV* v. *Romalpa Aluminium Ltd.*, widely known as the *Romalpa* case, which has caused bankers and others to question whether the floating charge can usefully survive as banking security in its present form. The full implications of this decision have still to be worked out and the brief notes on it in this edition must be regarded as provisional.

But the banks now appear in the law reports more often in the area of international trade than in any other: the law covering basic domestic banking, explored by the courts in depth over many years, appears to be reasonably settled. A number of new cases since the previous edition reflect the increasing importance of the finance of foreign trade in the business of banking. Four of the most recent have had to be treated briefly in the Appendix; the *Cebora* decision and the later decision of the House of Lords in the *Nova (Jersey) Knit* case are considered in the section concerned with the nature of the bill of exchange; other cases in this area fall within the sections on Discount of Bills and Bankers' Commercial Credits. This latter section we have expanded to include also earlier cases of importance;

it forms the most substantial part of a new chapter on Financing by Bankers. It is perhaps of interest to remark on the fact that the law reports have so little on other aspects of the banks' lending function, which clearly do not give rise to much litigation.

In the preface to the previous edition we remarked on the number of recent changes in banking practice not yet reflected in the law reports. Since then the credit card has made a notable appearance there in the *Charles* case, but it remains significant that the credit transfer, or bank giro credit, the legal implications of which are discussed in *Law of Banking*, seems to be so much less litigated than the cheque has been through the years.

In the immediate past, however, the bankers' main concern has been, not with possible difficulties of the new developments in banking practice, but with the implications of the Consumer Credit Act 1974. No attempt has been made in this edition to discuss the many aspects of the Act that seem likely to affect banking development in the future: much of the Act still awaits implementation, and we have felt that speculation as to its possible effects would be premature in a book of this kind.

It may be hoped that the White Paper on *The Licensing and Supervision of Deposit Taking Institutions* will have fathered a statute before any further edition of this book is necessary. Then *United Dominions Trust Ltd.* v. *Kirkwood* will be of historic interest only; but we have for the present left the notes to the case unchanged, even though the Consumer Credit Act repeals the Moneylenders Acts referred to there, the repeals taking effect at dates to be appointed.

The Administration of Justice Act 1977, which received the royal assent as our text was passed for press, has *inter alia* repealed section 72(4) of the Bills of Exchange Act, as to which see *Barclay Bank (International) Ltd.* v. *Levin Bros. (Bradford) Ltd.* and in amending section 106 of the Land Registration Act 1925 has removed the proviso that caused difficulty in *Barclays Bank Ltd.* v. *Taylor*.

Again we thank reviewers of the previous edition for useful comment and criticism. And we are most grateful to Mr E. C. Woods, Ll.M., Principal of the Solicitors and Legal Department of the Midland Bank, for the many valuable suggestions which have helped to improve this new edition.

CHORLEY
P. E. SMART

LONDON
August 1977

PREFACE TO FIRST EDITION

THE absence of an elementary case book on the Law of Banking is a serious impediment to the successful study of the subject, especially where library facilities are not available, and this book is an attempt to fill the gap. Even professional law students working under expert supervision often encounter difficulties in the use of the different sets of law reports, and find it helpful to have recourse to the various volumes of leading cases which have appeared over the last thirty years or so. We think that this type of book is even more necessary for the young bank officer, struggling to understand a difficult branch of the law in which the decisions of the Courts are all-important, and working sometimes with little or no tutorial assistance.

The Institute of Bankers has, of course, long made available its own volumes of *Legal Decisions affecting Bankers*, admirable compilations produced under the most distinguished editorship, but more detailed and elaborate than is needed by any but the most gifted and industrious students, while their chronological arrangement does not lend itself to the study of any particular aspect of the subject.

We have had in mind in compiling this volume the needs of the ordinary candidate for the Diploma Examination of the Institute of Bankers. The method employed is that which has become usual in this type of book: a sufficient summary of the facts of a case to enable the student to grasp what it is about; the decision; and, where appropriate, an apposite quotation from one or more of the judgments of the Court. To this, the leading case, is appended a Note in which attention is drawn to other cases relevant to the decision, to passages in textbooks or articles which we think may help the student, and to any other material which appears likely to be useful. The general plan of the subject-matter follows the first author's *Law of Banking*, which embodies the results of a number of years of teaching in this subject.

We are most grateful to Mr. John Tonkyn, an Assistant General Manager of Barclays Bank Limited, who read the manuscript and made a large number of valuable suggestions. We are also grateful to the Incorporated Council of Law Reporting for England and Wales for permission to make use of their various series of law reports, to the proprietors of the All England Law Reports and *The Times* Law Reports for their like permission, to the Council of the Institute of Bankers for allowing quotation from their *Legal Decisions affecting Bankers*, and from the *Journal* of the Institute, and to Messrs. Benn Bros. for permission to quote from *The Miller*.

The first author, while accepting full responsibility for the contents of this book, would like to make it clear that the main burden and heat of the day in connection with its preparation have fallen upon the second one, who shouldered the onerous task not only of digesting the leading cases, but of preparing the materials for the Notes.

The second author, in his turn, wishes to record his grateful appreciation of the encouragement given to him by the Trustees of the Houblon-Norman Fund in their award of a grant to further the studies of which this book is in part the product; and to express his thanks for the unfailing co-operation he has found at the Library of the Institute of Bankers. Without this co-operation his share of the work would have been impossible.

CHORLEY
P. E. SMART

LONDON
August, 1952

CONTENTS

TABLE OF CASES

[*References in bold type indicate where the facts of a case are set out tn detail.*]

TABLE OF STATUTES

TABLE OF ABBREVIATIONS

Square brackets around the date in a citation indicate that the date is an essential part of the reference. Round brackets are used where the report is in a numbered series, the date being added for information only.

The Incorporated Society of Law Reporting have since 1865 published various series of reports of which the following are referred to in this book—

L.R.C.P.	Common Pleas	
L.R.Ch.	Chancery	
L.R.Eq.	Equity	
L.R.Ex.	Exchequer	
L.R.H.L.	English and Irish Appeal Cases	1865–75
L.R.P.C.	Privy Council Appeal Cases	
L.R.Q.B.	Queen's Bench	
Ch.App.	Chancery Appeals	
App.Cas.	Appeal Cases (House of Lords)	
Q.B.D.	Queen's Bench Division	1876–90
Ch.D.	Chancery Division	
A.C.	Appeal Cases (House of Lords)	
Ch.	Chancery Division	1891—current
Q.B. or K.B.	Queen's or King's Bench Division	
W.N.	Weekly Notes	1866–1952
W.L.R.	Weekly Law Reports	1953—current

Other series of reports cited in this book, and the years covered by them, are—

A. & E.	Adolphus and Ellis	Q.B. 1834–42
All E.R.	All England Reports	1936—current
B. & A.	Barnewall and Alderson	K.B. 1817–22
B. & Ad.	Barnewall and Adolphus	K.B. 1830–34
B. & C.	Barnewall and Creswell	K.B. 1822–30
B. & S.	Best and Smith	Q.B. 1861–70
Bing.	Bingham	C.P. 1822–34
Bing.N.C.	Bingham's New Cases	C.P. 1834–40
Bli.(N.S.)	Bligh, New Series	H.L. 1827–37
Bro.C.C.	Brown's Chancery Reports	1778–94
Burr.	Burrow	K.B. 1757–71
C.B.	Common Bench Reports	1845–56
C.B., N.S.	Common Bench Reports New Series	1856–65
C. & P.	Carrington and Payne	N.P. 1823–41
Cl. & Fin.	Clark and Finelly	H.L. 1831–46
Com.Cas.	Commercial Cases	1895–1941
Cox C.C.	Cox's Criminal Cases	1843–1940
Cr. & M.	Crompton and Meeson	Exch. 1832–34
De G.M. & G.	De Gex, Macnaghten and Gordon	Ch. 1851–57
E. & B.	Ellis and Blackburn	Q.B. 1852–58
Esp.	Espinasse	N.P. 1793–1807
Ex.	Exchequer Reports (Welsby, Hurlstone and Gordon)	1847–56
H. & N.	Hurlstone and Norman	Exch. 1856–62
H.L.Cas.	House of Lords Cases (Clark)	1847–66
Hare	Hare's Vice Chancellor's Reports	1841–53
I.R.	Irish Law Reports	1894—current
Jur.N.S.	The Jurist, New Series	1855–66
L.J.Ch.	Law Journal, Chancery Reports	1831–1949
Ll.L.R.	Lloyd's List Law Reports	1919–50

Lloyd's Rep.	Lloyd's List Law Reports	1951–current
L.T.	Law Times Reports	1859–1947
Macq.	Macqueen	1851–65
M. & G.	Manning and Grainger	C.P. 1840–45
M. & R.	Moody and Robinson	N.P. 1830–44
M. & W.	Meeson and Welsby	Exch. 1836–47
Mer.	Merivale	Ch. 1815–17
Moo.J.B.	J.B. Moore's Common Pleas Reports	1817–27
N.I.	Northern Ireland Reports	1925—current
Q.B.	Queen's Bench Reports (Adolphus and Ellis, New Series)	1841–52
Russ.	Russell	Ch. 1823–29
S.C.	Court of Session Cases, Scotland	1906—current
Sid.	Siderfin	K.B. 1657–70
Sol.J.	Solicitors' Journal	1856—current
T.L.R.	Times Law Reports	1885–1952
T.R.	Term Reports (Durnford and East)	1785–1800
Taun.	Taunton	C.P. 1808–19
V.L.R.	Victoria (Australia) Law Reports	1874—current
Ves. Jr.	Vesey Junior	Ch. 1789–1816

Other abbreviations used are—

C.L.Y.	*Current Law Yearbook*
J.B.L.	*Journal of Business Law*
J.I.B.	*Journal of the Institute of Bankers*
L.D.B.	*Legal Decisions affecting Bankers*

Textbooks mainly cited are—
Chorley, *Law of Banking* (6th ed.).
Hart, *Law of Banking* (4th ed.).
Holden, *Securities for Bankers' Advances* (4th ed.).
Paget, *Law of Banking* (8th ed.).

INTRODUCTION

As far as possible legal technicalities have been avoided in this book, but the reader with little previous knowledge of the English legal system may find the following notes useful. The dangers of attempting to deal with so wide a subject in so short a space are obvious, as is the desirability of further reading for anyone who wishes to obtain a clearer picture of the law.[1]

The present structure of the courts was established by the Administration of Justice Act 1970, and the Courts Act 1971. It comprises (1) the magistrates' courts; (2) the county courts; (3) the Crown Court, a superior court of record, which can sit anywhere in England and Wales; (4) the High Court, organised in three divisions—Queen's Bench, Chancery and Family—which can also sit anywhere in England and Wales, thus replacing the earlier assize courts; (5) the Court of Appeal; and (6) the House of Lords. Broadly speaking appeal lies from the magistrates' courts and the county courts to the Crown Court and the High Court. Appeal thence lies to the Court of Appeal (or in certain special circumstances direct to the House of Lords). The House of Lords in any case takes appeals from the Court of Appeal.

In this book we are principally concerned with the High Court, the Court of Appeal and the House of Lords, which need further elaboration.

The House of Lords has for centuries been the highest court in the realm. Only a small number of legally qualified peers take part in the judicial work of the House of Lords. They are mostly life peers, and are known as Lords of Appeal in Ordinary. The Lords of Appeal serve also as members of the Judicial Committee of the Privy Council, which hears, *inter alia*, appeals from such parts of the Commonwealth as have not removed themselves from its jurisdiction. Its opinions are given great weight by English and Scottish courts, but are not formally binding on them, in contrast to decisions of the House of Lords, which are binding upon all courts, and normally upon itself, although the House is now prepared exceptionally to overrule an earlier decision.

In the absence of any precedent in the English cases the courts will consider precedents from other jurisdictions, especially Scotland, Ireland, the Dominions, and the United States, but of course none

[1] *Learning the Law*, by E. Glanville Williams, gives an admirable outline of the whole subject, with bibliographies of each topic.

of these is in any way binding: they are in greater or less degree persuasive merely.

A High Court judge is "Mr. Justice Smith," and this is written "Smith J." The regular members of the Court of Appeal have the title of Lord Justice: Smith J., becomes Smith L.J. The Chairman of the Court of Appeal is the Master of the Rolls—M.R. Upon elevation to the House of Lords as a Lord of Appeal in Ordinary, Smith L.J. becomes Lord Smith (or whatever other title he chooses). There are a number of examples in the pages that follow of individual judges referred to variously as J., L.J., or Lord, as they have moved from High Court to Court of Appeal, or from Court of Appeal to House of Lords.

The head of the Queen's Bench Division is the Lord Chief Justice, who normally sits in this court, although he is entitled to, and sometimes does, sit in the House of Lords, or even in the Court of Appeal. The Lord Chancellor is the head of the whole judicial system.

The only change in this part of the legal system effected by the 1970 Act was in the organisation of the divisions of the High Court, one of which had previously been Probate, Divorce and Admiralty. This is now replaced by the Family Division, Admiralty jurisdiction being transferred to the Queen's Bench, which also includes the Commercial Court.[3]

Queen's Bench,[4] Chancery and Probate, Divorce and Admiralty dated from 1875, when the Judicature Act of 1873 radically reformed the whole legal system. There were initially five divisions of the High Court, but Exchequer and Common Pleas were merged with Queen's Bench in 1880.

Before 1875 the whole legal system was much more complicated than it is now, and it is not possible to summarise it adequately in the space of this note. There were then a larger number of uncoordinated courts; the banking student is concerned mainly with the decisions of Queen's Bench, Common Pleas, and Exchequer (the Common Law Courts), Exchequer Chamber (a court of appeal for certain common law cases) and the Courts of Chancery, which administered the separate body of law known as Equity. Trusts and mortgages were within the equitable jurisdiction, and are still the concern of the Chancery Division; contract (including the relationship of banker and customer) was a common law matter, and is still

---

[3] The so-called Commercial Court is merely one of the courts of the Queen's Bench Division to which a judge specially conversant with commercial law has been assigned for duty. Naturally many cases involving points of banking law are dealt with in this court.

[4] King's Bench from 1901 to 1952.

dealt with mainly in the Queen's Bench Division.[5] But since 1875 there is no conflict between the two jurisdictions, judges in either being competent to deal with matters touching upon the other, and precedence being given to equitable rules where there would otherwise be conflict between equitable and common law rules.

The simplification of the legal system brought about by the Judicature Act was preceded by a formalisation of what had been previously a highly individual system of reporting the law. The Table of Abbreviations includes such of the earlier reports as are cited in this book, and it will be seen that they are nearly all named after the reporters themselves. In 1865 the Incorporated Council of Law Reporting started the Law Reports, and the "private" reporters began to be superseded. Certain series belonging to firms of publishers, *e.g.* the *Law Journal* reports, have continued to the present day, and others have been started since.

Thus *The Times Law Reports* (not to be confused with the law reports that appear in *The Times* newspaper) were published from 1885 until 1952, the *All England Reports* have been published since 1936, and the *Lloyd's List Reports* since 1919.

There can be discrepancies between different reports of the same case (although these are minimal in the major series), and it is sometimes desirable to examine two or more reports of the same case in order to discover its true effect. As this book is chiefly designed for students it has not been considered necessary to give a multiplicity of citations in the text. The Table of Cases includes, however, all the major references as well as the appropriate citation for every case which is to be found in *Legal Decisions affecting Bankers.*

The reporting of any case depends upon its importance as extending or explaining the law, and many cases which do neither are not reported in any of the series Sometimes a case of real importance is omitted, and although this happens less often today than ever before, it will be seen that some cases in this book have as their only citation the *Journal of the Institute of Bankers*, or *Legal Decisions affecting Bankers.* These are cases which are not reported, or are not reported in any detail, elsewhere. One case, *Chatterton* v. *London & County Banking Co. Ltd.*,[6] is of particular interest: the trade paper, *The Miller*, contained the only full report of it.

In a few cases in this book[7] the plaintiff or the defendant is described as the "public officer" of a bank partnership. Until 1826

---

[5] But since company law and some important aspects of security work, such as mortgage and charges, are normally dealt with in the Chancery Division, the banking student is often concerned with that Division also.

[6] *Post*, p. 136.

[7] Cf. *post*, pp. 159, 235, and 272.

an action by or against a banking partnership involved the recital of all the partners' names, and this, as the joint stock principle slowly developed, became a troublesome matter. The Bank Act of 1826 made provision for such banking partnerships (which must not be within 65 miles of London) to sue or be sued through a duly appointed and registered officer, the "public officer." In 1858 banks of limited liability were first permitted but the public officers continued to act for those registered under the 1826 Act (or the 1833 Act, which made similar provision) that did not avail themselves of the new privilege.

It may be added finally that while in a High Court action the role of plaintiff and defendant is clear enough, care is sometimes needed to distinguish, in appeal reports, between the appellant, who is bringing the appeal against the decision of the lower court, and the respondent. The appellant of course may have been the plaintiff or the defendant in the court below: thus in the *Savory* case the bank were defendants in the High Court, and appellants in the Court of Appeal and the House of Lords. And the *Savory* case is an example also of the way in which the name of a case may change: on appeal to the Court of Appeal the name is unchanged, even when the defendant is appellant, but in the House of Lords the appellant is named first. So it was *E. B. Savory and Co.* v. *Lloyds Bank Ltd.* in the High Court and the Court of Appeal, but *Lloyds Bank Ltd.* v. *E. B. Savory & Co.* in the House of Lords.

An unusual change took place when *Gallie* v. *Lee* reached the House of Lords, for there the original plaintiff had died and the second defendant did not appeal, so the case reached the Lords as *Saunders* v. *Anglia Building Society*[8]: *i.e.* the executrix of the original plaintiff and the building society which had been the second defendant.

---

[8] *Post*, p. 241.

Chapter 1

RELATIONSHIP OF BANKER AND CUSTOMER

Foley v. Hill
(1848) 2 H.L. Cas. 28

Joachimson v. Swiss Bank Corporation
[1921] 3 K.B. 110

The relationship between banker and customer is that of debtor and creditor; but one of the terms of the implied contract is that money lent to the banker is not payable except on demand

Facts of Foley v. Hill

In 1829, an account in the name of the plaintiff was opened with the defendant banker, the initial credit being for £6,117 10s. It was agreed that 3 per cent. per annum interest should be allowed. There were later two debits on the account, for £1,700 and £2,000. Interest entries were shown in a separate column, and interest was not credited to the main account.

In 1838, the plaintiff sought to recover the money outstanding by an action in Chancery for an account. The account, being so simple, was held not to be *ex facie* a matter for a Court of Equity, and the plaintiff thereupon claimed that the relationship of a banker with his customer was analogous to that of an agent and his principal, and that he was entitled to an account on that basis; and that therefore, the relationship being of a fiduciary nature, the Statute of Limitations did not apply.

Decision

The House of Lords held that the relationship was that of debtor and creditor, and that therefore the matter was not a suitable one for an account in Equity.

In the course of his judgment, Lord Cottenham L.C. said:

> Money, when paid into a bank, ceases altogether to be the money of the principal; it is then the money of the banker, who is bound to return an equivalent by paying a similar sum to that deposited with him when he is asked for it. The money paid into the banker's is money known by the principal to be placed there for the purpose of being under the control of the banker; it is then the banker's money; he is known to deal with it as his own; he makes what profit of it he can, which profit he retains to himself, paying back only the principal, according to the custom of bankers

in some places, or the principal and a small rate of interest, according to the custom of bankers in other places. The money placed in the custody of a banker is, to all intents and purposes, the money of the banker, to do with it as he pleases; he is guilty of no breach of trust in employing it; he is not answerable to the principal if he puts it into jeopardy, if he engages in a hazardous speculation; he is not bound to keep it, or deal with it, as the property of his principal, but he is of course answerable for the amount, because he has contracted, having received that money, to repay to the principal, when demanded, a sum equivalent to that paid into his hands.

That has been the subject of discussion in various cases. . . . That being established to be the relative situations of banker and customer, the banker is not an agent, or factor but he is a debtor.[1]

And Lord Brougham said:

This trade of a banker is to receive money, and use it as if it were his own, he becoming debtor to the person who has lent or deposited with him the money to use as his own. . .[2]

Facts of Joachimson v. Swiss Bank Corporation

The plaintiff firm was a partnership between two Germans and a naturalised Englishman, carrying on business in Manchester. On August 1, 1914, one of the Germans died and the partnership was thus dissolved. On the outbreak of war three days later the other German became an enemy alien. On August 1, the firm's account with the defendant bank was £2,321 in credit.

On June 5, 1919, the naturalised partner commenced an action in the name of the firm to recover this sum, the cause of action being alleged to have arisen on or before August 1, 1914. The firm had not made any demand on or before that date for payment of the sum in question and the bank (which had counter-claimed for a larger sum than the balance of the account) pleaded on the point here at issue (*inter alia*) that there had thus accrued no cause of action to the firm on August 1, 1914, and that therefore the action was not maintainable.

Decision

On appeal, the Court of Appeal held that where money was standing to the credit of a customer on current account at a bank, a previous demand was necessary before an action could be maintained against the bank for the money, and the Court therefore entered judgment for the defendant bank.

---

[1] At pp. 1005–1006.

[2] At p. 1008.

In his judgment, Atkin L.J. said:

I think that there is only one contract made between the bank and its customer. The terms of that contract involve obligations on both sides, and require careful statement. They appear upon consideration to include the following provisions. The bank undertakes to receive money and to collect bills for its customer's account. The proceeds so received are not to be held in trust for the customer, but the bank borrows the proceeds and undertakes to repay them. The promise to repay is to repay at the branch of the bank where the account is kept, and during banking hours. It includes a promise to repay any part of the amount due against the written order of the customer, addressed to the bank at the branch, and as such written orders may be outstanding in the ordinary course of business for two or three days, it is a term of the contract that the bank will not cease to do business with the customer except upon reasonable notice. The customer on his part undertakes to exercise reasonable care in executing his written orders so as not to mislead the bank or to facilitate forgery. I think it is necessarily a term of such contract that the bank is not liable to pay the customer the full amount of his balance until he demands payment from the bank at the branch at which the current account is kept. Whether he must demand it in writing it is not necessary now to determine.[3]

And Bankes L.J. said:

Having regard to the peculiarity of that relation there must be, I consider, quite a number of implied superadded obligations beyond the one specifically mentioned in *Foley* v. *Hill*[4] and *Pott* v. *Clegg*.[5] Unless this were so, the banker, like any ordinary debtor, must seek out his creditor and repay him his loan immediately it becomes due—that is to say, directly after the customer has paid the money into his account—and the customer, like any ordinary creditor, can demand repayment of the loan by his debtor at any time and place. . . . It seems to me impossible to imagine the relation between banker and customer as it exists today, without the stipulation that, if the customer seeks to withdraw his loan, he must make application to the banker for it.[6]

Notes [7]

The importance of *Foley* v. *Hill* was that it authoritatively established the legal basis of the relationship of banker and customer as that of debtor and creditor, a position which on the earlier cases was by no means clear. Originally the goldsmith-banker had accepted gold and valuables for safe custody, and his position had been that of a bailee. As the relationship began to assume its modern form, the fundamental aspect of which is that the customer

[3] At p. 127.
[4] *Supra.*
[5] (1847) 16 M. & W. 321.
[6] At pp. 119–121.
[7] The nature of the contract between banker and customer is discussed at length in Chorley, *Law of Contract in Relation to the Law of Banking* (Gilbart Lectures, 1964).

draws bills of exchange (now usually in the form of cheques) upon the banker, the bailment basis became quite inadequate for the solution of the legal problems arising, and an attempt was made to equate the position with that of agent and principal. An agent holding the moneys of his principal is under very strict obligations, and in particular must meticulously account for its use within the terms of his authority. If bankers had so to account the practice of banking as we know it today would be hardly possible. The decision in *Foley* v. *Hill* definitely rejected this view of the matter and established a basis for the relationship which left the banker quite free in his use of the moneys received from his customers. It is accordingly a case of the first importance.

The simple debtor–creditor relationship was accepted as fundamental, but it is not altogether satisfactory without refinements on the ordinary rules of debtor and creditor. For example, the enforcement of the rule that the debtor must seek out his creditor would give rise to obvious difficulty. The second case, *Joachimson* v. *Swiss Bank Corporation*, initiated the development of these refinements and carried the implications of *Foley* v. *Hill* a stage further, in deciding not only that the money is lent to the banker, who is thus able to do what he likes with it, but also that it is not repayable until demand is made. If the rule as to the debtor seeking out his creditor were applied to the banker, not only would his customer be entitled at any time to issue a writ against him for the balance of his account (as happened in effect in the *Joachimson* case) but on his side the banker could close the account without notice by repaying that balance. Either proposition would clearly not be in accord with the recognised function of the banker, and the (theoretical) dislocation of business which would have resulted from any other ruling was a reason which weighed with the Court in reaching the decision they did.

In *Arab Bank Ltd.* v. *Barclays Bank* (*D.C. & O.*) [8] the appellants had an account with the Jerusalem branch of the respondent bank, and had been unable to operate it when war broke out between the new state of Israel and the Arabs. The balance, some half million pounds, was in due course paid to the Custodian of the Property of Absentees in Israel; but the appellants now claimed the money from the respondents, basing their claim in part on the *Joachimson* principle. They contended that as, on the outbreak of hostilities, no demand had been made, there was thereafter no debt that could be properly transferred to the Custodian; and, the contract between banker and customer being wholly frustrated, a new right accrued

[8] [1954] A.C. 495.

to the customers to be paid the balance of the account as money had and received for a consideration that had wholly failed. This right, being independent of the contract, did not depend on prior demand and could be claimed away from the branch at which the account had been kept. The House of Lords unanimously rejected this argument, holding that while partly-performed contracts are frustrated by the outbreak of war, which prevents further performance, executed contracts in which only payment of a debt remains to be made, are merely suspended. In the case of a banking account, although demand is needed before action can be brought, a debt is owing by the bank to its customer before any demand for payment is made.

This decision of the House of Lords carries a little further the elucidation of a question that has been discussed ever since the *Joachimson* decision—what the effect of that decision was on garnishee proceedings.[9] The basis of the procedure, Order 45, rule 1, authorises the order nisi only when there is a debt " owing or accruing due " to the judgment debtor. Did the *Joachimson* decision establish that there was no such debt until demand was made? Atkin L.J. thought not; he said " this expression (debts owing or accruing) includes debts to which the judgment debtor is entitled though they are not presently payable." Bankes and Warrington L.JJ. considered that the service of the garnishee order would itself operate as sufficient demand, and this opinion was approved and extended in the *Rekstin* case[10] and accepted as settled law in *Bagley* v. *Winsome.*[11] In the *Arab Bank* case Lord Reid said (although not in connection with garnishee procedure) " the existence of a debt does not depend on there being a present right to sue for it. *Debitum in praesenti, solvendum in futuro* is a familiar concept, and a demand for payment is in my view merely that which makes the debt *solvendum.*"

The point has been fully discussed on more than one occasion,[12] but it is to some extent an academic one. In practice bankers have continued to treat garnishee orders as they had treated them before the *Joachimson* decision, and the *Arab Bank* decision probably makes it even more unlikely than it was before that the courts would now apply the demand rule to inhibit the garnishee procedure.

The *Joachimson* decision was concerned with current accounts; in the case of deposit accounts there are usually other considerations

[9] For an explanation of garnishee proceedings see Chorley, *Law of Banking* (6th ed.), p. 64 and *cf. post*, pp. 50 *et seq.*

[10] *Post*, p. 53.

[11] *Post*, p. 54.

[12] Chorley, *op. cit.*, p. 65; Paget, *Law of Banking* (8th ed.), p. 147.

precedent to the right to withdraw—a fixed period of notice (seldom enforced, an appropriate deduction of interest taking its place) and the production of deposit receipt or deposit book where either has been issued. In such cases the balance is clearly not payable until the conditions have been fulfilled, but the rule in the *Joachimson* case would presumably apply in the case of a demand deposit if the book was (as quite often happens) left in the hands of the bank.

The demand must be at the branch at which the account is kept —*cf.* in addition to the statement of Atkin L.J. itself, *Isaacs* v. *Barclays Bank Ltd. and Barclays Bank (France) Ltd.*,[13] where the position was discussed but not decided, and the *Arab Bank* case.[14]

A rather surprising attempt to extend the banker–customer relationship to one of general agency failed in *Midland Bank Ltd.* v. *Conway Corporation*,[15] when the corporation sought to serve on the bank an abatement notice in respect of a statutory nuisance. The bank had paid rates on the property in question on the instructions of their customer, the owner, who lived overseas; they had also received rent, knowing it to be rent. But a Divisional Court held that they had acted only as bankers, and their actions did not constitute them agents for the general management of the property: there was no super-added special relationship of this kind. In other words, the basic relationship is still one of debtor and creditor.

Tournier v. National Provincial and Union Bank of England

[1924] 1 K.B. 461

It is a further term of the implied contract that the bank enters into a qualified obligation not to disclose information concerning the customer's affairs without his consent

Facts

The plaintiff was a customer of the defendant bank. In April 1922, his account being £9 8s. 6d. overdrawn, he signed a document agreeing to pay this amount off by weekly instalments of £1. On the document the plaintiff wrote the name and address of a firm, Kenyon & Co., whose employ he was about to enter as a traveller, on a three months' contract.

When the agreement to repay was not observed the manager of the branch telephoned Kenyon & Co. to ascertain the plaintiff's

---

[13] [1943] 2 All E.R. 682.
[14] *Supra.*
[15] [1965] 1 W.L.R. 1165.

private address, and there followed conversation between him and two of the company's directors. The plaintiff said that in this conversation the manager had disclosed the facts of the overdraft and that promises for repayment were not being carried out, and had expressed the opinion that the plaintiff was betting heavily, the bank having traced a payment or payments passing from the plaintiff to a bookmaker. The plaintiff said that as a matter of fact the payment to the bookmaker was in respect of goods bought, and not of betting. The branch manager's version of the telephone conversation differed from that of the plaintiff in accent rather than in fact.

As a result of the conversation, Kenyon & Co. refused to renew the plaintiff's employment when the three months had expired. The plaintiff sued the defendant bank for slander, and also for breach of an implied contract that they would not disclose to third persons the state of the account or any transactions relating to it. Judgment was entered for the bank, and the plaintiff now appealed.

Decision

The Court of Appeal allowed the appeal and ordered a new trial. In the course of his judgment, Bankes L.J. said:

> At the present day I think it may be asserted with confidence that the duty [of non-disclosure] is a legal one arising out of contract, and that the duty is not absolute, but qualified. It is not possible to frame any exhaustive definition of the duty. . . . On principle, I think that the qualifications can be classified under four heads: (*a*) where disclosure is under compulsion by law; (*b*) where there is a duty to the public to disclose; (*c*) where the interests of the bank require disclosure; (*d*) where the disclosure is made by the express or implied consent of the customer.[16]

And Atkin L.J. said:

> The first question is: To what information does the obligation of secrecy extend? It clearly goes beyond the state of the account, that is, whether there is a debit or a credit balance, and the amount of the balance. It must extend at least to all the transactions that go through the account, and to the securities, if any, given in respect of the account; and in respect of such matters it must, I think, extend beyond the period when the account is closed, or ceases to be an active account. . . . I further think that the obligation extends to information obtained from other sources than the customer's actual account, if the occasion upon which the information was obtained arose out of the banking relations of the bank and its customers —for example, with a view to assisting the bank in conducting the customer's business, or in coming to decisions as to its treatment of its customers. . . .

[16] At pp. 471–473.

In this case, however, I should not extend the obligation to information as to the customer obtained after he had ceased to be a customer. . . . I do not desire to express any final opinion on the practice of bankers to give one another information as to the affairs of their respective customers, except to say it appears to me that if it is justified it must be upon the basis of an implied consent of the customer.[17]

Notes

In *Sunderland* v. *Barclays Bank Ltd.*,[18] the customer, a woman, issued a cheque to her dressmaker. The bank dishonoured it, as there were insufficient funds on the account; as they knew of the customer's bookmaking transactions they did not wish to allow any overdraft on the account. The customer protested about the dishonour to her husband, a doctor, and he told her to take the matter up with the bank. She did so, by telephone, and after a while the husband interrupted the conversation to add his own protest. The bank then disclosed to him that cheques had previously been drawn payable to bookmakers. Upon the wife's bringing an action against the bank for breach of duty in making this disclosure, the bank contended that the conversation with the husband was a continuation of that with the wife, and that they had her implied consent to the disclosure. This the wife denied; but it was held by du Parcq L.J. sitting as an additional King's Bench judge, that on the facts the bank must succeed, the disclosure being in their interests, within the third of the qualifications on the duty of secrecy in the *Tournier* case.

As we have seen, the scope of the implied contract between banker and customer is a wide one, and the term recognised in the *Tournier* decision as a part of it is in addition to those outlined by Atkin L.J. in the *Joachimson* case. It is of course obvious that no such obligation of secrecy attaches to the normal relationship of debtor to his creditor, so that this additional qualification is of substantial importance. An agent is under the duty not to disclose information acquired in the course of his agency and in the *Tournier* case the Court of Appeal seem to have treated the banker as in this respect under the obligation of an agent. It would appear therefore that *Foley* v. *Hill* did not destroy the fiduciary aspect of the relationship of banker and customer as completely as had been supposed.[19] This point of view is reinforced by the decisions relating to the customer's duty to his banker in relation to the operation of the account,[20] the drawing of the mandate,[21] and countermand of the mandate.[22]

---

[17] At pp. 485–486.

[18] *The Times*, November 25, 1938; 5 L.D.B. 163.

[19] *Cf. Lloyds Bank Ltd.* v. *Bundy*, *post*, p. 14.

[20] *Greenwood's* case, *post*, p. 66.

[21] *Macmillan's* case, *post*, p. 43.

[22] *Westminster Bank Ltd.* v. *Hilton*, *post*, p. 69.

The general secrecy covering the customer's account, which of course continues after the account is closed, is recognised in practice as fundamental. A most important point in the present decision is the scope of the qualifications on the duty, and all the four classes of qualification outlined by Bankes L.J. need the careful consideration of bankers. The first, compulsion by law, is considered in the next section.[23] The second qualification is much less frequently seen in practice. The banker who knew that an account on his books was that of a revolutionary body, for example, or that it was being used in time of war in connection with trade with the enemy, would owe a duty to the public to report the facts to the proper authorities; but he would clearly need to be extremely circumspect in his actions. There are many examples of the third qualification, one of which is when, upon suing a guarantor, the state of the account guaranteed must be shown—as it must, also when the bank sues the customer on his overdraft; and the *Sunderland* decision [24] is another such example.

The last type of permissible disclosure, with the customer's consent, is of course the one most often seen in practice. The customer may instruct his banker to give some or all of the particulars of his account to, say, his accountant; and in such a case there is no difficulty. It is sometimes less easy to deal with the questions asked by a proposing guarantor about the account he is to guarantee: has the customer in such a case given his implied consent to disclosure (where his express consent is lacking) by seeking to obtain the guarantee or should this properly be regarded as another example of the third group? This is a matter in which the reasonableness or otherwise of the questions must be the chief criterion, for while the guarantee may be avoided by misrepresentation there must clearly be no unnecessary disclosure.[25]

The greatest difficulty, however, and that most often discussed, has been caused by the answering of credit inquiries. Bankers' references are a useful part of the machinery of commerce, and the practice of using them has more than once received judicial approval, perhaps most notably in *Parsons* v. *Barclay & Co. Ltd.*,[26] where Cozens-Hardy M.R. spoke (at p. 252) of:

> . . . that very wholesome and useful habit by which one banker answers in confidence, and answers honestly, to another banker, the answer being given at the request and with the knowledge of the first banker's customer. . . .

There are however obvious dangers for the banker answering the inquiry. In the passage just quoted the customer's request and

---

[23] *Post*, p. 11.
[24] *Supra*.
[25] *Cf. post*, pp. 235 *et seq*.
[26] (1910) 2 L.D.B. 248.

knowledge are seen (in 1910) as essential parts of the " wholesome habit." Atkin L.J. in the passage quoted from his judgment in the *Tournier* case, 14 years later, saw the practice as justified only with the implied consent of the customer. His consent is plainly enough implied when he himself gives his banker as a referee; but the practice has grown up of answering all inquiries, provided that they come from other banks, with no knowledge whether the customer has himself given the bank as referee, or indeed whether he would or would not wish the inquiry to be answered. The banks could easily enough, if challenged, prove the existence of this usage, but it might not be possible to prove that it is understood and accepted by the general public—or, indeed, that it is in essence reasonable: for if A cannot be answered when he asks questions direct about B's finances (as the *Tournier* case demonstrates that he cannot) why may he be answered merely because he makes his inquiry at second hand?

It was pointed out some years ago [27] that the danger may be even greater in the practice amongst firms whose business makes a large number of credit inquiries necessary, of addressing such inquiries direct to the bankers of the subjects of them, with a request that the replies be sent to the inquirer's bankers. Whatever sanction custom has given to normal inquiry procedure may rest in part upon the fact that the inquirer's banker supervises the inquiry, and can indeed refuse to make any he has reason to regard as improper. Although in fact this supervision is very little exercised, the power of supervision exists so long as inquiries are made in this way, and its theoretical importance might be considerable in resisting a customer aggrieved by an unfavourable answer; while the banker's defence that the answering of inter-bank inquiries is common usage cannot be easily extended to a modification of the practice that may be too new for the public generally to be aware of it.

The position cannot be said to be clear; in the absence of decided cases the banker can merely follow normal usage and hope that it does not prove to be legally unjustified. Certainly any departure from that usage should be entertained only with a full appreciation of the dangers of such departure.[28]

---

[27] In an article, " Changes in Banking Law and Practice," by John Tonkyn (June 1950) 71 J.I.B. 148; and see Mather, *Banker and Customer Relationship*, pp. 31 *et seq*. *Cf.* Chorley, *op. cit.*, pp. 248 *et seq.*

[28] *Cf. post*, pp. 295 *et seq.*, as to the position, *vis-à-vis* the inquirer, of the banker answering a credit inquiry concerning his customer.

Williams and Others v. Summerfield
[1972] 2 Q.B. 513

Disclosure of information concerning the customer's affairs by compulsion of law

Facts

When the Bristol police sought to inspect the banking accounts of certain defendants in a criminal prosecution the magistrate made the order required under section 7 of the Bankers' Books Evidence Act 1879. The defendants appealed, arguing, *inter alia*, that the Act was intended only to provide a procedural method to allow evidence not otherwise admissible, and did not alter the fundamental proposition that a defendant in criminal proceedings should not be required to incriminate himself.

Section 7 provides:

> On the application of any party to a legal proceeding a court or judge may order that such party be at liberty to inspect and take copies of any entries in a banker's book for any of the purposes of such proceedings. . . .

Decision

The Divisional Court dismissed the appeal. Lord Widgery C.J. pointed out that acceptance of the appellants' argument would mean in practice that the Act does not apply to any criminal proceedings, whereas the Act is explicit that it does. But, he said:

> . . . one must I think recognise that an order under section 7 can be a very serious interference with the liberty of the subject. It can be a gross invasion of privacy; it is an order which clearly must only be made after the most careful thought and on the clearest grounds. . . . I think that in criminal proceedings, justices should warn themselves of the importance of the step which they are taking in making an order under section 7; should always recognise the care with which the jurisdiction should be exercised; should take into account amongst other things whether there is other evidence in the possession of the prosecution to support the charge; or whether the application under section 7 is a fishing expedition in the hope of finding some material on which the charge can be hung.[29]

Notes

As Lord Widgery remarked, this was the first case in close on a 100 years since the Bankers' Books Evidence Act was passed in which its application to criminal proceedings had been tested. In

[29] At p. 518.

civil cases, he said, " the courts have set their face against section 7 being used as a kind of searching inquiry or fishing expedition beyond the ordinary rules of discovery," and it may be taken that his statement regarding the care that should be exercised in the making of a section 7 order is relevant to civil as well as to criminal cases.

The Act is probably the best known example of the first of the four qualifications to the " no disclosure " rule set out by Bankes L.J.[30] In fact the primary purpose of the Act was, in Lord Widgery's words, " to enable entries in a banker's books to be proved in legal proceedings without the disruption of the bank which would result if the original books had to be taken away and kept in court," and it is not until section 7, " that one finds any kind of provision in this Act whereby an application of a hostile character can be made." Even here there was no change in substantive law: " the ordinary rules of discovery " cannot be extended by means of the section.

There are other circumstances in which the banker's duty of secrecy is qualified by compulsion of law. Thus by the Companies Act 1948 the banker is obliged to make what disclosures are relevant when an officer of a company is prosecuted, or when an investigation into the affairs of a company is undertaken by the Department of Trade, or in winding-up proceedings.

The income tax legislation gives what appears to be increasing access to the banker's books. As long ago as 1928, in *Att.-Gen.* v. *National Provincial Bank Ltd.*,[31] it was held that under section 103 of the Income Tax Act 1918 (now s. 22 of the 1952 Act) the bank must, in certain circumstances, name all persons for whom it receives interest on certain government stocks.

The 1952 Act gave the Revenue extensive powers of inquiry when tax evasion was suspected, and these provisions, and further extensions in subsequent legislation, were consolidated in the Taxes Management Act 1970 and the Income and Corporation Taxes Act 1970. Thus in *Royal Bank of Canada* v. *I.R.C.*[32] the bank was required to provide extensive information regarding transactions in securities carried out for their customer, a company registered in the Bahamas. The Revenue relied on section 414 of the 1952 Act, empowering the Commissioners to call for " such particulars as they think necessary," and Megarry J. held that the bank must provide the information sought; the proviso in the section protecting " ordinary banking transactions " covered only transactions in the ordinary course of banking business, which the

---

[30] *Ante*, p. 7. [31] (1928) 44 T.L.R. 701. [32] [1972] C.R. 669.

transactions in question were not. In *Clinch* v. *I.R.C.*[33] where the plaintiff, the managing director of the London subsidiary of a Bermuda bank, had been required to give the names and addresses of all customers for whom he had acted " in or in connection with any transaction or operation of a kind " listed under five heads, Ackner J. rejected his argument that the Act did not authorise questions to an intermediary about unidentified transactions on behalf of unidentified principals. He considered that the wording of the Act covered the kind of wide-ranging inquiry in question. (He did not accept the Revenue's initial contention, however, which questioned the court's power to interfere with an act of executive authority: " One of the vital functions of the courts is to protect the individual from any abuse of power by the executive, a function which nowadays grows more and more important as governmental interference increases.")

By s. 17 of the Taxes Management Act 1970, the Revenue can require a bank to disclose interest exceeding £15 per annum paid to any customer; and Schedule 6 of the Finance Act 1976, has significantly enlarged the Revenue's powers to call for documents in the possession of a bank in relation to a taxpayer's liability for tax arising from any business carried on by him or his wife.

However, it is important in the whole of this area that the banker should disclose no more than the law compels him to. An interesting example of a bank's caution in this regard is *Eckman* v. *Midland Bank Ltd.*[34] When the Amalgamated Union of Engineering Workers refused to pay the fine of £5,000 imposed by the National Industrial Relations Court, a sequestration order was made, and the Union's bankers, Midland Bank and Hill, Samuel Ltd., were required to disclose the assets held by them and to pay the fine. The banks argued that while the writ of sequestration entitled them to give the information sought, it did not oblige them to give it. The relationship between banker and customer was not one that consisted wholly of legal rights and duties, and a banker should not take any action of this kind of which his customer would disapprove unless compelled (in this case by an order of the court) to do so. Donaldson J. agreed " that strict compliance with obligations which bind in honour only is one of the hall marks of the most respected members of the banking community," but he rejected the argument in the present case: the third party in a writ of sequestration must not knowingly take any action that would obstruct the operation of the writ, and a demand by sequestrators for disclosure of property must be answered promptly, fully and accurately.

---

[33] [1974] Q.B. 76.

[34] [1973] 1 Q.B. 519.

It is also to be noted that Donaldson J. discussed in some detail, albeit *obiter*, the general effect of a sequestration order in connection with a banking account. He remarked that where there has been an agreed overdraft limit which has not been fully taken up " this facility is part of the property of the contemnor which the sequestrators are entitled to have transferred to them and which they can operate by authority of the writ of sequestration." Securities lodged to secure borrowing are also subject to the sequestration order, as to any margin not required to cover the borrowing.

Lloyds Bank Ltd. v. Bundy
[1975] Q.B. 326

There can be a special relationship between banker and customer over and above that of contract

Facts

The defendant was a farmer who had guaranteed his son's overdraft of £1,500 with the plaintiff bank, who were also his bankers, the guarantee being supported by a charge on his farm. When the son's business ran into difficulties the bank called for further security, and the father agreed to increase his guarantee and to charge the farm for £6,000. On that occasion the papers were left with the father, who showed them to his solicitor. The solicitor advised him not to commit himself beyond £5,000, half the value of the farm; but he went ahead with the £6,000 charge.

The son's business deteriorated further, and to support an overdraft limit of £10,000 the bank took the father's further charge. This time the papers were signed immediately in the presence of the assistant manager of the branch, who accepted that the father relied upon him for advice as bank manager.

Some months later a receiving order was made against the son, and the bank sought to sell the property. As the father remained in possession these proceedings were for his eviction.

Decision

The Court of Appeal allowed the father's appeal against the decision of the County Court in favour of the bank. The guarantee and the charge were set aside: the bank was in breach of the fiduciary duty of care which resulted from the special relationship between themselves and their customer.

Sir Eric Sachs said:

It not infrequently occurs in provincial and country branches of great banks that a relationship is built up over the years, and in due course the senior officials may become trusted counsellors of customers of whose affairs they have an intimate knowledge. Confidential trust is placed in them because of a combination of status, goodwill and knowledge. . . . The documents which [the defendant] was being asked to sign could result, if the company's troubles continued, in the defendant's sole asset being sold, the proceeds all going to the bank, and his being left penniless in his old age. That he could thus be rendered penniless was known to the bank—and in particular to [the assistant manager]. That the company might come to a bad end quite soon . . . was not exactly difficult to deduce (less than four months later . . . the bank were insisting that Yew Tree Farm be sold). The situation was thus one which to any reasonable person . . . cried aloud the defendant's need for careful independent advice.[35]

Notes

This decision is noteworthy as giving legal recognition to a "special relationship" which bankers have long recognised (more widely than "in provincial and country branches" only) and normally valued highly. Once the relationship commences and reliance is placed by the customer upon the banker as his financial adviser, the greatest care is necessary when the customer is required to give security to the bank; in particular, customers who may not understand the implications of the transaction must have an opportunity to obtain independent legal advice.

Lord Denning based his judgment primarily on inequality of bargaining power; only if that were wrong did he regard the case as also within the more restricted area of undue influence, in which the special relationship is relevant.

But Sir Eric Sachs concentrated on undue influence and the "confidentiality" which is an essential ingredient of the special relationship upon which undue influence is founded. And Cairns L.J. said that he had had doubts as to the existence of a fiduciary duty in the case, "but in the end . . . for the reasons given by Sir Eric Sachs . . . I have reached the conclusion that in the very unusual circumstances of the present case there was such a duty."[36]

All three judgments emphasised that the decision depended on the "very unusual circumstances." Lord Denning said: "Let me say at once that in the vast majority of cases a customer who signs a bank guarantee or charge cannot get out of it"[37] The special relationship, however, has possible relevance in other circumstances than those of guarantee or charge—cases like *Woods* v. *Martins Bank Ltd.* and *Wilson* v. *United Counties Bank Ltd.*[38] could be brought within its ambit (the dictum of Salmon J. in the former case,

---

[35] At pp. 344–345.
[36] At p. 340.
[37] At p. 336.
[38] *Post*, pp. 299–301.

quoted on page 301, is clearly relevant) and the continuing line of cases that originated with the *Hedley Byrne* decision [39] depend also on the establishment of special relationships to found liability for financial loss resulting from negligent statements.

It is to be remarked that the establishment of undue influence does not depend on fraud. Both Lord Denning and Sir Eric Sachs made it clear that they considered that the assistant manager had acted in good faith. The decision may not have the serious effect on banking practice which counsel for the bank had suggested " in somewhat doom-laden terms," but it does provide a warning that the relationship has its responsibilities as well as its clear benefits.[39a]

United Dominions Trust v. Kirkwood
[1966] 2 Q.B. 431

The definition of a banker is not static, but depends on current practice

Facts

The defendant was managing director of a company that had financed the purchase of cars in its garage business through " stocking loans " from United Dominions Trust, the company accepting bills for £5,000 drawn by UDT, and the defendant indorsing them. When the bills were not met and the company went into liquidation, UDT brought the present action against the defendant as indorser. His only defence was that as unlicensed moneylenders UDT were not entitled to recover the debt.

The Moneylenders Act 1900, which requires moneylenders to be licensed, provides in section 6 for the exemption from this requirement of, *inter alia*, bankers.

And the plaintiffs claimed to be within this banking exemption, producing evidence that they received money on deposit, and operated current accounts; that other bankers recognised them as bankers; and that the Inland Revenue allowed them to account for stamp duty on cheques by composition fee.

Mocatta J. finding for the plaintiffs, the defendant appealed.

Decision

The Court of Appeal upheld the finding in favour of the plaintiffs by a majority. Lord Denning M.R. said:

---

[39] *Post*, p. 295.
[39a] *Cf.* Woods, *Lloyds Bank* v. *Bundy* (December, 1976) 97 J.I.B. 219.

There are therefore two characteristics usually found in bankers today: (i) They accept money from, and collect cheques for, their customers and place them to their credit; (ii) They honour cheques or orders drawn on them by their customers when presented for payment and debit their customers accordingly. These two characteristics carry with them also a third, namely, (iii) They keep current accounts, or something of that nature, in their books in which the credits and debits are entered. Those three characteristics are much the same as those stated in Paget's *Law of Banking* (6th ed., 1961), p. 8: "No-one and nobody, corporate or otherwise, can be a ' banker ' who does not (i) take current accounts; (ii) pay cheques drawn on himself; (iii) collect cheques for his customers." [40]

Notes [41]

Generations of banking students have been amused when they first came upon section 2 of the Bills of Exchange Act, which states that "' Banker ' includes a body of persons whether incorporated or not who carry on the business of banking." The purpose of that section was, not to define the business of banking, but to make it clear at a time when joint stock banks were still not as familiar as they are today that companies and firms, as well as individuals, could be bankers. But the several other statutory references [42] do not carry definition appreciably further, and the Jenkins Committee [43] declined the invitation of the Board of Trade to provide a definition that would relieve the Board of its duty under the Companies Act of deciding which companies do and which do not rank as banking companies.

The question had not come before the courts in recent years until in 1966 United Dominions Trust were to everyone's surprise challenged in this remarkable case—remarkable not least because the plaintiffs' success was plainly contrary to the court's view as to the proper definition of banking. All three judges found that on the evidence before them UDT fell short of the requirements that all three agreed must be satisfied to constitute a banker; but Lord Denning and, with less conviction, Diplock L.J. based their finding in favour of the plaintiffs on their reputation as bankers: the banking community should know a banker when they see one. Harman L.J., perhaps more consistently, could not go with his brethren here, and although he recognised the unfortunate consequences that would have followed his decision, he would have

[40] At p. 447.

[41] The commentary that follows is unchanged from the previous edition. It may be hoped that the banking legislation currently proposed will resolve the problems discussed.

[42] As to which, and generally on this topic, see Ryder, Gilbart Lectures, 1970.

[43] *Cf. post*, p. 183; and (October 1962) 83 J.I.B. 318.

rejected the UDT case. And Lord Denning made it clear that other companies in the same situation as UDT could not rely upon a similar decision being reached again: they should seek a certificate from the Board of Trade. The Companies Act 1967 expressly provided that such a certificate should be conclusive evidence of the status of banker for the purposes of the Moneylenders Act.

It is reasonable to believe that the legal definition of banking, based on the three criteria of Paget and Lord Denning, is now established as currently sound. It is interesting to note that the UDT decision was based on an examination of current practice; thus the receipt of deposits not withdrawable by cheque, which was formerly regarded as a further requirement, found no place in the new list. At least as interesting was the importance placed upon the opinion of other bankers.

Unfortunately definition is not the end of the matter. It was pointed out some years ago [44] that " the changing face of modern banking activities and the emulation of banking by other institutions may cause the problem to demand solution." The position has certainly not improved since then, and the curious mixture of remedies produced by the ad hoc treatment of the problem is still with us. The Moneylenders Act 1927 forbids moneylenders to suggest either directly or by implication that they are carrying on a banking business; but Board of Trade control for purposes of the Companies Act (and, by cross reference, the Protection of Depositors Act) applies only to the use of the word " bank " in the company name, and then only if it is registered under the Companies Act—the use of " banking " in the description of the company's business goes unchecked, and the Jenkins Committee rejected the Board of Trade's suggestion that some restriction should be imposed.[45] The Building Societies Act 1960 permits building societies to keep uninvested funds only in banks designated by the Chief Registrar, whose list is a severely restrictive one; but there is no legal bar to an individual or a partnership trading as X.Y.Z. Co., Bankers.

Lord Denning, in his judgment, suggested that Board of Trade registration could form the basis of a register of bankers—" and people will know where they stand." Registration, coupled with prohibition of the use of " bank," " banking " or " bankers " by unregistered businesses, may eventually be necessary. Clearly the protection of gullible investors would be the primary justification for such a step. A secondary reason can be found in the embarrassment caused to the clearing banks when an individual, trading as a

[44] Ryder, " The Legal Meaning of Bank " [1965] J.B.L. 34.
[45] Para. 446.

bank, or a company registered outside the strict confines of the United Kingdom, asks the bank at which the account is kept for clearing facilities. These can of course be refused; but a cheque drawn on X.Y.Z. Co., Bankers, and tendered for collection by a Barclays' customer in Newcastle or a Lloyds' customer in Penzance can be rejected only at the risk of offending good customers, and clearing facilities of at least a minimum nature can thus be exacted from the clearing banks by anyone who issues his own cheques and persuades people to open accounts with him. The paying banker, bound by section 79 (2) of the Bills of Exchange Act to pay his customers' crossed cheques only to other bankers, is in even greater difficulty, for if, with section 79 in mind, he refuses to pay a crossed cheque presented by X.Y.Z. Co., whom he refuses to recognise as bankers, and the firm later establishes that they are in fact a bank, he may be in breach of his contract with his customer. If on the contrary he pays the cheque, and X.Y.Z. Co. are not a bank, he is in breach of section 79.

The fact that the founding fathers of English banking commenced business in much the same way as the small pretenders to banking status of today may properly inhibit today's great banks from any too heated objections to newcomers. But just as "bank" and "banking" are useful bait for deposits, so less directly is the current account cheque book; and it would seem no unreasonable interference with free enterprise to have the kind of register envisaged by the Master of the Rolls.

Great Western Railway Co. Ltd. v. London and County Banking Co. Ltd.

[1901] A.C. 414

Commissioners of Taxation v. English, Scottish and Australian Bank

[1920] A.C. 683

A customer of a bank is one who has an account with that bank; but the relationship is not one of which duration is the essence

Facts of Great Western Railway Co. Ltd. v. London and County Banking Co. Ltd.

One Huggins, over a course of years, exchanged cheques with the respondent bank, although he had no account with them. In 1898 he obtained from the appellant company, by false pretences, a cheque drawn in his favour and crossed "Not Negotiable," for

£142 10s., and this too he exchanged, as to £117 10s. for cash, the balance of £25 being credited by the branch manager, at Huggins's request, to the local Council. The cheque was paid on presentation.

Upon discovery of the fraud, Huggins was convicted and action brought against the bank to recover the money, on the grounds, *inter alia*, that Huggins was not a customer of the bank within section 82 of the Bills of Exchange Act 1882.[46]

Bigham J. gave judgment for the bank, and this judgment was upheld by the Court of Appeal. The railway company now further appealed.

Decision

The House of Lords allowed the appeal, holding that Huggins was not a customer of the bank.

In the course of his judgment, Lord Lindley said:

> I cannot think that Huggins was in any sense a customer of the bank; no doubt he was known at the bank as a person accustomed to come and get cheques cashed, but he had no account of any sort with the bank. Nothing was put to his debit or credit in any book or paper kept by the bank. . . . Lord Justice Romer thought he was a customer because the bank had for years collected cheques for him; but in my view the bank collected money for themselves, not for him, in this particular transaction, and the evidence only shows that previous transactions were similar to this.[47]

Facts of Commissioners of Taxation v. English, Scottish and Australian Bank

On June 6, 1917, an Australian taxpayer delivered to the offices of the Commissioner of Taxation, in Sydney, a cheque payable to bearer for £786 18s. 3d., in payment of taxes owing. The Commissioner required all payments made at his office to be in cash, and it was for this reason that the cheque was made payable to bearer. The cheque was stolen from the offices by some person unknown.

On June 7 a person calling himself Stewart Thallon opened an account with the respondent bank, with a deposit of £20 in cash, and gave as his address certain well-known residential chambers in the town. On June 8 he paid in the stolen cheque for £786 18s. 3d. On June 9, 11, 12, cheques were presented for £483 16s. 6d., £260 10s., and £50 12s. 6d. Thallon was not seen again; the name was unknown at the address given and was presumably fictitious.

The Commissioner of Taxation brought an action against the bank for conversion. The bank pleaded section 88 of the Bills of

[46] Now s. 4 of the Cheques Act 1957.

[47] At p. 425.

Exchange Act 1909 (Commonwealth of Australia) (which substantially reproduces section 82 of the Bills of Exchange Act 1882). The Commissioner contended that (*a*) the bank had been negligent and (*b*) Thallon was not a customer within the meaning of the Act. The trial judge and, on appeal, the Supreme Court for New South Wales, found for the bank. The Commissioner now further appealed.

Decision

The Judicial Committee of the Privy Council dismissed the appeal, holding that the bank had not been negligent and that Thallon was a customer within the meaning of the Act.

In delivering their judgment Lord Dunedin said:

> Their Lordships are of opinion that the word " customer " signifies a relationship in which duration is not of the essence. A person whose money has been accepted by a bank on the footing that they undertake to honour cheques up to the amount standing to his credit is, in the view of their Lordships, a customer of the bank in the sense of the statute, irrespective of whether his connection is of short or long standing. The contrast is not between an habitué and a newcomer, but between a person for whom the bank performs a casual service, such as, for instance, cashing a cheque for a person introduced by one of their customers, and a person who has an account of his own at the bank.[48]

Notes

In a line of cases, including the first case above, it had been held that an account is necessary to the relationship of banker and customer, in addition to some degree of use and custom. In *Ladbroke* v. *Todd*[49] the plaintiffs were bookmakers, who posted to a client, Jobson, a cheque drawn to his order and crossed " Account Payee." The cheque was stolen, and the thief, fraudulently endorsing Jobson's name upon it, took it to the defendant banker and with it opened an account in Jobson's name. At his request the cheque was specially cleared, and on the following day he drew the proceeds and disappeared. The plantiffs issued a new cheque to Jobson and sued the bank to recover the proceeds of the first cheque as money had and received to their use, contending that the thief was not a customer of the bank within the meaning of section 82 and that the defendants were therefore not entitled to the protection of the section. They argued that " a person does not become a customer of a bank until the first cheque is collected." Judgment was given for the plaintiffs, on the grounds of the banker's negligence in not taking reasonable precautions to safeguard the interests of persons who might be the true owners of the cheque; but Bailhache J. said

---

[48] At p. 687.

[49] (1914) 19 Com. Cas. 256.

that, in his opinion, but for the negligence, the defendant would have been entitled to the protection of the section as having received payment for a customer:

> It is true that it was the first transaction that had taken place between them; but I have to look at the relationship between the parties created by the receipt of the cheque. Was he a customer of the bank when he handed the cheque to the defendant? I think he was. There must be a time when he began to be a customer. In my opinion a person becomes a customer of a bank when he goes to the bank with money or a cheque and asks to have an account opened in his name, and the bank accepts the money or cheque and is prepared to open an account in the name of that person; after that he is entitled to be called a customer of the bank. I do not think it is necessary that he should have drawn any money or even that he should be in a position to draw money. I think such person becomes a customer the moment the bank receives the money or cheque and agrees to open an account.[50]

This decision was criticised as being in conflict with previous decisions, but the Privy Council decision in the second case here dealt with goes far to confirm the view of Bailhache J. Privy Council cases are not technically binding on the other English courts, but the greatest weight short of binding precedent is attached to them, and more recently, in *Barclays Bank Ltd.* v. *Okenarhe*,[51] Mocatta J. quoted Bailhache J.'s dictum with approval.

The older view is probably now of academic interest only—that the word " customer " implies some course of dealing maintained over a period, and that an isolated transaction can never of itself make a customer. If that were so, the first collection on an account would *not* be made for a customer, but if it were followed by further transactions the relationship would be established and would be considered to " relate back." Nowadays the Bailhache view is to be preferred: anyone who ostensibly intends to continue the relationship may be regarded as a customer. Indeed, it has been argued [52] that the mere offer by the prospective customer to open an account, and its acceptance by the bank, creates as binding a contract as any other offer and acceptance.

This reasoning is in line with common banking usage. A person who has given satisfactory references and completed the bank's other formalities would be regarded as a customer even if he had not paid in at all; if he had been suitably introduced, and after the references had been taken up, a cheque book would be issued to

[50] At p. 261.

[51] *Post*, p. 195.

[52] See Chorley, Gilbart Lectures, 1955, cited by Mocatta J. in *Barclays Bank Ltd.* v. *Okenarhe*, *supra*.

such a person even before any credit was received, although an initial credit is the normal course of events upon the opening of an account.

In *Woods* v. *Martins Bank Ltd.*,[53] Salmon J. took the matter further, holding that when the bank, several weeks before an account was opened, accepted instructions to receive money and invest it on behalf of the plaintiff, the relationship of banker and customer was set up. Although limited to its special facts this decision must make the older view even less tenable; and although the banker would still be reluctant to regard as a customer a person for whom he merely exchanged cheques from time to time, it may be that even here a banker/customer relationship will some day be imported. It may be noted, however, as a point of academic interest, that the crediting to an account headed " Sundry Customers' Account " of cheques thus cashed for persons with no account does not make those persons customers.[54]

In the light of the increasing diversity of the business of the commercial banks, a question may arise in the future as to whether a person dealing with a specialist division of a bank is a customer of the bank in the full sense. The holder of a bank credit card who has no bank account would presumably not be a customer of the bank where the credit card operation is entirely separate from the bank, but, where the credit card is operated by the bank, it could clearly be argued that the card holder is a customer of the bank, even though he has no banking account in the accepted sense.

With regard to the apparent negligence of the bank in the *Commissioners of Taxation* case, in not taking up references regarding their customer, see *post*, p. 99.

It may be noted that a bank can itself be the customer of another bank. In *Importers Company Ltd.* v. *Westminster Bank Ltd.*,[55] Atkin L.J. said:

> The remaining point was that Heilmanns, being a bank, could not be a " customer." In my opinion, on the evidence, they were customers in every sense of the word. They had a drawing account with the respondents. But if they were in a different position, it seems to me that if a non-clearing bank regularly employs a clearing bank to clear its cheques, the non-clearing bank is the " customer " of the clearing bank.[56]

Stony Stanton Supplies (Coventry) Ltd. v. *Midland Bank Ltd.*[57] is an

---

[53] *Post*, p. 299. *Cf.* Chorley, Gilbart Lectures, 1964, for further discussion of the point here referred to.
[54] *Matthews* v. *Brown & Co.* (1894) 10 T.L.R. 386.
[55] [1927] 2 K.B. 297. *Cf. post*, p. 118.
[56] At p. 310.
[57] [1966] 2 Lloyd's Rep. 373.

interesting but quite exceptional case of an account opened in the name of a company eventually proving to have founded no banker/customer relationship at all. In 1960, one Fox, an undischarged bankrupt, formed a company which later had the name Stony Stanton Supplies (Coventry) Ltd., the two directors being the proprietors of the company registration firm through which he had formed the company. Fox had entered into negotiations for the purchase of an old-established wholesale grocery business, R. H. Taylor (Coventry) Ltd. Mr. Taylor agreed to sell, and introduced Fox to the manager of his own branch of the Midland Bank. Fox in due course produced to the branch manager the forms necessary for opening an account in the name of the Stony Stanton Company, the forms purporting to be signed by the two directors as chairman and secretary. These signatures were forgeries. Money thereafter coming into the Taylor business was paid in to the new account, and drawn upon by Fox, on forged signatures, for his own purposes. When the fraud was discovered Fox received a prison sentence, and Mr. Taylor's company obtained a winding-up order against the Stony Stanton Company. The present action was for the recovery of some £9,000, the amounts drawn by Fox from the account in the company's name. The Court of Appeal, upholding the decision of McNair J. in favour of the bank, held that the company had given no authority to Fox to buy the grocery business, no contract between the company and R. H. Taylor Ltd. had been signed, the company had never had any title to the funds passing through the account (in the opening of which, in the circumstances, there had been no negligence), and there had been no banker/customer relationship between the bank and the company, to which therefore the bank owed no duty.

Reference may be made here to *Burnett* v. *Westminster Bank Ltd.*,[58] widely commented upon as the first case concerning the banks' automated book-keeping, which is of legal interest primarily in its relevance to the contract between banker and customer.

On the introduction of automated book-keeping the bank printed on the covers of cheque books a warning that the cheques (and credit slips) in the books, all of which bore magnetic ink characters, would " be applied to the account for which they have been prepared. Customers must not, therefore, permit their use on any other account." The plaintiff, who had accounts at two branches of the bank, at only one of which the book-keeping was automated, altered a cheque on this branch with the intention of drawing on his account at the other branch. He later instructed the non-

[58] [1966] 1 Q.B. 742.

automated branch to stop payment of the cheque; but the magnetic ink coding took the cheque to the automated branch, where it was paid, no one noticing the handwritten alteration. Mocatta J. held that the wording on the cover of the cheque book was not adequate notice to alter the pre-existing contractual relationship, unless the bank could show that the customer had read the words, or had agreed in writing to their effect. He said that he would have been prepared to accept the signature on the cheque as signifying such agreement if the warning had been printed on the cheque itself (in the way, it will be noted, that the right to refuse payment against uncleared effects is reserved on credit slips: *cf. post*, p. 83 *et seq.*); he said also that the position *might* have been different if the cheque book had been the first issued to a new customer, instead of one issued to an established customer who had previously received other cheque books that did not bear any of the terms of the contract.

The case raises points of interest only regarding the nature of the cheque as a mandate, and the possibility, not at issue before the Court, that a bank might be held to be negligent in not scrutinising automated cheques.[59]

---

[59] *Cf.* Chorley, Gilbart Lectures, 1966, and *The Banker* (August 1965), Vol. 55, p. 528.

Chapter 2

CHEQUES

Bavins Junr. & Sims v. London and South Western Bank

(1899) 81 L.T. 655

A cheque must be an unconditional order

Facts

An instrument in the form of a cheque, but with the order to pay followed by the words: " Provided the receipt form at foot hereof is duly signed, stamped and dated," was stolen from the plaintiffs, the payees of the instrument, and was later paid in for the credit of a customer of the defendant bank, which duly collected it for his account. The receipt and the indorsement were not made by or under the authority of the plaintiffs, but there was no evidence that the customer for whom the instrument was collected knew that it had been stolen.

When the plaintiffs sought to recover the money as damages for conversion and alternatively as money had and received, the bank claimed the protection of section 82 of the Bills of Exchange Act 1882 (now s. 4 of the Cheques Act 1957). Kennedy J. at first instance, held that, as the instrument was payable only upon the signing of the receipt, it was not an unconditional order within section 3 of the Act, (defining a bill of exchange) and as section 82 thus could not apply he gave judgment for the plaintiffs. The bank appealed, claiming that by section 17 of the Revenue Act 1883 (now s. 5 of the Cheques Act 1957), the provisions of section 82 of the Bills of Exchange Act were extended to instruments other than cheques.

Decision

The Court of Appeal approved the view that such instruments as that in question, being conditional orders, are not cheques. They found, however, that the bank had been negligent in not detecting an irregularity in the indorsement, so that even though the Revenue Act extended the protection of section 82 the bank here lost its protection.

Notes

The use of receipt forms on cheques, whether combined with endorsements or, as here, in addition to them, has very substantially diminished since the passing of the Cheques Act in 1957 made it generally known that the paid cheque is itself prima facie evidence of payment. Thus the earlier cases on the subject are now of largely academic interest.

They established that the effect of such receipts depended on the wording of the document. Instruments " payable only upon signature by the payees of a form of receipt at the foot of the instrument and not drawn upon the appellant bank . . . are clearly not bills of exchange"—*London, City and Midland Bank Ltd.* v. *Gordon.*[1] But in *Nathan* v. *Ogdens Ltd.*[2] the words, " the receipt at back hereof must be signed," were held to be addressed to the payee, not the banker, so that the order to the banker was unconditional; and in *Thairlwall* v. *Great Northern Railway Co.*,[3] a dividend warrant bearing the words, "Note: this warrant must be signed by the person to whom it is payable, and presented for payment through a banker. It will not be honoured after three months from the date of issue unless specially endorsed by the secretary," was held to be a cheque.

In practice the banks have long required of customers using any such form of receipt an indemnity which puts them, as regards the protective sections of the Bills of Exchange Act and the Cheques Act, in the same position as if they were handling ordinary cheques. It is to be noted also that as the Cheques Act relieves the banker of the liability to examine indorsements on cheques, that small minority of cheques for which receipt/indorsements are required carry a large R on the face.

The interest of the *Bavins* case as regards section 17 of the Revenue Act is entirely academic since the Cheques Act incorporated that section.

Slingsby and Others v. District Bank Ltd.

[1932] 1 K.B. 544

The effect of material alterations within section 64 of the Bills of Exchange Act 1882

Facts

The plaintiffs, who were executors of an estate, had as solicitors a firm, Cumberbirch and Potts, who assisted them in work connected with the estate, the partner Cumberbirch being the acting

[1] [1903] A.C. 240; *post*, pp. 130 *et seq.*
[2] (1905) 93 L.T. 553; (1906) 94 L.T. 126.
[3] [1910] 2 K.B. 509.

partner. The plaintiffs had an account with the defendant bank. Cumberbirch, who regularly drew cheques for the plaintiffs' signatures, drew one such for £5,000 representing an investment of trust funds, in the form "Pay John Prust & Co. . . . or order," with a space between the word "Co." and the word "or." The executors signed the cheque, and Cumberbirch then added in the blank space the words "per Cumberbirch and Potts." The whole of the cheque with the exception of the signatures being in Cumberbirch's writing, there was no apparent alteration or addition. He then indorsed the cheque "Cumberbirch and Potts" and paid it to the credit of an account with the Westminster Bank in the name of the Palatine Industrial Finance Co. Ltd., in which he was interested. The cheque was duly collected and paid.

When the fraud was discovered the plaintiffs brought an action against the collecting bank, the Westminster Bank, which they lost.[4] For technical reasons they did not appeal but brought the present action against the District Bank, and Wright J. finding for them, the bank appealed.

Decision

The Court of Appeal upheld Wright J.'s decision, holding, *inter alia*, that:

(i) The cheque having been materially altered within section 64 of the Bills of Exchange Act it was avoided as between the plaintiffs and the defendants, and the latter therefore lost the protection both of sections 60 and 80.

(ii) If the description of the payee as altered was a permissible one, the indorsement without mention of John Prust & Co. was invalid, and defendants were negligent in honouring the cheque.

In the course of his judgment, Scrutton L.J. said:

> The cheque, having been signed by the executors in a form which gave Cumberbirch no rights, was fraudulently altered by Cumberbirch before it was issued and, it was not disputed, altered in a material particular. . . . The cheque was thereby avoided under section 64 of the Bills of Exchange Act. A holder in due course might not be affected by an alteration not apparent, such as this alteration. But [the Westminster Bank were not holders in due course and] could not therefore justifiably claim on the District Bank, and the cheque when presented to the District Bank was invalid, avoided, a worthless piece of paper, which the District Bank was under no duty to pay. This invalidity comes before any question of indorsement. Secondly I am of opinion, as already stated, that if valid the cheque was not properly indorsed. The indorsement should have been "John

---

[4] *Slingsby* v. *Westminster Bank Ltd.* (*No. 2*) [1931] 2 K.B. 583.

Prust & Co., *per pro* Cumberbirch and Potts." Any attempt to prove a custom failed.[5]

Notes

The Bills of Exchange Act 1882, s. 64 (1), provides that a bill (or of course a cheque) materially altered without the assent of all parties liable upon it is avoided. If the banker pays a void instrument he cannot debit his customer with the amount of it.[6]

Section 64 (2) of the Act provides:

> In particular the following alterations are material, namely any alteration of the date, the sum payable, the time of payment, the place of payment, and, where a bill has been accepted generally, the addition of a place of payment without the acceptor's assent.

This leaves a number of points that may or may not be material, including for example the alteration of " bearer " to " order " in *Attwood* v. *Griffin* [7] (where the alteration was held in the circumstances to be not material), and an alteration of the place of drawing, as in *Koch* v. *Dicks* [8] (where the alteration from London to a German town was held to be material, Greer L.J. pointing out that an alteration from London to Southampton would not be material as it would not affect rights in the bill). The test of what is material is clear enough: in *Suffell* v. *Bank of England*,[9] Brett L.J. said: " Any alteration of any instrument seems to be material which would alter the business effect of the instrument. . . ." [10] But it is plainly undesirable that bills and cheques should be altered at all, and in *Koch* v. *Dicks*, Scrutton L.J. in placing upon the person setting up the altered instrument the onus of proving the non-materiality of the alteration, provided a salutary check upon any tendency to regard any such alterations as immaterial.

The significance of this one of the three *Slingsby* decisions [11] lies in its emphasis that a cheque materially altered as the cheque for £5,000 was altered becomes a nullity upon which the paying banker cannot properly pay, even though the position of a holder in due course *vis-à-vis* the drawer might not be affected by a non-apparent alteration; and in the fact that it lays down the correct form of indorsement for a cheque made out in the unusual, but by no means unknown, form of the £5,000 cheque.[12] The placing by Scrutton

[5] At p. 559.
[6] *Cf.* Chorley, *op. cit.*, p. 93.
[7] (1826) 2 C. & P. 368.
[8] (1932) 49 T.L.R. 24.
[9] (1882) 9 Q.B.D. 555.
[10] At p. 568.
[11] *Cf. post*, pp. 45, 116, 131.
[12] *Cf. Marquis of Bute* v. *Barclays Bank Ltd.*, *post*, p. 114.

L.J. of the principal's name before "*per pro*," although etymologically accurate, is not in accordance with common usage; "*per pro* Prust & Co., Cumberbirch and Potts" is the normal form. In any case, the important point is that the fact that it is an agent's signature must be apparent in the indorsement itself.

Reference should be made to p. 45 regarding the refusal of the Court here to apply the principle of the *Macmillan* case to facts only slightly different from those in that case.

The "opening" of a crossed cheque is the alteration most commonly seen in practice. Its dangers led to the resolution of the Committee of London Clearing Bankers in 1912 under which no such cheque was to be cashed without the full signature of the drawer to the alteration, and even so only for the drawer personally or his known agent. This rule is too often broken, and too often with unfortunate results for the bank concerned.

Griffiths v. Dalton

[1940] 2 K.B. 264

An undated cheque may be completed by the holder, but the completion is fully effective only if it is done within a reasonable time

Facts

In August, 1931, the defendant gave the plaintiff a cheque, undated, for £750. Nothing was done with the cheque until February, 1933, when the plaintiff filled in the date, February 20, 1933, and paid the cheque to his credit at a Brighton branch of the Midland Bank. The cheque was dishonoured, and the plaintiff brought this action upon it.

Decision

The Court found for the defendant.

In his judgment, Macnaghten J. said:

The plaintiff, by section 20 of the Bills of Exchange Act 1882, following what, I think, was the common law before the passing of that Act, had a prima facie authority to fill in the date, but by the common law he was bound to do so within a reasonable time. The question what is a reasonable time is a question of fact, and on the facts of this case I am satisfied that the reasonable time had long since elapsed. There was, therefore, no authority to fill in the date as it appeared on the cheque and no liability on the bank to meet it.[13]

---

[13] At p. 265.

Notes

Section 20 (1) provides that ". . . when a bill is wanting in any material particular, the person in possession of it has a prima facie authority to fill up the omission in any way he thinks fit."

The practice of bankers in refusing payment of undated cheques has been questioned, but although a cheque is not invalid merely because it is undated,[14] section 20 (2) provides that the filling up of any omission must be " strictly in accordance with the authority given," and " it is difficult to see what authority the customer can be supposed to have given to the banker in the circumstances." [15]

In *Griffiths* v. *Dalton*, 18 months was held to be unreasonable delay in completing the cheque. The position would have been different had the cheque been negotiated to a third party, who took it in good faith and for value, for section 20 (2) provides further that " if any such instrument after completion is negotiated to a holder in due course it shall be valid and effectual for all purposes in his hands, and he may enforce it as if it had been filled up within a reasonable time. . . ."

Bank of England v. Vagliano Bros.
[1891] A.C. 107

North & South Wales Bank Ltd. v. Macbeth
[1908] A.C. 137

The meaning of a " fictitious or non-existing person " under section 7 (3) of the Bills of Exchange Act 1882

Facts of Bank of England v. Vagliano Bros.

Vagliano carried on business in London as a merchant and foreign banker in the name of Vagliano Brothers, and banked with the Bank of England. One of his clerks, by name Glyka, with another clerk managed the foreign correspondence of the firm, and over a period forged the signature of Vucina, an Odessa correspondent of Vagliano, as drawer of a number of bills on Vagliano to a total of £71,500. All these bills were drawn in favour of a firm, Petridi & Co., in whose favour Vucina had drawn genuine bills on Vagliano. Glyka also forged letters of advice from Vucina, and the bills were duly accepted by Vagliano in the course of routine of the office, which also involved monthly advice to the

[14] Bills of Exchange Act s. 3 (4) (*a*).
[15] *Questions on Banking Practice* (10th ed.), p. 187.

Bank of England of these and other bills due to become payable during the month. Glyka obtained the forged bills again after acceptance and forged the indorsements of Petridi & Co., making the bills payable to B. Maratis or N. Maratis, non-existing persons, and obtained payment of the bills in cash at the Bank of England. He was later arrested, admitted the forgeries, and was sentenced to 10 years' penal servitude.

The bank had debited Vagliano's account with the amounts of the bills, and Vagliano now claimed that the bank must recredit him with such amounts. The bank contended, *inter alia*, that the bills were, in the circumstances, payable to fictitious or non-existing persons within the meaning of section 7 (3) of the Bills of Exchange Act 1882, and were therefore payable to bearer.

That subsection provides that:

> Where the payee is a fictitious or non-existing person the bill may be treated as payable to bearer.

Decision

On appeal the House of Lords held (on this point) that the payees named on the bills were fictitious or non-existing within the meaning of the subsection, that the bills were payable to bearer, and that the bank was therefore entitled to debit Vagliano with the amounts paid by them on the bills. In the course of his judgment, Lord Macnaghten said:

> On behalf of Vagliano Brothers it was contended that a bill payable to a fictitious person is not payable to bearer unless the acceptor is proved to have been aware of the fiction; and further it was contended that nothing but a creature of the imagination can properly be described as a fictitious person. I do not think that either of these contentions . . . can be maintained. . . . Then it was said that the proper meaning of " fictitious " is " imaginary." I do not think so. I think the proper meaning of the word is " feigned " or " counterfeit." It seems to me that the C. Petridi & Co. named as payees on these pretended bills were, strictly speaking, fictitious persons. When the bills came before Vagliano for acceptance they were fictitious from beginning to end. The drawer was fictitious; the payee was fictitious; the person indicated as agent for presentation was fictitious. One and all they were feigned or counterfeit persons put forward as real persons, each in a several and distinct capacity; whereas, in truth, they were mere make-believes for the persons whose names appeared on the instrument. They were not, I think, the less fictitious because there were in existence real persons for whom these names were intended to pass muster.[16]

[16] At pp. 160–161.

Facts of North & South Wales Bank Ltd. v. Macbeth

One White fraudulently induced Macbeth to draw a cheque for £11,250 in favour of Kerr or order. Kerr was an existing person, and Macbeth, although in fact misled by the fraud, intended him to receive the money. White obtaining the cheque, forged Kerr's indorsement and paid the cheque into his account with the appellant bank who in due course received payment of it. On discovering the fraud, Macbeth brought action against the bank to recover the money on the basis that by collecting a cheque to which their customer had no title they were guilty of the tort of conversion. Since the cheque had not been crossed, the bank were unable to rely for protection upon section 82 of the Bills of Exchange Act 1882.[17] However, they contended, *inter alia*, that the payee was a fictitious person within the meaning of section 7 (3) of the Act, and that as the cheque must therefore be regarded as payable to bearer, they could not have been guilty of conversion in collecting it.

Decision

The House of Lords held that the subsection did not apply; as the drawer of the cheque intended that the payee or his transferee should receive the money it could not be said, although this intention was induced by fraud, that the payee was fictitious.

In his judgment, Lord Loreburn L.C. said:

If the argument for the appellants were to prevail, namely, that the payee was a fictitious person because White (who was himself no party to the cheque) did not intend the payee to receive the proceeds of the cheque, most serious consequences would ensue. It would follow, as it seems to me, that every cheque to order might be treated as a cheque to bearer if the drawer had been deceived, no matter by whom, into drawing it. To state such a proposition is to refute it. . . . As to the authorities, I agree with the Court of Appeal in thinking that neither *Bank of England* v. *Vagliano*,[18] nor *Clutton* v. *Attenborough*[19] governs the present case. I will not discuss the former of those authorities beyond saying that it was not a case in which the drawer intended the payee to receive the proceeds of the bill. And in the latter authority the payee was a non-existent person whom no one either could or did mean to be the recipient of the proceeds of the cheque.[20]

Notes [21]

In *Clutton* v. *Attenborough* the appellants, a firm of land agents,

[17] Now s. 4 of the Cheques Act 1957, which extends the protection to uncrossed cheques.

[18] *Supra*. [19] [1897] A.C. 90. [20] At pp. 139–140.

[21] As to the effect of the *Vagliano* decision on the law regarding indorsements, see *post*, p. 78.

were fraudulently induced by their clerk to draw cheques in favour of Brett, there being actually no such person. The clerk forged indorsements in the name of Brett, and induced a third party to cash the cheques for him; the third party, the respondents in the present case, who acted in good faith, eventually obtained payment of the cheques, and upon Cluttons' suing them for the money they had received it was held that the cheques, being payable to a person who by any showing was fictitious, could be considered as payable to bearer, and that Cluttons' could not therefore recover.

In *Vinden* v. *Hughes* [22] a cashier filled in a number of cheques with the names of customers of his employers, obtained the firm's signature, forged the indorsements and negotiated the cheques to an innocent third party, who obtained payment from the firm's bankers. When the firm sued the third party for the amounts he had received, it was held that on the facts of the case the payees could not be regarded as fictitious or non-existing.

The importance of the rule that a bill payable to a fictitious or non-existing payee may be treated as payable to bearer arises from the fact that it enables any indorsement which may be forged upon it to be disregarded. The decision in the *Macbeth* case, however, deprives it of most of its practical value, since banks are for the most part concerned with cheques, and it will rarely be the case that a person who signs a cheque as drawer will do so without some knowledge of the payee. In this connection the reports of *Clutton* v. *Attenborough* are not at all satisfactory, but the case is intelligible only on the basis that Brett did not in fact exist. Occasionally, however, the whole business may be fictitious from the opening of the account, as in *Robinson* v. *Midland Bank Ltd.*[23] In that case, the report of which is of unusual interest for reasons not here relevant, there had been a blackmailing conspiracy against an Eastern potentate, called in the case Mr. A, who had been discovered in compromising circumstances with the wife of the plaintiff. The plaintiff was held not to have been a party to the conspiracy. Mr. A issued a cheque for £150,000 to prevent the plaintiff from bringing divorce proceedings, and the conspirators, without the plaintiff's knowledge, opened an account with the defendants in the name of the plaintiff. They paid into this account the cheque in question, and later drew out the proceeds. The plaintiff's action for money had and received failed because, *inter alia*, it was held that the bank was dealing with a fictitious customer, notwithstanding the use of plaintiff's name.

---

[22] [1905] 1 K.B. 795.

[23] (1924) 41 T.L.R. 170. *Cf. Stony Stanton Supplies (Coventry) Ltd.* v. *Midland Bank Ltd.* [1966] 2 Lloyd's Rep. 373; *ante*, p. 23.

In the *Vagliano* case the drawer of the bill was in fact the forger, only the acceptance being genuine. But since it is the intention of the drawer which is vital, the bill could properly be regarded as payable to a fictitious payee. This situation could not arise in the case of a cheque, because if the drawer's signature is forged it is quite immaterial that the payee is fictitious, since the paying bank must, unless there is an estoppel against the customer, be liable in any event.

It may be noted that the drawers of the cheques could not recover from their own banks because of the protection given to the paying banker by section 60; but this covers cheques only and there is no such protection either for the acceptor of a bill who pays the wrong person on a forged indorsement or for the banker who debits to his customer's account such a bill which has been accepted payable at the bank.[24] Lord Bramwell's dissenting judgment in the *Vagliano* case was based on a principle which would have left the banker unprotected even in the circumstances of that case: ". . . [A] banker cannot," he said, " charge his customer with the amount of a bill paid to a person who had no right of action against the customer, the acceptor." The banker may be grateful that the majority of the Court considered this an over-simplification of the law.

It may be noted also that had the cheques signed by Macbeth been crossed the defendant bank would in all probability have been able to plead section 82 of the Bills of Exchange Act 1882, successfully (see pp. 94 *et seq.*). The protection given by that section is extended by section 4 of the Cheques Act 1957, which replaces it, to uncrossed cheques.

Orbit Mining & Trading Co. Ltd. v. Westminster Bank Ltd.

[1963] 1 Q.B. 794

An order to a banker in the words " Pay Cash or Order " is not a cheque but merely a mandate

Facts

The plaintiff company had two directors, who were authorised to sign cheques jointly on the company's account. One of them, Epstein, had some years prior to his joining the plaintiff company

[24] See *Robarts* v. *Tucker* (1851) 16 Q.B.D. 560; *post*, p. 77.

opened an account with the defendant bank. The bank was not informed of his new employment when he joined Orbit.

Epstein's co-director, on going abroad for short visits, left crossed cheques with Epstein signed in blank, and in August, 1957, and August and October, 1958, Epstein paid in three of these cheques, completed with his own (virtually illegible) signature and made payable to " Cash or Order," for the credit of his private account. He was not authorised to issue the company's cheques otherwise than for the business of the company, and he was not entitled to the money represented by these cheques. When his fraud was discovered the company brought an action against the bank for conversion of the cheques, totalling some £1,800.

MacKenna J. held that the three instruments were not cheques within section 73 of the Bills of Exchange Act, but were documents intended to enable a person to obtain payment from a banker within section 17 of the Revenue Act 1883, and section 4 (2) (*b*) of the Cheques Act 1957.[25] But he held further that the bank had lost the protection of section 4 (1) of the 1957 Act by their negligence.

Decision

The Court of Appeal, allowing the bank's appeal on the negligence issue, upheld MacKenna J.'s finding as to the nature of the documents.[26]

Harman L.J. said:

In order to be a cheque within section 73, the document must be a bill of exchange. This is defined by section 3 (1) of the Act of 1882, under which there must be a sum payable " to the order of a specified person or to ' bearer '." Clearly " cash " is not a specified person, and I do not think that unless made expressly in favour of the bearer it is enough to argue that " cash or order " in the end as a matter of construction means " bearer," and I agree with the judge below that the mandate to pay bearer must be expressed and not implied. As to section 4 (2) (*b*), this is clearly a document intended to enable a person to obtain payment of the sum mentioned in the document. " Person " here means any person, and does not require a named person; therefore " cash " is good enough. The question is whether the document was " issued by a customer of a banker." In my opinion, this clearly was so issued. It was a good cheque so far as the plaintiff company was concerned. . . . A written document is intended

[25] The subsection applies the protection of s. 82 of the 1882 Act, as extended by s. 4 (1) of the 1957 Act to:

any document issued by a customer of a banker which, though not a bill of exchange, is intended to enable a person to obtain payment from that banker of the sum mentioned in the document.

[26] *Cf. post*, pp. 98 and 105, for other points involved.

to bring about that which its written terms indicate. It is not legitimate to inquire into the mind of the creator of the document.[27]

Notes

In *North and South Insurance Corporation Ltd.* v. *National Provincial Bank Ltd.*[28] an instrument in the form " Pay Cash or Order " was paid by the defendant bank a few days after a winding-up petition had been presented, unknown to the bank, and the liquidator claimed that the bank had wrongly paid an order instrument without an indorsement. Branson J. held that the document was not a cheque, and that it must therefore be construed in accordance with the apparent wishes of the drawers. The words " or Order " must therefore be ignored as being inconsistent with the apparent intention, and the document was thus a valid order to the bank.

> It cannot have been intended that " Cash," which is a purely impersonal collection of letters, should indorse this draft. That being so, I think the four words " Pay Cash or Order " cannot be read so as to give any sensible meaning to the whole four, and the result is that the printed words " or Order " must be disregarded, and we have a direction to pay cash—by necessary implication, to pay it to the bearer of the document. . . ."[29]

There was some discussion following the *North and South Insurance* decision as to whether instruments in the form in question (and " Pay Wages or Order " is analogous) could be treated as equivalent to " Pay Bearer " cheques. On the one hand, the rule that a bill payable to a fictitious payee is regarded as a bearer bill could be viewed as supporting the wider view, as indeed could the words of Branson J. just quoted. On the other hand it was argued that the decision should be treated with caution, and regarded as meaning no more than that if the amount of the instrument is received by the person intended to receive it the drawer cannot claim it back from the bank. This narrower view received support from the decision in *Cole* v. *Milsome*,[30] where Lloyd-Jacob J. held that the plaintiff, who had innocently received a " Pay Cash or Order " instrument from a fraudulent third party, was not entitled to recover from the defendant as drawer of the instrument; he considered that the *North and South Insurance* case " did not decide that . . . a payment [in this form] was a payment to bearer."

The decision of the Court of Appeal in the *Orbit* [31] case confirms this view: instruments in this form are *not* to be regarded as pay-

---

[27] At pp. 821–822.
[28] [1936] 1 K.B. 328.
[29] At pp. 335–336.
[30] [1951] 1 All E.R. 311.
[31] *Cf.* Megrah, Gilbart Lectures, 1962, where the case is discussed at some length.

able to bearer, although for some purposes the practical effect is the same as if they were. It will be noted that the period during which the fraudulent cheques in the *Orbit* case were issued included the passing of the Cheques Act 1957, so that the provisions of that Act fell to be applied to the later cheques; but the 1957 Act has not affected the position as regards the point here discussed, and it is still appropriate to quote the advice given on the matter in 72 J.I.B. at p. 200 (October 1951):

The following rules may, perhaps, be taken as a guide in dealing with an instrument drawn "pay cash or order" (which is assumed to be otherwise in order)—

(*a*) if uncrossed it may safely be paid over the counter only to the drawer or his known agent and whether indorsed or not (the indorsement of the drawer does not make the instrument transferable);

(*b*) if crossed and bearing no sign of having been transferred, it may be paid through the clearing or over the counter to another bank without question, whether indorsed by the drawer or not;

(*c*) it should not be collected, if uncrossed, except for a responsible customer, who, anyhow, should be asked to cross it.

Re Hone (a bankrupt), Ex parte the Trustee v. Kensington Borough Council

[1951] Ch. 85

Payment of a debt by cheque: when effected

Facts

The debtor was the occupier of certain property, in respect of which she issued a cheque for £55 5s. payable to the borough council, representing six months rates on the property. This cheque was issued on November 3, 1949, and received by the borough treasurer on the same day. It was paid into the council's account on November 4, and after passing through the clearing was paid by the debtor's bankers, the National Provincial Bank, Colchester, on November 8. On November 4, after the cheque had been paid into the council's account, the debtor had filed her petition in bankruptcy, was made bankrupt at once, and adjudicated on the same day.

The trustee in bankruptcy sought a declaration that the sum of £55 5s. was part of the property of the bankrupt, and the council contended, *inter alia*, that it was protected by section 45 of the Bankruptcy Act 1914, which provides: ". . . nothing in this Act shall invalidate, in the case of a bankruptcy—(*a*) Any payment by the bankrupt to any of his creditors . . . Provided that . . . the payment . . . takes place before the date of the receiving order. . . ." In the present circumstances, the council submitted, payment had been made within the meaning of the section on November 3.

Decision

It was held that payment had not been made until the cheque had been collected. In his judgment Harman J. said:

[In *Marreco* v. *Richardson*] Farwell, L.J., made some observations which may be said to be near this case. He said [32]: " There is no doubt the cheque was given in part payment of the debt, and if it was so given in due time, that is, within six years of the commencement of this action, the case is taken out of the statute; if not, the debt is statute-barred." Then he quotes *Pearce* v. *Davis*,[33] a case before Patteson, J., and adds ". . . the payment is made at the time when the cheque is given, and I infer from the judgment of Patteson, J., that the giving of a cheque would support a plea of payment." He refers with approval to Byrne, J.'s decision in *Hadley* v. *Hadley*,[34] and adds: ". . . the giving of a cheque for a debt is payment conditional on the cheque being met, that is, subject to a condition subsequent, and if the cheque is met it is an actual payment ab initio and not a conditional one." It is therfore said that here the cheque was met and that there was an actual payment ab initio, namely, before the bankruptcy.

I cannot take that view as between the trustee in bankruptcy and the bankrupt. It may be that, as between debtor and creditor, in certain circumstances that might be so. In both [the *Hadley* case and the *Marreco* case, *supra*] the *ratio* of the decision was that the promise to pay was what counted; but I cannot think that here the council did receive payment when the piece of paper passed to them. They got the money when they were richer by £55. It is quite true that, having accepted the cheque, they could not have sued for the debt unless and until the cheque was dishonoured. Nevertheless, it was not until the cheque was honoured that they were paid.[35]

Notes

The moment at which payment by cheque is effected is perhaps less certain in law than in common usage. Since the passing of the Cheques Act 1957, receipts are not issued so regularly for payments made by cheque as they are previously [36]; but it is normal business

[32] [1908] 2 K.B. 592.

[33] (1834) 1 M. & R. 365.

[34] [1898] 2 Ch. 680.

[35] At pp. 88–89.

[36] It was a curious side effect of the Cheques Act that s. 3, intended merely to preserve for the unindorsed paid cheque the value as evidence of receipt that had always attached to the indorsed paid cheque, drew the attention of the business community for the first time to this aspect of the cheque. It was an unjustifiable *non sequitur* that led further to the omission of stamps from many acknowledgements of payment.

practice for such receipts as are issued to be sent on the generally understood condition that if the cheque is dishonoured the receipt is ineffective; and the increasing tendency to issue such receipts without qualification is possibly a recognition of the fact that in any event the payee has an action against the drawer on the dishonoured cheque itself, irrespective of the original debt.[37]

However, in such circumstances as those of *Re Hone* the moment of payment can be material; and there have been other cases in the courts which turned on the same point.

In *Chambers* v. *Miller* [38] a clerk was sent to the bank by his employer to cash a third party's cheque. The cashier handed him notes, which he checked, and, thinking at first that there was an error, checked again. During the time he was checking the money the cashier discovered that the amount on which the cheque was drawn had become overdrawn, and an attempt was made to recover the cash from the clerk. The House of Lords held that when the money passed over the counter the property in it passed too and emphasised that the property passed from transferor to transferee according to the intention of the parties.[39]

The circumstances of that case were comparatively simple. A more modern decision on quite different circumstances was that in *Re Owen Decd.*, *Owen* v. *Inland Revenue Commissioner.*[40] Here the deceased had intended some years before his death to make certain gifts, and accordingly cheques were issued on May 21, 1941, to the three donees. The first cheque was presented for payment on June 4, the second on June 5, and the third on July 2. The donor died on June 1 1944, and the question arose as to whether the gifts were subject to estate duty, or whether they had been made more than three years before the death. It was held that they were so subject, as the gifts were not complete until the cheques had been paid by the drawee bank.

Despite these and similar cases, the decision in *Re Hone* provoked

---

[37] *Cf.* the cases discussed at pp. 125 *et seq.* where the principle is established that only in exceptional circumstances will the courts consider any kind of counter-claim as entitling the acceptor to postpone payment on a bill of exchange: the bill is a contract separate from the underlying transaction.

[38] (1862) 13 C.B.(N.S.) 125. *Cf. post*, p. 83.

[39] An interesting example of the same principle was the New Zealand case *Balmoral Supermarket Ltd.* v. *Bank of New Zealand* [1974] 2 Lloyd's Rep. 164, where robbers stole $ NZ 3,260 which the plaintiffs' clerk had placed on the bank counter preparatory to paying in. The plaintiffs' claim that the property in the money had passed to the bank was rejected by the Supreme Court of New Zealand, which held that the debtor-creditor relationship was not created until a deposit was made, and merely placing money on the counter did not constitute a deposit.

[40] [1949] 1 All E.R. 901.

some discussion, and the student is referred to April 1951 72 J.I.B. 89, for a summary of the opposing points of view and for the opinion of the Editor of the *Journal* that the decision was a sound one. It may be noted that *Re Owen* was decided at least in part on the well-established doctrine that in English law a cheque does not operate as an assignment of funds. The critics of *Re Hone* argue,[41] on the lines of Farwell L.J. as cited by Harman J. in the judgment in that case, that payment subject to a condition subsequent becomes, upon fulfilment of that condition, valid *ab initio*. This argument, which does not conflict with the no-assignment doctrine, would if adopted in *Re Owen* have given a decision contrary to that in fact reached: the condition-subsequent argument makes it reasonable to hold that a cheque effectively transfers money upon delivery without at all infringing the no-assignment doctrine.

In *The Brimnes: Tenax Steamship Co. Ltd.* v. *The Brimnes (Owners)* [42] all three judges in the Court of Appeal accepted that payment would have been effected immediately upon receipt of a cheque by the beneficiary's bankers. There had been no discussion of the point, which was not necessary to the decision in the case, the Court merely rejecting a suggested analogy with such payment. But the opinion must be given the weight attaching even to the *obiter dicta* of a unanimous Court of Appeal, and it may be regarded as pointing towards a reversal of the tendency of the Courts to regard the date of payment by the paying bank as the effective date upon which a debt is settled by cheque.

The time at which payment is effected can be questioned in regard to other forms of money transfer in the banking system. Thus in *The Brimnes* the payment in issue was a transfer from one account to another in the books of Morgan Guaranty Trust in New York, the transfer being effected by a telex message from Hambros in London. The Court of Appeal held that payment was effected, not when the telex was received, but some two hours later, after the message had been "processed" and the decision to effect the transfer made.

This decision might seem to be in conflict with that in *Mardorf Peach & Co.* v. *Attica Sea Carriers Corp. of Liberia.*[43] Here the instrument involved was a payment order issued under the London Currency Settlement Scheme. Such payment orders are regarded as equivalent to cash by the banks operating the scheme, even though beneficiaries cannot draw against them until they are "processed." The Court of Appeal held by a majority that payment was effected

[41] *Cf. e.g.* Chorley 14 M.L.R. 65.
[42] [1974] 3 All E.R. 88.
[43] [1976] Q.B. 835.

when the payment order was received by the beneficiary's bankers, any paper work thereafter being irrelevant. The House of Lords reversed their decision in favour of the plaintiffs,[44] but this was on other grounds, while dicta of Lord Russell and Lord Salmon seem to support the majority view of the Court of Appeal on the point here discussed, Lord Salmon remarking that " no doubt a certain amount of processing or paper work has to be done even in relation to a cash payment before it finds its way as a credit into the haven of the customer's account." [45]

For consideration for a cheque, see Appendix.

---

[44] [1977] 2 W.L.R. 286.

[45] See *The Banker* (April 1977), Vol. 127, p. 141, " Two Questions of Time," where also is discussed the question whether a payment due on a Sunday, when the banks are closed, must be made on the Friday. This was accepted without argument in the *Mardorf Peach* case, only Lord Denning, in the Court of Appeal, suggested that the assumption was wrong. It may be thought that his view finds support in the provision of the Banking and Financial Dealings Act 1971, which makes bills of exchange due on any non-business day payable on the succeeding business day.

CHAPTER 3

THE PAYING BANKER

London Joint Stock Bank Ltd. v. Macmillan & Arthur
[1918] A.C. 777

In drawing a cheque, the customer owes a duty to the bank to take reasonable precautions against possible alteration of the cheque

Facts

The respondents, customers of the London Joint Stock Bank, entrusted to their confidential clerk the duty of filling in cheques for signature. The clerk presented a cheque to one of the partners for his signature, drawn in favour of the firm or bearer; there was no sum written in words, and in the space for the figures were the figures " 2.0.0." The partner signed the cheque, and the clerk thereafter inserted the figures " 1 " and " 0 " respectively before and after the figure " 2," and added the words " one hundred and twenty pounds." He presented the cheque at the bank and received £120 in cash, the bank debiting the plaintiffs' account with that sum.

The firm contended that the bank could debit their account with £2 only, and brought this action for a declaration to that effect. The bank alleged that the firm had been negligent in drawing and signing the cheque.

Decision

The House of Lords held that the relationship of banker and customer imposed a special duty on the customer, in drawing a cheque, to take reasonable and ordinary precautions against forgery, and that the alteration in this case was the direct result of a breach of that duty by the firm, whose account the bank was therefore entitled to debit with the full amount of £120 paid by them on the cheque.

In his judgment, Lord Finlay L.C. said:

A cheque drawn by a customer is in point of law a mandate to the banker to pay the amount according to the tenor of the cheque. It is beyond dispute that the customer is bound to exercise reasonable care in drawing the cheque to prevent the banker being misled. If he draws the cheque in a manner which facilitates fraud, he is guilty of a breach of duty as between himself and the banker, and he will be responsible to the banker for any loss sustained by the banker as a natural and direct consequence of this breach of duty. . . . As the customer and the banker are under a contractual relation in this matter, it appears obvious that in drawing a cheque the customer is bound to take usual and reasonable precautions to prevent forgery. . . . If the cheque is drawn in such a way as to facilitate or almost to invite an increase in the amount by forgery if the cheque should get into the hands of a dishonest person, forgery is not a remote but a very natural consequence of negligence of this description.[1]

Notes

This is perhaps the most important case ever decided upon the law relating to cheques, because it makes clear for the first time the dual function of the cheque. The cheque is primarily an instrument of authority or a mandate from customer to banker used for the purpose of obtaining repayment of the customer's moneys held by the banker. Since it was at a very early stage convenient for the customer not only to be able to obtain the money, or part of it, himself, but also to have it, or part of it, paid to some third party or third party's order, it became customary to draw the mandate in the form of a bill of exchange, or, as this particular form of bill came to be called, a cheque.

The function of the cheque as a mandate was recognised as early as 1827 in *Young* v. *Grote*,[2] where the plaintiff, on going away on business, left with his wife for the purpose of his business five blank cheques signed by himself. The wife required £50 2s. 3d. to pay wages, and got one of the clerks to fill in one of the cheques for that amount. He did so, but in such a way as to allow him to make subsequent additions, and after showing it to the wife, who told him to cash it, he increased the amount to £350 2s. 3d. The bank cashed the cheque, and it was held that the loss must fall on the plaintiff.

In spite of the fact that *Young* v. *Grote* was plainly founded on the mandate principle,[3] the cheque's form as a bill of exchange tended for long to obscure its mandate aspect, which becomes of such great importance when any question arises, as it did in the *Macmillan* case, as to the customer's obligation to take care of his banker's interests when making out the mandate.

---

[1] At pp. 789–790.

[2] (1827) 4 Bing. 253.

[3] The decision in *Young* v. *Grote* was based on principles earlier eunnciated by Pothier. In *Scholefield* v. *Earl of Londesborough* (*infra*), Watson L.J. cited Pothier as discussing " the nature of the contract which is constituted between the drawer and the acceptor of a bill, which he asserts to be *un vrai contrat de mandat, mandatum solvendae pecuniae*." In the *Macmillan* case itself Lord Finlay said: " Pothier treats the question [of the right of the drawee to be recouped by the drawer when by reason of a fraudulent alteration in the draft he has been led to pay more than the sum really drawn for] as one of the law of mandate."

It must be here remarked that there is some difference as to the effect of the *Macmillan* decision. It clearly established (as indeed *Young* v. *Grote* had established earlier) that a customer drawing an incomplete cheque and leaving the completion of it to his agent cannot object to his banker's debiting him with the fraudulently raised amount of it. It is generally considered, however, that the decision went further than this, and set up a wider duty of care in the drawer, so that even when he completes the cheque he must not leave spaces facilitating fraudulent raising.[3a] Hart[4] argues against this view, although he admits that Lord Finlay (as in the citation from his judgment, *supra*) and Lord Shaw did go this far. But the full proposition has been approved by most of the textbooks[5] and, more than once, by the Courts, and is almost certainly the correct view. Indeed, Lord Shaw in his judgment went still further, and suggested that the customer is liable for the condition of the cheque until it is presented, and might therefore even be responsible for an erasure and substitution: in the words of the headnote to the case, "in the case of a customer's cheque, admittedly genuine, no responsibility rests upon the banker for what has happened to the cheque before its presentation to the bank, but the responsibility for what has happened to it between the dates of signature and presentation rests upon the customer."

However, in *Slingsby* v. *District Bank Ltd.*,[6] the banker was denied any such complete immunity as was contemplated in Lord Shaw's opinion and in the headnote just quoted. In this case the cheque was payable to John Prust & Co., with a blank between those words and "or order," the fraudulent solicitor adding the words "per Cumberbirch and Potts" in the blank so left. It was held that such an alteration was a form of fraud that could not reasonably be anticipated by the customer, and that therefore the customer could not be held to have been negligent in leaving the blank space in the cheque. This decision has been criticised, but it is to be noted that some banks, at least, give printed warnings in their cheque books of the danger of gaps in the words and figures of the amount, but say nothing of the danger of blanks in the designation of the payee.

As to the possibility of the customer's being liable in a case of erasure, an early decision in *Hall* v. *Fuller*[7] was to the effect that where a cheque had been altered in this way from £3 to £200, the customer could be debited with the sum of £3 only.

[3a] *Cf. Lumsden & Co.* v. *London Trustee Savings Bank, post*, p. 106.
[4] *Law of Banking* (4th ed.), pp. 384 *et seq.*
[5] *Cf. e.g.* Paget, *op. cit.* p. 293.
[6] [1932] 1 K.B. 544; *ante*, p. 27, for facts and decision on other points involved.
[7] (1826) 5 B. & C. 750.

It may be said that there is apparent, since the establishment of the customer's duty to take care in drawing the cheque, a tendency to establish duties of a general character in relation to the handling of the account; see, for example, the *Greenwood* case,[8] *Westminster Bank Ltd.* v. *Hilton,*[9] and the *Orbit* case.[10] It is possible that another case on the lines of *Slingsby* v. *District Bank* would now be decided differently.

The distinction between the liability of the drawer of a cheque and that of the acceptor of a bill of exchange is seen in comparing the *Macmillan* decision with that in *Scholefield* v. *Earl of Londesborough.*[11] In this last case, the defendant accepted a bill drawn upon him for £500, but which was stamped £2—sufficient to cover a bill for £4,000. After acceptance the drawer fraudulently increased the amount of the bill to £3,500, inserting the figure " 3 " and the words " three thousand " in appropriate spaces which he had left in the bill when he drew it. He then indorsed the bill to a third party, who negotiated it to the plaintiff, who took it in good faith and for value. The plaintiff sued the defendant for the amount of the bill as altered. The defendant paid £500 into Court, the amount of the bill as accepted by him, and denied any further liability. The plaintiff contended (*inter alia*) that the defendant was negligent in accepting the bill in that form, and with a £2 stamp upon it.

On appeal the House of Lords decided that the acceptor of a bill of exchange was not under any duty to take precautions against a subsequent alteration of the bill, and that the defendant had not been negligent, Lord Watson saying:

The duty which the appellant's argument assigns to an acceptor is towards the public, or what is much the same thing towards those members of the public who may happen to acquire right to the bill, after it has been criminally tampered with. Apart from authority, I do not think the imposition of such a duty can be justified on any sound legal principle. In many if not most cases which occur in the course of business, the bill is written out by the drawer, and sent by him to the acceptor, who is under an obligation to sign it. Assuming the appellant's argument to be well founded, it would be within the right of the acceptor to return the bill unsigned, if it were not drawn so as to exclude all reasonable possibilities of fraud or forgery. The exercise of that right might lead to very serious complications in commercial transactions. . . . I am therefore unwilling in

[8] *Post,* p. 66.

[9] *Post,* p. 69. But in *Place & Sons Ltd.* v. *Turner, The Times,* February 7, 1951, it was held *inter alia* by Devlin J. that the drawer of a cheque owes no duty to the drawee or to the general public to avoid such carelessness in his business (including the drawing of cheques) as may injure another financially .

[10] *Ante,* p. 35.

[11] [1896] A.C. 514.

the case of an acceptor to affirm the doctrine, upon which the appellant relies, unless it can be shown to be established by authority as part of the English law merchant. . . . The result of the English authorities is, in my opinion, decidedly adverse to the appellant.[12]

The contrast between cheque and bill in this connection may be otherwise expressed: between a banker and his customer there is a contractual relationship under which the discharge of the banker's primary obligation is effected by means of the mandate, in the drawing up of which the customer can reasonably be expected to take care. But between the acceptor of a bill and the payee or holder of the instrument there is no such relationship, under which it would be proper to hold the acceptor responsible for the drawing of the instrument.

Selangor United Rubber Estates Ltd. v. Cradock (a bankrupt) and Others. (No. 3)

[1968] 1 W.L.R. 1555

The paying banker owes a duty to his customer to exercise reasonable care and skill in carrying out his part of the contract. He may also be liable as a constructive trustee if funds on the account are misapplied

Facts

The plaintiff company was in 1958 a " shell," with assets of some £235,000. The first defendant's bid for the shares was accepted by a majority of the shareholders, and he arranged with the branch of the District Bank at which he had an account, and to which Selangor's account was transferred, to issue a draft for £200,000 to the company through which he had made the bid, so that they could go ahead with the take-over. His account was in turn credited with a Selangor cheque payable to yet another company and indorsed to him. The bank was told that this represented a loan by Selangor to the payee company at 8 per cent., and a loan by them to Cradock at 9 per cent. In fact Selangor's money had been used to buy Selangor's shares.

In 1961 the company was in compulsory liquidation and the present action was brought by the Board of Trade against the first defendant and nine others, including the District Bank, as well as directors of all three companies. The case against the bank, with which alone we are here concerned, was (*a*) in equity that they

[12] At pp. 537–542.

were constructive trustees of the money paid out, and had actual knowledge that it was being wrongly applied, their officials having seen the whole transaction; and (*b*) in contract, that they were negligent in paying the cheque on Selangor's account without inquiring as to its purpose.

Decision

Ungoed-Thomas J. upheld the claim against the bank under both heads. He said:

The evidence showed that the banks put severe limits, as is common knowledge, on powers of bank managers to grant overdrafts and thus risk the bank's money—limits which bear no comparison at all with the amounts at risk of the plaintiff on the Woodstock cheque. The evidence also showed that District gave explicit instructions to avoid their being liable for conversion of cheques, when acting as collecting banks. For my part I can see no substantial difficulty in banks providing against such exceptional transactions, involving substantial amounts, as in this case, being carried through by officials completely inexperienced in such transactions and unqualified to deal with them. If a bank allows such officials to conduct such business it is asking for the kind of trouble which it has got in this case.[13]

Notes

Section 54 of the Companies Act 1948, provides:

(1) Subject as provided in this section, it shall not be lawful for a company to give, whether directly or indirectly, and whether by means of a loan, guarantee, the provision of security or otherwise, any financial assistance for the purpose of or in connection with a purchase or subscription made or to be made by any person of or for any shares in the company, or, where the company is a subsidiary company, in its holding company.

The provision has been criticised, and the Jenkins Committee,[14] noting that it is anyhow widely disregarded, recommended that subject to conditions which they drafted to protect minority shareholders and creditors, a company should be permitted to purchase its own shares. No action has been taken on this recommendation, and the prohibition is still in force.

The *Selangor* decision,[15] remarkable if only for the 50,000 word judgment that its considerable complications required, may be regarded as far as its banking aspects are concerned either as merely a special example of accepted banking principles or as an alarming

[13] At p. 1634.

[14] *Cf. post*, p. 183.

[15] Followed by Brightman J. in *Karak Rubber Co. Ltd.* v. *Burden* (*No. 2*) [1972] 1 W.L.R. 602.

extension of the banker's danger of being found negligent in the handling of his customer's account. The second view would seem to be justified.[16]

It is to be noted that the finding of the court in contract included the proposition that the fact that the cheque was signed by properly authorised signatories did not exclude the bank's obligation to exercise care—in this case to inquire as to the purpose of the payment. Nor was the bank excused this duty by the fact that the answer would probably be false if in fact the transaction was irregular. As to the finding in equity, the principle that a banker can be a constructive trustee of funds on a customer's account, and that in such circumstances he cannot necessarily pay his customer's cheque without inquiry, is clear enough [17]; but the circumstances in which a bank had previously been held to have been in breach of their constructive trust were considerably simpler than those of the *Selangor* case.

It is of course true that the case was decided on its special facts, which are not of every day occurrence. But the principles upon which it was decided are applicable to the relationship between the paying banker and his customer generally; while it is at least as important to the banker to recognise that there are other circumstances in which the bank manager's familiarity with or ignorance of the complexities of company finance must now be significant.

In *S.B.A. Properties* v. *Cradock and Others*,[18] an earlier case in the group of actions of which *Selangor* (No. 3) is the principal, the Bank of Nova Scotia successfully resisted a claim that they had been negligent in not making sufficient inquiry as to the purpose of payments out of the account. But that action was brought by the Board of Trade under section 169 (4) of the Companies Act 1948, which is concerned with fraud and misfeasance "in connection with . . . the management" of the company affairs, and Goff J. dismissed the action on the grounds, *inter alia*, that acting as a company's bankers, even negligently, was not acting in connection with the management of the company. Bankers can thus draw little comfort from this decision, which depended entirely on the wording of the section under which it was brought.[18a]

---

[16] *Cf.* Paget, *op. cit.* p. 288.

[17] *Cf. Re Gross, post,* p. 146.

[18] [1967] 1 W.L.R. 716.

[18a] *Cf.* Ryder, "Payment of Cheques—a New Source of Liability" [1975] J.B.L. 195.

Rogers v. Whiteley
[1892] A.C. 118

Plunkett v. Barclays Bank Ltd.
[1936] 2 K.B. 107

The effect of a garnishee order nisi

Facts of Rogers v. Whiteley

There was standing to the credit of Rogers's account with the banking department of Whiteley's a balance of more than £6,800. One Elizabeth Holloway, a judgment creditor of the appellants for £6,000, obtained a garnishee order nisi ordering that " all debts owing or accruing due " from Whiteley's to Rogers be attached. In consequence the bank dishonoured cheques drawn by Rogers on the balance between £6,000 and his credit balance. Rogers brought action against Whiteley's for damages for injury to credit by these dishonours. Pollock B. found that the bank was bound by the order. An application to set aside this judgment on the ground, *inter alia*, of misdirection was refused by the Divisional Court, that decision was affirmed by the Court of Appeal, and the appellant appealed to the House of Lords.

Decision

The House of Lords dismissed the appeal, holding that the whole balance was attached by the order. In his judgment Lord Watson said:

> Many nice questions may arise in the application of Order xlv, but I do not think the point which we are called upon to decide in this case is attended with the least difficulty. The effect of an order attaching " all debts " owing or accruing due by him to the judgment debtor is to make the garnishee custodier for the Court of the whole funds attached; and he cannot, except at his own peril, part with any of those funds without the sanction of the Court. Whether the Order can in the first instance issue in other terms than those prescribed by the rules, it is not necessary for the purposes of this case to decide; but I entertain no doubt that when the attachment has been made in these terms it is within the power of the Court to restrict its operation to such an amount of the debts owing by the garnishee as will satisfy the judgment debt; but so long as such restriction is not made and the attachment is unreleased the garnishee is under no obligation to disregard the attachment and to pay the excess to his creditor.[19]

[19] At pp. 121–122.

And Lord Halsbury said:

The order appears to me to have been in such terms that it would have been a disobedience to the order on [the banker's] part if he had paid anything after it had been served upon him.[20]

In his concurring judgment Lord Morris discussed the evils possibly resulting from this judgment: for example, that of a credit balance of £50,000 attached for a £5 or £10 debt. He submitted that it was in fact competent for a judge to make an order attaching only a limited sum, although the order in this case was not so worded.[21]

Facts of Plunkett v. Barclays Bank Ltd.

In 1935 the plaintiff, a solicitor, opened two accounts at the Kingsway branch of the bank, one being distinguished as a " Client Account," in compliance with the Solicitors Act 1957,[22] and the Solicitors' Accounts Rules, 1935. On September 7, 1935, £48 5s. was paid in, in cash, to the credit of the Client Account, this sum representing rent and costs due to a third party. On September 6, a cheque for the same amount was sent to the solicitor acting for the third party to whom the money was due. On September 9, application was made for a garnishee order by the plaintiff's former wife, for costs in her successful divorce proceedings against him. The order was made in the usual form, and served on the defendant bank. On September 10, the chief clerk at the branch informed the plaintiff that the bank must regard both accounts as being attached by the order; and on September 11, the bank dishonoured the cheque for £48 5s. with the marking " Refer to drawer." This action was brought for alleged breach of contract by the dishonour and alleged libel in writing the words " Refer to Drawer."

Decision

The court held that the balance of the Client Account was attached by the order, and that in the circumstances " Refer to Drawer " was not libellous.[23]

In his judgment du Parcq J. after holding that the £48 5s. was, to the knowledge of the defendants, trust money, went on to say:

---

[20] At p. 120.

[21] It is now possible to word the order in this restrictive manner, and where it is so worded the banker can, of course, pay away any surplus over the amount expressly attached. Even if the costs prove unexpectedly high, and the amount attached is in fact insufficient, the bank cannot be held liable for paying away the surplus.

[22] *Cf. post*, p. 155. [23] *Cf. post*, pp. 75 *et seq.*

I find it impossible to say that money paid into a Client Account kept with a bank in the name of a solicitor is not a debt owing from the banker to the solicitor. It cannot be denied that the relation of debtor and creditor subsists between the bank and the solicitor. The solicitor may at any time draw a cheque upon the account and the bank must honour it. As a general rule, the bank is not entitled to set up a supposed *jus tertii* against the customer: see *per* Lord Westbury, *Gray* v. *Johnston*.[24] The service of the order nisi gives the judgment creditor, in the worlds of Farwell, L.J., in *Galbraith* v. *Grimshaw and Baxter*,[25] an equitable charge on the debt, and I cannot think that it was ever intended that the garnishee should be compelled to adjudicate upon conflicting equities, even though the problem presented by the conflict might appear to the lawyer to be a simple one.[26]

Notes [27]

The effect of *Joachimson* v. *Swiss Bank Corporation* [28] on garnishee proceedings has already been discussed.

The order must clearly designate the judgment debtor, and where the designation is incorrect the bank is entitled to ignore the order.

In *Koch* v. *Mineral Ore Syndicate* [29] the bank informed the solicitors of the judgment creditor that they had no account in the name given. The solicitors asked them to attach a different account, which they said was the judgment debtor's, and the bank refused. Later the order was amended, but the bank was not liable for having paid cheques on the account in the meantime.

In *Heppenstall* v. *Jackson, Barclays Bank Ltd., Garnishees*,[30] moneys paid into the credit of the judgment debtor after service of the order nisi were held not to be attached; an accruing debt does not include " anything which *may* be a debt, however probable, or however soon it may be a debt." [31] It is clearly convenient that upon receipt of the order the bank should rule off the account and start a new one for subsequent transactions, but it does not seem that this is a legal duty. The customer should be advised of the receipt of the order.

Similarly, money which has gone from the account at the time of the service of the garnishee order will not be attached; but the

---

[24] (1868) L.R. 3 H.L. 1, 14; *post*, p. 150.
[25] [1910] 1 K.B. 399 at p. 343.
[26] At pp. 118–119.
[27] In the cases discussed in these notes it is important to distinguish between those in which a bank is directly concerned, and those in which the parties are judgment creditor and judgment debtor. The latter do not concern the bank, which has observed the terms of the order nisi and awaits the issue, normally having paid the money attached into court.
[28] *Ante*, p. 1.
[29] (1910) 54 S.J. 600.
[30] [1939] 1 K.B. 585.
[31] *Per* Lord Blackburn in *Tapp* v. *Jones* (1875) L.R. 10 Q.B. 591.

passing of such money from the account must have been completed before the service of the order. In *Rekstin* v. *Severo Sibirsko, etc., and the Bank for Russian Trade* [32] the first respondents instructed the second, their bankers, to transfer the whole of their credit balance to the account of the Trade Delegation of the U.S.S.R., a body enjoying diplomatic immunity. This transfer was completed in the books of the bank, and the amount closed; but a quarter of an hour later a garnishee order nisi was served on the bank purporting to attach the balance which had been transferred. The bank had not communicated the transfer to the Trade Delegation, nor did this body have any knowledge that it was contemplated. On the question whether the bank was in fact still indebted to the first respondents when they received the order, the Court of Appeal held that mere book entries without communication to the transferee were revocable, and that a garnishee order nisi operates to revoke any such revocable transfer.[33]

In *Hirschorn* v. *Evans* [34] the account which it was sought to garnishee was a joint account of a husband and wife. The garnishee order was against the husband only, and the Court of Appeal held, by a majority, that, as the debt owed by the bank was to husband and wife jointly, it could not be attached for the husband's debt. Mackinnon L.J. said:

> It is true that there was an authority on the bank to honour cheques upon that joint account if the cheques were signed by one or other of them. That simply means " Either of us has authority on behalf of and as agent for both of us to sign cheques." It would amount to no more than an authorisation to the bank: " Upon this our joint account you are authorised to honour cheques drawn by our clerk or agent, John Smith." But such an authorisation would not make the bank the debtor of John Smith.[35]

In *Bower* v. *Foreign and Colonial Gas Co. Ltd., Metropolitan Bank, Garnishees,*[36] a garnishee order being served upon the bank they sought to reserve £500 of the balance attached to meet two bills under discount but not yet due. It was held that they could not do this; the discount of the bills was in effect a separate advance to the customer, which would have been nullified by any such lien as was claimed.

---

[32] [1933] 1 K.B. 47.

[33] But *cf. Momm* v. *Barclays Bank International Ltd. post*, p. 65, where the bank was held not to be entitled to reverse entries on the morning after they had been made, even though the credit had not been communicated to the beneficiary.

[34] [1938] 2 K.B. 801. *Cf. post*, p. 170.

[35] At p. 814.

[36] (1874) 22 W.R. 740.

In *Jones & Co.* v. *Coventry*,[37] it was sought to attach the balance of an account, £17 12s. 6d. of which represented a pension warrant issued by the Paymaster General and paid in earlier on the day the garnishee order was served. It was held that the warrant, which called for a declaration of entitlement and a receipt, was not a negotiable instrument, despite a statement on it that it might be " negotiated in the country or abroad." It remained the property of the Paymaster General until it was paid at his office, and so was not attachable.

In *Bagley* v. *Winsome* [38] it had been sought to attach a deposit account, one of the terms of which was that 14 days' notice of withdrawal should be given, and another that the deposit book should be produced on withdrawal. The depositor had himself given a notice of withdrawal 14 days before the garnishee summons was issued, but the Court of Appeal held that, although following on the *Joachimson* decision it had been established that a garnishee order could operate as a demand by the judgment debtor, this principle could not be extended to make the order satisfy other conditions precedent to payment.

However, in order to remove the anomaly of the debtor's being frustrated by such conditions, section 38 of the Administration of Justice Act 1956 provides that such balances can now be attached.

The importance of the decision in *Plunkett's* case is that it clarified the banker's position when funds that he knows are trust funds are attached by a garnishee order: the fact that he knows there is a trust does not entitle him to ignore the order. The judgment does not, of course, affect the rights of the *cestui que trust* [39]; upon representation being made, the court will amend the order to exempt the trust funds, and du Parcq J. emphasised that it is the bank's duty in such a case to make the position known to the court, as well as advising the customer of the receipt of the order. (The learned judge also emphasised the propriety of restricting the order where a client account is involved, and suggested that applicants for orders might properly be warned that extra costs might be incurred in the attachment of a trust account.) It need hardly be said that the trouble involved for the banks in this procedure is slight in comparison with that which would have resulted from a contrary decision.

An example of circumstances in which the court's ruling had to

---

[37] (1909) 2 K.B. 1029.

[38] [1952] 2 Q.B. 236. *Cf. ante*, p. 5.

[39] *Cf. Hancock* v. *Smith* (1889) 41 Ch.D. 456, where an account in the name of a stockbroker consisted entirely of clients' money, and *Lancaster Motor Co.* (*London*) *Ltd.* v. *Bremith Ltd.* [1941] 1 K.B. 675, where the creditors unsuccessfully sought to attach the liquidator's account.

be sought was *Harrods Ltd.* v. *Tester.*[40] There the respondent had opened an account with the Westminster Bank in the name of his wife. All credits to the account had been paid by him, he had authority to draw on the account, and his wife drew cheques on it only with his permission. The appellants obtained a garnishee order nisi against her, but the husband contended that in fact all the moneys on the account were his own, and the Court of Appeal upheld his contention. Lord Wright M.R. said that, although payments into an account in the name of another are prima facie gifts, this is merely a presumption which can be rebutted, and the evidence in the present case made it clear that a trust in favour of the husband had been created.

Arab Bank Ltd. v. Ross

[1952] 2 Q.B. 216

Requirements of a regular indorsement

Facts

In part payment for certain shares the defendant gave two promissory notes for £10,000 each, made payable to Fathi and Faysal Nabulsy Co. These notes were indorsed to the plaintiff bank, who claimed that they had given value for them, and were holders in due course. The indorsements were in the form "Fathi and Faysal Nabulsy," and the defendant contended, *inter alia*, that the notes were therefore not complete and regular on their face.

Decision

The Court of Appeal held on this point that the indorsement was irregular, that this prevented the bank from succeeding as holders in due course, but that as holders for value they were entitled to recover payment from the defendant.

In the course of his judgment, Denning L.J., after pointing out that "regularity is a different thing from validity" and that it "is also different from liability," continued:

> Once regularity is seen to differ both from validity and from liability, the question is when is an indorsement irregular? The answer is, I think, that it is irregular whenever it is such as to give rise to doubt whether it is the indorsement of the named payee. A bill of exchange is like currency. It should be above suspicion. But if it is asked: When does an indorsement

[40] [1937] 2 All E.R. 236.

give rise to doubt? I would say that that is a practical question which is, as a rule, better answered by a banker than a lawyer. Bankers have to consider the regularity of indorsements every week and every day of every week, and every hour of every day, whereas the judges sitting in this court have not had to consider it for these last 20 years. So far as I know, the last occasion was in *Slingsby's* case.[41]

The Law Merchant is founded on the custom of merchants, and we shall not go far wrong if we follow the custom of bankers of the City of London on this point. . . .

They insist on strict conformity, it was said, so as to be able to avail themselves of the protection of sections 60, 79, 80 and 82 of the Act of 1882, which they feared they might lose if they paid on an indorsement which does not correspond exactly with the name of the payee. But it is to be noticed that this usage of bankers goes back to times long before those sections were part of the law. The usage certainly existed in 1834 (see *Leonard* v. *Wilson*[42]), whereas section 60 did not appear, even in its original form, until 1853, and sections 79, 80 and 82 not till 1878. The truth is, I think, that the bankers adopted this strict attitude both in their own interests and also in the interests of their customers. It would be quite impossible for them to make inquiries to see that all the indorsements on a bill are, in fact, genuine; but they can at least see that they are regular on the face of them: see *Bank of England* v. *Vagliano Brothers*,[43] *per* Lord Macnaghten. That is some safeguard against dishonesty. It is a safeguard which the bankers have taken for the past 120 years at least, and I do not think we should throw any doubt today on the correctness of their practice.[44]

Notes

The rules regarding indorsements are extensive, and used to occupy much space in banking textbooks,[45] but they have produced very little litigation, and the judgments in the *Arab Bank* case are the most important summary of indorsement law that the courts have yet given. The statement of Denning L.J. here cited, that bankers are the people best equipped to decide as to the regularity of indorsements, lends welcome emphasis to a common-sense point of view on a matter which is essentially one of practice. Some of the more subtle rules have an appearance of artificiality, and there is something less than complete unanimity amongst bankers on some of the practice involved,[46] but the general principle underlying them

---

[41] [1932] 1 K.B. 544; *post*, p. 27.

[42] *Supra*.

[43] [1891] A.C. 157; *ante*, p. 31.

[44] At pp. 227–228.

[45] *e.g.* Sheldon, *Practice and Law of Banking* (6th ed., 1949) gave 13 pages of examples of correct and incorrect indorsements, while questions 538–614 of *Questions on Banking Practice* (10th ed.) were concerned with the same topic.

[46] There is perhaps discernible a tendency to move from the extreme strictness of earlier years.

is clear enough: that the indorsement should prima facie show that the payee and no other made it.[47]

The importance of indorsements to the banker has been very greatly reduced, although not entirely removed, by the Cheques Act 1957.[48] Indorsements are still scrutinised by the paying banker when cheques are paid over the counter,[49] and by the collecting banker when cheques are paid in for the credit of persons other than the payees,[50] while on certain instruments other than cheques indorsements are still generally required. In these circumstances, in which the overwhelming majority of instruments handled by the banks do not require indorsement, it is perhaps even more necessary than it was before for the banker to keep in mind the requirements for the indorsements that remain necessary.

Carpenters' Company v. British Mutual Banking Co. Ltd.

[1938] 1 K.B. 511

The protection of section 60 of the Bills of Exchange Act 1882, may be lost if the paying bank is also the collecting bank, and through its negligence forfeits the protection of section 4 of the Cheques Act 1957

Facts

The plaintiffs were the trustees of a home, and kept an account in this connection with the defendant bank. The plaintiffs' clerk, Blackborow, was secretary of the committee administering the home, and as such regularly obtained cheques to pay tradesmen. Blackborow himself had an account with the defendants.

In 1920 he commenced to misappropriate the funds of the company, usually cheques drawn in favour of tradesmen who had supplied goods, in other cases cheques purporting to be in settlement of forged invoices. All the cheques so misappropriated were crossed

---

[47] *Cf. Slingsby & others* v. *District Bank, ante*, p. 27, for an example of a particular indorsement requirement.

[48] See Chorley, *op. cit. passim*, for the effects of the Cheques Act. *Cf. Jones and Holden's Studies in Practical Banking* (6th ed.), pp. 296 *et seq.*; and *Chalmers on Bills of Exchange* (13th ed.), pp. 300 *et seq.*, for events leading to the passing of the Act, and discussion of its provisions.

[49] *Cf.* Chorley, *op. cit.* p. 78, and Paget, *op. cit.* p. 210, as to whether such " indorsements " are strictly necessary.

[50] *Cf. Westminster Bank Ltd.* v. *Zang, post*, p. 91. In *Midland Bank Ltd.* v. *R. V. Harris Ltd. post*, p. 92, the bank was unsuccessfully challenged on the absence of indorsement on a cheque paid in for the credit of the payee's account.

and properly drawn, Blackborow forging the indorsements of the payees and paying the cheques to the credit of his own account. These frauds continued over a period of years before they were discovered.

The company brought an action against the bank for the amount of the cheques, and Branson J. found as a fact that the bank did not act without negligence, and so had lost the protection of section 82 of the Bills of Exchange Act (now section 4 of the Cheques Act 1957), but that as they *paid* the cheques in good faith and in the ordinary course of business they were, notwithstanding their negligence in collection, protected by section 60. The company appealed.

Decision

The Court of Appeal held (Mackinnon L.J. dissenting) that the defendant bank had converted the cheques; as Branson J. had found that they did this negligently they could not rely on section 82, and were liable to the plaintiffs for the face value of the cheques so converted in the previous six years.

In his judgment, Greer L.J. said:

> . . . when the cheques were presented to the defendant bank they had never ceased to be the property of the drawers, the Carpenters' Company, as they had never in fact been indorsed by the payees. The defendant bank was then asked by Blackborow to receive the cheques, and to place the amounts to the credit of his private account with it. This the bank did, and by so doing it in my judgment converted the cheques to its own use and became liable to the Carpenters' Company, the drawers of the cheques, for the face value of the cheques.
>
> In my judgment section 60 of the Bills of Exchange Act, 1882, only protects a bank when that bank is merely a paying bank, and is not a bank which receives the cheque for collection.[51]

Notes [52]

The essential point of this decision, that a banker who acts as both paying and collecting banker cannot avoid his responsibility for negligence as collecting banker on the grounds that as paying banker he is protected by section 60, is a comparatively simple one. It may be noted that Mackinnon L.J. dissented solely on the grounds that he considered the Court bound by the *Gordon* decision,[53] which the

---

[51] At p. 529.

[52] See *post*, p. 104, for the relevance of this case to the " lulling to sleep " doctrine.

[53] See *post*, p. 84. In that case the point was settled in the Court of Appeal, and was not before the House of Lords.

majority of the Court distinguished on the grounds that there was there no negligence.

It may be noted, too, that the bank in this case claimed to be protected by section 19 of the Stamp Act 1853, which reads:

> . . . any draft or order drawn upon a banker for a sum of money payable to order on demand, which shall, when presented for payment, purport to be indorsed by the person to whom the same shall be drawn payable, shall be a sufficient authority to such banker to pay the amount of such draft or order to the bearer thereof; and it shall not be incumbent on such banker to prove that such indorsement, or any subsequent indorsement, was made by or under the direction or authority of the person to whom the said draft or order was or is made payable either by the drawer or any indorser thereof.

The lower court upheld this claim, but the Court of Appeal held that the section had been impliedly repealed, as regards cheques and bills, by section 60 of the Bills of Exchange Act. The effect of the present case, in this connection, is therefore to restrict the effect of section 19 of the Stamp Act to drafts other than cheques and bills.[54]

Raphael and Another v. Bank of England
(1855) 17 C.B. 161

The meaning of " good faith "

Facts

In November, 1852, some bank-notes issued by the defendants were stolen in Liverpool, and payment of the notes was stopped forthwith. The loss was advertised.

The plaintiff, St. Paul, was a money-changer in Paris, whose firm habitually changed English notes. There was some evidence that notice of the loss of the notes in question reached him in the spring of 1853. In June, 1854, one of the missing notes, for £500, was presented to St. Paul for changing, and after seeing the passport of the person presenting the note, and getting him to write his name and address on the note, he changed it into French money. St. Paul did not look at the file of notices of lost and stolen notes.

The plaintiffs (Raphael being St. Paul's English correspondent) now sued the defendants for the amount of the note and interest. The defendants pleaded *inter alia* that the plaintiffs were not bona fide holders for value of the note, because they had received notice that it was stolen. The jury found that St. Paul's firm gave value for

---

[54] *Cf. post*, pp. 75, 130 *et seq.*

the note; that they had notice of the robbery; that they had no knowledge of the loss when they took the note, but that they had means of knowledge; and that they took the note bona fide. Judgment was entered for the plaintiffs, and the defendants appealed.

Decision

The Court of Common Pleas upheld the decision, and the appeal failed.

Cresswell J. said:

A person who takes a negotiable instrument bona fide for value has undoubtedly a good title, and is not affected by the want of title of the party from whom he takes it. His having the means of knowing that the security had been lost or stolen, and neglecting to avail himself thereof, may amount to negligence: and Lord Tenterden at one time thought negligence was an answer to the action. But the doctrine of *Gill* v. *Cubitt* [55] is not now approved of. I think, therefore, there is no reason to find fault with the verdict on that ground. Then, the jury have found, in substance, that the note in question was taken by St. Paul bona fide and for value. He could not have taken it bona fide, if at the time he took it he had notice or knowledge that the note was a stolen note.[56]

And Willes J. said:

[In the case of *May* v. *Chapman* [57]] it is laid down by Parke, B., that " notice and knowledge " means not merely express notice, but knowledge, or the means of knowledge to which the party wilfully shuts his eyes—a suspicion in the mind of the party, and the means of knowledge in his power wilfully disregarded.[58]

Notes

In sections 1 and 3 of the Cheques Act 1957, which provide protection for respectively the paying and the collecting banker, that protection depends upon the banker having acted in good faith and (*a*) in the ordinary course of business, when he is the paying banker; (*b*) without negligence, when he is the collecting banker. Section 90 of the Bills of Exchange Act 1882 (with which the Cheques Act is construed as one) provides:

A thing is deemed to be done in good faith within the meaning of this Act, where it is in fact done honestly, whether it is done negligently or not.

Negligence by itself does not imply absence of good faith.

In the normal course of collecting and paying cheques the banker is unlikely to act otherwise than in good faith and there seems to

---

55 (1824) 3 B. & C. 466.
56 At p. 171.
57 (1847) 16 M. & W. 355.
58 At p. 174.

be no reported case in which a bank has been challenged on this score. The possible relevance of constructive, as opposed to actual, notice was discussed in *Jones* v. *Gordon*,[59] where a person had taken bills (issued for a fraudulent purpose) at a gross undervalue and had deliberately refrained from making inquiries, Lord Blackburn said:

> I consider it to be fully and thoroughly established that if value be given for a bill of exchange, it is not enough to show that there was carelessness, negligence, or foolishness in not suspecting that the bill was wrong, when there were circumstances which might have led a man to suspect that. All these are matters which tend to show that there was dishonesty in not doing it, but they do not in themselves make a defence to an action upon a bill of exchange. I take it that in order to make such a defence, whether in the case of a party who is solvent and *sui juris*, or when it is sought to be proved against the estate of a bankrupt, it is necessary to show that the person who gave value for the bill, whether the value given be great or small, was affected with notice that there was something wrong about it when he took it. I do not think it is necessary that he should have notice of what the particular wrong was. . . . But if the facts and circumstances are such that the jury . . . came to the conclusion that he was not honestly blundering and careless, but that he must have had a suspicion that there was something wrong, and that he refrained from asking questions . . . I think that is dishonesty.[60]

And in *Auchteroni & Co.* v. *Midland Bank Ltd.*[61] Wright J. quoted Lord Herschell in *London Joint Stock Bank* v. *Simmons* [62]:

> I should be very sorry to see the doctrine of constructive notice introduced into the law of negotiable instruments. But regard to the facts of which the taker of such instruments had notice is most material in considering whether he took in good faith. If there be anything which excites the suspicion that there is something wrong in the transaction, the taker of the instrument is not acting in good faith if he shuts his eyes to the facts presented to him and puts the suspicions aside without further inquiry.[63]

---

[59] (1877) 2 App.Cas. 616.
[60] At pp. 628–629.
[61] [1928] 2 K.B. 294; *cf. post*, p. 63.
[62] [1892] A.C. 201; *post*, p. 225.
[63] At p. 302.

Baines v. National Provincial Bank Ltd.
(1927) 32 Com.Cas. 216

The ordinary course of business

Facts

The plaintiff, a bookmaker, banked with the Harrogate branch of the defendant bank. On August 14, 1925, he drew a cheque for £200, payable to G. A. Wood, and handed it to the payee, shortly before 3 p.m. In the ordinary course the bank closed at 3 p.m., and the cheque could not have been presented before that time. Wood presented it, however, and for the purposes of this case the bank admitted cashing it at 3.5 p.m. Plaintiff later wished to stop payment of the cheque, and on the opening of the bank the next morning he sent his son to countermand payment. As the cheque had already been paid, the bank debited his account, however, and he then brought this action for a declaration that they were not entitled to do so, and that in cashing it after closing time they had committed a breach of their duty to him as his bankers.

Decision

It was held that a bank is entitled to deal with a cheque within a reasonable business margin of time after their advertised time of closing, and that in cashing the cheque as they did in this case, the bank had acted within their rights.

In the course of his judgment, Lord Hewart C.J. said:

What precisely are the limits of time within which a bank may conduct business, having prescribed, largely for its own convenience, particular times at which the doors of the building will be closed, is a large question which is not raised here. What is contended on behalf of the defendants is that they are entitled within a reasonable business margin of their advertised time for closing to deal with a cheque, not of course in the sense of dishonouring it, but in the sense of doing that which the cheque asks them to do, namely, to pay it. In my opinion their contention is right, and the plaintiff's case fails entirely.[64]

Notes

In the *Joachimson* case [65] Atkin L.J. said that it was part of the banker's obligation to pay cheques of the customer in normal business hours. In the present case, the court was not prepared to make it part of the obligation *not* to pay the cheques outside normal banking hours. It seems certain, however, that the ordinary course

[64] At p. 218.
[65] *Ante*, p. 1.

of the banker's business could not reasonably be extended more than a short time after the advertised time of closing; it would not, for example, be within the ordinary course of business to pay a cheque at midnight.[66]

In practice it is, of course, impracticable to finish the counter work of the branch immediately upon the closing of the doors, and it frequently happens that a quarter of an hour, or longer, elapses before the last customer (who may be waiting to present a cheque) is attended to. A difficulty might arise if a person entered the bank unobserved, while there were still customers awaiting attention, at, say, 3.20 p.m., and the bank cashed a cheque presented by such a person under the impression that he had been waiting since before closing time.

The ordinary course of business is so largely a question of what is reasonable in the particular circumstances that it is not possible to lay down firm rules. Thus, in *Auchteroni & Co.* v. *Midland Bank Ltd.*[67] Wright J. said:

> The law merchant has always recognised such presentation [of a bill, complete and regular on its face, and indorsed in blank by what the cashier knew to be the customer's genuine indorsement] as due presentation sufficient to require the bankers, in the absence of very special circumstances of suspicion, such as presentation by a tramp, or a postman or an office boy, to pay. To lay down any different principle and to treat that which is merely infrequent or unusual as irregular by the law merchant would be, I think, to make an inroad on the established rules of the law merchant without any sufficient ground.[68]

The encashment of cheques by open credit (*i.e.* " under advice "), or by cheque card, at branches other than that at which the account is kept is so common a practice that it would almost certainly be held to be within the ordinary course of business. Paget doubts [69] whether a cheque cashed by open credit by a third party instead of by the drawer himself would be within the ordinary course of business. It is to be noted, however, that this practice has been substantially increased, at least in a specialised form, by the growth of payment of wages by cheque; arrangements are often made for cheques in payment of wages or salaries to be cashed at branches convenient for the payees instead of the branch on which they are drawn.

In the same context Paget says that the cashing of a cheque by another bank (as opposed to another branch of the same bank) is

---

[66] See Chorley, *op. cit.* p. 92.
[67] [1928] 2 K.B. 294.
[68] At p. 304.
[69] *Op. cit.* p. 334.

outside the ordinary course of business, and this view is taken also in *Questions on Banking Practice.*[70] Until the point comes before the courts it must remain doubtful, but a bank under attack would presumably call in aid both the fact that this practice too is common, and the argument that the cashing bank is the agent of the bank on which the cheque was drawn, from which, of course, it will have had instructions as to payment.

The absence of litigation on open credits seems to indicate that in practice little trouble arises; and in any event this service to customers is so popular that were any legal impediment to it to be discovered it is probable that it would be overcome by some such expedient as the opening of temporary accounts at the branches or banks at which it was desired to establish the credits.

In an Irish case in 1962, *Royal Bank of Ireland* v. *O'Rourke,*[71] the Supreme Court considered the positions of both the paying and the collecting bank, on the dishonour of a cheque. A cheque had been exchanged for cash by the plaintiff bank at Dun Laoghaire on a Wednesday, taken in by hand to Dublin and presented to the College Green branch of the National Bank on the Thursday, and received back unpaid at Dun Laoghaire on Saturday. Notice of dishonour was telephoned on Monday to the defendant, who then pleaded that there had been delay both in presentation and in notice of dishonour. The court, finding for the bank, held that presentation on the day following receipt was sufficient,[72] and that notice of dishonour received on the day following dishonour by the person to whom it must be given was in good time [73]; while as regards the time taken by the National Bank in dishonouring the cheque (assumed but not proved to be the result of the deferred posting system) they held that they need not decide whether there had been unreasonable delay. This would seem to be the first time that deferred posting has come before the courts, even indirectly; it may be noted that while the Bills of Exchange Act makes no express provision as to the time within which a cheque must be paid or dishonoured, the court here said that regard must be had to the nature of the bill, the usage of trade with bills of that nature, and the facts of the particular case.

The fate of cheques presented through the Bankers Clearing House must normally be decided on the day of presentation, but the rules of the Clearing House allow cheques dishonoured for other

[70] (10th ed.) p. 168.
[71] [1962] I.R. 159.
[72] *Hare* v. *Henty* (1861) 10 C.B.N.S. 65.
[73] *Cf.* (Aug., 1964) 85 J.I.B. 290 where it is pointed out that s. 49 (14) of the Bills of Exchange Act gave the bank an even stronger defence.

than technical reasons to be returned on the morning after presentation (with telephone advice if the cheque is over £30), where by inadvertence return has not been made on the day of presentation. This exception to the basic rule presumably originated with delayed posting and continues with computerisation, but it was not referred to in the evidence of banking practice in the payment of cheques summarised in some detail by Brightman J. in his judgment in *Karak Rubber Co. Ltd.* v. *Burden (No. 2)*.[74]

Computerisation was not accepted as justification for late dishonour in the special circumstances of *Momm & others* v. *Barclays Bank International Ltd.*,[75] where Kerr J. held that the bank, having passed debit and credit entries between two customers' accounts on June 26, 1974, were not entitled to reverse those entries on the morning of June 27, even though the credit had not been communicated to the beneficiary. He rejected the bank's argument that the final balances for the day were not available from the computer until the following morning. He said:

> A day is a day. For banking purposes it ends at the close of working hours, and otherwise at midnight. Commerce requires that it should be clearly ascertainable at the end of a day whether a payment to be made on that day has been made or not. Whether that has happened or not cannot be held in suspense until the following morning. The only result will be that the defendants will no longer be able to rely, as against their own payee customers, on the possibility of having second thoughts on the following morning.[76]

The judgment in this case is of considerable interest to bankers. It concerned an " in house " transaction [77]; two " out house " payments, made at the same time on the instructions of the debtor company, were " irrevocably despatched " before the close of business.

The case was not concerned with, and the judgment did not touch upon, the cheque clearing process, but that the same reasoning might be applied to postponed return of dishonoured cheques is clearly a possibility.

---

[74] [1972] 1 W.L.R. 602.

[75] [1976] 3 All E.R. 588; also *sub nom. Delbrueck & Co.* v. *Barclays Bank International Ltd.* [1976] 2 Lloyd's Rep. 341.

[76] At p. 598.

[77] *Cf. The Brimnes, ante,* p. 41, considered by Kerr J. in the *Momm* judgment as not countering his view that communication to the payee is not an essential of a completed payment.

Greenwood v. Martins Bank Ltd.

[1933] A.C. 51

A banker has normally no authority to debit his customer when that customer's signature to a cheque or a mandate has been forged; but the customer may be estopped from denying the genuineness of the signature

Facts

The plaintiff had an account with the defendant bank. His wife kept the pass book and cheque book, and gave him cheques as he required them. In October, 1929, he asked her for a cheque, saying that he wished to draw £20. She thereupon told him that there was no money in the bank, as she had drawn it all out to help her sister in legal proceedings in which she was involved. The wife had in fact forged her husband's name on cheques over a period. Upon the urgent request of the wife, the husband refrained from notifying the bank of the frauds.

Eight months later he discovered that the explanation his wife had given him, regarding her sister's legal proceedings, was false, and he then told her that he would notify the bank, whereupon she committed suicide. The plaintiff afterwards brought an action against the defendants for the amount paid by them on the forged signatures.

Decision

The House of Lords held that the plaintiff owed a duty of disclosure to the bank on his first discovery of the fraud, and that as his conduct had, in the event, deprived them of their right of action against the forger he was estopped from asserting the forgery.

In his judgment Lord Tomlin, after summarising the essentials of estoppel—a representation, an act or omission resulting from that representation by the person to whom it was made, and detriment suffered by him as a result—went on to say:

> The deliberate abstention from speaking in those circumstances seems to me to amount to a representation to the respondents that the forged cheques were in fact in order, and assuming that detriment to the respondents followed there were, it seems to me, present all the elements essential to estoppel.[78]

In the Court of Appeal, Scrutton L.J. had said[79]:

> [There is] a continuing duty on either side to act with reasonable care to ensure the proper working of the account. It seems to me that the banker, if a cheque were presented to him which he rejected as forged, would be

[78] At p. 58.

[79] [1932] 1 K.B. 371.

under a duty to report this to the customer to enable him to inquire into and protect himself against the circumstances of the forgery. This, I think, would involve a corresponding duty on the customer, if he became aware that forged cheques were being presented to his banker, to inform his banker in order that the banker might avoid loss in the future. If this is correct there was in the present case silence, a breach of duty to disclose.[80]

Notes

Where the customer's signature has been forged the instrument is a nullity, and the banker cannot debit his customer's account because he has no mandate to do so.[81] But there may be cases where the customer is estopped from setting up the forgery as against the banker.

The three essentials of estoppel set out by Lord Tomlin are to be seen in an old case, *Leach* v. *Buchanan*.[82] There, a person who was asked to give value for a bill of exchange sent a messenger to the acceptor to ask if the acceptance was good. The acceptor said that it was; and when, on presentation for payment, he asserted that it was in fact a forgery it was held that he was estopped from setting up the forgery against the person who had acted on his representation to the contrary.

It may be remarked that *Greenwood's* case arose before the passing of the Law Reform (Married Women and Tortfeasors) Act 1935. As husbands were then still liable for their wives' torts, Greenwood would himself have been liable had the bank been able to bring an action against the wife. However, the fact that this " circular " effect would not arise today does not affect the important general principle of the decision.

Estoppel cannot normally be set up as a defence by the person whose negligence was the cause of the loss, and in the *Greenwood* case the trial judge found against the bank on the grounds that they had been negligent in not detecting the forgeries. The Court of Appeal and the House of Lords, however, considered that, while the bank's negligence was the proximate cause of their loss in paying the forged cheques, it was not the proximate cause of the loss of their right of action against the forger.

The facts were different, but no less favourable to the bank, in *Brown* v. *Westminster Bank Ltd.*[83] Here the bank had several times, through two successive managers of the branch concerned, drawn the attention of their customer, an old lady, to the number of

---

[80] At p. 381.

[81] *Cf.* dictum of Kerr J. in *National Westminster Bank Ltd.* v. *Barclays Bank International Ltd. post*, p. 79.

[82] (1802) 4 Esp. 226.

[83] [1964] 2 Lloyd's Rep. 187.

cheques passing through her account payable to her servant, Carless. On the first such occasion she said that she was in the habit of asking Carless to cash cheques for her at the British Legion Club; and on other occasions she did not deny drawing the cheques. Eventually the second manager discussed the matter with the customer's son, who held her power of attorney; and in due course the present action was brought against the bank in respect of 329 cheques alleged to have been forged. Roskill J. held that the plaintiff was estopped from setting up the forgeries against the bank; even those that occurred before the bank first queried the cheques had been represented as genuine by the customer's statement to the manager, so that she was thereafter debarred from setting up the true facts.

The *Greenwood* and *Brown* cases may be compared with two older cases, where the bank failed in their defences based on their customers' negligence. In *Lewes Sanitary Steam Laundry Co. Ltd.* v. *Barclay & Co. Ltd.*,[84] the secretary of the company forged a large number of cheques on the company's account. The company sued the bank for the money paid out on the forgeries, and the bank alleged that the company had been negligent both in a system that did not provide for adequate scrutiny of the company's books and in their appointment as secretary of a person whom they knew to have been previously guilty of forgery. This defence failed, Kennedy J. remarking that " negligence to make an estoppel must be in, or immediately connected with, the transaction itself which is complained of."[85] And in *Kepitigalla Rubber Estates Ltd.* v. *National Bank of India Ltd.*,[86] where the secretary of a company over a period of two months drew cheques by forging the signatures of the directors, it appeared that during this period the directors had not examined the pass book or the company's cash book; but it was held that the plaintiffs were under no duty so to organise their business that forgery of cheques could not take place.

These two cases were decided before the *Macmillan* case had brought out the duty of care that the customer owes to his banker.

---

[84] (1906) 11 Com.Cas. 255.

[85] At p. 267. *Cf.* Lord Finlay, in *London Joint Stock Bank Ltd.* v. *Macmillan and Arthur* (*ante*, p. 43): " Of course the negligence must be in the transaction itself, that is, in the manner in which the cheque is drawn. It would be no defence to the banker, if the forgery had been that of a clerk of the customer, that the latter had taken the clerk into his service without sufficient inquiry as to his character. Attempts have often been made to extend the principle of *Young* v. *Grote* beyond the case of negligence in the immediate transaction, but they have always failed " (at p. 795). *Cf.* also Scrutton L.J., quoted *post*, pp. 103–104.

It is interesting to compare the courts' insistence on this point with the gradual extension of the scope of the banker's duty to circumstances far removed from the immediate transaction; *cf. post*, pp. 84 *et seq.*

[86] [1909] 2 K.B. 1010.

But the facts in the *Macmillan* case, and in the *Greenwood* and *Brown* cases, were more favourable to the bank than those in the two earlier cases, and the courts so far have not extended the customer's duty of care to take in negligence less directly concerned with the transaction. It may be noted that McNair J. in *Brewer* v. *Westminster Bank Ltd.*,[87] expressly rejected the argument that *Greenwood's* case had weakened the *Kepitigalla* decision: " In my judgment," he said, " there is no inconsistency between the two decisions."

Curtice v. London, City & Midland Bank Ltd.

[1908] 1 K.B. 293

Westminster Bank Ltd. v. Hilton

(1926) 43 T.L.R. 124

Countermand of payment is effective only when it is brought to the notice of the banker and when it is unambiguous in terms

Facts of Curtice v. London, City & Midland Bank Ltd.

The plaintiff was a customer at the Willesden Green branch of the defendant bank. He drew a cheque for £63 in payment for horses bought from one, Jones, but as the horses were not delivered, he sent a telegram stopping the cheque, and this telegram was delivered by the G.P.O. in the letter box of the bank at 6.15 p.m. On the next day the telegram was missed when the letter box was cleared, and during the day the cheque was paid. The following morning the telegram was found, together with the written confirmation of the countermand which the plaintiff had posted. He was notified that the " stop " had arrived too late to be effective, whereupon he drew a cheque for the whole of his balance, including the sum of £63, and, upon this cheque being dishonoured, brought the present action for money had and received. In the county court, judgment was given for the plaintiff, and a Divisional Court dismissed the bank's appeal. The bank further appealed.

Decision

The Court of Appeal held that there had been no effective countermand of payment within section 75 of the Bills of Exchange Act; and this was so even though the negligence of the bank was the cause of it.

---

[87] [1952] 2 All E.R. 650, at p. 656, *post*, pp. 172 *et seq.*

In the course of his judgment, Cozens-Hardy M.R. said:

There is no such thing as a constructive countermand in a commercial transaction of this kind. In my opinion, on the admitted facts of this case, the cheque was not countermanded, although it may well be that it was due to the negligence of the bank that they did not receive notice of the customer's desire to stop the cheque. For such negligence the bank might be liable, but the measure of damage would be by no means the same as in an action for money had and received. I agree with the judgment of A. T. Lawrence, J., on this point, and that is sufficient to dispose of the appeal. But as we have had an argument addressed to us as to the effect upon the duty of a bank of the mere receipt of a telegram, I wish to add a few words on that. A telegram may, reasonably and in the ordinary course of business, be acted upon by the bank, at least to the extent of postponing the honouring of the cheque until further inquiry can be made. But I am not satisfied that the bank is bound as a matter of law to accept an unauthenticated telegram as sufficient authority for the serious step of refusing to pay a cheque.[88]

And Fletcher Moulton L.J. said:

It has long been held that an order must be unambiguous. If a master chooses to give an order to his servant that bears two meanings, he cannot find fault with his servant for having taken the meaning which it was not in fact intended to bear; and that applies to a banker when receiving orders as much as to agents generally. Now that principle which applies to the duty of conveying the mandate in a form in which the meaning is unambiguous applies, in my opinion, *mutatis mutandis*, to the question of its authenticity. If the mandate is sent in a form in which a servant, acting reasonably, has no security that the mandate comes from his employer, the employer cannot grumble that he did not act upon it. Authenticity and meaning appear to me, in the general law of agency, to stand on the same footing, subject, of course, to the broad difference of circumstances which are due to the difference of nature of the two.[89]

Facts of Westminster Bank Ltd. v. Hilton

The plaintiff, who had an account with the defendant bank, drew a cheque for £8 1s. 6d., payable to one, Poate. The cheque, which was drawn on July 31, 1924, was numbered 117285, and post-dated August 2. On August 1, the plaintiff wired to the bank to stop payment of cheque No. 117283, giving the payee and the amount of the cheque No. 117285. In fact, cheque No. 117283, to another payee and for another amount, had previously been paid by the bank. On August 6, cheque No. 117285 was presented and, the bank supposing that it had been drawn in place of the one that had been stopped, paid it. The plaintiff brought an action for negligence

[88] At pp. 298.
[89] At pp. 299–300.

against the bank, and when it was decided in favour of the bank he appealed. The Court of Appeal found in his favour, whereupon the bank appealed.

Decision

The House of Lords held that, as the one certain item of identification was the number of the cheque, the bank was not guilty of negligence.

In the course of his judgment, Lord Shaw of Dunfermline said:

When a banker is in possession of sufficient funds to meet such a cheque from a customer, the duty of the bank is to honour that cheque by payment, and failure in this duty may involve the bank in serious liability to its customer. This duty is ended, and on the contrary when the cheque is stopped another duty arises—namely, to refuse payment. In a case of that character it rests upon the customer to prove that the order to stop reached the bank in time and was unequivocally referable to a cheque then in existence, and signed and issued by the customer before the notice to stop. It would, of course, be intolerable in business to permit the form of stoppage to be applied to a non-existent and non-issued cheque. Further, in the ordinary course of trade a cheque is signed on the date it bears. This being so the notice of stoppage on reaching the bank will properly be treated as only applying to a cheque bearing a date the same as, or anterior to, the date of stoppage. To carry the scope of stoppage further and to make it apply to the case (exceptional and out of the ordinary course of business transactions)—the case of cheques which though subsequent to stoppage in date were yet anterior to stoppage at the time of signature and issue, namely, post-dated cheques—it is, in my view, necessary for the customer to prove and explain the post-dating, but further to prove that this fact was brought clearly home to the mind of the banker so as to bring the post-dated cheque within the order of stoppage. If these last things are not clearly proved (and the onus of doing so is no light one), then the bank acts rightly in declining to dishonour a cheque which *ex facie* bears a date subsequent to the stoppage.[90]

Notes

It is to be remarked that, in the Curtice case, the opinions concerning the use of the telegram as a method of countermanding payment were *obiter*: the case was decided on the fact that the countermand was not in fact received. In *Westminster Bank* v. *Hilton* the *ratio decidendi* of Lord Shaw's judgment was not that of the four other Law Lords, which was based on the facts of the particular case. The judgments here quoted are valuable, however, in that they provide basic principles for the law of countermand of payment; and although not of binding force, they are yet of great authority.

[90] At pp. 129–130.

It must be noted too, in the *Curtice* case, that the bank succeeded in the action brought against them for money had and received. An action on the same facts for negligence might well have had a different issue.

A stop sent to one branch of a bank is not an effective stop of a cheque drawn on another branch of that bank.[91]

Gibbons v. Westminster Bank Ltd.

[1939] 2 K.B. 882

Upon the wrongful dishonour of his cheque a customer who is not a trader must prove special damage before he can be awarded substantial damages

Facts

The plaintiff was a woman customer of the defendant bank, who, after paying in a sum of money to her account, drew a cheque which was dishonoured as a result of the bank's having put the credit to another account instead of to hers. Upon the dishonour, she called on the manager of the branch at which the account was kept, and he paid her £1 1s.—in full satisfaction, as the bank claimed, of any claim she might have against them. The jury found, however, that she did not so accept the payment.

The defendant bank contended that the plaintiff was entitled to nominal damages only, as she had not pleaded any special or actual damage. The jury awarded substantial damages, however, in the sum of £50, and after they had then been discharged, the court heard further argument regarding damages.

Decision

It was held that as the plaintiff was a non-trader, who had not proved any special damage, she was entitled to nominal damages only. 40 shillings were awarded.

In the course of his judgment, Lawrence J. said:

The authorities which have been cited in argument all lay down that a trader is entitled to recover substantial damages for the wrongful dishonour of his cheque without pleading and proving actual damage, but it has never been held that that exception to the general rule as to the measure of damages for breach of contract extends to any one who is not a trader. The cases cited in which this view has been taken are *Marzetti* v. *Williams*,[92]

[91] *London Provincial & South Western Bank Ltd.* v. *Buszard* (1918) 35 T.L.R. 142; *post*, p. 344, *cf. Burnett* v. *Westminster Bank Ltd.*, *ante*, p. 24.

[92] (1830) 1 B. & Ad. 415.

Rolin v. *Steward*,[93] *Bank of New South Wales* v. *Milvain*,[94] and *Kinlan* v. *Ulster Bank Ltd.*[95] The rule is so put in Grant's *Law of Banking* (7th ed.), at pp. 88–89, and in Smith's *Leading Cases* (13th ed.), Vol. 2, at p. 574, where it is also stated that the exception to the general rule is one which ought not to be extended, reference being made to the speech of Lord Atkinson in *Addis* v. *Gramophone Co. Ltd.*[96] In my opinion, this matter should be treated as covered by these authorities, and I hold accordingly that the corollary of the proposition laid down by them, is the law—namely, that a person who is not a trader is not entitled to recover substantial damages for the wrongful dishonour of his cheque, unless the damage which he has suffered is alleged and proved as special damage.[97]

Notes

The rule that a trader, and so far only a trader, can recover substantial damages for the wrongful dishonour of his cheque without proof of actual damage is, as Lawrence J. pointed out, an exception to the general rule as to the measure of damages for breach of contract. It is of comparatively recent development, and may still be capable of extension; there are other classes of the community likely to suffer at least as serious damage as the trader.[98]

In *Evans* v. *London and Provincial Bank Ltd.*[99] the plaintiff, the wife of a naval officer, drew a cheque on her husband's behalf payable to the mess steward of the ship on which he was serving. This cheque was wrongfully dishonoured, and Lord Reading C.J. directed the jury that the only question was what damages were due to the lady for the bank's mistake, as she had not suffered any special damage. The jury returned a verdict of one shilling damages.

Rolin v. *Steward*[1] is an example of the trader's obtaining substantial damages without proof of special loss. In that case three cheques and a bill were dishonoured in error; they were re-presented the next day, and paid. In the plaintiff's subsequent action a jury awarded him £500 damages, and on appeal it was held that, although in the circumstances this amount was excessive, yet he was entitled to substantial damages, and £200 was awarded.

In *Baker* v. *Australia and New Zealand Bank Ltd.*[2] the plaintiff, a company director, was awarded only nominal damages for breach of contract in the wrongful dishonour of her cheques, and a sum of £100 in her action for libel.

---

[93] (1854) 14 C.B. 595; *infra*.
[94] (1884) 10 V.L.R. 3.
[95] [1928] I.R. 171.
[96] [1909] A.C. 488 at p. 495.
[97] At p. 888.
[98] *Cf.* Chorley, *op. cit.* p. 111.
[99] (1917) 3 L.D.B. 152.
[1] *Supra*.
[2] [1958] N.Z.L.R. 907; *post.* p, 75, 76.

Davidson v. Barclays Bank Ltd.

(1940) 56 T.L.R. 343

When a cheque is wrongfully dishonoured it may be possible to bring an action for libel against the bank; and the defence of privilege cannot be relied upon by the bank in such circumstances

Facts

The plaintiff, a bookmaker, drew a cheque for £2 15s. 8d. upon the Kennington branch of the defendant bank. Owing to the fact that the bank had previously paid in error a cheque which the plaintiff had countermanded there were not sufficient funds on the account to meet the later cheque, which was accordingly returned marked "Not sufficient."

The plaintiff brought the present action against the bank, complaining that the words meant that he had drawn a cheque knowing that he had insufficient funds, that he was unable to pay £2 15s. 8d., and that it was unsafe to transact business with him and give him credit. The defendant bank pleaded, *inter alia*, that the words were published only to the payee of the cheque, who had an interest in knowing the reason why the cheque had not been met, and to whom they were under a duty to communicate that reason; that the words were published in the honest though mistaken belief that they were true, and that the occasion of publication was therefore privileged.

Decision

It was held that in fact the bank owed no duty of communication to the payee of the cheque; that there was no common interest between bank and payee calling for communication; and that the occasion was not privileged.

In the course of his judgment, Hilbery J. said:

It seems obviously fallacious for the bank to say that, because they had made a mistake as a result of which they thought the occasion to be one when the cheque must be returned, therefore the occasion was one where they had to make the communication explaining why the cheque was returned. . . . What the bank seek to do here is to create an occasion of qualified privilege after making a mistake which appeared to make a communication on their part necessary. That is where the essential difference lies between this case and that which counsel for the defendants instanced in argument—namely, where one person inquires of another about the character of a third person, or where the customer of a bank gives his bank manager as a reference to a person from whom he proposes to rent premises. In either of these examples, when the request for the information is made, the occasion of qualified privilege is already constituted. If on such an occasion . . . a communication is made which is mistakenly defamatory . . . the communication is privileged and, subject to the well-known qualification, no action will lie. In each of those examples the privileged occasion is already there when the communication is made . . . it is not the mistake which creates the occasion; it is the occasion which is followed by the mistake.[3]

Notes

It is open to the injured customer, in some cases, to frame his action in libel, either alone, as in the *Davidson* case, or jointly with his contractual claim, as in *Plunkett* v. *Barclays Bank Ltd.*[4] *and Baker* v. *Australia and New Zealand Bank Ltd.*[5] If the rule is established that only a trader can succeed in a claim for substantial damages without proof of special damage, this alternative course of action may be more used than it has been in the past. The banks are at risk in the matter only when cheques have been wrongfully dishonoured, but the risk then is a real one, and the cases suggest that it is now virtually impossible for them to avoid it.

For many years the banker could argue that his most common answer on dishonoured cheques, " Refer to drawer," had no necessarily defamatory meaning. In *Flach* v. *London and South Western Bank Ltd.*[6] the plaintiff's cheque was returned unpaid during the moratorium at the outbreak of the First World War. The bank succeeded in their first defence to her action against them, that they were protected by the terms of the moratorium; they succeeded also in their contention that the words " Refer to drawer " were not libellous, Scrutton J. saying on this point that in his opinion the words in their ordinary meaning amounted to a statement by the bank, " We are not paying; go back to the drawer and ask why," or else, " Go back to the drawer and ask him to pay."

In *Plunkett's* case [7] du Parcq J. adopted the view of Scrutton J. as to the libel issue before him, but as time passed it became increasingly unrealistic to expect contemporary opinion to agree; and by 1950 the decision of the Irish Supreme Court (not binding on English courts, but to be treated with respect) in *Pyke* v. *Hibernian Bank Ltd.*[8] was not unexpected. Three cheques were wrongly dishonoured with the answer " Refer to drawer," two of the cheques bearing also the word " re-present." A jury awarded £1 damages for breach of contract and £400 for libel, and this verdict was affirmed in the Supreme Court, where although two of the judges accepted the bank's argument that the words were incapable of a

[3] At p. 349.
[4] [1936] 2 K.B. 107; *ante*, p. 51.
[5] *Ante*, p. 73.
[6] (1915) 31 T.L.R. 334.
[7] *Ante* p. 51.
[8] [1950] I.R. 195.

defamatory meaning, the other two rejected it, and distinguished the *Flach* decision on the grounds that there the dishonour was not in fact wrongful.

In England *Jayson* v. *Midland Bank Ltd.*[9] has probably settled the matter. Here the plaintiff claimed that the dishonour was wrongful and that " Refer to drawer " was libellous. The jury found that the words were (in the words of the question the judge put to them) likely " to lower the plaintiff's reputation in the minds of right thinking people." This did not avail the plaintiff, because the jury found also that the dishonour was justified, and the Court of Appeal dismissed the plaintiff's appeal on that point. But it seems unlikely that any bank could succeed in future in a plea that " Refer to drawer " is not defamatory, especially as the jury's view in *Jayson's* case is almost certainly shared by most people today.

The answer in the *Davidson* case, " Not sufficient," was clearly defamatory; so are such other answers as " Exceeds arrangements." Again it has been held by the Supreme Court of New Zealand (and again the decision is not binding in England, but is of great weight) that " Present again " is capable of bearing a defamatory meaning,[10] and the decision of the Court of Appeal in 1906, in *Frost* v. *London Joint Stock Bank Ltd.*[11] that the absence of any stated reason for dishonour could not give rise to a presumption of one meaning rather than another especially when the meaning suggested is libellous, is of academic interest in view of the rule of the London Clearing House requiring written answers on all dishonoured cheques passing through the clearing. It may be questioned therefore whether any wording (other than those marking technical irregularities) can avoid the danger of a libel action if the dishonour is not in fact justified.

There is a secondary point of interest in *Pyke's* case. Black J. one of the judges finding for the bank, differed from Hilbery J.'s finding as to privilege in *Davidson's* case: he considered that Hilbery J.'s view of the authorities was too limited, and that on a wider range there was authority for holding that privilege can apply even when the occasion has arisen because of the mistake of the person claiming the privilege. But that opinion, persuasively reasoned as it was, can give the banker no comfort until it is followed in an English court.

---

[9] [1968] 1 Lloyd's Rep. 409.

[10] *Baker* v. *Australia and New Zealand Bank Ltd.* [1958] N.Z.L.R. 907, *ante*, p. 73.

[11] (1906) 22 T.L.R. 760.

Robarts v. Tucker

(1851) 16 Q.B. 560

Payment after a forged endorsement

Facts

A branch of the Pelican Life Insurance Company (of which company Tucker was secretary) drew on its head office a bill for £5,000 in settlement of a claim under a life policy. The indorsements to the bill were forged by the solicitor for the claimants under the policy, and the bill was presented at the head office of the company for acceptance. After scrutiny the bill was accepted payable at the firm's bankers, Robarts, Curtis & Co., and it was later paid there. Upon the forgeries being discovered, the insurance company paid £5,000 to the defrauded beneficiaries, and brought this action against the bank.

The bank in its defence argued (i) that they owed no duty, beyond that of reasonable care, in inspecting indorsements; (ii) that in this case the insurance company, in accordance with their usual practice, had inspected the indorsements before accepting the bill, and so had vouched for them. Upon losing the case in the Queen's Bench Division, the bank appealed.

Decision

The Court of Exchequer Chamber dismissed the appeal.

In the course of his judgment, Parke B. said:

If this were the ordinary case of an acceptance made payable at a banker's, there can be no question that making the acceptance payable there is tantamount to an order, on the part of the acceptor, to the banker to pay the bill to the person who is according to the law merchant capable of giving a good discharge for the bill. . . . The bankers cannot charge their customer with any other payments than those made in pursuance of that authority. If bankers wish to avoid the responsibility of deciding on the genuineness of indorsements, they may require their customers to domicile their bills at their own offices and to honour them by giving a cheque upon the banker. [In the present case] reliance is placed on the evidence which shows that the company were accustomed to take precautions before accepting a bill. But that custom was never communicated to the bankers; and there is no evidence, direct or indirect, of any communication to the bankers from which an authority to pay this bill without examination could be inferred.[12]

---

[12] At p. 579.

Notes

The banker's loss of the right to debit his customer arises, not from negligence in failing to detect the forgery of a signature which he cannot be expected to know, but from his failure to obey his customer's mandate: he has not paid to the designated payee.

This inability to debit the customer's account, clearly established in *Robarts* v. *Tucker*, would have been of considerable and ever-increasing danger to bankers as the use of cheques developed. It was this which gave rise to the statutory protection provided, *in the case of cheques*, by section 19 of the Stamp Act 1853, later substantially re-enacted by section 60 of the Bills of Exchange 1882.[13]

There are two cases, apart from section 60, when the banker can debit his customer's account with instruments on which the indorsement has been forged: (i) when the payee was fictitious or non-existing, and, as a result, the bill can be treated as payable to bearer under section 7 (3) of the Act: the forgery of the indorsement is then irrelevant; (ii) when, rarely, the customer is estopped from denying the authenticity of the indorsement. *Bank of England* v. *Vagliano* [14] is an example of both exceptions; in addition to the finding already set out [15] the House of Lords held that by accepting the bill payable at his bank, Vagliano represented it to be genuine, although the bill was in fact a forgery throughout. The distinction on this point between *Vagliano's* case and *Robarts* v. *Tucker* is in the fact that in the latter case the bill itself was a good one, only the indorsements being forged, while in the former the whole instrument was forged save for Vagliano's signature; this alone gave the bill any value, as there was not even a drawer to whom recourse could be had.

In this connection, Lord Halsbury L.C. said:

> I am not intending to throw any doubt upon the propriety of the decision in *Robarts* v. *Tucker*, nor am I prepared to assent to the proposition that it is a harsh decision. A customer tells his banker to pay a particular person; the banker pays someone else, and it would seem to follow as a perfectly just result that the banker should be called upon to make good the amount he has so erroneously paid. But what relation has such a decision to a case where a thing which bears the form and semblance of a known commercial document like a bill of exchange gets by the act of the customer into the hands of a banker, where there is no real drawer, no real transaction between himself and the supposed drawer, and where, as a matter of fact, there is no person who in the proper and ordinary sense of the word is a payee at all? It seems to me that if all these circumstances, acting upon and inducing the bankers to make the payments they did make, are acts which are the fault of the customer, it is the customer and not the banker who ought to bear the loss.[16]

[13] *Cf. ante*, p. 130 *et seq.*
[14] [1891] A.C. 107.
[15] *Ante*, p. 31.
[16] At p. 117.

It will be seen, however, how rarely such circumstances as those of the *Vagliano* case are likely to occur; for no protection can be drawn from that decision where the document is genuine apart from the forged indorsement. This must have been placed on the bill after the customer's acceptance, and he cannot be made responsible for it. It is to be noted, too, that the banker will in such a case be liable to pay the true owner, and he will have no such protection as section 60 of the Bills of Exchange Act gives him with regard to cheques.

National Westminster Bank Ltd. v. Barclays Bank International Ltd. and Another

[1975] Q.B. 654

The recovery of money paid under a mistake of fact

Facts

The second defendant was Mr. Ismail, a Nigerian businessman anxious to move substantial funds out of Nigeria, in evasion of the strict exchange control regulations in force there. He bought, at a premium, a cheque for £8,000 on the National Westminster Bank, St. James's Square, London, but before paying for it he sent it to his own bank in London, Barclays Bank International, for special collection and advice of payment. The cheque was duly presented and paid, and Mr. Ismail paid for it in Nigeria. A fortnight later it was established that the cheque, which had been stolen from the owner's cheque book, was a clever forgery. The paying bank brought the present action for recovery of the money, which still stood to Mr. Ismail's credit in his London account. Barclays took no part in the trial, but Mr. Ismail resisted, arguing that (*a*) by paying the cheque the plaintiffs had represented that it was genuine, he had acted to his detriment on this representation and the plaintiffs were therefore estopped from recovering; (*b*) even apart from estoppel, the fact that he had acted to his detriment in reliance on the payment barred recovery; (*c*) the paying bank owes a duty of care to payees in honouring cheques, and the plaintiffs had been negligent in this duty; and (*d*) the plaintiffs were anyhow estopped by their negligence.

Decision

Kerr J. held that the plaintiffs were entitled to recover. He rejected all the defendant's arguments, and held further that even apart from the issues thus raised, in view of the suspicious circumstances in which the cheque had been obtained, which were not disclosed to the plaintiffs, he could not regard their payment of the cheque as a representation that it was genuine.

On the first of the defendant's arguments he said:

> . . . Mr Ismail can in the present case only succeed in raising an estoppel against the plaintiffs if the mere fact of a banker honouring a cheque on which his customer's signature has been undetectably forged carries with it an implied representation that the signature is genuine I cannot see any logical basis for this. At most, it seems to me, the paying banker is thereby representing no more than that he believes the signature to be genuine. . . . Furthermore, I think that the law should be slow to impose on an innocent party who has not acted negligently an estoppel merely by reason of having dealt with a forged document on the assumption that it was genuine. In the context of forged share transfers this contention has been rejected as against companies which register a transfer in the belief of its authenticity: see *Simm* v. *Anglo-American Telegraph Co.*[17]

Notes

This very interesting case is noteworthy for the number of propositions, welcome to bankers, for which the judgment is authority. Thus, Kerr J. after carefully examining the several heads of the allegation of negligence, and holding that the bank had not in fact been negligent, rejected also the contention that the special presentation of the cheque should have put the paying bank especially on guard. " Special presentation," he said, " is usually the result of uncertainty as to the availability of funds, and does not ' imply anything sinister or suspicious which in itself should put the paying bank on guard.' "

He held also, rejecting the defendant's third argument, that the paying banker owes no " duty of care to a payee in deciding to honour a customer's cheque, at any rate when this appears to be regular on its face," while his comment on " the common aphorism that a banker is under a duty to know his customer's signature "—that it " is in fact incorrect even as between the banker and his customer. The principle is simply that a banker cannot debit his customer's account on the basis of a forged signature, since he has in that event no mandate from the customer for doing so "—should help to lay the recurrent superstition to rest.[18]

On the defendant's second argument, namely the detriment suffered, he said:

> The mere fact that the defendant has acted to his detriment by spending

[17] (1879) 5 Q.B.D. 188; and *cf. The Lord Mayor of Sheffield* v. *Barclay and Others*, *post*, *p*. 285. *Per* Kerr J. at p. 674.

[18] *Cf.* Chorley, *op cit.* p. 95.

or paying away the money in reliance on having received the payment is not sufficient to bar the plaintiff's right to recover it: see *e.g.* *Standish* v. *Ross*,[19] *Durrant* v. *Ecclesiastical Commissioners*[20] and *Baylis* v. *Bishop of London*.[21] There are exceptions to this rule if in the circumstances the plaintiff represented to the defendant that he might treat the money as his own, or if he was under a duty as against the payee to inform him of the true state of account between them, or if the mistake was in some way induced or contributed to by the payee: see *e.g.* *Holt* v. *Markham*,[22] the review of the authorities by Asquith J. in *Weld-Blundell* v. *Synott*,[23] and *Larner* v. *London County Council*.[24] But none of these have any application here.[25]

How far detriment to the defendant is relevant in resisting claims for repayment is essentially the point of apparent conflict between the decision of Mathew J. in *London and River Plate Bank* v. *Bank of Liverpool*[26] and that of the Judicial Committee of the Privy Council in *Imperial Bank of Canada* v. *Bank of Hamilton*.[27] In the first of these two cases the defendant bank paid bills accepted by the plaintiff bank, which were later found to bear forged indorsements. By then the defendants had by the lapse of time lost their right to give notice of dishonour to other parties. But in holding that the plaintiffs could not recover, Mathew J. seemed to recognise no possibility of recovery except on immediate discovery of the mistake. He said:

> In *Cocks* v. *Masterman*[28] the simple rule was laid down in clear language for the first time that when a bill becomes due and is presented for payment the holder ought to know at once whether the bill is going to be paid or not. If the mistake is discovered at once, it may be the money can be recovered back; but if it be not, and the money is paid in good faith, and is received in good faith, and there is an interval of time in which the position of the holder may be altered, the principle seems to apply that money once paid cannot be recovered back. That rule is obviously, as it seems to me, indispensable for the conduct of business.[29]

But in the *Imperial Bank of Canada* case, which concerned a fraudulently raised cheque, Lord Lindley said:

> The rule laid down in *Cocks* v. *Masterman* and recently reasserted in even wider language by Mathew J. . . . had reference to negotiable instruments, on the dishonour of which notice has to be given to someone . . . who would be discharged from liability unless such notice were given in proper time. Their Lordships are not aware of any authority for applying so stringent a rule to any other cases. Assuming it to be as stringent as is alleged in such

---

[19] (1849) 3 Ex. 527.
[20] (1880) 6 Q.B.D. 234.
[21] [1913] 1 Ch. 127.
[22] [1923] 1 K.B. 504; *post*, pp. 82, 140.
[23] [1940] 2 All E.R. 580.
[24] [1949] 2 K.B. 683; *post*, p. 140.
[25] At pp. 675–676.
[26] [1896] 1 Q.B. 7.
[27] [1903] A.C. 49; *infra*.
[28] (1829) 9 B. & C. 902.
[29] At p. 11.

cases as those above described, their Lordships are not prepared to extend it to other cases where notice of the mistake is given in reasonable time, and no loss has been occasioned by the delay in giving it.[30]

In the course of a detailed examination of these two cases, Paget suggests [31] that the Privy Council decision, " in so far as [it] conflicts with the judgment of Mathew J. . . . has lost any authority it may have had." This opinion is based upon the Court of Appeal decision in *Morison's* case,[32] where the principle in the *Bank of Liverpool* case was approved and applied, but it may be suggested that the adoption of Mathew J.'s decision by the Court of Appeal was not in such terms as to emphasise the absolute nature of the principle—Buckley L.J. for example, emphasised rather that the bank had in fact altered its position. On the other hand, the Privy Council was considering an excellent " stringent " interpretation of the principle, for in the case in question, in the Court of Appeal for Ontario, Armour C.J. had said, in his dissenting judgment: " The application of this rule does not at all depend on whether the holder of the bill is or is not prejudiced by the delay." It was this absolute interpretation that the Privy Council was at pains to set aside; and the Court of Appeal, in *Morison's* case, would not appear to have supported such an interpretation. Indeed, Mathew J. himself, after stating the principle emphatically, went on to show that the position of the defendant bank had been affected by the delay.[33]

In these circumstances it is submitted that the principle in question must still be read subject to the Privy Council " gloss," and so indeed does Kerr J. seem to have regarded it in his review of the cases in the *National Westminster Bank* case. It is to be noted that there the instrument in question, being a forgery, was a nullity in law, so that the English cases, all of them concerned with negotiable instruments, were anyhow to be distinguished. But Kerr J.'s statement of principle, that detriment is relevant only as an exception to the general rule, would seem to be good law.[34]

For money paid in mistake to be recoverable at all, the mistake must be one of fact, not law. Thus, in *Holt* v. *Markham*,[35] Holt & Co., acting as Army agents, overpaid Colonel Markham as a result of misinterpreting the relevant Army regulations. The Court of

---

[30] At p. 58.

[31] *Op. cit.* pp. 356 *et seq.*

[32] *Post*, p. 101.

[33] As has been more than once pointed out, it is hard to follow his statement that the Bank of Liverpool had lost their right of giving notice to Larrinaga and Co.

[34] *Cf. post*, pp. 139 *et seq.*, for the relevance of detriment to the customer in cases on wrong entries in the customer's account.

[35] [1923] 1 K.B. 504; *cf. post*, p. 140.

Appeal held *inter alia* that this was a mistake of law, and the money therefore not recoverable. But in *Admiralty Commissioners* v. *National Provincial and Union Bank of England Ltd.*,[36] where pay had been credited to an officer's account for some time after he had, first, been transferred to the Royal Air Force and, later, killed, the plaintiffs were held entitled to recover the money so paid; the bank had contended that they were not entitled to release the amount in question until the consent of the personal representatives had been obtained, but this argument was rejected. It will be noted that the bank had not altered its position after receipt of the credits—for example, by paying out any part of them to, or on behalf of, their customer.

The mistake must be one between the party paying and the party receiving the money. *Chambers* v. *Miller*[37] was a case of a bank paying a cheque when it was presented to them, but immediately discovering that there was not sufficient funds on the account to meet it. It was held that the mistake here was between the bank and its customer, and could not affect the rights of the person paid, who need not repay the money.

It is of course difficult, if not impossible, for the defendant to resist payment where he did not take in good faith.[38] Kerr J.'s secondary finding in the *National Westminster Bank* case may be regarded as in part supporting this proposition.

The position of Barclays Bank International as collecting bank was not in issue, in view of their submission to whatever the court decided, but Kerr J. suggested that had they parted with the money they would have had a good defence " on the basis that as the collecting bank they were in the same position as agents who have parted with the money to their principal." As they had not parted with the money they could not have resisted the plaintiffs' claim.

---

[36] (1922) 38 T.L.R. 492.
[37] (1862) 13 C.B. (N.S.) 125; *cf. ante*, p. 40.
[38] *Kendal* v. *Wood* (1870) L.R. 6 Ex. 243.

CHAPTER 4

THE COLLECTING BANKER

Capital and Counties Bank Ltd. v. Gordon

[1903] A.C. 240

The banker as holder for value

Facts

The respondent, Gordon, trading as Gordon & Munro, was in business as a manufacturer of coffin furniture. Between 1895 and 1899, his clerk, Jones, opened letters addressed by customers to Gordon, and stole cheques contained in them. Of these cheques he paid 32 to the credit of an account opened with the appellant bank in the name of Warner & Co. The bank placed them to his credit immediately upon receipt, and he was allowed to draw against them at once, the bank presenting the cheques to the drawee banks and receiving payment for them.

Upon the fraud being discovered Gordon brought an action against the bank, and another against the London, City and Midland Bank Ltd., who had similarly collected for the fraudulent clerk 116 cheques belonging to Gordon. (In the latter case there were other points involved, as well as that at issue in the present case.[1]) The bank set up section 82 of the Bills of Exchange Act 1882,[2] and, the jury finding no negligence, judgment on further consideration was entered for the bank. The Court of Appeal reversed this judgment, and the bank now appealed to the House of Lords.

Decision

The House of Lords held that the bank, having credited the cheques to their customer's account before receiving the proceeds, did not collect those cheques for their customer, but had received payment for themselves, as holders for value.

In his judgment, Lord Macnaghten said:

But the protection conferred by section 82 is conferred only on a banker

[1] *Cf. ante*, p. 27; *post*, p. 130.

[2] Now s. 4 of the Cheques Act 1957: see *post*, p. 349. In the collection cases before 1957 that follow, reference is made to s. 82, except where the context otherwise requires. As to the effects of s. 4, see Chorley, *op. cit.*, pp. 137 *et seq.* For the history of the topic, see Chorley, Gilbart Lectures, 1953, *The Law relating to the Collection of Cheques*.

who receives payment for a customer—that is, who receives as a mere agent for collection. It follows, I think, that if bankers do more than act as such agents they are not within the protection of the section. It is well settled that if a banker before collection credits a customer with the face value of a cheque paid into his account the banker becomes holder for value of the cheque. It is impossible, I think, to say that a banker is merely receiving payment for his customer and a mere agent for collection when he receives payment of a cheque of which he is the holder for value. . . . It appears to me that [Collins M.R. in the Court of Appeal] has accurately summed up the whole case. " The protection afforded by section 82 must," he says, be limited to that which is necessary for the performance of the duty which by the legislation as to crossed cheques was imposed on bankers. If bankers deal with crossed cheques in the ordinary way in which bankers dealt with cheques before the legislation as to crossed cheques and in which they deal with cheques other than crossed cheques at the present time, namely, by treating them as cash, and upon receipt of them at once crediting the customer with the amount of them in the ordinary way instead of making themselves a mere conduit pipe for conveying the cheque to the bank on which it is drawn and receiving the money from that bank for their customer, I think they are collecting the money, not merely for their customer, but chiefly for themselves, and therefore are not protected by section 82." [3]

Notes

The *Gordon* decision has lost some of its interest to bankers since the passing of the Cheques Act in 1957, though recent cases show that it must still be kept in mind. By section 4 (1) of the Cheques Act the protection formerly given by section 82 of the Bills of Exchange Act 1882, to the banker who received payment of a crossed cheque for a customer, is given both to him and to the banker who:

(*b*) having credited a customer's account with the amount of such an instrument, receives payment thereof for himself

in both cases irrespective of whether the instrument is crossed or not. The aspect of the *Gordon* decision that took bankers and lawyers by surprise, and led to the passing of the Bills of Exchange (Crossed Cheques) Act 1906, is now largely of historic interest.

The question as to whether the banker can establish a title as holder of a cheque which has been paid in by a customer can, however, still be of importance to him, as for instance when he has lost the protection of section 4 of the Cheques Act by his negligence. The purchase or discount of a cheque by a banker differs fundamentally in law from the collection of it on behalf of a customer, but the two processes may not be easy to distinguish in practice, for in

[3] At pp. 246–249.

both cases the banker will credit his customer's account with the amount of the cheque. In the *Gordon* case the Court of Appeal and the House of Lords reasoned that an agent collecting would be unlikely to credit the account until the cash was actually received. Later decisions have modified this rather simple view of the matter.[4]

The best known and most far-reaching of these decisions was that in *A. L. Underwood Ltd.* v. *Barclays Bank Ltd.*[5] In that case, Underwood was the director of what was, in effect, a one-man company and he paid into his account with the defendant bank cheques drawn in favour of the company, which he endorsed "A. L. Underwood Ltd., A. L. Underwood, sole director." The bank duly collected the cheques. Upon Underwood's death a receiver was appointed, and when action was brought against the bank for conversion they pleaded, *inter alia*, that they received payment of the cheques as holders in due course. It was shown that they had credited Underwood with the amount of the cheques immediately upon receiving them. It was also shown, however, that there was no agreement with Underwood that he should be allowed to draw against the cheques before clearance, and that on some of the bank's credit slips appeared a warning to customers that the bank reserved the right to postpone payment of cheques drawn against uncleared effects. Upon judgment being given for the plaintiffs, the bank appealed, and the Court of Appeal upheld the judgment of the lower court, Atkin L.J. saying in his judgment:

> I think it sufficient to say that the mere fact that the bank in their books enter the value of the cheques on the credit side of the account on the day on which they receive the cheques for collection does not, without more, constitute the bank a holder for value. To constitute value there must be in such a case a contract between banker and customer . . . that the bank will before receipt of the proceeds honour cheques of the customer drawn against the cheques . . . neither [the *Gordon* decision] nor the statute [the 1906 Act] lay down the rule, judicial or statutory, that if a bank credits a cheque at once in its books that fact without more makes the bank a holder for value.[6]

It is claimed by Paget,[7] and with some justification, that the decision in *Underwood* v. *Barclays Bank Ltd.* cannot be reconciled with the *Gordon* decision and that *Gordon* was in fact wrongly decided. *Underwood* certainly went further than any previous case to negative the effect of that decision; in practice such a contract

[4] *Cf. e.g. Akrokerri (Atlantic) Mines Ltd.* v. *Economic Bank* [1904] 2 K.B. 465; *Lloyds Bank Ltd.* v. *Hornby* (October, 1933) 54 J.I.B. 372.

[5] [1924] 1 K.B. 775.

[6] At pp. 305–306.

[7] *Op. cit.* p. 389.

as that envisaged by Atkin L.J. is of rare occurrence, and might be difficult to prove. It appears also to be inconsistent with an earlier case in the House of Lords, not cited or considered in the *Underwood* cases, *viz. Sutters* v. *Briggs*,[8] where the question arising under the Gaming Act 1835, was whether a collecting banker is the holder of the cheque he collects. It was held that he is; and in his judgment, delivered on behalf of himself and Lords Buckmaster and Carson, Viscount Birkenhead L.C. said:

> It is, as is well known, usual for bankers, in the case of substantial customers at least, to constitute themselves holders in due course, as was the case in *Capital and Counties Bank Ltd.* v. *Gordon*, the result of which case led to the passing of the Bills of Exchange (Crossed Cheques) Act, 1906.[9]

Later, Lord Birkenhead said:

> The Bills of Exchange (Crossed Cheques) Act, 1906, confers the same protection on bankers who by their action have made themselves not merely " holders " but " holders in due course ": see *Capital and Counties Bank* v. *Gordon* and *per* Bowen, L.J., *National Bank* v. *Silke*.[10]

This interpretation of the *Gordon* case (in which, of course, there was no question of agreement to pay against uncleared effects) is in apparent conflict with that of the Court of Appeal two years later. Lord Birkenhead's opinion would seem to have been *obiter* only, but the *obiter dicta* of the House of Lords must carry considerable weight. The argument in support of the view there taken is developed at some length by Paget, who argues further that Lord Birkenhead's dictum is not to be regarded as *obiter*, but as the considered opinion of the whole House.

However, it is unlikely that any bank will in future be able to establish that it was a holder for value on facts as simple as those of the *Gordon* case. In *Westminster Bank Ltd.* v. *Zang*[11] the cheque of which the bank claimed to be holder for value had, when paid in, reduced a substantial overdraft. Roskill J. at first instance, found that there was an implied agreement to pay against uncleared effects; but all three judges in the Court of Appeal considered that the printed words on the bank's credit slips, reserving the right to refuse payment against uncleared effects, precluded any such implication of agreement. And in the House of Lords also the bank lost their case, it being unanimously held that they had not established that they were holders for value. Only Viscount Dilhorne

[8] [1922] 1 A.C. 1.
[9] At p. 15.
[10] [1891] 1 Q.B. 435 at p. 439. *Per* Lord Birkenhead, pp. 17–18.
[11] *Post*, p. 91, where the facts of the case are set out.

discussed the point: he considered that (1) the reduction of the overdraft was irrelevant, in view of the fact that the bank charged interest on the amount of the cheque until it was cleared. 'In these circumstances it is hard to see that by crediting it to the account and reducing the overdraft the bank gave value for it'[11a]; (2) no implied agreement could be read into the circumstances of the case; (3) the printed words on the credit slip negatived such an agreement; and (4) no evidence was given "that cheques drawn by the company and presented between April 27 and May 2, were only honoured in consequence of the uncleared effects." Viscount Dilhorne dealt only with the facts before him, without reference to any earlier decisions. But it must be assumed now that a bank can establish a claim to be holder for value of a cheque paid in for collection only by providing the kind of express agreement envisaged by Atkin L.J. or by showing that cheques were in fact honoured specifically against the uncleared effects.

On this point Salmon L.J. had said in the Court of Appeal:

> In *Underwood's* case there had been no drawings against the uncleared cheques. There had merely been book entries crediting the customer with their proceeds. It was in those circumstances that this Court was considering how a bank could become holders for value of the uncleared cheques. In my judgment this Court certainly did not lay down that in no circumstances could a Bank become holders for value save by an express or implied contract to honour cheques drawn against the uncleared cheques. An obvious way of becoming a holder for value is to give value by honouring a cheque drawn against an uncleared cheque whether or not there is an antecedent contract to do so. Whether the bank has honoured a cheque drawn against uncleared effects is a matter of fact . . . on the evidence of the bank manager and of the ledger to see how any such finding could have been made.[12]

But it will be noted that Viscount Dilhorne's judgment, at (4) above, if read strictly, set bounds to this argument: on this reading value is given only if it can be shown that cheques were paid that would have been dishonoured had the effects in question not been paid in.

An example of such circumstances is to be found in *Barclays Bank Ltd.* v. *Harding*,[13] where there was no doubt that the bank would have dishonoured substantial cheques unless covering effects had been provided. A further example is seen in *Barclays Bank Ltd.* v. *Astley Industrial Trust Ltd.*[14] where Milmo J. distinguished the *Zang* decision as being on materially different facts—" in particular

[11a] At p. 118.

[12] [1966] A.C. 182 at p. 210.

[13] (April 1962) 83 J.I.B. 109.

[14] [1970] 2 Q.B. 527, *cf. post*, p. 224.

there was no question of the bank having a lien such as there admittedly was in the present case " [15]—but where in fact on one of the bank's contentions there was no need to distinguish it. The bank's customers, a garage company, had received cheques from the defendant company in respect of hire purchase agreements. Upon discovering that the agreements were fictitious the defendants stopped payment of the cheques, but the bank had paid their customers' cheques both before receipt of the Astley cheques (upon the assurance that they were coming) and after they were paid in, pending their clearance. The bank now claimed to be holders for value (*a*) in respect of both the antecedent debt—the overdraft—and the cheques paid pending collection; and (*b*) to the extent of an overdraft, by virtue of section 27 (3) as having a lien on the cheques. They succeeded in all three contentions.

It may be noted that Milmo J. expressly rejected the defendants' argument that the bank could not be at once an agent for collection of a cheque and a holder of that cheque for value.

> It seems to me that the language of section 2 of the Cheques Act 1957 negatives this proposition since it presupposes that a banker who has been given a cheque for collection may nevertheless have given value for it. It is, moreover, a commonplace occurrence for a banker to allow credit to a customer against an uncleared cheque . . . I readily accept that if a banker holds a cheque merely—and I emphasise the word " merely "—as his customer's agent for collection he cannot be a holder for value and still less a holder in due course; but that is an entirely different proposition.[16]

He also refused to accept the argument that the fact of the bank charging interest on the uncleared effects prevented them from being holders for value. In the light of Viscount Dilhorne's view this last finding cannot pass unquestioned; while the reasoning based on section 2 of the Cheques Act may prove to have been an over-simplification. But one welcomes the reinforcement given to the finding of Ungoed-Thomas J. in *Re Keever*,[17] that the bank obtained a lien for the amount of the overdraft on cheques paid in for collection, the antecedent debt represented by the overdraft itself constituting consideration for the lien.

It will be apparent that the present position of the law on this whole question remains both uncertain and unsatisfactory. The position in practice is of course that although bankers reserve the right to refuse payment against uncleared effects, they regularly make such payment as a normal course (admittedly charging interest), and they scrutinise effects only in the case of customers of

---

[15] At p. 540. [16] At p. 538. [17] *Post*, p. 310; but *cf. post*, p. 224.

doubtful credit: the word "substantial" in Lord Birkenhead's proviso can be interpreted in its widest sense.[18] The banker normally assumes that his customer is honest and solvent until there is reason to believe otherwise, and it is submitted that although it may now be difficult to establish Lord Birkenhead's view of the matter as good law, that view is still more in accord with banking practice than the contrary reasoning that has followed it.

It will have been apparent in these notes that the terms "holder in due course" and "holder for value" seem often to be used as though they were interchangeable.[19] In the context of the collection cases they often are, but the distinction between them is sometimes important, as for example when a banker has collected a cheque which to his knowledge was issued in payment of a gaming debt,[20] or one crossed "Not negotiable" in connection with which he has lost the protection of section 4 of the Cheques Act by his negligence in some other respect (there is no negligence *per se* in collecting a cheque so crossed for a person other than the payee).[21] In such a case proof that he was holder for value will be no defence against a charge of conversion; if he knew the cheque to be a gaming payment, or if his customer's title to the "Not negotiable" cheque was defective, he will not be a holder in due course, the only status that would help him.[22]

---

[18] It should perhaps be said here that the banker paying against uncleared effects on a substantial account is in fact granting accommodation to a customer upon whose standing he relies rather than upon the cheques paid in. It need hardly be added that, although such cheques are not "scrutinised," the banker is alert to notice any unusual movement on any of his accounts. *R.* v. *Kritz* [1949] 2 All E.R. 406, was a notable example of the dangers that surround uncleared effects. It was a "cross-firing" case, and Lord Goddard C.J. said:

> "Drawing against uncleared cheques is one of the oldest forms of fraud. Generally, bank managers are too much on their guard to let it go on, but in this case, because of the specious lies which the appellant told to the bank manager and of the fact that the bank manager did not have that degree of suspicion which bank managers ought to have, the appellant managed to defraud the bank to a very considerable extent."

The difference between that kind of uncleared effects and those more generally seen on private and trading accounts alike hardly needs emphasis.

[19] Defined in s. 27 (2) and s. 29 (1) of the Bills of Exchange Act 1882. *Cf.* Chalmers, *op. cit.* pp. 89 *et seq.*

[20] *Woolf* v. *Hamilton* [1898] 2 Q.B. 337.

[21] *Cf. post*, p. 119.

[22] *Cf. Arab Bank Ltd.* v. *Ross*, *ante*, p. 55.

Westminster Bank Ltd. v. Zang

[1966] A.C. 182

The effect of section 2 of the Cheques Act 1957

Facts

The defendant, having lost heavily at cards, borrowed £1,000 from a friend, Mr. Tilley, and gave him his cheque in exchange. The loan was money belonging to the company which Mr. Tilley controlled, and he subsequently paid the cheque to the credit of the company's account, together with others. He did not indorse any of the cheques, although the cheque for £1,000 was payable to him personally and not to the company. The clearing banks in 1957, after the passing the Cheques Act, had laid down a rule that " indorsement will be required as heretofore if the instrument is tendered for the credit of an account other than that of the ostensible payee."

On the day the cheque was paid in the company account was overdrawn more than £1,000 in excess of the agreed overdraft limit, but not to an extent that caused the bank alarm; and further cheques were paid on the account on the same day. The cheque for £1,000 was dishonoured.

When their customer issued a writ against the defendant the bank surrendered the cheque to his solicitors, for the purpose of enabling him to enforce his claim, against their undertaking to return it on demand. This action was not proceeded with, and in due course the bank commenced their own action, claiming as holders for value by virtue of section 2 of the Cheques Act. The defendant, having unsuccessfully pleaded the Gaming Act, took four further points—

(i) that the cheque was delivered to the bank by Mr. Tilley, not as the " holder " within section 2, but as the agent of the company;

(ii) that the words of the section, " which the holder delivers for collection," could not apply to an unindorsed cheque paid in to an account which was not that of the payee;

(iii) that the bank had not given value for the cheque; and

(iv) that the bank had ceased to be " holder " of the cheque when they gave it up to Mr. Tilley's solicitors.

Roskill J. having found for the bank, the defendant appealed. Upon the Court of Appeal finding for the defendant, the bank appealed further.

Decision

The House of Lords dismissed the appeal, holding that the bank had not established their claim to be holders for value. The respondent's first two points were rejected, and in view of the finding on the third point their Lordships did not discuss the fourth.

On the second point Viscount Dilhorne said:

> The acceptance of a paid unindorsed cheque as evidence of its receipt by the payee of the sum payable by the cheque does not appear to be as cogent evidence of receipt by the payee as production of a paid cheque indorsed by him. But this is, in my opinion, no ground on which one would be entitled to construe section 2 in the way contended for by the respondent. I regard the language of that section as clear and unambiguous. I can see nothing in the section nor in the other sections of the Act from which it is to be inferred that " collection " in section 2 means collection only for the payee's account. If that had been the intention of Parliament, it could easily have been expressed. If the protection given to the drawer by section 3 is inadequate, that is a matter for Parliament to rectify.[24]

Notes

The *Zang* case was decided, as has been seen, on the fact that the bank was held not to be holders for value. But the decision is important also as regards section 2 of the Cheques Act, and also for the Court of Appeal's finding on the effect of the bank having given up possession of the cheque.

There had been an earlier challenge to the banks on section 2. Thus in *Midland Bank Ltd.* v. *R. V. Harris Ltd.*[25] the argument was that as the bank were neither payees nor indorsees of cheques that they had received unindorsed, they could not be holders. Megaw J. had no difficulty in holding that the section was adequate to protect the bank, which in this case had received the unindorsed cheques for the credit of the payee.

The *Zang* case was more difficult, for here the respondent was arguing that an unindorsed cheque could be " collected " within the terms of section 2 only for the payee; and this argument had the attraction that any wider view must weaken the position of the drawer seeking to establish that the payee has received his money. As Lord Reid put it:

> If the payee denies that he ever received the cheque, how is the payer to support the prima facie evidence afforded by section 3? There is no indorsement and no easy way to find out whether the payee ever received the cheque.[26]

But only Lord Denning M.R. in the Court of Appeal was prepared to say that the Act requires indorsement of cheques paid in to accounts other than those of the payees; while the rest of the Court, and Viscount Dilhorne and Lord Reid in the House of Lords,

---

[24] At p. 218. [25] [1963] 1 W.L.R. 1021. [26] At p. 222.

recognised the problem, they regarded the wording of the section as conclusive. It is for Parliament to amend the law if the drawer's position is regarded as seriously prejudiced. In practice, of course, the clearing banks' refusal to accept cheques for third party accounts without indorsement goes most of the way to redress the position, but the fact that this rule was inadvertently broken in the *Zang* case shows that the danger does exist.

The respondents' fourth point in the *Zang* case is of more moment to bankers than their immunity in respect of third party cheques. The House of Lords, as has been pointed out already, did not pronounce on the point, but two of the judgments in the Court of Appeal found conclusive the argument that the cheques were returned to the payee in order that he should be able to sue—as holder. When he, in due course, handed it back to the bank it was not for collection, nor did the bank that time have any claim to have given value.

This point also had had a preliminary airing in *Midland Bank Ltd.* v. *R. V. Harris Ltd.*[27] There the defendants were unable to produce evidence as to what had actually happened to the cheques (which, by the time the case came on for hearing, were in the possession of the bank). Megaw J. was therefore

> unable to hold that the defendants have laid the foundation for any argument on this point, apart from any other difficulties (and I think they might have been formidable) in the way of the defendants in establishing the point.[28]

But any comfort the banks may have found in his comment in parentheses was removed by the finding of Lord Denning and Salmon L.J. in the *Zang* case.

In the normal course of business there is no problem: a cheque received back dishonoured is returned to the customer for whom it was collected and his account is debited. When trouble can be clearly foreseen it is open to the bank to retain the cheque, surrendering it, if at all, only subject to reservation of their own rights. But where trouble is not foreseen, as must often be the case, it would seem that the banks can find themselves at risk if they follow their normal routine.

---

[27] *Supra.*
[28] At p. 1029

NEGLIGENCE UNDER SECTION 4 OF THE CHEQUES ACT

Lloyds Bank Ltd. v. E. B. Savory & Co.
[1933] A.C. 201

Marfani & Co. Ltd. v. Midland Bank Ltd.
[1968] 1 W.L.R. 956

The negligence may refer back to the opening of the account

Facts of Lloyds Bank Ltd. v. E. B. Savory & Co.

The respondents were a firm of stockbrokers, who had in their employ two clerks, Perkins and Smith. In accordance with Stock Exchange practice, the firm was in the habit of issuing crossed bearer cheques representing payments to jobbers, and between March 1924 and March 1930 first Perkins and then Smith stole a number of these cheques and paid them into the appellant bank, in the case of Perkins for the credit of his account at Wallington, in the case of Smith for the credit of his wife's account at Redhill and later at Weybridge. Making use of the " branch credit " system used by all the large banks, the two clerks paid in the cheques at city branches of the bank and, while the cheques were cleared with the drawee bank, the credit slips were forwarded to the branches at which the accounts were kept. As the credit slips bore no particulars of the cheques, the branches receiving them through the post did not know the drawers of the cheques thus being credited. Moreover, neither branch had made inquiries as to who were the employers, in the one case of Perkins and in the other of the husband of Mrs. Smith.

When the frauds were discovered the respondents brought an action against the appellant bank for damages for conversion or, alternatively, for money had and received. The bank pleaded in defence section 82 of the Bills of Exchange Act, and sought to establish that they had not been negligent. It was shown in evidence that the " branch credit " system was commonly used by bankers, and had been so used for many years. The evidence as to the inquiries normally made upon the opening of a new account varied, but the bank's rule book was shown to lay down that no new account should be opened " without knowledge of or full inquiry into the circumstances " of the customer.

Judgment was given for the bank (except in the case of one cheque, which had been paid in and collected before Mrs. Smith's account had been opened). The appeal of Savory & Co. was allowed by the Court of Appeal, and the bank now appealed to the House of Lords.

Decision

The House of Lords held (Lord Blanesborough and Lord Russell of Killowen dissenting) that the bank had not discharged the burden of proving that they had acted without negligence, and the appeal was dismissed.

In his judgment in the Court of Appeal, Lawrence L.J. said:

Mr. Rayner Goddard [counsel for the bank] . . . submitted that to bring the bank within the protection of section 82 it was not necessary to do more than prove that it had acted according to the ordinary practice of bankers and that, whatever step might have to be taken in the future to guard against a repetition of similar frauds, it would not be right to convict the bank of negligence for having in good faith acted in accordance with such a long-established practice. In support of his argument Mr. Rayner Goddard cited *Chapman* v. *Walton*,[29] and *Commissioners of Taxation* v. *English Scottish and Australian Bank Ltd.*[30] In my judgment, neither of the pronouncements so relied on was intended to cover such a case as the present, where bankers, solely for the convenience of their customers, have adopted a system with an inherent and obvious defect which no reasonably careful banker could fail to observe.[31]

And in his judgment in the House of Lords, Lord Wright said:

I think . . . that at least where the new customer is employed in some position which involves his handling, and having the opportunity of stealing, his employers' cheques, the bankers fail in taking adequate precautions if they do not ask the name of his employers . . . because they fail to ascertain a most relevant fact as to the intending customer's circumstances. This is specially true of a stockbroker's clerk; it may be different in the case of an employee whose work does not involve such opportunities, as, for instance, a technical employee in a factory. But in the case of a stockbroker's clerk or other similar employment, the bank are dealing with something which involves a risk fully known to them. . . . It is clear that they ask information as to the man's occupation and if they find that he is (for instance) a stockbroker's clerk, they surely should go on and ask who his employers are, since otherwise they cannot guard against the danger fully known to them of his paying in cheques stolen from his employers. It is argued that this is not the ordinary practice of bankers and that a bank is not negligent if it takes all precautions usually taken by bankers. I do not accept that latter proposition as true in cases where the ordinary practice fails in making due provision for a risk fully known to those experienced in the business of banking.[32]

Facts of Marfani & Co. Ltd. v. Midland Bank Ltd.

The office manager of the plaintiff company introduced himself to a restaurant proprietor, Mr. Akaddas Ali, and in the course of

---

[29] (1834) 10 Bing. 57.
[30] *Ante*, p. 19.
[31] [1932] 2 K.B. 122 at pp. 143–144.
[32] At p. 231.

several conversations, in which he said his name was Eliaszade, he spoke of his intention to open his own restaurant. Subsequently, on the eve of Mr. Marfani's departure on a visit to Pakistan, he drew a cheque for £3,000 on the company payable to Eliaszade, a London firm with which Marfanis did business, and obtained Mr. Marfani's signature to it. This cheque he paid into an account with the Midland Bank which he opened in the name of Eliaszade, giving as one of his two referees the name of Mr. Ali. When Mr. Ali, himself a good customer of the bank, who had introduced other satisfactory customers, confirmed that in his view the man would be good for the conduct of a bank account, the bank issued a cheque book, and over the following fortnight the balance of the account was withdrawn. When the fraud was discovered the company brought an action against the bank for damages for conversion of the cheque.

The company alleged negligence under several heads, in particular that the bank had not made sufficient inquiry upon the opening of the account, and that they should have had two references (the second referee did not reply to the bank's inquiry). Upon Nield J. finding that the bank had not been negligent the company appealed.

Decision

The Court of Appeal upheld the finding in the lower court. In his judgment Diplock L.J. said:

> What the court has to do is to look at all the circumstances at the time of the acts complained of, and to ask itself were those circumstances such as would cause a reasonable banker possessed of such information about his customer as a reasonable banker would possess, to suspect that his customer was not the true owner of the cheque.[33]

Notes

The tort of conversion takes place wherever one person wilfully and without justification interferes with the chattel, *i.e.* movable property, of another in a manner inconsistent with that other's rights, and in such a way as to deprive him of possession of it.[34]

Section 4 of the Cheques Act 1957 confers protection on collecting bankers against the risk of action for conversion to which they are prima facie liable should the customer whose cheque is being collected turn out not to have a good title to it. This protection is, however, conditional upon the banker's being able to show (*inter*

---

[33] At p. 973.

[34] See Chorley, Gilbart Lectures, 1956; and *cf.* decision of McNair J. in *Marquess of Bute* v. *Barclays Bank Ltd.*, *post*, p. 114.

alia) that he conducted the collection ("received payment") without negligence.

Although the words of the section appear to refer only to the actual business of collection, the courts have held that the obligation to take care applies from the very beginning of the relationship, at which stage information must be obtained not only as to the customer's respectability but as to all matters relating to him which are obviously relevant to the possibility of his using his account to obtain payment of cheques which he has fraudulently converted to his own purposes. Such frauds can be guarded against only if precautions are taken, not only to see that everything is prima facie in order with the transaction at the time when it occurs—for example, that the indorsement is correct—but also that the surrounding circumstances, as discovered at the opening of the account and in the whole handling of it, do not throw any suspicion upon the transaction.

No more instructive illustration of the extreme responsibility which the courts have put upon the banks can be found than the case of *Lloyds Bank Ltd.* v. *E. B. Savory & Co.*, which is perhaps the most important of all the section 4 cases. It will be observed that there were two distinct grounds upon which the bank failed to prove that due care had been taken. The judgments in the Court of Appeal were in the main based upon the deficiencies in the branch credit system [35]: that is to say, on negligence in connection with the handling of the account. In the House of Lords, however, all five judgments recognised in varying degrees that there was negligence involved in the use of the branch credit system only if the information concealed by it would put the bank on notice of irregularity if it were not so concealed: the negligence here in question was negligence occurring at the time the account was opened. The dissenting judgments were based on this point: since the customer's employer, and equally the employer of the husband of the woman customer, might admittedly be changed on the day after the account was opened, was there any useful purpose in inquiring about them? Lord Russell of Killowen said, in this connection:

> I know of no authority before the present case, justifying that proposition, and I can conceive no logical basis on which one can rest an obligation on A to make an inquiry (for the purpose of regulating and guiding his future

[35] One of the large banks uses special credit slips for the branch credit system, and requires them to bear the names of the drawers and the payees of every cheque paid in in this way. The fact that this has not become general banking practice presumably indicates that this particular *Savory* risk is not found to be a serious one in practice; it does not appear to have come before the courts again in the 33 years since the *Savory* decision.

action during an indefinite period of time) the answer to which may cease to be correct immediately after it is given.[36]

But if there was no negligence in omitting to ask for the employer's name there was, *in the circumstances of the case*, no negligence in omitting to pass on the name of the drawers of the cheques paid in. It would be otherwise, of course, if, for example, a customer, the secretary or director of a company, paid into his account through the branch credit system cheques belonging to his company, for in such a case the information concealed by the system from the customer's branch would have put them on inquiry had it not been concealed, in that they would certainly have ascertained their customer's own employment.

The dissenting judgments in this case are of interest, for the case marks one of the extreme limits to which the courts have extended the duty of care in the collection of cheques, and it is still open to the House of Lords, in circumstances only a little different from those of the present case, to adopt the somewhat broader outlook of Lords Blanesborough and Russell of Killowen. It may be remarked that in the *Orbit* case [37] Harman L.J. said:

> I must say that it seems to me to be a quite impossible obligation to put on the cashiers of a collecting bank to scrutinise the signatures of the drawers of incoming cheques, more especially the signatures to cheques of a limited company. Hundreds of these come in every day. In the latest case in the House of Lords on this subject, *Lloyds Bank Ltd.* v. *E. B. Savory & Co.*, it was held by the majority that a collecting bank had acted with negligence in not inquiring when two accounts were opened as to the employers of the customer. This seems to me a hard doctrine, but it has no application here. . . . It cannot at any rate be the duty of the bank continually to keep itself up to date as to the identity of a customer's employer.[38]

The criticism of the *Savory* decision was, as is clear from this quotation, *obiter*, but it may perhaps be regarded as symptomatic of a rather less strict view of the banker's duty.

This changing view has found its clearest expression so far in the *Marfani* case, where Diplock L.J. referred to the *Savory* decision and said:

> There were many other matters calculated to arouse suspicion in the social conditions of the 1920s. It was decided upon expert evidence, not of what is now current banking practice, but of what it was nearly 40 years ago. I find in it no more than an illustration of the general principle that a banker must exercise reasonable care in all the circumstances of the case.[39]

[36] (1932) 49 T.L.R. at p. 121.
[37] *Ante*, p. 35.
[38] [1963] 1 Q.B. 794 at pp. 824–825.
[39] [1968] 1 W.L.R. at p. 976.

He also took a point that had been rejected in some of the earlier cases:

> It does not constitute any lack of reasonable care to refrain from making inquiries which it is improbable will lead to detection of the potential customer's dishonest purpose if he is dishonest, and which are calculated to offend him and maybe drive away his custom if he is honest.[40]

But the decision is perhaps principally significant for the Court of Appeal's endorsement of the principle that the current practice of careful bankers is not lightly to be considered negligent. Counsel for the plaintiffs had argued that the court should examine that practice and decide whether it complied with the standard of care expected of a prudent banker. Diplock L.J. agreed that this was so, " but I venture to think that this court should be hesitant in condemning as negligent a practice generally adopted by those engaged in banking business." [41] It is interesting to compare this view with that of Lord Wright in the *Savory* case: there is no contradiction between the two, but the difference in accent is noticeable.

Of course, the *Marfani* decision is not to be regarded as removing all the dangers that await the careless banker. It recognises in part at least that negligence is to be measured by the standards of the present day; but every case must still be considered on its merits, and while the attitude of the courts today is different from that of 45 years ago (as indeed is the banking system that they have to consider), bankers will have noted the warning sounded by Cairns J. With Diplock and Danckwerts L.JJ. he found for the bank, but with some hesitation: " if the defendant bank here exercised sufficient care, it was in my view only just sufficient." [42] And he remarked that the decision should not encourage any loosening of the rules that banks had made as a result of earlier, adverse, decisions. It is still necessary for the banker to study those decisions.

In them were set varying standards of care. As long ago as 1903, in *Turner* v. *London and Provincial Bank Ltd.*,[43] tried by Walton J. and a jury, carelessness in opening the account was one of the circumstances of the bank's negligence, and in *Ladbroke* v. *Todd* [44] the bank was held negligent for the same reason. Yet in the *Commissioners of Taxation* case [45] the bank successfully contested liability, despite apparent absence of inquiry regarding their customer, and Lord Dunedin went so far as to say: " It is not a question of negligence in opening an account, though the circumstances connected

---

[40] *Ibid.* at p. 977.
[41] *Ibid.* at p. 975.
[42] *Ibid.* at p. 982.
[43] (1903) 2 L.D.B. 33.
[44] *Ante*, p. 21.
[45] *Ante*, p. 19.

with the opening of an account may shed light on the question of whether there was negligence in collecting a cheque." [46]

In a later case, *Hampstead Guardians* v. *Barclays Bank Ltd.*[47] an account was opened in the name of Donald Stewart with the defendant bank. A reference was given, and in the course of the post a reply was received purporting to be from the referee but in fact a forgery. On the day the reply was received the customer brought in two orders drawn on the plaintiffs and payable to " D. Stewart & Company," with the explanation that this was his trading name. There was only one firm of the name in London, at an address different from that given when the account was opened. He later drew the proceeds of the orders and disappeared. Acton J. held that the bank had been negligent, and said that the reference, even had it been genuine, would have been good only for a genuine Donald Stewart. While this fact was not important on the day the account was opened, it became so when on the following day the orders were paid in. It is to be noted, however, that he went on to describe the negligence associated with the actual orders, and it is doubtful whether the circumstances of the opening alone would have been held to be sufficient negligence.

In *Nu-Stilo Footwear Ltd.* v. *Lloyds Bank Ltd.*[48] the circumstances were similar to those of the *Hampstead Guardians* case, the customer here opening his account in a false name, giving his own name as referee. Sellers J., however, distinguished the earlier decision on the grounds that in the present case the bank took up the reference by telephone and in writing, thus confirming that the referee was what he purported to be, and also inquired of the referee's bank (where he had earlier opened an account) as to his suitability as a referee. He found the bank negligent, nevertheless, in that the second cheque paid in to the customer's account, for £550 10s. 1d., payable to a third party, and other subsequent cheques, some of them payable to the customer, some to third parties, were of amounts inconsistent with his stated occupation of free-lance agent, newly started in business:

> Each further personal cheque should have prompted an inquiry as to what the customer was doing as a free-lance agent, as the receipt by him of large sums was quite out of harmony with the description of his trade or prospects as revealed by him to the bank.[49]

The extent to which the bank's own rule book was cited in the *Savory* case in the judgments both in the Court of Appeal and in the

---

[46] *Ibid.* at p. 688.
[47] (1923) 39 T.L.R. 229.
[48] (1956) 7 L.D.B. 121.
[49] At p. 127.

House of Lords, is noteworthy. Viscount Buckmaster emphasised (as did Goddard J. in even more precise terms in the *Motor Traders* case [50]) that a bank's own rules do not themselves establish a legal standard of care; but " they afford a very valuable criterion of obvious risks against which the banks think it is their duty to guard." [51]

It may be remarked finally that Sir John Paget, in his note to the *Turner* case in the volume of *Legal Decisions affecting Bankers* cited above, said: " The lack of inquiry into the standing and habits of the customer seems somewhat remote from the actual transaction." [52] This comment has today some historic interest, in its reflection of the extent to which standards of negligence under section 82 have been tightened in the past 70 years.[53]

Morison v. London County and Westminster Bank Ltd.

[1914] 3 K.B. 356

Lloyds Bank Ltd. v. Chartered Bank of India, Australia and China

(1928) 44 T.L.R. 534

Negligence in collecting for agents or employees where the principal or employer is the drawer of the cheques

Facts of Morison v. London County and Westminster Bank Ltd.

Plaintiff was an insurance broker, carrying on business under the name of Bruce Morison & Co. From 1888 onwards his clerk, Henry Abbott, had authority to sign cheques for the firm, *per procuration*—and the plaintiff's bankers, the National Provincial Bank, were so instructed. In 1900 Abbott was appointed manager of the business. In 1905 Abbott opened a private account with the defendant bank, and between 1907 and 1911 drew some 50 cheques, some payable to the firm—" Selves "—and some to himself, to a total value of £1,885 3s. 9d., which he paid into his private account, and which were duly collected by the bank. He had no authority to use the cheques in this way.

It was shown that some at least of the frauds were discovered by the plaintiff, and others were probably known to the plaintiff's auditors.

Upon the full extent of the frauds being discovered the plaintiff

[50] *Post*, p. 109. [51] At p. 117. [52] (1903) 2 L.D.B. 33 at p. 34.
[53] *Cf.* Chorley, Gilbart Lectures, 1955, *Opening the Account and other Problems.*

brought an action for conversion against the defendant bank. The bank claiming that they were protected by section 82, Lord Coleridge J. held that they had been negligent on the grounds that, reading section 25 with section 82, they were put on inquiry by the fact that the cheques bore a "*per pro*" signature, and further that apart from section 25, the fact that a prima facie agent was paying in to his private account cheques which he had drawn *per pro* his principal should have caused the bank to make inquiries. The bank appealed.

Decision

The Court of Appeal allowed the appeal, holding, *inter alia*, that, assuming the bank to have been negligent in the case of the first cheques paid in, the fact that such cheques over a period of more than two years, had not been questioned was enough to negative negligence in the collection of later, similar, cheques.

In the course of his judgment, Lord Reading C.J. said:

With reference to the earlier transactions, limited to the years 1907 and 1908, I agree with the decision of Lord Coleridge J. that the defendants did not act without negligence. The proceeds of six cheques were collected in these two years for Abbott by the defendants. . . . The most cursory examination would have shown the defendants that they were collecting payment for their customer of cheques drawn by him as agent upon the account of his principal at another bank, and that the first three of these crossed cheques were made payable on the face of the instruments to the principal or order and issued to the bank by means of the indorsement of the agent purporting to act for the principal. . . . Different considerations apply, however, to the collection of the later cheques issued in 1909, 1910, and 1911. No question had been raised in reference to the cheques paid into Abbott's account in the preceding two years and any doubt or suspicion which the defendants ought to have had of these earlier transactions would have disappeared. . . . It is true that the plaintiff owed no duty to the defendants to examine his passbooks or check his accounts with them or with Abbott, but, when we are asked to find as a fact that the defendants were negligent, it is necessary to consider all the circumstances, and in my judgment, as these transactions were only repetitions of those of the previous years which had passed unchallenged, the defendants should not be deprived of the protection of the statute.[54]

And Buckley L.J. said:

The position after (say) the end of 1907, was such that any suspicion which they ought to have had would have been lulled to sleep by the action of Morison himself. Such a sufficient time had then elapsed during which the customer had received back his passbook and his cheques, and had

---

[54] At pp. 368–369.

raised no question as to the validity of the cheques, as that the defendants were entitled to assume that there was no cause for suspicion or inquiry.[55]

Facts of Lloyds Bank Ltd. v. Chartered Bank of India, Australia and China

The plaintiff bank had as their chief accountant in their Bombay office one Lawson, who had authority to sign on behalf of his employers. He drew a series of 19 cheques, between March, 1922, and January, 1924, to a total value of more than £17,000, all payable to the defendant bank, and these he sent to the bank, requesting them to credit the private account he kept with them. This they did, collecting the cheques (which were drawn on the Imperial Bank of India); and upon the fraud's being discovered, the plaintiff bank brought an action for conversion. The defendants relied particularly upon section 131 of the Indian Negotiable Instruments Act 1881, corresponding to section 82 of the Bills of Exchange Act. Upon the main issue of negligence, judgment was given for the plaintiffs, and the defendants appealed.

Decision

The Court of Appeal held that, although the cheques were payable to the defendants themselves, they had received payment "for a customer"; but that they had not discharged the burden of proving due care, and the appeal failed.

In the course of his judgment, Scrutton L.J. said:

The learned judge finds, after careful consideration, that the defendant bank failed to prove absence of negligence. He rests his judgment on the payment by Lawson of large cheques of his bank into his private account, and failure to make inquiries of the manager of the plaintiff bank as to the regularity of the transactions. I agree in this finding, and would add that I think examination of Lawson's account (and I am sure that general examination of the accounts of every customer takes place from time to time in all well-managed banks) should, I think, have put the defendant bank on inquiry as to the source from which these heavy payments to stockbrokers were being made, in the case of an account generally in low water, except for these payments in, immediately reduced by payments out.

The only remaining defence was that the defendant bank was "lulled to sleep" by the failure of the plaintiff bank to detect these frauds. The learned judge has dismissed this on the ground that no one from the defendant bank came to say he was "lulled to sleep"; their attitude was that they remembered nothing about the matter. This is enough to dispose of the matter, but though a similar defence succeeded in *Morison*'s case [56] I am not at all satisfied as to the grounds of such a decision. It does not seem consistent with the decisions in *Bank of Ireland* v. *Trustees of Evans'*

---

[55] At p. 377.

[56] *Supra.*

Charities in Ireland,[57] and *Swan* v. *North British Australasian Company*,[58] that negligence, to act as estoppel, must be the proximate cause of the loss. If my butler for a year has been selling my vintage wines cheaply to a small wine merchant, I do not understand how my negligence in not periodically checking my wine book will be an answer to my action against the wine merchant for conversion. However, the ground of the learned judge's decision is enough to dispose of this point. This, I think, substantially exhausts the points taken on the appeal, which must be dismissed with costs.[59]

And Sankey L.J. said:

In my view, a bank cannot be held to be liable for negligence merely because they have not subjected an account to a microscopic examination. It is not to be expected that the officials of banks should also be amateur detectives. It is not easy, nor is it desirable, to define the degree of negligence which would render them liable. Many factors have to be taken into consideration, the customer, the account, and the surrounding circumstances. But, whilst it is difficult to draw the line, the problem upon which side of the line a particular case falls does not present such difficulties. Having regard to the uncommon nature of the cheques in question, having regard to the fact that Lawson was an employee of the plaintiffs, as was well known by the defendants, and having regard to the heavy payments made at crucial times to persons known to be brokers, I cannot come to any other conclusion but that the defendants were negligent in this case.[60]

Notes

On its own exceptional facts the *Morison* decision may be justified, but it seems unlikely that any development of the " lulling to sleep " doctrine will take place. The doctrine has received no approval in later cases, and the remarks of Scrutton L.J.[61] may be compared with those of Greer L.J. in the *Carpenters Company* case,[62] where he said:

It was suggested . . . the bank was entitled to suppose that the Carpenters Company had no objection to the long standing practice of [their clerk] paying cheques made out in favour of customers to the credit of his own account. It seems to me that this argument ought not to succeed. Each transaction . . . must fall to be determined on the facts relating to such transaction. It might well be that the earlier transactions were not fraudulent. . . . There are some parts of the decision in *Morison's* case[63] which appear to indicate that after a number of transactions had appeared in the books of the defrauded company, and had been passed by the auditors of the defrauded company, the bank would be entitled to think when the next

[57] (1855) 5 H.L. Cas. 389.
[58] (1863) 10 Jur.(N.S.) 102.
[59] At pp. 536–537.
[60] At p. 540.
[61] *Supra*.
[62] *Ante*, p. 57.
[63] *Supra*.

cheque came in that it was freed from the necessity of any inquiry, and its failure to inquire would not be negligence. This view is inconsistent with the case of *A. L. Underwood Ltd.* v. *Bank of Liverpool & Martins.*[64]

The circumstances in the *Morison* case may be distinguished from those in the other two cases here compared, in that here the plaintiff had knowledge of the earlier frauds and failed to disclose them to the bank; and on this point the case may be compared with the *Greenwood* case.[65] But Lord Wright's remark in *Lloyds Bank Ltd.* v. *Savory & Co.*[66] " no one from the bank came to say he was ' lulled to sleep,' or indeed had given his mind to the question at all " [67] applies with equal force in the circumstances of the *Morison* case, and it must be considered doubtful whether even in similar circumstances the decision would now be in favour of the bank.[68]

But a bank is not defenceless in such circumstances. In the *Orbit Mining Co.* case [69] the Court of Appeal held that the bank had not been negligent, and Sellers L.J. said:

> If the standard required goes beyond reasonable precautions in the interests of true owners of instruments which may, it must be admitted, be so readily converted where dishonesty holds sway . . . and goes to a standard which safeguards any fraud from being overlooked, it leaves a bank no remedy for conversion. It is clear in this case that, if Mr. Woolf had not filled in blank forms and disobeyed the requirements of Orbit's bank and had shown ordinary diligence in supervising what had happened to the cheques he had irregularly signed, these frauds would have been rendered at least more difficult and would probably never have arisen. It seems one-sided to blame the bank. Honest trading requires vigilance and proper conduct on the part of all involved.[70]

More recently, in a decision that may prove of considerable value to the banks, Donaldson J. held that the Law Reform (Contributory Negligence) Act 1945, which had previously been considered to apply only to cases of negligence, applied also to the tort of conversion. (It will be remembered that negligence is only

[64] [1924] 1 K.B. 775, *post*, p. 189. *Per* Greer L.J. at p. 540.

[65] *Ante*, p. 66.

[66] *Ante*, p. 94.

[67] At p. 124.

[68] And *cf.* the remarks of the Judicial Committee of the Privy Council in *Bank of Montreal* v. *Dominion Gresham Guarantee and Casualty Company Ltd.* [1930] A.C. 659: " In this connection the so-called doctrine of lulling to sleep has been invoked. Neglect of duty does not cease by repetition to be neglect of duty. If there be any doctrine of lulling to sleep it must depend upon and can only be another way of expressing estoppel or ratification " (at p. 666).

[69] *Cf. ante*, p. 35 for facts, and decision on another point.

[70] *Per* Sellers L.J. at pp. 817–818. *Cf.* Harman L.J. quoted at p. 98.

relevant in conversion cases in the negative, in the bank's defence). Dr. Holden, in the first edition of his *Law and Practice of Banking*, had suggested that this was the law, and had cited in support a New Zealand decision, based on the New Zealand equivalent of the English 1945 Act. In *Lumsden & Co.* v. *London Trustee Savings Bank*,[71] where the plaintiffs' action was for the conversion of certain cheques, Donaldson J. accepted Dr. Holden's view of the Act and reduced the plaintiffs' damages by 10 per cent., holding that while the bank had been negligent in not fully establishing their customer's credentials when the account was opened, the plaintiffs had also been negligent in leaving spaces in their cheques which allowed additions to be made to the payees' names.

This decision, and that of the New Zealand Court of Appeal, so far stand unsupported, but while confirmation by a higher court will be needed to put the matter beyond doubt, there seems to be no reason to assume that this new defence will be lost to the banks.[72]

In *Australia and New Zealand Bank Ltd.* v. *Ateliers de Construction Electriques de Charleroi*[72a] the cheques in question were payable to, not drawn by, the agent's employers. He was the Australian agent of a Belgian company, and he paid into his own account cheques payable to the company and indorsed for them by himself. Before the Privy Council the bank's defence was not that there had been no negligence, but instead the assertion that there had been no conversion. The agent, the bank claimed, had implied authority to deal with the cheques; his employers knew that he had handled large sums for them previously by paying into his own account and later accounting to the company; they had given no instructions as to how cheques were to be handled, nor had they complained about the agent's methods; and they had no banking account in Australia. The Privy Council held that in the circumstances authority could, as the bank contended, be implied.[73]

---

[71] [1971] 1 Lloyd's Rep. 114.

[72] *Cf.* Chorley, *op cit.* pp. 135 *et seq.* See also Drover, Gilbart Lectures 1972, where it is suggested that, the Act may apply also to the tort of breach of contract—*e.g.* the payment of a forged cheque.

[72a] [1966] 2 W.L.R. 1216.

[73] On not dissimilar facts, in an Australian case, *Souhrada* v. *Bank of New South Wales* [1976] 2 Lloyd's Rep. 444, the bank succeeded in the Supreme Court of New South Wales in their plea that there had been no conversion. Yeldham J. said: " There cannot be a conversion where the agent, on whose instructions the proceeds of the cheque were collected by the defendants, was authorised by the true owner of them to give such instructions " (at p. 452).

Midland Bank Ltd. v. Reckitt and Others
[1933] A.C. 1

The fact that the agent drawing the cheques has a power of attorney, under which he draws cheques to his own order, does not remove the need for inquiry by the bank

Facts

Lord Terrington carried on business as a solicitor as H. J. S. Woodhouse & Co., and was authorised by power of attorney given by Sir Harold Reckitt to draw cheques on the latter's banking account at the Hull branch of Barclays Bank. Lord Terrington fraudulently drew 15 cheques to a total value of nearly £18,000 on this account in the form " Harold G. Reckitt by Terrington, his attorney," and paid these cheques to his credit with the Midland Bank, Cornhill, where he had an overdraft. It was shown that throughout the Midland Bank were pressing Lord Terrington for money, and were uneasy about the overdrawn state of his two accounts with them.

When Sir Harold Reckitt brought an action against them for conversion, the bank relied upon section 82, and upon the ratification clause in the Power of Attorney, which was as follows:

> And the principal hereby for himself his heirs executors and administrators ratifies and confirms and agrees to ratify and confirm whatsoever the attorney or any such person as aforesaid acting as the agent of or substitute for or in place of the attorney shall do or purports to do by virtue of these presents including in any such confirmation whatsoever shall be done between the time of the death of the principal or the revocation by any other means of this power of attorney and the time of such death or revocation becoming known to the attorney or any such person as aforesaid.

Upon judgment being given for the bank, on the grounds that they had not been negligent, the plaintiff appealed, and the Court of Appeal allowed the appeal. The bank now further appealed.

Decision

The House of Lords held that the bank were negligent in not inquiring concerning the drawing of the cheques, the form of which put them on notice that the money was not Lord Terrington's. The ratification clause did not affect the plaintiff's right to maintain the action.

In the course of his judgment Lord Atkin said, on the latter point:

> It remains to deal with contentions of the bank based upon the terms of the power of attorney. The bank never in fact asked for or saw the terms of

the document; and, for my part, I venture to doubt whether in such circumstances they could ever rely on any other than an actual authority. Ostensible authority appears to be excluded when the party averring it cannot show that any appearance of authority other than the actual authority was ever displayed to him by the principal. . . . It was said, however, that the clause of the power of attorney whereby the principal " ratifies and confirms and agrees to ratify and confirm whatsoever the attorney shall do or purports to do by virtue of these presents " protects the bank. The clause in some such form is of long standing. It does not appear to be happily worded; for a ratification in advance seems to contradict the essential attributes of ratification as generally understood. It cannot, I think, be construed as extending the actual authority given by the power of attorney; it may amount to a promise to adopt acts done within the ostensible authority; and this strengthens the position of those who rely on the ostensible authority by an express promise as well as by an estoppel. If this be so it is difficult to see how the promise could be available except to someone who was aware of it, and who acted on the strength of it. But in any case it would appear to be a highly improbable construction to suppose that a principal using this form has precluded himself from objecting to a dealing with his property by a person who had notice in ordinary circumstances that the agent was exceeding his authority actual and ostensible. . . . Such a construction would make powers of attorney a danger instead of a business facility and would certainly defeat the intention of any reasonable principal. I think, therefore, that the notice in this case defeats this defence.[74]

Notes

This decision is an example of the danger that a signature purporting to be within a power of attorney may in fact be outside its limits, and as a result as completely inoperative as any other unauthorised signature. The bank is clearly put on notice by the form of the signature that the attorney is dealing with moneys not his own; and a ratification clause in the terms which are normally used is here established as not extending the scope of the power.

Unless the power is expressed to be given under section 10 of the Powers of Attorney Act 1971 (when the attorney has authority to do anything that the donor of the power can lawfully do), the attorney must not act outside the powers granted in terms. Unless there is express power to borrow, the attorney must not do so—and power to draw on a banking account does not necessarily permit drawing on an overdrawn account, unless there is also a borrowing power; while a general clause in a power of attorney does not add to the powers given in the rest of the document.[75] But the principal danger to the banker remains that demonstrated in *Midland Bank Ltd.* v. *Reckitt*, the principle of which had already been applied in *Reckitt* v.

[74] At pp. 17–18.

[75] *Attwood* v. *Munnings* (1827) 7 B. & C. 278.

Barnett, Pembroke and Slater Ltd.,[76] in which Lord Terrington had paid a personal debt to the respondents with a cheque drawn on Sir Harold Reckitt's account. It was held that the fact that the cheque was drawn by Lord Terrington as attorney, and the knowledge that the debt was a personal one, debarred the respondents from retaining the proceeds of the cheque.

In the *Reckitt* case, as in *Morison's* case,[77] the effect of section 25 of the Bills of Exchange Act was considered. The section provides:

> A signature by procuration operates as notice that the agent has but a limited authority to sign, and the principal is only bound by such signature if the agent in so signing was acting within the actual limits of his authority.

In both the cases in question the bank had notice, not merely from the form of the signature, but from their knowledge of the parties, that the agent was paying his principal's money to his private account; and it may be presumed that a collecting banker who has no such knowledge need not make inquiries merely because his customer pays in a cheque drawn by an ostensible agent. The *Crumplin* decision [78] supports this view; the *Morison* case was there advanced in connection with two of the cheques in dispute, which had been signed "*per pro*"; but Pickford J. refused to hold that this form of signature, with no more, had any special concern for the collecting bank.

Ross v. London County Westminster and Parr's Bank Ltd.

[1919] 1 K.B. 678

Motor Traders Guarantee Corporation Ltd. v. Midland Bank Ltd.

[1937] 4 All E.R. 90

Negligence in the collection of cheques payable to third parties

Facts of Ross v. London County Westminster and Parr's Bank Ltd.

The Overseas Military Forces of Canada set up an Estates Office under the Accountant-General to collect the estates of members of those forces who died during the first world war. One of the officials employed by the Estates Office was de Volpi, a quartermaster-sergeant, who in 1916 opened a private account with the Herne Hill branch of a bank which later formed part of the defendant bank.

[76] [1929] A.C. 176. [77] *Ante*, p. 101. [78] *Post*, p. 119.

From May 1917 to April 1918 de Volpi paid into this account at first over the counter at Herne Hill, and later through the Berners Street branch of the bank for credit of the account at Herne Hill, 33 cheques to a total value of £3,916 16s., all of them except one for £10 7s. 8d. being payable to "The Officer in Charge, Estates Office, Canadian Overseas Military Forces," and indorsed by that officer under that description. De Volpi was not entitled to handle the cheques in this way, and in November 1918 he was convicted of larceny. The Paymaster-General brought the present action against the bank to recover the amount of the cheques, but afterwards withdrew his claim in respect of the cheque for £10 7s. 8d. The defendants relied upon section 82.

In his evidence, the manager of the Herne Hill branch said that the staff of the branch who took cheques from customers and kept the ledgers was constantly changing and consisted in part of women, and that he did not himself see the cheques paid in at his branch by de Volpi, while those paid in at Berners Street did not come to his branch, which merely received advice of the credits; he admitted that if a private customer were to present to him a cheque payable to and indorsed by a public official he would regard it as his duty to make inquiries before allowing the credit.

Decision

It was held that the fact that the cheques were drawn payable to and indorsed by a public official should have put the bank upon inquiry whether their private customer was entitled to the cheques, and the bank had therefore not proved absence of negligence. Judgment was given for the plaintiff.

In his judgment, Bailhache J. said:

I recognise that the same degree of intelligence and care cannot be looked for in a cashier as in an official higher in authority, such as a manager, and I am told that during the period in question the cashiers and clerks at these branches were being constantly changed, and that some of them could not have had very long experience of their work. I must, however, attribute to the cashiers and clerks of the defendants the degree of intelligence and care ordinarily required of persons in their position to fit them for the discharge of their duties. . . . Each of the cheques in question was drawn payable to "The Officer in Charge, Estates Office, Canadian Overseas Military Forces," and was indorsed by that officer under the same description. Each cheque bore upon its face the fact that it was payable to the officer of a public department and not to a private person, and the indorsement on each cheque showed that it was being negotiated by that officer. It is not in accordance with the ordinary course of business that a cheque so drawn and indorsed should be used for the purpose of paying the debt of a private individual. It was highly improbable that the officer in charge of the Estates Office would hand to de Volpi cheques in this form with the intention that the latter should pay them into his private account. It therefore seems to me that when de Volpi presented these cheques with a view to having them credited to his private account a cashier of ordinary intelligence and experience should have been put on inquiry whether or not the credit ought to be made.[79]

Facts of Motor Traders Guarantee Corporation Ltd. v. Midland Bank Ltd.

A certain motor trader in Bristol, by name Turner, had an account with the defendant bank. He induced the plaintiffs to make out a cheque for £189 5s., crossed " not negotiable," to a firm of car dealers in Bristol, Welsh & Co., representing that this sum was the purchase price of a car which was to be let on hire purchase to him. He forged the indorsement of Welsh & Co. and paid the cheque to his account with the defendants, saying that it had been negotiated to him. The cashier asked for an explanation, and a plausible one was offered; the cashier examined Turner's account in the ledger and saw that there had been several previous substantial transactions with Welsh & Co., including one payment to them of £484 10s., which Turner stated was in connection with the present transaction. In these circumstances, the cashier accepted the cheque for Turner's credit, and it was duly presented and paid.

In the six months the account had been open, some 35 cheques had been dishonoured, only some of them being paid on re-presentment.

The rules of the bank laid upon branch managers the duty of deciding whether or not such " third party " cheques should be accepted for the credit of customers.

The plaintiff brought this action for damages for conversion of the cheque, and the bank claimed to be protected by section 82.

Decision

It was held that (i) a breach of the bank's own rules is not conclusive proof of negligence, nor is even a customer entitled to demand literal performance of them, but (ii) in view of Turner's banking record, further inquiry should have been made before taking the cheque for his credit. The bank thus failed to prove that they had not been negligent within section 82, and so were liable.

In his judgment, Goddard J. said:

I am far from saying, and I do not intend to lay down until there is some authority which compels me to so hold, that it can be stated that there is an absolute duty upon a banker, even where he is put on inquiry, to inquire

[79] At pp. 685–686.

of the payee of the cheque or of the drawer of the cheque. The circumstances may be such that that is the only course that he can take to get satisfactory information. What I mean to say is that it would be going too far to hold that in every case a banker can discharge the onus which is upon him, if he wishes to take the protection of section 82, only by showing that he has inquired of one or other of these people. It may very well be that, in certain cases, the information that he gets is enough, and, as I have already said, I think that, if Turner's banking history had been different from what it is now shown to have been, I should have been inclined to hold, and I think that I probably should have held, that the inquiries which were made by [the cashier] were enough. But with a man who had this history of dishonoured cheques, and dishonoured cheques for considerable sums, I think it is obvious that [the cashier] should have consulted the manager, which is the course of conduct which the bank regulations set out. I again say that I am far from saying that the plaintiffs, or any other person whose property has been converted, are entitled to rely upon a literal performance, or are entitled to require a literal performance, by the bank of these regulations. The bank does not owe a duty to them to carry out this rule, that rule, or the other rule. Indeed, I doubt whether they owe their own customers the duty of carrying out all the rules which they may lay down as counsels of perfection. The question in every case is not whether the bank require a particular standard of conduct, but whether the particular acts which are done are enough to discharge the onus which is upon the bank either in respect of their own customer or in respect of some other customer.[80]

Notes

These cases are examples of the many which show the danger of accepting for the credit of private accounts cheques which are payable to companies, firms or public bodies.[81] The danger is now well recognised by bankers, and clear instructions are given by most banks to their employees as to the necessity for inquiry.

Comparison between the facts of these two cases, however, throws into relief the significance of the second as marking a further, albeit subtle, increase in the extent of the banker's liability in collection. To the contemporary banker the circumstances of the first case appear to represent gross negligence on the part of the defendant bank, and, indeed, no bank would today defend an action brought against it on such facts. The circumstances of the second case are quite otherwise, and closely correspond to the regular practice of many banks. The limits of the decision may be emphasised: it established, not that there is necessarily negligence in collecting a " third party " cheque for a customer, even where the customer has a doubtful banking record, but that in such a case the bank cannot

[80] At p. 96.

[81] *Cf. e.g. A. L. Underwood Ltd.* v. *Barclays Bank Ltd., ante*, p. 86 and *Penmount Estates Ltd.* v. *National Provincial Bank Ltd., post*, p. 121.

be excused, as it otherwise might, for not observing its own regulations. Even thus limited, however, the decision appears to go somewhat further than earlier cases, for it does provide a precedent for the view that a number of unpaid cheques on an account is a factor to be considered in deciding whether a particular cheque can safely be collected without further inquiry, a suggestion which had not previously appeared in the negligence cases.

The case is unusual in that it was concerned, not as are most of the negligence cases with whether the circumstances put the bank on inquiry—the cashier made inquiry at least as exhaustive as would appear reasonably possible, short of actually getting into touch with the drawer of the cheque—but with whether that inquiry was sufficient.

On the other hand, in the later case of *Smith and Baldwin* v. *Barclays Bank Ltd.*[82] we find inquiry by the bank of a character held by the court to be sufficient to satisfy the requirements of section 82. The plaintiffs were associates in a printing firm, the Argus Press, who took into an informal partnership one Bray. Over a period of two years Bray fraudulently paid into his private account with the defendants five cheques payable to the Argus Press, one of them representing an entirely fraudulent transaction of which the plaintiffs knew nothing, the others being genuine payments of debts owing to the firm. In October 1941 the manager of the branch at which Bray banked questioned him concerning the payment in of cheques payable to the firm, and Bray said that he had bought the business from the plaintiffs. The following day he showed the manager a certificate of registration under the Registration of Business Names Act. The plaintiffs, who themselves had never had a partnership agreement, had not registered the name of their business. It was held, with regard to the cheques other than the first (in respect of which the circumstances prevented any claim against the bank) that the bank had not been negligent, and were protected by section 82. Stable J. said:

> The plain fact of the matter was that there was his customer who, as [the manager] believed and as the fact was, was registered as the proprietor of the Argus Press. He was the only person in the wide world who was registered as the proprietor of the Argus Press, and what more natural that into his account cheques made payable to that business should be paid. In my view, to say that if [the manager] had embarked on a prolonged and detailed scrutiny of every available piece of material that there was he might have discovered that Bray had not bought out Mr. Smith and Mr. Baldwin . . . seems to me to throw a wholly wrong standard of care on banks in a matter of this kind.[83]

[82] (1944) 5 L.D.B. 370.

[83] *Ibid.* at p. 375.

To have gone further would have been to require the bank in the words of Sankey L.J. in the *Chartered Bank of India* case to play the part of " amateur detectives." [84]

But in *Baker* v. *Barclays Bank Ltd.*[85] the bank's inquiries were not sufficient. The plaintiff was in partnership with one Bainbridge, and each partner was authorised to indorse cheques alone. Nine cheques payable to the firm were indorsed by Bainbridge and handed by him to a customer of the defendant bank, Jeffcott, who paid them to the credit of a previously dormant account in his name. The manager of the branch asked him how it happened that he was paying in these third party cheques, and he explained that Bainbridge was the sole partner in the firm and that he, Jeffcott, was helping him in the business with a view to becoming a partner. The manager accepted this explanation and made no inquiry of Bainbridge; and in the subsequent action for conversion of the cheques the bank was held to have been negligent in not making further inquiries. It is interesting to note that Devlin J. came to this decision in spite of the fact, which he acknowledged, that inquiry of Bainbridge might well have been fruitless as far as the interests of the plaintiff were concerned; the manager should have inquired why Bainbridge had no account of his own into which to pay the cheques, and he should have recognised that in accepting the cheques in the way he did he was in effect opening an account for Bainbridge, who was not his customer.

Marquess of Bute v. Barclays Bank Ltd.

[1955] 1 Q.B. 202

Negligence in the collection of cheques payable " to A for B "

Facts

The plaintiff had had in his employ as manager of three sheep farms in the Island of Bute one McGaw. McGaw resigned in April 1949 but in September 1949 the Department of Agriculture for Scotland sent him three warrants totalling £546 in respect of hill sheep subsidy which McGaw had quite properly claimed on behalf of the plaintiff four months before his resignation. The plaintiff had not notified the Department of Agriculture of the termination of McGaw's employment.

The warrants were readdressed by the local post office and McGaw, who was now living at Barnsley, opened an account with the

---

[84] *Ante*, p. 101.
[85] [1955] 1 W.L.R. 822; *cf. post*, p. 172.

defendant bank, which received the three warrants as the first credit on the account and, after references had been taken up, allowed him to draw against them.

The warrants were expressed to be payment of hill sheep subsidy, and were drawn payable to Mr. D. McGaw, Kerrylamont, Rothesay, Bute. This name and address were in a printed rectangle, and outside this box, in brackets, were the words " for Marquess of Bute."

The plaintiff claimed the amount of the warrants as damages for conversion or as money had and received to his use. The defendant bank raised the defences (*a*) that the warrants were not the property of the plaintiff, or that they bore no indication that McGaw was not entitled to receive the proceeds; (*b*) that the plaintiff was estopped from denying that he had intended the warrants to be received by McGaw; and (*c*) that the bank was protected by section 82.

Decision

McNair J. rejected all three defences. He held that:

(*a*) (i) to claim in conversion the claimant need only establish that at the material time he was entitled to immediate possession, which (McNair J. held) the plaintiff here could do;

(ii) in any event, the test as to true ownership is the intention of the drawer, and here the Department of Agriculture knowing that the subsidy was due to the plaintiff had indicated their intention in the words in parentheses;

(*b*) the estoppel argument could succeed only if the documents were in a form that could reasonably be understood as an unequivocal representation that McGaw was entitled to the proceeds. Hill sheep subsidy from the Department of Agriculture in Scotland, tendered by a complete stranger in Barnsley, was not such a representation; and

(*c*) the same reasoning defeated any defence under section 82.

Notes

It is unfortunate that this decision,[86] on the peculiar facts of a particular case, also extends the scope of negligence under section 4 of the Cheques Act 1957.

Until the *Marquess of Bute* decision it was possible to argue (as most bankers would have argued) that " Pay A for B " entitled A to receive the proceeds, though he would be accountable to B; that it was the drawer's intention that A should have the money; and that A was entitled to immediate possession—though always accountable to B. In the circumstances of the present case it would have seemed

[86] The case is examined in some detail in Chorley, Gilbart Lectures, 1956.

that the Department of Agriculture, without notice that McGaw was no longer entitled to receive the money, must have intended him to receive it, even though they knew that the Marquess of Bute was entitled to the ultimate benefit of it; otherwise there seems little point in drawing the warrants in the form in which they were drawn, instead of directly payable to the Marquess of Bute with the intention that McGaw should indorse *per pro*. In the light of McNair J.'s ruling, however, this view of the matter can no longer be supported.

It is to be noted that no question of the bank's negligence could arise until the plaintiff had established conversion; had McGaw indeed been the true owner of the warrants and entitled to immediate possession of them the bank could not have been negligent in collecting them for him.

The form in which the warrants were drawn may be compared with that of the cheque in *Slingsby* v. *District Bank Ltd.*[87] As McNair J. said in his passing reference to that case, however, there is a difference between the two. It will be remembered that in the earlier *Slingsby* action on the cheque, against the collecting bank,[88] the plaintiff lost—not on a form of drawing more in his favour than the " Pay A for B " form, but on facts much more favourable to the bank. Finlay J. said, in finding for the bank, that Mr. Cumberbirch was of high repute and well known to the defendant bank. There was nothing to arouse suspicion in the fact that Mr. Cumberbirch was paying in the cheque to the account of the company of which he was chairman, rather than to his private account. Finlay J. felt that, with subsequent knowledge, it might appear that inquiries ought to have been made, but, given the large number of cheques with which banks have to deal every day, they could not be expected to scrutinise each one with the skill and care of detectives.

This decision represented what has been called [89] " a valiant attempt to stem the stream " of " hard treatment " that the collecting banker has received from the courts. But in *Slingsby* v. *District Bank Ltd.*, Scrutton L.J. said:

> There are, of course, difficulties as to how in law you should deal with money claimed by a customer from a bank because the bank has collected it from the customer's bank on a document which does not authorise such collection, but I thought that all those difficulties had been settled by the decision in *Morison's* case,[90] followed by this court in *Underwood's* case [91];

---

[87] *Ante*, p. 27.
[88] *Slingsby* v. *Westminster Bank Ltd.* (*No.* 2); *ante*, p. 28.
[89] Jacobs, *Bills of Exchange* (4th ed.), p. 248.
[90] [1914] 3 K.B. 356, *post*, pp. 101 *et seq.*
[91] [1924] 1 K.B. 775, *ante*, pp. 86 *et seq.*

in the *Lloyds Bank* case [92]; and in *Reckitt* v. *Midland Bank*, lately affirmed in the House of Lords.[93] *Slingsby* v. *Westminster Bank Ltd.*[94] is, in my opinion, wrongly decided and should not be followed by any court in preference to those decisions of the Court of Appeal . . .[95]

This emphatic disapproval checked the "stemming" at once; the effect of this disapproval is no doubt as complete as though the decision had been reversed on appeal. The words of Finlay J. just quoted, were to find their first substantial echo, in other circumstances, in the Court of Appeal in the *Orbit* case, 30 years later.[96]

House Property Co. of London Ltd. and Others v. London County and Westminster Bank Ltd.

(1915) 31 T.L.R. 479

Negligence in connection with cheques crossed "Account payee"

Facts

The plaintiff company were dealers in real property, the other plaintiffs being the trustees for the time being of a trust known as the Bingley Trust, to which the plaintiff company, in the course of their business, had mortgaged certain property. In 1912, Norman, the solicitor to the trustees, wrote to the company calling in the mortgage on grounds of depreciation. This was done fraudulently, no instruction having been given to him. After negotiation, the plaintiff company arranged to repay £800 of the mortgage moneys, and sent to the solicitor a cheque for this amount, payable to the trustees "or bearer," and crossed "Account payee." The solicitor paid the cheque to the credit of his account at the St. Mary Axe branch of the defendant bank, and it was collected for him.

The present action was brought on the grounds that the bank had been negligent in collecting a cheque so crossed for one who was not the named payee. The bank contended that (if the crossing had any effect as far as they were concerned) as the cheque was a bearer cheque they had in fact collected for the payee.

Decision

It was held that the bank had been negligent. In his judgment, Rowlatt J. said that:

---

[92] [1929] 1 K.B. 40, *ante*, pp. 103 *et seq.*
[93] (1932) 48 T.L.R. 271, *ante*, pp. 107 *et seq.*
[94] *Slingsby* v. *Westminster Bank Ltd.* (*No.* 2) [1931] 2 K.B. 583.
[95] [1932] 1 K.B. 544 at p. 558.
[96] *Ante*, p. 105.

[counsel for the defendants] had argued that the cheque was made out to Hanson and others or bearer, and that Norman was the bearer, and that the defendants in collecting it for his account were collecting it for the payee. That was a shallow argument, as " payee " did not mean the owner of a cheque at the time it was presented, but the name written across the face of the cheque—in this case, F. S. Hanson and others. No evidence had been called by the defendants, and they contended that they had not been guilty of negligence in allowing this cheque to be collected for a gentleman whom they knew to be a solicitor to be credited to his own account. The defendants offered no sort of excuse for so doing, and if he (his Lordship) were to say that they were entitled to do so without any explanation, he would be practically saying that a bank could not be negligent in respect of a cheque of that kind.[97]

Notes

The marking " Account payee " or " Account . . . only " is at least as old as *Bellamy* v. *Marjoribanks* [98] and is now widely used. It is not part of the crossing (although it does not constitute an unlawful addition to an authorised crossing within section 79 of the Bills of Exchange Act),[99] and it does not restrict the negotiability of the cheque [1]; but the collecting banker ignores it at his peril.

The effect of the words is, however, merely to put the banker on inquiry, and he does not lose the protection of section 4 of the Cheques Act if his inquiries are reasonably answered. In *Bevan* v. *National Bank, Ltd.*,[2] for example, where some of the cheques payable to Malcolm Wade & Co. and collected for Malcolm Wade's private account were crossed " account payee," it was held that the bank had not been negligent in so collecting them, as it had been reasonable for them to accept Wade's statement that he was trading as Malcolm Wade & Co., although in fact he was only the manager of that firm. Again, in *Importers Co.* v. *Westminster Bank Ltd.*,[3] where the defendant bank collected as agents for a German bank, all the cheques concerned being payable to German payees, the plaintiffs' contention was that, as it was impossible for the Westminster Bank to know to what account " account payee " cheques had been credited, the bank accepted such business at their own risk. This was rejected by the Court of Appeal, and it was held that the bank had not been negligent so as to lose their statutory protection.

The crossing " Account payee " was at one time much criticised,[4]

---

[97] At p. 680.
[98] (1852) 7 Ex. 389.
[99] *Cf. Akrokerri (Atlantic) Mines Ltd.* v. *Economic Bank* [1904] 2 K.B. 465.
[1] *National Bank* v. *Silke* [1891] 1 Q.B. 435.
[2] (1906) 23 T.L.R. 65.
[3] [1927] 2 K.B. 297. *Cf. ante*, p. 23.
[4] *Cf.* Paget, *op. cit.* pp. 417 *et seq.*

but it is clearly a most useful additional protection for the customer, however inconvenient it may be for bankers. It may be noted that the addition of the words to *bearer* cheques, as in the *House Property Company* case, is a practice which is now less frequent than it was before the passing of the Cheques Act. Until 1957 many large concerns requested their customers to make out cheques in this way: the customer sending his cheque was protected from loss by the crossing, while the creditor firm avoided having to indorse the cheques received by it, both at the expense of the collecting banker's vigilance.

Crumplin v. London Joint Stock Bank Ltd.

(1913) 30 T.L.R. 99

Negligence in connection with cheques crossed " Not negotiable "

Facts

The plaintiff was a stockbroker, who employed as manager, book-keeper and cashier one Rands. Rands from time to time introduced business, receiving half commission, and in 1909 he introduced in this way a Mr. Davies, for whom a small transaction was properly carried out. Between 1909 and 1913 Rands, speculating on his own behalf, used the name of Davies as a cover and, when the differences were in his favour, drew cheques payable to Davies which were duly signed by the plaintiff and crossed " Not negotiable." Two of the cheques were signed " *Per pro.*" Having endorsed Davies's name, Rands paid the cheques into his account with the Fenchurch Street branch of the defendant bank.

When the fraud was discovered the plaintiff brought this action, claiming that the bank had been negligent in accepting for the credit of one person cheques marked " Not negotiable " and payable to another person.

Decision

It was held that a " Not negotiable " crossing is merely one factor among others to be considered in deciding whether a collecting banker has been negligent, and that in the circumstances of the present case there had not been negligence.

In his judgment, Pickford J. said that:

. . . the mere taking of a " not negotiable " cheque ought not to be held to be evidence of negligence. It would be remarkable if, while the section provided that bankers were protected if they took a crossed cheque in good faith and without negligence that it should be possible to hold that the bankers were negligent merely from the fact that they took such a cheque, unless they gave rebutting evidence that they had made proper inquiries before taking it. His Lordship thought it was a matter which ought to be taken into consideration together with all the other matters, and that it did not go higher than that. In the present case evidence was given by persons of importance in the banking world, who said that transactions of this kind were not uncommon . . . it was quite clear from that evidence that the practice for cheques of this description to be paid in was so common as not to raise suspicion. It came down to a mere question whether, looking at the total number of the payments in, the number of these cheques that were paid in, their amount, and the period over which they were paid in, those circumstances were sufficient to put the defendants upon inquiry . . . He thought that if the account had been opened with a small sum, followed by a succession of large cheques similar to Davies's cheques, he would have had no difficulty in holding that this ought to have put the bank upon inquiry But when, as in this case, the cheques were for small amounts, and when they were paid in at such long intervals, it was not negligence in the bank not to have made inquiry.[5]

Notes

Bankers are interested in negotiability in other ways besides their concern with cheques and bills of exchange, and the principle is discussed later.[6] But it is in connection with cheques and bills that the principle is seen in its clearest form. It was widely canvassed in the discussion that preceded the passing of the Cheques Act [7]: the non-transferable instrument that was advocated then on grounds of safety would have taken the majority of money transfers out of the negotiable area. In the event the Cheques Act got rid of most indorsements while preserving the negotiability of cheques, and the effect of the limitation of that negotiability by the addition of restrictive wording is a matter of interest, though seldom of direct concern, to bankers.

The paying banker as such cannot normally know whether the cheque has been negotiated before it reaches him. The collecting banker who receives for the credit of A, a cheque payable to and duly indorsed by B, knows of the negotiation and may be, but usually is not, affected by that knowledge. In *Great Western Railway Co. Ltd.* v. *London and County Banking Co. Ltd.*[8] there was a suggestion in Lord Brampton's judgment that section 82 might not give the same protection to the banker collecting " not negotiable " cheques as it does where the crossing is simple. The decision in the *Crumplin* case, in which the " not negotiable " was the main point at issue,

---

[5] At p. 101. [6] *Post*, p. 124.
[7] See Holden, *Jones and Holden's Studies in Practical Banking* (6th ed.), pp. 287 *et seq.*
[8] [1901] A.C. 414; *ante*, p. 19.

was therefore important, even though it must not be given more than its proper weight. In the following year, in the *Morison* case,[9] Lord Reading referred to the question, *obiter*, in terms which left it open. He said:

> It is certainly not conclusive evidence of negligence against a banker who collects crossed cheques so marked. Even if I assume that the taking of a crossed cheque bearing these words would be some evidence of negligence, it could not affect my decision upon the later cheques. . . .[10]

There has been much discussion of the point.[11] The balance of argument is clear—as Paget puts it: " the ' not negotiable ' crossing has nothing to do with the collecting banker or he with it." [12]

Penmount Estates Ltd. v. *National Provincial Bank Ltd.*[13] is one of the more recent cases which may support the *Crumplin* decision. There a solicitor paid into his Clients' Account with the defendant bank a cheque crossed " not negotiable," payable to the plaintiff, whose indorsement had been forged. When the bank had queried previous " third party " cheques paid in, the solicitor had told them that the payees had no accounts; on this occasion he said that he had arranged for the payees to indorse the cheque in order that he might pay it into his account and issue his cheque for the amount less his costs. The bank succeeded in their defence that they had not been negligent, Mackinnon J. saying: " It is true that, in the light of after events, the explanations given . . . may sound improbable to anyone in a suspicious frame of mind; but in my opinion the officials of the bank, doing their duty under section 82, have not to be abnormally suspicious." [14] The " not negotiable " crossing was not considered in the judgment, but it may be noted that the bank did not contest liability in respect of similar cheques crossed " Account payee only."

In the light of the above authorities it seems unlikely that a court would be prepared to hold a banker negligent merely because he collected a " not negotiable " cheque without inquiry.

In *Wilson & Meeson* v. *Pickering* [15] it was held that the payee of a cheque crossed " not negotiable " is within section 81 of the Bills of Exchange Act 1882. In this case, a partner in the plaintiff firm handed a cheque so crossed, and signed in blank, to the secretary of

---

[9] *Ante*, p. 101.
[10] [1914] 3 K.B. 356 at p. 373.
[11] *Cf.* Paget, *op. cit.*, pp. 415 *et seq.*
[12] *Op. cit.* p. 417; *cf.* Chorley, *op. cit.*, p. 132.
[13] (1945) 173 L.T. 344.
[14] (1945) 173 L.T. 344 at p. 346. *Cf. ante*, p. 116 for Finlay J.'s similar view.
[15] [1946] 1 All E.R. 394.

the firm with instructions to complete it for £2, payable to the Inland Revenue. Instead the secretary made it out for £54 4s., payable to the defendant, to whom the secretary owed money. It was held that section 81 prevented the defendant from having any better right than the fraudulent secretary; and the plaintiffs were not estopped by their conduct from denying the validity of the cheque, as they owed no duty of care to the defendant. In any event, the defendant would not, in restoring the amount of the cheque, lose her original right against the secretary. The Court of Appeal pointed out also that the rule of estoppel as to the filling up of blanks in negotiable instruments [16] applies only to such instruments; the cheque in this case was, on its face, not negotiable.

Because of its ineffectiveness *vis-à-vis* the collecting banker, the " not negotiable " crossing does not provide as complete protection to the drawer as is sometimes thought. If the drawer stops a cheque so crossed, whether because of a dispute with the payee or because it has been misappropriated, the crossing will prevent any third party into whose hands the cheque comes obtaining a right of action on it, as he might have if it were not so crossed. But if such a third party, innocent holder or thief, has paid it in for collection and it is paid before the stop becomes effective, the drawer normally has no recourse against either collecting or paying banker, and while he can, by reason of the simple crossing, discover to whose account it was credited, that may be of little value to him.

In practice virtually complete protection can be obtained only by using such words as " Pay John Smith only " (deleting " or Order "), or by a combination of " not negotiable " and " account payee only." (As to the rare failure, in the drawer's interest, of " account payee only," see *ante*, p. 118, where also its inconvenience to the banks is referred to). The non-transferable instrument mentioned earlier would of course have resolved the problem; in its absence it is not easy to explain to customers the differing consequences of additional crossings. But it remains unsatisfactory that the simple crossing of cheques is so widely regarded as providing drawers with protection much more complete than in fact it is.

CHAPTER 5

OTHER INSTRUMENTS USED IN BANKING

Goodwin v. Robarts

(1876) 1 App. Cas. 476

Mercantile usage can confer negotiability

Facts

The plaintiff had bought certain bearer Russian and Hungarian Government scrip, expressed to be exchangeable for bonds. He deposited the certificates with his broker, Clayton, who fraudulently lodged them with the defendant, his banker, as security for a loan to himself. In this action by the plaintiff to recover the scrip the defendant banker claimed that title in it had passed to him, and proved 50 years' usage by which such scrip had been treated as negotiable by delivery.

Decision

The House of Lords upheld the decision of the Court of Exchequer Chamber that such usage did in fact make the scrip negotiable legally, and that the plaintiff's case failed.

In the Court of Exchequer Chamber,[1] Lord Cockburn C.J. said:

It is true that the law merchant is sometimes spoken of as a fixed body of law, forming part of the common law, and as it were coeval with it. But as a matter of legal history, this view is altogether incorrect. The law merchant, thus spoken of with reference to bills of exchange and other negotiable securities, though forming part of the general body of the *lex mercatoria*, is of comparatively recent origin. It is neither more nor less than the usages of merchants and traders in the different departments of trade, ratified by the decisions of Courts of Law, which, upon such usages being proved before them, have adopted them as settled law with a view to the interests of trade and public convenience. . . . Why is it to be said that a new usage which has sprung up under altered circumstances, is to be less admissible than the usages of past times? . . .

We must by no means be understood as saying that mercantile usage, however extensive, should be allowed to prevail if contrary to positive law. . . . But so far from that being the case, we are, on the contrary, in our opinion, only acting on an established principle of that law in giving legal effect to a usage, now become universal, to treat this form of security. . . as assignable by delivery.[2]

[1] (1875) L.R. 10 Ex. 337.

[2] At pp. 346, 352, 357.

Notes

The negotiability of cheques and bills of exchange is largely taken for granted by bankers, but they are concerned with the principle in other areas of their work, not least where other instruments may or may not have the quality of negotiability.[3]

To be negotiable an instrument must be " capable of being sued upon by the holder of it *pro tempore* in his own name; and it must be, by the custom of trade, transferable like cash by delivery (including indorsement and delivery in the case of an instrument payable to order)." [4] Mercantile custom had long recognised cheques, bills and promissory notes as negotiable when statutory recognition was accorded in 1882 by the Bills of Exchange Act,[5] but until *Goodwin* v. *Robarts* was decided in 1876 there had been considerable doubt as to whether mercantile usage was fixed or expandable. In particular, in *Crouch* v. *Crédit Foncier of England*,[6] a case concerning a bearer debenture, it was held that the instrument could not be regarded in law as negotiable merely because the business community had so treated it. The decision in *Goodwin* v. *Robarts*, three years later, showed that this proposition could not be maintained; and in *Rumball* v. *Metropolitan Bank*,[7] scrip certificates for shares in an English company were similarly held to be negotiable. In *Bechuanaland Exploration Co.* v. *London Trading Bank Ltd.*,[8] where the question was again of bearer debentures, Kennedy J., on the grounds that *Goodwin* v. *Robarts* had virtually overruled the *Crédit Foncier* decision, held that they were negotiable.

The combined effect of these decisions is to make all such documents, whether English or foreign, negotiable,[9] provided always that they satisfy the general requirements of negotiability. But they are of wider importance in that they established, finally, that proof of mercantile usage can confer legal negotiability on instruments not previously so recognised.[10]

In *Jones & Co.* v. *Coventry*,[11] Darling J., holding that the warrant in question was not negotiable, laid emphasis on the absence in it

---

[3] *Cf. post*, pp. 225 *et seq.*, as to the pledge of negotiable securities. *Cf.* also pp. 119 *et seq.*

[4] Halsbury's *Laws of England*, Vol. 4, p. 513.

[5] See Holden, *The History of Negotiable Instruments in English Law*, for the development of the principle of negotiability, and *cf.* Chorley, *op. cit.*, pp. 151 *et seq.*

[6] (1873) L.R. 8 Q.B. 374.

[7] (1877) 2 Q.B.D. 194.

[8] [1898] 2 Q.B. 658.

[9] See Chorley, *op. cit.*, p. 154, for a description of these documents, with which bankers are mainly concerned as security for loans.

[10] *Cf.* Holden, *The History of Negotiable Instruments in English Law*, pp. 151 *et seq.*

[11] *Ante*, p. 54.

of a promise to pay. He was not, of course, suggesting that such a promise is an essential of negotiability: the cheque itself has no promise, and although English bank notes still include the word, they would be negotiable without it—as indeed would any other document that Parliament chose to make so. Paget's reference to the *Coventry* case makes the point thus: the negotiable instrument " must embody a promise or a ground of action in itself."

In this connection it may be noted that in *Akbar Khan* v. *Attar Singh*,[12] a Privy Council case concerning deposit receipts, Lord Atkin said that negotiable instruments " come into existence for the purpose only of recording an agreement to pay money and nothing more, though of course they may state the consideration." [13] The implied promise to pay, in the documents in question, was not enough to make them promissory notes.

Cebora S.N.C. v. S.I.P. (Industrial Products) Ltd.

[1976] 1 Lloyd's Rep. 271

The cash equivalence of the bill of exchange

Facts

The plaintiffs, an Italian manufacturing company, entered into an agreement with the defendants, an English company, granting them exclusive rights to sell the plaintiffs' products in the United Kingdom. Following disputes between the parties the plaintiffs terminated the agreement and set up their own distributing company in England. The defendants gave instructions that five outstanding bills of exchange, for a total of £56,000, should be dishonoured. Upon the plaintiffs claiming summary judgment on the bills, the defendants counterclaimed for delivery of defective goods and loss of profit. The District Registrar entered judgment for the plaintiffs on the bills, and the defendants appealed, applying for a stay pending trial of the counterclaim, and alleging that in all the circumstances, including the fact that the plaintiffs were outside the jurisdiction, there was considerable doubt whether any judgment that might be obtained on the counterclaim would be enforceable. But May J. refused the stay, and the defendants appealed.

Decision

The Court of Appeal dismissed the appeal. Sir Eric Sachs said:

Any erosion of the certainties of the application by our Courts of the law

[12] [1936] 2 All E.R. 545.

[13] At p. 550.

merchant relating to bills of exchange is likely to work to the detriment of this country, which depends on international trade to a degree that needs no emphasis. For some generations one of those certainties has been that the bona fide holder for value of a bill of exchange is entitled, save in truly exceptional circumstances, on its maturity to have it treated as cash, so that in an action upon it the Court will refuse to regard either as a defence or as grounds for a stay of execution any set off, legal or equitable, or any counterclaim, whether arising on the particular transaction upon which the bill of exchange came into existence, or, a fortiori, arising in any other way. This rule of practice is thus, in effect, pay up on the bill of exchange first and pursue claims later. . . .

In my judgment, the Courts should be really careful not to whittle away the rule of practice by introducing unnecessary exceptions to it under the influence of sympathy-evoking stories, and should have due regard to the maxim that hard cases make bad law. Indeed, in these days of international interdependence and increasing need to foster liquidity of resources, the rule may be said to be of special import to the business community. Pleas to leave in Court large sums to deteriorate in value while official referee proceedings are fought out may well to that community seem rather divorced from business realities, and should perhaps be examined with considerable caution.[14]

Notes

It is clear that the courts have a discretion to order a stay of execution in an action on bills of exchange, even apart from the fraud, duress or failure of consideration which can found defences to bills of exchange.[15] But the *Cebora* decision underlines the fact that this discretion will be exercised only in "truly exceptional circumstances."

All three judgments in the Court of Appeal were based on the decisions in *James Lamont & Co. Ltd.* v. *Hyland* (*No.* 2) [16] and *Brown Shipley & Co. Ltd.* v. *Alicia Hosiery Ltd.*[17] In the *Lamont* case the defendants sought leave to defend a claim on a bill of exchange on the grounds that they were counter-claiming unliquidated damages, larger than the amount of the bill, for breach of the contract in respect of which the bill had been given. The Court of Appeal reviewed the authorities and upheld the trial judge's refusal of a stay: unliquidated damages cannot found a defence to a bill of exchange. And in the *Brown Shipley* case Lord Denning cited the rule formulated in *Lamont* thus:

Where there is an action between immediate parties to a bill of exchange, then in the ordinary way judgment should be given upon that bill of exchange as for cash and it is not to be held up by virtue of some counter-

[14] At pp. 278–279.
[15] *Cf.* Chalmers, *op. cit.*, pp. 99 *et seq.*
[16] [1950] 1 All E.R. 929.
[17] [1966] 1 Lloyd's Rep. 668.

claim which the defendant may assert even, as in that case [*Lamont*] a counterclaim relating to the specific subject-matter of the contract.[18]

The rule was conclusive in *Cebora*, but two months earlier the Court of Appeal had recognised a specific exception to the rule. In *Nova (Jersey) Knit Ltd.* v. *Karngarn Spinnery GmbH*[19] there was a dispute between the English plaintiffs and the German defendants, and the defendants resisted immediate payment of dishonoured bills of exchange on the grounds that German arbitration was pending on the whole issue in dispute. The Court of Appeal granted the stay, but on appeal the House of Lords reversed their decision by a majority,[20] Lord Wilberforce saying:

I fear that the Court of Appeal's decision, if it had been allowed to stand, would have made a very substantial inroad upon the commercial principle on which bills of exchange have always rested.[21]

That principle he had described thus:

. . . I must emphasise, since it seems to be suggested that all the merits require the whole dispute to go to arbitration in Germany, that it is not mere technicality that supports the appellants' claim. When one person buys goods from another, it is often, one would think generally, important for the seller to be sure of his price: he may (as indeed have the appellants here) have bought the goods from someone else whom he has to pay. He may demand payment in cash; but if the buyer cannot provide this at once, he may agree to take bills of exchange payable at future dates. . . . Unless they are to be treated as unconditionally payable instruments . . . which the seller can negotiate for cash, the seller might just as well give credit. And it is for this reason that English law (and German law appears to be no different) does not allow cross-claims, or defences, except such limited defences as those based on fraud, invalidity, or failure of consideration, to be made.[22]

But the decision in this case does not mean that the cash equivalence rule can never be affected by pending arbitration proceedings.[22a] The argument in the House of Lords turned largely on whether the arbitration agreement, which was governed by German law, and on which there was conflicting expert evidence, could be held to cover the bills of exchange. Lord Wilberforce considered that it could not, and his brethren agreed, with the exception of Lord Salmon, who delivered a dissenting judgment and would have dismissed the appeal. He too recognised the basic rule (and made a particular point on it: " certainly there could be no question of a

[18] At p. 669.
[19] [1976] 2 Lloyd's Rep. 155.
[20] [1977] 2 All E.R. 463.
[21] At p. 470.
[22] At p. 470.
[22a] *Cf. Barclays Bank Ltd.* v. *Aschaffenberger Zellstoffwerke AG*, *post*, p. 199.

stay if the bills had been discounted and the holders in due course were the plaintiffs in the action " [23]). But he held that the agreement covered the bills, and he seemed to accept the defendants' argument " that if the circumstances of this case were not exceptional, it is difficult to imagine any that could be." It seems clear that if the majority had agreed with him on both points the stay would have been granted.

Eaglehill Ltd. v. Needham Builders Ltd.

[1973] A.C. 992

Notice of dishonour of a bill of exchange

Facts

The defendants were drawers of a bill of exchange for £7,660 on a furniture company, payable on December 31, 1970, and accepted payable at Lloyds Bank, High Wycombe. It was discounted by the plaintiff company. By December 28, the furniture company was in liquidation, and both plaintiffs and defendants knew this, and that the bill could not be paid. But notice of dishonour is necessary regardless of the knowledge of the parties, and Eaglehill prepared a notice, dating it January 1, the day after the bill was to be presented. The secretary of the company mistakenly posted it on December 30, and it reached the defendants by the first post on December 31. On the same day the bill was delivered to the bank by the first post.

The defendants argued that notice is ineffective if it is given before the dishonour takes place. Here it could not be proved that this had not happened, and therefore they could not be liable on the bill. A majority of the Court of Appeal reluctantly accepted this argument, Lord Denning dissenting.

Decision

The House of Lords unanimously allowed the appeal, holding that (1) a notice of dishonour is not vitiated by the mere fact that it was posted before the due date for payment of the bill; it constitutes a good notice unless it is received before the bill itself is dishonoured; and (2) a notice of dishonour is given at the time when the drawers receive it, which (*per* Lord Cross) " when it is opened in the ordinary course of business, or would be so opened if the ordinary

[23] At p. 475.

course of business was followed." [24] And in the absence of evidence as to the precise times at which notice and bill were received, Lord Cross said:

> If two acts have been done, one of which ought to have been done after the other if it was to be valid and the evidence which could reasonably be expected to be available does not show which was done first they will be presumed to have been done in the proper order.[25]

Notes

The bill of exchange is now much less frequently seen in domestic banking than it once was, but its continuing use in international commerce [25a] makes it important for bankers still to be familiar with the formalities of its handling, so long as the laws of England apply, while it has always to be remembered that the cheque is itself a bill of exchange. The *Eaglehill* case, although no bank was directly involved, provides a good example of one of the formalities. In the event, the House of Lords, on the special and unusual facts of the case, unanimously upheld Lord Denning's powerful dissenting judgment in the Court of Appeal. But the judgments in the latter, of Sachs and Stamp L.JJ. should not be forgotten. Sachs L.J. said:

> It is now a very long time since Lord Mansfield stressed the importance of certainty in the law merchant. For well over a century there has been certainty that to establish due notice of dishonour it must be shown that it was notice after presentment and dishonour. In this technical sphere of the law merchant it would be no good service to introduce complexity and uncertainty by grafting artificial exceptions on to a well-known rule—exceptions moreover which run contrary to the plain meaning of the words of the 1882 Act and which would make an inroad on its provisions.[26]

It is to be noted that he made the same point in a different context in the *Cebora* case.[27] The two different approaches to the facts of the present case may be regarded as reflecting the recurring difference between what may be termed the strict and the liberalising schools of thought in the law. In practice the prudent course is to seek to satisfy the former.

---

[24] At p. 1011.
[25] At p. 1011.
[25a] *Cf. post*, pp. 199 *et seq.*
[26] [1972] 2 A.C. 8 at p. 24.
[27] *Ante*, p. 125.

London City and Midland Bank Ltd. v. Gordon
[1903] A.C. 240

Bankers' drafts

Facts

Here, as in *Capital and Counties Bank Ltd.* v. *Gordon*,[28] the clerk of the respondent, Gordon, had stolen a number of cheques sent to his employer, and the appellant bank had collected them for him, Included with them were four drafts, to a total value of £32 15s. 9d., drawn by a country branch of the appellant bank on its own head office, and not crossed.

This case, heard with the *Capital and Counties* case (with which it was largely parallel) followed the same course as that case, and the appeal of the bank against the decision of the Court of Appeal was heard by the House of Lords.

Decision

The bank's appeal was dismissed in respect of all the instruments concerned except the bankers' drafts. It was held, with regard to these, that the bank was protected.

In his judgment, Lord Lindley said:

. . . I agree with the Court of Appeal in thinking that the bank, which is both drawer and drawee of these instruments, is not entitled to treat them as bills of exchange as defined in section 3 of the Bills of Exchange Act, although a holder may sue the bank upon them and treat them either as bills of exchange or as promissory notes.[29] An instrument on which no action can be brought by the drawer can hardly be a bill of exchange within section 3 of the Act, whatever it may be called in ordinary talk. Next it was contended that section 17 of the Revenue Act of 1883 [30] extended to these documents and brought them within the protecting clauses of the Bills of Exchange Act. But, as pointed out by the Court of Appeal, section 17 of the Revenue Act, 1883, only applies to drafts issued by a customer of a bank, whilst these drafts were issued, not by a customer, but by a bank to a customer. I agree, therefore, with the Court of Appeal on this point. But then reliance was placed on the Stamp Act of 1853, section 19, which relates to drafts or orders drawn on bankers and payable to order on demand. The section exonerates the bankers drawn upon from liability if they pay such drafts or orders to holders claiming under endorsements which are forged. This Statute was passed before crossed cheques were regulated by statute, and it has no special reference to them, nor does it refer to any bankers except those on whom the instruments are drawn.[31]

[28] *Ante*, p. 84

[29] See s. 5 (2).

[30] Now replaced by s. 5 of the Cheques Act 1957.

[31] At pp. 250–251.

After reviewing the history of the section, and its relation to later legislation, Lord Lindley continued:

> . . . section 19 of the Act of 1853 appears to me to be purposely preserved in order to protect bankers cashing drafts or orders on them, and which are not bills of exchange or cheques as defined in the Act of 1882, in the same way as section 60 of that Act protects them from cashing documents drawn on them, and which are bills of exchange and cheques as defined in it.[32]

And he therefore considered that the bank was protected in respect of these particular drafts.

Notes

Paget [33] argues at some length that the inclusion of bankers' drafts within the protection of the only surviving section of the Stamp Act, 1853,[34] was not justified. But, as he remarks, " it is not for bankers to complain of its retention and application to drafts other than bills and cheques " and there is no doubt, in the light of this decision, that the protection exists.

Until 1932 it was not possible effectively to cross a banker's draft. In that year the Bills of Exchange Act (1882) Amendment Act provided that the crossed cheque sections of the principal Act should apply to bankers' drafts as if the drafts were cheques. The 1932 Act was repealed and re-enacted in section 5 of the Cheques Act 1957.

In the *Gordon* case Lord Lindley referred to a doubt which had been expressed as to whether the protection of section 19 extends to foreign as well as to inland drafts. As the drafts in the *Gordon* case were inland only it was not necessary for him to decide the point. The argument which has been advanced against the inclusion of foreign bills is that, as there was at the time of the passing of the Act no stamp duty on foreign bills, no such protection could have been in the mind of the draftsman of the Act, which was concerned with stamp duties. Paget [35] convincingly marshals the arguments in favour of the full protection being available; and in the course of business today a bank is more likely to require protection in the case of a draft drawn by an overseas branch upon the head office than for a purely inland bill.

An exception to the general rule that a draft drawn by a banker upon himself is not a cheque was seen in *Slingsby* v. *Westminster Bank Limited* [36]; there the interest warrants on 5 per cent. War Stock, 1929–47, were drawn by the Chief Accountant of the Bank of

---

[32] At p. 252.
[33] *Op. cit.*, pp. 212 *et seq.*
[34] Reproduced, *ante*, p. 59.
[35] *Op. cit.*, pp. 273 *et seq.*
[36] [1931] 1 K.B. 173.

England upon the Bank of England itself, but Finlay J., who held the documents to be dividend warrants, and so within section 95 of the Bills of Exchange Act, expressed the opinion also that the Chief Accountant in drawing them was acting as an agent of the Government, and not in his capacity as an officer of the Bank.

It may be noted finally that a banker's draft must always be to order: a bearer draft would be in effect a bank-note, and no bank in this country now retains the right of note issue except the Bank of England.

Fine Art Society Ltd. v. Union Bank of London Ltd.

(1886) 17 Q.B.D. 705

Postal orders are not negotiable instruments

Facts

The plaintiffs had an account with the defendant bank. The plaintiffs' secretary stole from them certain Post Office orders which he paid into the private account which he maintained with the defendants, who cashed them and credited him with the proceeds. The Post Office regulations, which provided that such orders should be signed by the payee, before payment, also provided that such signature might be dispensed with when the postal orders were paid through a bank and bore the bank's crossing stamp.

The plaintiffs brought the present action to recover the amount of the orders.

Decision

The Court of Appeal held that the defendants had wrongfully converted the orders; that there was no custom of negotiability nor were the orders made quasi-negotiable by the Post Office regulations as to the bank's crossing—this merely substituted the bank's signature for that of the payee; and that there was no estoppel to prevent the plaintiffs from enforcing their claim.

In his judgment, Lord Esher M.R. said:

> I do not think it can be said that the documents here in question have obtained the same position as that of the documents in *Goodwin* v. *Robarts*.[37] It seems clear that they have not been treated as negotiable instruments by the general practice in England. I do not think it is shown that bankers or merchants or the Post Office have, for all purposes and with regard to all persons, so treated them. They have none of the attributes of negotiable

[37] *Ante*, p. 123.

instruments. It is urged that the doctrine of estoppel, as stated in *Goodwin* v. *Robarts*, ought to be applied to this case. The House of Lords there said that, even if the instruments were not negotiable, the mode in which they had been treated both here and abroad was such that it must be taken that the plaintiff was aware of it, and that in handing them over to another person he put it in his power to hand them over as negotiable instruments. I think that the proposition as there stated was only stated as applicable to the facts of the special case, which contained a statement that the form of instrument then in question had been treated as a negotiable instrument by the mercantile world, and by all parties dealing with it, both in this country and abroad. It does not seem to me that there is anything in this case upon which such an estoppel could be founded against the plaintiffs.[38]

Notes

The Post Office Act 1969, s. 76, provides:

> Any person acting as a banker . . . who, in collecting in that capacity for any principal, shall have received payment . . . of any postal order or of any document purporting to be a postal order, shall not incur liability to anyone except that principal by reason of having received the payment. . . .

It is not entirely clear whether this section provides protection for the banker who receives postal orders for the credit of his customer's account. It has been pointed out [39] that the section reproduces an enactment of 1880, which was therefore operative when the *Fine Arts* case was heard, although there was no reference to it in that case. Moreover, as Sheldon remarks,[40] the normal practice of bankers is to credit such postal orders as cash, which raises the question whether the " collecting " of section 25 can protect them. This question parallels the discussion which is outlined in the notes to the *Gordon* case.[41]

In any case, the section provides no protection in the case of money orders. Money orders also fall short of negotiability and here there is somewhat greater risk for the banker, in that the Post Office regulations governing them allow the Post Office to recoup themselves for any money orders found to be irregular, which have been presented through a bank. In *London and Provincial Bank* v. *Golding*,[42] a Chinese, whom the Post Office refused payment of certain money orders sent from abroad, cashed them with the defendant, who paid them into his account with the plaintiff bank, asking them to let him know when the orders were " all right." The bank did this upon receiving the money from the Post Office. Upon

---

[38] At pp. 710–711.
[39] Paget, *Law of Banking* (7th ed.), p. 264.
[40] *Practice and Law of Banking* (10th ed.), p. 155.
[41] *Ante*, pp. 84 *et seq.*
[42] (1918) 3 L.D.B. 161.

an irregularity being subsequently discovered by the Post Office, the money was claimed back by them under the above-mentioned regulation, and the bank debited the customer with the amount, in accordance with the normal practice of banks upon the return of unpaid instruments. The Chinese had by now left the country, and the customer refused to be debited. The Court of Appeal found in favour of the bank, but it has often been pointed out that banks would be well advised to make it clear to customers paying in these documents that, in view of the Post Office regulations, the right is reserved of debiting the account at any future time should the orders be dishonoured.

Gowers and Others v. Lloyds and National Provincial Foreign Bank Ltd.

[1938] 1 All E.R. 766

The collection of pension warrants

Facts

A pensioner of the Colonial Service, named Gibson, lived in France and banked with the Paris branch of the defendant bank. His pension was paid by the Crown Agents for the Colonies, by warrant sent through the post to him, and the warrants were forwarded to the bank for collection, each with a certificate duly completed to the effect that Gibson was still living. Mrs. Gibson had a power of attorney to draw on Gibson's account.

Gibson died in 1929, but this fact did not become known to the defendants until 1935, when Mrs. Gibson also died. During the six years, pension warrants continued to be received by the bank, and were collected by them for credit of the Gibson account, the bank supposing Gibson to be living, as he had previously lived, at Vichy, whence the warrants were received. Each warrant bore the forged signature of Gibson, and a certificate of existence apparently regular. It was sought to recover from the bank the amount of the warrants wrongly paid on the ground, *inter alia*, that in presenting the documents for payment the bank implicitly warranted the continued life of the pensioner.

Decision

The Court of Appeal affirmed the decision of the lower Court in favour of the bank, and on the point here dealt with Sir Wilfred Greene M.R. said:

What does the document on its face convey to such a bank? It conveys quite clearly, as it seems to me, that the evidence of life, and the evidence of the authenticity of the signature, which the Crown Agents require, which is the only evidence which they require, is the certificate, filled up and apparently in order. The alternative proposition, for which [counsel for the plaintiffs] contends involves that the bank whose case I am considering, when a document of this kind is presented to it, with a certificate apparently in order, is bound at its peril, before it forwards the certificate to the Crown Agents, itself to ascertain the very matters with which the certificate deals. It must ascertain whether or not the pensioner is alive, it must ascertain whether or not the signature upon the document is really his signature, and I apprehend that it must ascertain whether or not the person who purports to have signed the certificate is in fact the person who signed it, and that he held the necessary qualification. . . . It seems to me quite impossible to extract from this document, intended to be used in the way in which it is intended to be used, evidence of any such obligation upon the bank.[43]

Notes

In this case the bank successfully repelled the suggestion that by merely presenting a document for payment they had implicitly warranted the truth of a certificate which the document contained. Had the bank failed in this case the dangers of collecting such documents would have been greatly increased; already there are inherent risks in the more usual practice of the bank itself signing the certificate of existence of the payee. Often the latter lives abroad, and where this is so, and especially where the account concerned is a joint account, on which all recent drawings may have been by the other party, there is an obvious possibility that the banker may sign carelessly. It must be emphasised that the *Gowers* decision is not at all relevant to such facts, and would give the banker no protection. Where, as sometimes happens, the bank signs a standing certificate of existence (upon the understanding that a pension will be paid until the certificate is cancelled) the danger that the banker will be " lulled to sleep " is still greater.

---

[43] At pp. 771–772.

Chapter 6

THE ACCOUNT

Chatterton v. London & County Banking Co. Ltd.

[1891] *The Miller*, February 2

A customer owes his banker no duty to examine his passbook or statement; nor, when he does in fact check it, does that checking estop him from later claiming that entries in it are wrong

Facts

Chatterton was a customer of the defendant bank who had in his employ a clerk, one Noad. It was Chatterton's custom to have his passbook from the bank weekly, and to check the items in it, Noad calling them to him from the ledger and he ticking them in the passbook. In due course Chatterton discovered that 25 cheques, which had been paid by the bank over a period, had been forged, presumably by the clerk. The cheques were stated to have disappeared, but the plaintiff claimed that the bank should refund to him the total amount of them. The bank contended that if the cheques were forgeries (which they did not admit) then the plaintiff had by his conduct misled them.

The jury at the first hearing found, *inter alia*, that " the plaintiff had by his conduct contributed to the loss or the cheques being paid," and judgment was given for the bank. The plaintiff appealed, and in the Queen's Bench Denman, Charles and Vaughan Williams JJ. ordered a new trial. The bank in their turn appealed against this order, but the Court of Appeal (the Master of the Rolls, and Lindley and Lopes L.JJ.) upheld the order.

Decision

In his summing up at the new trial, Mathew J. wondered if it was the regular practice of customers to examine and tick their passbooks and counterfoils. Would it be considered negligent for the customer to allot the task of examining his passboook to a clerk?

The plaintiff denied he had misled the bank in any way, claiming, indeed, to have taken greater precautions than was normally the case. Mathew J. said that one of the questions the jury must ask itself was whether the plaintiff had acted in a manner likely to encourage the bank to honour cheques now acknowledged as forgeries and, if so, had the bank in fact acted on such encouragement in paying the forged cheques.

If they did think that the bank so acted, then the judge said he would ask them to say what the acts of the plaintiff were which misled the bank.

The jury, without retiring, returned a verdict for the plaintiff.

Notes

This important case is reported at length only in *The Miller*, although there is a report of the new trial in *The Times* for January 21, 1891. It is unfortunate that in *Legal Decisions affecting Bankers* only the first trial, which the bank won, is reported [1]; the effect of the case is, of course, to the contrary.

The student is referred to Paget [2] for a detailed discussion of the case. The argument there advanced is against the tenor of the *Chatterton* decision and those which have followed it. As is there pointed out, the bank did not make, or at any rate did not press, the argument in which a bank's only hope would now lie, that of the account settled—that in returning the passbook the customer had accepted as binding the balance there shown. But on the argument that *was* mainly pressed, that the bank had somehow been misled (the comparison is plain with the "lulling to sleep" doctrine, as to which see *ante*, p. 104), the correctness of the decision seems clear.

It is to be noted that the account-settled argument, although it might be useful to the bank when the customer wishes to disavow entries, would by analogy (unless confused with the "duty to check" argument, from which it is properly distinct) be equally useful to the customer in circumstances such as those of the *Holland* case,[3] when he is claiming to have been misled by an erroneous credit entry.

It would obviously be satisfactory for the banks if they could establish the customer's duty to check his passbook, or, more normally now, his statement, but in the light of the *Chatterton* decision, which has been more than once approved and followed, it seems unlikely that they can do so [4]; and to equate the passbook with the account settled would seem to have dangers as great as its advantages.

Certainly the virtual replacement of passbooks by statements has

---

[1] At Vol. 1, p. 110.

[2] *Op. cit.* pp. 119 *et seq.*

[3] *Post*, p. 138.

[4] *Cf. e.g. Kepitigalla Rubber Estates Ltd.* v. *National Bank of India Ltd.*, *ante*, p. 68, and *Brewer* v. *Westminster Bank Ltd.*, *post*, p. 172.

made even more unlikely than it was before the development of any automatic protection for the banker. The statement is not returned to the bank, and in the absence of such return it seems impossible to attempt to establish that degree of agreement which is essential to the account stated. Within a banking framework in which the statement is the only form of communication to the customer of the state of his account, the banks must seek protection, if they desire it, in some express agreement with their customer.[5]

Holland v. Manchester and Liverpool District Banking Co.

(1909) 25 T.L.R. 386

Where the customer acts, in good faith, upon a wrong entry made in the statement or passbook, so altering his position, the banker is estopped from claiming to have the error adjusted

Facts

The plaintiff had an account with the defendant bank. On September 21, 1907, after examining his passbook, which showed a balance to his credit of £70 17s. 9d., the plaintiff issued a cheque for £67 11s., in payment of a trade debt to Reynolds & Co. On presentation this cheque was dishonoured, as the actual credit balance was only £60 5s. 9d., a credit for £10 12s. having been entered twice in the passbook. Although the bank apologised to Reynolds, when the circumstances were disclosed, this firm refused the plaintiff any further credit and, the facts becoming known, other creditors also refused him credit. The plaintiff brought the present action for damages.

Decision

The jury assessed the damages at £100, subject to the court's decision as to whether the plaintiff was entitled to draw the cheque in such circumstances. The Lord Chief Justice held that, although the bank were entitled to have the wrong entry ultimately adjusted, the plaintiff, not having been negligent or fraudulent, was entitled, until the correction was made, to act upon the bank's statement in the passbook. Having so acted, and suffered damage thereby, he was entitled to recover the amount of the damage.

In the course of his judgment, Lord Alvertsone C.J. said that the effect of a passbook entry did not seem to have been clearly decided

---

[5] See Chorley, *op. cit.* pp. 175 *et seq. Cf.* as to money paid by mistake generally, Paget, *op. cit.* pp. 361 *et seq.*

in the Courts, but he considered that, whilst the bank in this case were entitled to have any wrong entry ultimately corrected, until the correction was made the customer had the right to act upon the bank's statements in the passbook, and to receive them as statements by the bank that there was so much money to his credit. The passbook in all cases although subject to adjustment was prima facie evidence against the bank of the amount standing to the credit of a customer, upon which that customer, in the absence of negligence or fraud on his part, was entitled to rely.

Notes

In *Skyring* v. *Greenwood & Cox* [6] the plaintiff was the administratrix of Major Skyring R.A. and the defendants were paymasters of the Royal Artillery. In error over a period of years the defendants had credited Major Greenwood with pay in excess of the sums authorised. Early in 1821 a statement of running account between the parties was rendered, including pay not authorised. A few months later the defendants wrote claiming repayment of the excess. Major Skyring died in December, 1822, and the defendants rendered a statement to the plaintiff, carrying forward the balance from the previous statement, but showing the excess pay as a debit against that balance. Abbot C.J. in giving judgment for the plaintiff, said:

> It is of great importance to any man, and certainly not less to military men than others, that they should not be led to suppose that their annual income is greater than it really is. Every prudent man accommodates his mode of living to what he supposes to be his income; it therefore works a great prejudice to any man, if after having had credit given him in account for certain sums, and having been allowed to draw on his agent on the faith that those sums belonged to him, he may be called upon to pay them back.[7]

It will be noted, however, that in the *Holland* case Lord Alverstone considered that the bank had the right to call ultimately for adjustment of their mistake. Clearly, as had been established as long ago as 1860, in *Commercial Bank of Scotland* v. *Rhind*,[8] a credit entry to the customer's account is no more than prima facie evidence against the bank, which the banker can show to have been erroneous. But it is unlikely that Lord Alverstone intended to suggest (the point was not directly in issue in the *Holland* case) that the bank has any absolute right to adjust the error, irrespective of the customer's bona fide actions upon the strength of it.

Some difficulty has been found in deciding whether or not the

---

6 (1825) 4 B. & C. 281.
7 At p. 289.
8 (1860) 3 Macq. 643 (H.L.).

mere spending of the money wrongly credited can be such detriment to the customer as will estop the payer from reclaiming it. In *Holt* v. *Markham*,[9] where estoppel was one of the grounds of the decision against the bank, Scrutton L.J. said:

> I think this is a simple case of estoppel. The plaintiffs represented to the defendant that he was entitled to a certain sum of money and paid it, and after a lapse of time sufficient to enable any mistake to be rectified he acted upon that representation and spent the money. That is a case to which the ordinary rule of estoppel applies.[10]

In *Lloyds Bank Ltd.* v. *Brooks*,[11] a case heard at Manchester Assizes on a question of amounts wrongly credited, counsel for the bank contended strongly that as the defendant had merely used the money for her own purposes the bank could not be estopped merely because she would not have so spent it had she not been misled. In his judgment in favour of the defendant, Lynskey J. reviewed the authorities, and quoted the judgment of Denning L.J. in *Larner* v. *L.C.C.*,[12] in which he said:

> This defence of estoppel, as it is called—or more accurately, change of circumstances—must, however, not be extended beyond its proper bounds. Speaking generally, the fact that the recipient has spent the money beyond recall is no defence unless there was some fault—as, for instance, breach of duty—on the part of the paymaster and none on the part of the recipient.[13]

Lynskey J. distinguished the cases upon which counsel for the bank had based his argument on the grounds that in them the overpayment had been made by persons owing no duty to the persons paid; the bank, however, owed a duty not to over-credit her, and not to induce her by their representation to draw more than she was entitled to.

In earlier editions of this book it was suggested that it would be difficult for a commercial customer to prove that he had acted on a wrong credit, especially if it was for a substantial amount. An attempt to do so in *United Overseas Bank* v. *Jiwani*,[14] exemplifies the difficulty created by the conditions that must be satisfied. Here the defendant, a resident in Uganda, had opened an account with the plaintiffs, a Swiss bank in Geneva, in order to build up assets outside Uganda. His balance in October 1972 was $10,000, when the bank received a telex message from Zurich that $11,000 had been paid to his credit. He was in process of buying a hotel, and in this connection he issued his cheque for $20,000. When the bank received

---

[9] *Ante*, pp. 82 and 140.
[10] At p. 514.
[11] (1950) 72 J.I.B. 114.
[12] *Ante*, p. 81.
[13] At p. 688.
[14] [1976] 1 W.L.R. 964.

written confirmation of the telex they mistakenly treated it as a second credit, credited the defendant's account and so advised him. He issued a further cheque for $11,000 towards the hotel purchase; and when the bank discovered their mistake they sought to recover the resulting overdraft.

Mackenna J. in a judgment which bankers must welcome outlined the three conditions which the defendant must satisfy before he could resist repayment: (a) that the bank had misrepresented the state of his account; (b) that he had been misled by the misrepresentation; and (c) that as a result " he changed his position in a way which would make it inequitable to require him to repay the money." The first condition was clearly satisfied; on the second the defendant's evidence was not accepted. But, more importantly for bankers generally, even if that evidence had been accepted, the third condition was held not to have been met. Had the mistake not been made the defendant would still have continued with his purchase (which " was in itself a benefit, and a continuing benefit, unlike the investment in *Holt's* case "), finding the money elsewhere, as he would on the evidence have been able to do. By the same token, he was now able to repay the money to the bank.[15]

British and North European Bank Ltd. v. Zalzstein

[1927] 2 K.B. 92

Where the customer knows that the statement or passbook is wrong, the banker is not estopped from adjusting the error

Facts

In 1923 the defendant had two accounts with the plaintiff bank, overdrawn £900 in excess of the agreed limit, and to conceal this fact from the bank's auditors, the bank's manager transferred from another account, over which he had a power of attorney, the sum of £2,000 to the credit of Zalzstein. Later the same sum was transferred back to the account from which it had been taken. The defendant did not see his passbook until both these entries had been made, nor did he object to the entries when he did see them.

Eventually, when the defendant made no reductions in his overdraft, a writ was issued by the bank. The defendant then alleged that his guarantor had made a payment of £2,000 to his credit,

[15] *Cf. National Westminster Bank Ltd.* v. *Barclays Bank International Ltd., ante*, p. 79 for an example of detriment to the customer unsuccessfully pleaded in the context of money paid under a mistake of fact.

and an adjournment was granted in order that he might produce proof of this allegation. No such proof was offered, but instead the defendant claimed that when the sum of £2,000 was placed to his credit it formed a payment to him, and that his overdraft was reduced accordingly; and that the bank had no authority to make the later debit.

Decision

The court held that the entries were book entries merely, and that the defendant was not entitled to claim the benefit of the credit of £2,000.

In the course of his judgment, Sankey J. said:

. . . I am of opinion that the cases which have been decided on mistakes of fact have very little to do with the present case. . . . The law applicable to the subject is in my view rather to be found in that branch which deals with the effect of entries in pass books, and the real question is whether there has been payment in this case. The present position of the law as to bank pass books is said to be most unsatisfactory: see Paget on Banking, 4th ed., p. 344.[16] I do not think it can be dogmatically asserted that an entry made in a pass book is in all cases conclusive and binding on the bank, or conclusive or binding on the customer, but each case must be judged on its own particular facts, although the customer in whose favour the entry stands starts with the advantage that prima facie it is an admission by the bank in his favour, which cannot in some cases be rebutted.

Bigham J. has said that entries made in a pass book by the bank are "statements on which the customer is entitled to act": *Akrokerri* (*Atlantic*) *Mines* v. *Economic Bank*.[17] That may be so in certain events, but if a customer after some months examines his pass book and sees a credit of £2,000 and a debit of a similar amount immediately afterwards, and knows nothing about either entry, is he entitled to say, I will act on the credit and disregard the debit? . . . In my opinion he is not. I think too that in every case where it is sought to treat a mere book entry as a payment, some other circumstance must be present and relied upon to enable the customer in whose favour it is made to succeed, either some express previous authority to pay, or some communication of the making of the entry to the customer and some acting on it by him: *Eyles* v. *Ellis*[18] and *Skyring* v. *Greenwood*.[19]

Notes

This decision presents no difficulty, and is the obvious, common-sense view of the matter; but it is worth pointing out that, in normal circumstances of mistake as opposed to the unusual circumstances

[16] In the current, 8th ed., p. 114.
[17] [1904] 2 K.B. 465 at p. 470.
[18] (1827) 12 Moo.J.B. 306.
[19] (1825) 4 B. & C. 281, *ante*, p. 139. *Per* Sankey J. at pp. 96–98.

in the *Zalzstein* case, it may well be difficult to prove that the customer knew the entry to be wrong, as indicated in the case last given and the notes thereto.

Devaynes v. Noble, Clayton's Case

(1816) 1 Mer. 529, 572

In the case of a current account, payments in are, in the absence of any express indication to the contrary by the customer, presumed to have been appropriated to the debit items in order of date

Facts

Devaynes was the senior partner in a firm of bankers. Upon his death the surviving partners continued to carry on business under the former partnership name of Devaynes, Dawes, Noble & Co., despite written notice from Devaynes's son and from the trustees of the father that the continued use of the name Devaynes was without their consent. Upon the bankruptcy in the following year of the surviving partners, a number of questions of law fell to be argued in Chancery, one claimant being selected to represent each class of creditor.

In this way, Nathaniel Clayton represented those who, after Devaynes's death, continued to deal with the partners, both by paying in and drawing out, some withdrawals being made (after the death) before any credits were paid in, but the balance on the whole being increased by these transactions. In the case of Clayton himself, the balance of £1,713, at the death of Devaynes, was reduced within a few days to £453, no payments in being made in that time; and before the bankruptcy, withdrawals amounted to considerably more than the whole sum of £1,713. Clayton, however, claimed that the sum of £453 was due to him from Devaynes's estate, on the ground that subsequent withdrawals from the account were to be set against later credits.

Decision

Sir William Grant M.R. considered the general topic of appropriation of payments which, in the Civil Law, was primarily at the option of the debtor, and, in the absence of express appropriation by either debtor or creditor, was effected in the manner most beneficial to the creditor. In the English authorities there had been some conflict as to whether, instead, in the absence of appropriation by the debtor, the creditor had the option of appropriating whenever he thought fit, no matter how long after the payment. He continued:

> But I think the present case is distinguishable from any of those in which that point has been decided in the creditor's favour. They were all cases of distinct insulated debts. . . . But this is the case of a banking account, where all the sums paid in form one blended fund, the parts of which have no longer any distinct existence. Neither banker nor customer ever thinks of saying, this draft is to be placed to the account of the £500 paid in on Monday, and this other to the account of the £500 paid in on Tuesday. There is a fund of £1,000 to draw upon, and that is enough. In such a case there is no room for any other appropriation than that which arises from the order in which the receipts and payments take place, and are carried into the account. Presumably, it is the sum first paid in, that is first drawn out. It is the first item on the debit side of the account, that is discharged, or reduced, by the first item on the credit side. . . . You are not to take the account backwards, and strike the balance at the head, instead of the foot, of it. A man's banker breaks, owing him, on the whole account, a balance of £1,000. It would surprise one to hear the customer say, " I have been fortunate enough to draw out all that I paid in during the last four years; but there is £1,000, which I paid in five years ago, that I hold myself never to have drawn out; and, therefore, if I can find any body who was answerable for the debts of the banking-house, such as they stood five years ago, I have a right to say that it is that specific sum which is still due to me, and not the £1,000 that I paid in last week." This is exactly the nature of the present claim.[20]

Accordingly Clayton's claim was not substantiated.

Notes

In modern conditions the rule in *Clayton's* case is not likely to be applied again in the precise circumstances of *Devaynes* v. *Noble*. But the case is a landmark both in banking law and in the general law, and it is still constantly applied in a variety of circumstances in and out of banking. Several examples are to be found elsewhere in this book.[21]

The rule can of course work against as well as for the bank. In *Deeley* v. *Lloyds Bank Ltd.*[22] the bank had advanced money against a second mortgage. There was a subsequent mortgage to the borrower's sister, Mrs. Deeley, and the bank, which was held to have had notice of this third mortgage, did not break the account with their customer, despite the fact that it was a rule of the bank that this should be done. The account continued to work, and

[20] At pp. 608–609.
[21] *Cf.* pp. 158, 246, 273, 332, 339, 341.
[22] [1912] A.C. 756.

within three weeks credits paid in totalled more than the amount of the bank's mortgage, while within another fortnight credits totalled more than the whole of the indebtedness, secured and unsecured. Upon the customer's later bankruptcy the bank entered into possession of the mortgaged property, selling it for a sum just large enough to pay off the first and second mortgages. Mrs. Deeley subsequently claimed accounts as against a mortgagee in possession. Judgment was given for the bank, and a majority in the Court of Appeal dismissed the appeal, but the House of Lords allowed the further appeal, holding that payments to the credit of the account after notice of the third mortgage wiped out the advance outstanding at the time of the notice, while subsequent withdrawals had created a fresh advance to which Mrs. Deeley's mortgage had priority.

Lord Shaw of Dunfermline quoted with approval the words of Eve J. in the court of first instance:

> I understand that to mean this: according to the law of England, the person paying the money has the primary right to say to what account it shall be appropriated; the creditor, if the debtor makes no appropriation, has the right to appropriate; and if neither of them exercises the right, then one can look on the matter as a matter of account and see how the creditor has dealt with the payment, in order to ascertain how he did in fact appropriate it.[23]

There can be other bars to the application of the rule besides the breaking of the account; in the *Deeley* case Lord Atkinson said:

> It is no doubt quite true that the rule laid down in *Clayton's* case is not a rule of law to be applied in every case, but rather a presumption of fact, and that this presumption may be rebutted in any case, by evidence going to show that it was not the intention of the parties that it should be applied[24];

and such evidence may be provided by the terms of the contract. Thus in *Westminster Bank Ltd.* v. *Cond*[25] the guarantor contended that, as the bank had continued the account unbroken after making demand on him, the advance he had guaranteed had been paid off by the payments into the account. But the bank's guarantee form contained a clause that was held to cover these circumstances and prevent the operation of the rule.

A clause of this kind is included in many bank guarantee forms, but it is not usually relied upon, the account being usually broken. It is broken similarly on the death of one of the partners in a

---

[23] At p. 783.

[24] At p. 771.

[25] (1940) 46 Com.Cas. 60. See *post*, p. 237, for facts and decision on main point at issue.

partnership; in *Royal Bank of Scotland* v. *Christie* [26] is seen an example of the application of the rule in *Clayton's* case upon failure to do so.

In the case of *The Mecca* [27] the House of Lords held that the rule in *Clayton's* case did not apply when, instead of an account current between the parties, there were a number of separate transactions, nor when, from an account rendered or other circumstances, it appeared that the creditor intended to reserve the right of appropriation. They also held that, whereas appropriation by a debtor must be made at the time of payment, appropriation by the creditor may be made as late as he wishes, " up to the last moment " (so long as he has not made earlier election), and might be declared by the creditor bringing an action, or by any other method so long as his intention was clear.

A trustee who has mixed trust money with his own by paying both into the same banking account cannot rely upon the rule in *Clayton's* case as against the beneficiaries, for it will be presumed in such a case that the moneys first drawn out by him from the banking account were his own, so as to leave any remaining balance available for the beneficiaries.[28] But the rule will apply as between two different beneficiaries whose moneys have both been paid into the same account, when the trustee later has drawn out part of the trust moneys.[29]

Re Gross, Ex Parte Kingston

(1871) 6 Ch. App. 632

Bodenham v. Hoskins

(1852) 21 L.J. Ch. 864

When the banker knows that an account is composed of trust moneys, he must not deal with it in a manner which he knows to be inconsistent with the trust; and a benefit to the banker may be evidence of his privity to a breach of trust

Facts of Re Gross, ex p. Kingston

Gross was treasurer of the county rates for the eastern division of Suffolk. He kept private accounts with the National Provincial Bank of England in Ipswich, and, although the other county funds

---

[26] *Post*, p. 176.
[27] [1897] A.C. 286.
[28] See *Re Hallett's Estate, Knatchbull* v. *Hallett* (1879) 13 Ch.D. 696, *post*, p. 155.
[29] See *Re Stenning, Wood* v. *Stenning* [1895] 2 Ch. 433 and *Re Hallett*, *supra*.

were kept with Bacon's Bank, Gross kept the police rates mixed with his own principal account, and made drawings on this account for police-rate payments. Later, however, he opened two further accounts, called " Police Account " and " Superannuation Account," and transferred to them the moneys in question, thereafter keeping his private money entirely distinct from the public funds which he was handling, save that, interest being allowed on all the accounts, it was carried to his main private account.

Some time later Gross became insolvent, and disappeared. It was then found that the two police accounts were in credit to a total of £2,972 10s. 6d., but that the two other accounts in Gross's name were overdrawn to a total which left less than £300 net credit, if the four balances were amalgamated. The County Court judge at Ipswich made an order that the bank were entitled to a lien on the credit balances to satisfy the net indebtedness, and the magistrates, representing the County, appealed. The Chief Judge in Bankruptcy found against the bank, and the present case was a further appeal.

Decision

The appeal was dismissed, and it was held that in the circumstances the bank had no right of set-off.

In the course of his judgment, Sir W. M. James L.J. said:

The bankers opened the account, and dealt with the account, knowing that it was a county account. The fact that, when his private account was overdrawn, he drew from it sums made up of pounds, shillings, and pence, for the purpose of paying them into the police account, conclusively shews that he paid, out of moneys which his bankers were willing to lend him, the moneys which he knew to be due from him to the county. . . . In my mind this case is infinitely stronger than those referred to during the argument, in which a similar claim on the part of bankers was disallowed, for in those cases the banker relied on cheques drawn by the customers; and if a banker receives from a customer holding a trust account a cheque drawn on that account, he is not in general bound to inquire whether that cheque was properly drawn. Here the customer has drawn no cheque, and the bankers are seeking to set off the balance on his private account against the balance in his favour on what they knew to be a trust account.[30]

Facts of Bodenham v. Hoskins

The plaintiff was the owner of the Rotherwas estate, and Parkes, his receiver. Parkes had a private account with the defendant banker, and on being appointed Bodenham's receiver, opened another account called " the Rotherwas account." Evidence was given that Parkes had promised to bring this account to the bankers,

---

[30] At p. 639.

in consideration of their allowing him an overdraft on his private account; and that they were told that the account would be for the receipt of the rents of the estate. Later a cheque for £829 11s. 9d., drawn on the Rotherwas account, was paid to the credit of Parkes's private account, which was overdrawn, and on this being discovered, the plaintiff sought refund of the money, alleging that the bankers had knowledge not only of the fact that the money was trust money, but also that Parkes was, or was in danger of becoming, insolvent. The defendants in their defence denied all knowledge of the trust relationship.

Decision

Lord Kindersley V.-C. found for the plaintiff, and on appeal his judgment was upheld.[31] In the course of it he said:

All, I think, that I can impute to them [the defendants] is, that they were not aware that, according to the principles—the moral principles—of a court of equity . . . a person who deals with another, which other he knows to have in his hands, or under his control, moneys belonging to a third person, cannot deal with an individual holding those moneys for his own private benefit, when the effect of that transaction is, that that person commits a fraud on a third person. That Parkes was committing a fraud in appropriating to his own purpose the money of his employer, is beyond question. The bankers did not seem to feel or be aware that they had no right, and that Parkes had no right, to enter into any arrangement, the effect of which was to make the money . . . liable to any defalcation, any deficiency that might exist upon the private account of Mr. Parkes with the bankers.[32]

Notes [33]

It is often not clear whether or not an account is to be regarded as a trust account; a trust can be created without the use of any such words as " trust " or " confidence," as was confirmed in *Re Kayford Ltd.* (*in Liquidation*),[34] a case of considerable interest to bankers although no bank was directly involved in it. A mail order company had paid to a deposit account with the bank sums received from customers as payment in advance for goods ordered; as goods were despatched appropriate sums were transferred from the deposit to the company's current account. When the company went into liquidation the question arose whether the deposit balance, then £38,000, was held in trust for the customers or formed part of

[31] See (1852) 2 De G.M. & G. 903.
[32] At p. 872.
[33] For discussion of the question of third party claims, see Chorley, *op. cit.* pp. 181 *et seq.*
[34] [1975] 1 W.L.R. 279.

the company's general assets. Megarry J. held that on the evidence, including clear evidence of intention, the deposit was a trust account. He said " different considerations might perhaps arise in relation to trade creditors; but I am here concerned only with members of the public, some of whom can ill afford to exchange their money for a claim to a dividend on the liquidation. . . ."

A banker in such circumstances would lose his right of set-off if he had notice of the existence of the trust,[35] as he most probably would on the facts of the *Kayford* case. The banker's involvement is different where the claim is by a third party alleging breach of trust.

The main difficulty in reconciling the decisions on third party claims is the question of what exactly is required to fix the banker with notice of the breach of trust which is taking place: the Courts have recognised that it is not easy for the banker to decide whether his duty to pay the customer's cheque is in any particular case over-ridden by his duty to the *cestui que trust*; but it cannot be said that they have given very exact guidance as to what his decision should be, as will be seen if the cases in this section are compared.

Perhaps the strictest ruling was that of Fry J. in *Foxton* v. *Manchester and Liverpool District Banking Co.*[36] In this case an executorship account had been opened in the joint names of Edmund and Henry Hardman, both of whom had private accounts also with the defendant bank. Both private accounts were overdrawn, and substantial sums were transferred from the executors' account to the private accounts. After the deaths of the two executors, certain beneficiaries under the will sought to recover from the bank the sums which had been so transferred, and in giving his decision against the bank, Fry J. said:

> It appears to be plain that the bank could not derive the benefit which they did from that payment, knowing it to be drawn from a trust fund, unless they were prepared to show that the payment was a legitimate and proper one, having reference to the terms of the trust. It is said that they did not know what the trust was at that time. That appears to me, I confess, to be immaterial, because those who know that a fund is a trust fund cannot take possession of that fund for their own private benefit, except at the risk of being liable to refund it in the event of the trust being broken by the payment of the money.[37]

This judgment has been approved in later cases, but whether the " benefit " to the banker must be benefit deliberately sought (as in the pressure exercised on the executors in *Foxton's* case) or may be

---

[35] *Cf. Barclays Bank Ltd.* v. *Quistclose Investments Ltd., post*, p. 198.

[36] (1881) 44 L.T. 406.

[37] At p. 608.

merely incidental benefit, is not entirely clear. In *Coleman* v. *Bucks and Oxon Union Bank* [38] it was contended against the bank that even incidental benefit must fix them with notice of the breach of trust, but Byrne J. considered that the *Foxton* decision could not be pushed so far, and must mean rather that bankers were liable who " are going to derive a benefit from the transfer and intend and design that they should derive a benefit from it."

It is natural, in any event, that benefit gained by the person dealing with the trust funds must be a material factor in assessing his culpability. On this point reference may be made to *Midland Bank Ltd.* v. *Reckitt and Others* [39]; the fact that the bank had pressed strongly for repayment of the overdraft was held to be a fact materially against them. But benefit gained is still only one factor in the case for recovery of trust moneys. In the *Selangor* case [40] there was clearly no benefit to the bank; and in *John* v. *Dodwell & Co.*,[41] when Dodwell's manager had bought shares for himself with cheques on Dodwell's account, the firm was held to be entitled to recover the money from the brokers as being held in trust for them, on the grounds that the manner in which the cheques were drawn showed that the manager was using the firm's money for his own purposes, which left the brokers without any right to hold that money as against the firm; while further, the brokers were in the position of receiving property from someone they knew to be in a fiduciary position, knowing that he was in breach of his trust, and so were themselves under a fiduciary obligation to the agent's principal.

Gray v. Johnston
(1868) L.R. 3 H.L. 1

But in the absence of (a) *a breach of trust and* (b) *the banker's knowledge of it, neither the known existence of a trust nor an incidental benefit to the banker is enough to justify his dishonour of his customer's cheque*

Facts

The appellants were bankers of Dublin, and the respondent the son of one Thomas Johnston, a customer of theirs. The father by his will left a life interest in the whole of his property to his wife, with power of appointment amongst his children and grandchildren. At the time of his death, his business account was overdrawn against the

[38] [1897] 2 Ch. 243; *post*, p. 152.
[39] [1933] A.C. 1; *ante*, p. 107.
[40] *Ante*, p. 47.
[41] [1918] A.C. 563.

security of his life policies; and in order to realise the policies, the bankers had first the will and later the probate from the widow, who was also the executrix. Upon receipt of the policy moneys, the overdraft was paid off and a balance of £853 17s. 5d. left to the credit of the account. This sum was then drawn off by a cheque signed by the widow in her capacity as executrix, and payable to Johnston and Mayston, in which name she was carrying on the business with her son-in-law. The cheque was then paid into the new account in this firm name which had previously been opened with the Grays, and which at the time of the payment was overdrawn, although no complaint had been made by the bankers about the overdraft.

Johnston's son, the respondent here, brought the present action seeking a declaration that the money so transferred belonged to the estate of the deceased, and alleging that the transfer was a breach of trust by the widow, and that the bankers had known of and participated in the breach. The respondent bank denied all knowledge of the breach, and also contended that there was no custom amongst bankers of taking notice of trusts; that on the contrary they were bound to honour their customers' cheques, and not bound to inquire into the application of moneys so drawn.

Upon the Court of Chancery in Ireland deciding in favour of the plaintiff, the bank appealed.

Decision

The appeal was allowed. In the course of his judgment, Lord Cairns L.C. said:

> In order to hold a banker justified in refusing to pay a demand of his customer, the customer being an executor, and drawing a cheque as an executor, there must, in the first place, be some misapplication, some breach of trust, intended by the executor, and there must in the second place . . . be proof that the bankers are privy to the intent to make this misapplication of the trust funds. And to that I think I may safety add, that if it be shown that any personal benefit to the bankers themselves is designed or stipulated for, that circumstance, above all others, will most readily establish that the bankers are in privity with the breach of trust which is about to be committed.[42]

Applying these principles to the facts of the present case, the Lord Chancellor held that the respondent bankers had not been shown to be privy to the breach of trust, and that the benefit they had received in the reduction of the overdraft on the new firm account was incidental merely, and was not " designed or stipulated for."

[42] At p. 11.

Notes

Gray v. *Johnston* is the leading authority for the more moderate view of the banker's liability when trust funds in his hands are mishandled, and it is not easy to reconcile this decision with the full implications of the dictum of Fry J. in *Foxton's* case.[43] However, in *Coleman* v. *Bucks and Oxon Union Bank*,[44] Byrne J. attempted to limit those implications.

In *Coleman's* case, a sum of money was paid to the defendant bank by a firm of solicitors for the credit of "James Gurney Trust." Gurney, who was a prosperous auctioneer and estate agent, was the sole trustee of the will of one Bovingdon, but he had no separate trust account with the bank, who placed the credit to Gurney's only account with them. This account was overdrawn by an amount in excess of the credit. Three years later Gurney was adjudicated bankrupt, and new trustees of Bovingdon's will were appointed. The action was to recover the amount of the credit, the plaintiffs contending that the bank had notice of the existence of a trust, but despite this had taken the benefit of the moneys in reduction of the overdraft on Gurney's account.

In the course of his judgment, Byrne J. said, after quoting from the judgment of Fry J. in *Foxton's* case:

> I am asked to say that that amounts to a decision to this effect: that wherever there is an account which upon the face of it is a trust account, and the customer draws a cheque upon that account, and pays in the cheque to the credit of his own private account, the bankers are bound to see and inquire . . . that the customer is in point of fact entitled to the money which he so transfers from one account to another. I do not think that that was the meaning of the learned judge in that case. If bankers have the slightest knowledge or reasonable suspicion that the money is being applied in breach of a trust, and if they are going to derive a benefit from the transfer and intend and design that they should derive a benefit from it, then I think the bankers would not be entitled to honour the cheque drawn upon the trust account without some further inquiry into the matter. But the present case is not that case at all, and . . . notwithstanding certain considerations which suggested themselves to me, as, for instance, if this money had first been carried to a trust account it may be that the trustee would not so readily have committed the breach of trust . . . , and notwithstanding the fact that in point of law the money must be regarded as having been applied at the moment in reduction of the overdraft, I do not think that I can hold these defendants liable to make good this amount.[45]

In *John Shaw* (*Rayners Lane*) *Ltd.* v. *Lloyds Bank Ltd.*[46] an action was brought against the bank by the liquidator of a limited company

---

[43] *Ante*, p. 149.
[44] [1897] 2 Ch. 243.
[45] At pp. 253–254.
[46] (1944) 5 L.D.B. 396.

for the recovery of moneys paid out on the signature of a person purporting to be the receiver of the company. In fact he was not the receiver, and there was even doubt as to whether there had ever been a debenture under which he could have been so appointed; but the only account with the bank had been in his name as receiver and there was nothing in the actual transactions or the account to put the bank on suspicion. On the point here under discussion Hallett J. said:

> [Counsel for the defendants] then says that . . . I should apply to this case the principle laid down in such cases as *Gray* v. *Johnston*,[47] *Coleman* v. *Bucks*,[48] *Bank of New South Wales* v. *Goulburn*[49]; in other words, that I should hold that the bank were not liable for allowing [the receiver] to draw from the account by means of cheques signed by him although they knew that it was an account which he had in a fiduciary capacity, unless it can be shown that the bank were privy to the breach of trust on the part of [the receiver]. [Counsel] contends that such a case as *Bodenham* v. *Hoskins*[50] is clearly distinguishable, because there the decision depended upon the finding that the bank was in fact privy to the breach of trust. Taking the view that [he] is right upon this point, the question which I then have to decide is whether the bank was in fact . . . privy to the undoubted fraud. . . .;

and in fact the learned judge found that it was not.

Comparison may also be made with *London Joint Stock Bank Ltd.* v. *Simmons*.[51]

Thomson v. Clydesdale Bank Ltd.

[1893] A.C. 282

There is no presumption of a trust merely from the profession of the customer

Facts

The appellants were trustees under the will of Thomas Dunlop, and in the course of the trusteeship sold certain shares to the value of £2,900. The stockbroker, whose name was also Thomson, had been instructed by the trustees to deposit the proceeds in certain colonial banks in their names, but instead he paid them to the credit of his account with the respondent bank, at the same time representing to the appellants that he had not yet received the proceeds. A short time afterwards, Thomson absconded, and it was

---

[47] *Supra*.
[48] *Supra*.
[49] [1902] A.C. 543.
[50] (1852) 2 De G.M. & G. 903; *ante*, p. 146.
[51] *Post*, p. 225.

later found that he was insolvent, his account being considerably overdrawn even after receipt of the cheque in question.

The appellants sought to recover the amount of the cheque from the bank, who contended that it had been received by them in the ordinary course of business. It appeared from the evidence that Thomson was described in the bank's books as a stockbroker, but that the manager made no inquiries as to the source of money paid in. In the court below, the bank had been held not to be liable.

Decision

The House of Lords dismissed the appeal, and affirmed the decision of the Court of Session.

In the course of his judgment Lord Herschell L.C. said:

> The only point to which I have not alluded, and upon which stress was laid, is this: that in the bank books Mr. Thomson is described as a stockbroker; therefore, it was said, his account would be understood to be one relating to matters in which he was acting for principals, . . . My Lords, if a stockbroker who was receiving money in respect of transactions for his clients could never properly pay it to his account in discharge of liabilities incurred, there might be something in the case of the appellants; but obviously that is not so. . . . It seems to me that if, because an account is opened with bankers by a stockbroker, they are bound to inquire into the source from which he receives any money which he pays in, it would be wholly impossible that business could be carried on, and I know of no principle or authority which establishes such a proposition.[52]

Notes

Marten v. *Rocke, Eyton & Co.*[53] was a case of an auctioneer who after cattle sales habitually paid the proceeds into his account with the defendant bank, pending settlement with the various vendors. After one such sale the bankers, who knew their customer's business and the nature of the credits which he paid in, appropriated a substantial credit to the clearance of his overdraft. North J. remarking, on the " shabby conduct " of the bank (who had given no notice of their intention to withdraw the accommodation allowed), yet felt himself bound reluctantly to hold that the persons to whom the money was owed could not recover from the bankers.

In *Teale* v. *William Williams Brown & Co.*[54] the plaintiffs were solicitors who had two accounts with the defendant bank, named Private and Office respectively. It was shown in the evidence that clients' money was paid only into the office account. The bank sought to set off the credit balance on the office account against the

---

[52] At p. 288.
[53] (1885) 53 L.T. 946.
[54] (1894) 11 T.L.R. 56.

overdrawn private account, and in holding that they were entitled to do so, Wright J. said that it would be a strange thing if a bank was called upon to assume that moneys standing to an office account were affected with a trust. There was nothing to put the bank upon inquiry. The bank was justified in treating the accounts as mixed accounts.

However, by section 85 (ii) of the Solicitors Act 1957, re-enacting the similar provision in the 1933 Act, a banker has no right " by way of set-off, counter claim, charge or otherwise " against his solicitor-customer's client account.[54a]

This is, of course, a statutory exception to the general law, and *Teale's* case, while no longer applicable to solicitors' accounts, remains a good example of that general law.[55]

In re Hallett's Estate, Knatchbull v. Hallett
(1879) 13 Ch. 696

Banque Belge Pour L'Étranger v. Hambrouck and Others
[1921] 1 K.B. 321

When moneys on a customer's account are claimed by a third party, they can be followed into the account, so long as they are still traceable

Facts of Re Hallett's Estate, Knatchbull v. Hallett

Hallett was a solicitor who had paid into his banking account and there mixed with his own money funds which he held in a fiduciary capacity, (*a*) in respect of the property settled by him in his marriage settlement; and (*b*) as bailee of the property belonging to a client. The trustees of the settlement and the client whose property had been misappropriated each claimed to be entitled to the money in the hands of the bankers in preference to the general creditors of the estate.

Decision

It was held by the Court of Appeal that when money on an account is held in a fiduciary capacity, even though the customer is not a trustee proper, the person for whom he holds the money can follow it.

54a And see regulations made under the Employment Agencies Act, 1973, by which the agent must pay money on behalf of a worker client to the worker or into a clients' account: S.I. 1976 No. 715.

55 *Cf.* Chorley, *op. cit.* pp. 200 *et seq.* for a discussion of the position of the banker's relationship with solicitor customers.

Jessel M.R. said:

If the bailee sells the goods bailed, the bailor can in equity follow the proceeds, and can follow the proceeds wherever they can be distinguished, either being actually kept separate, or being mixed up with other moneys. I have only to advert to one other point, and that is this—supposing, instead of being invested in the purchase of land or goods, the moneys were simply mixed with other moneys of the trustee, using the term again in its full sense as including every person in a fiduciary relation, does it make any difference according to the modern doctrine of Equity? I say none. It would be very remarkable if it were to do so. Supposing the trust money was 1,000 sovereigns, and the trustee put them into a bag, and by mistake or accident or otherwise, dropped a sovereign of his own into the bag. Could anyone suppose that a Judge in Equity would find any difficulty in saying that the *cestui que trust* has a right to take 1,000 sovereigns out of that bag? I do not like to call it a charge of 1,000 sovereigns on the 1,000 sovereigns, but that is the effect of it. I have no doubt of it. It would make no difference if, instead of one sovereign, it was another 1,000 sovereigns; but if instead of putting it into his bag, or after putting it into his bag, he carries the bag to his bankers, what then? According to law, the bankers are his debtors for the total amount; but if you lend the trust money to a third person, you can follow it. If in the case supposed the trustee had lent the £1,000 to a man without security, you could follow the debt, and take it from the debtor. If he lent it on a promissory note, you could take the promissory note; or the bond, if it were a bond. If, instead of lending the whole amount in one sum simply, he added a sovereign, or had added £500 of his own to the £1,000, the only difference is this, that instead of taking the bond or the promissory note, the *cestui que trust* would have a charge for the amount of the trust money on the bond or the promissory note.[56]

Facts of Banque Belge Pour L'Étranger v. Hambrouck and others

A M. Pelabon, a customer of the plaintiff bank, was the owner of an engineering works, and Hambrouck was an accountant in his employ. Hambrouck by fraud obtained crossed cheques to the value of £6,000 payable to himself and drawn, or purporting to be drawn, by M. Pelabon. He paid them into his account at Farrow's Bank, who collected them from the plaintiff bank. Hambrouck drew cheques on his account in favour of the second defendant, Mlle. Spanoghe, with whom he was living, and who paid them to the credit of her account with the London Joint City and Midland Bank. When Hambrouck's frauds were discovered there was an amount of £315 to the credit of Spanoghe's account, the whole amount being part of the proceeds of the cheques in question. No

[56] At pp. 710–711.

consideration had been given for the cheques, beyond the illegal consideration of continuing to cohabit with Hambrouck.

The plaintiff bank claimed to recover the balance of £315, and brought the present action against the male and female defendants, joining the London Joint City and Midland Bank as defendants. The bank paid the money into Court and were dismissed from the action.

Decision

The Court of Appeal held that the money was recoverable by the plaintiffs.

In the course of his judgment, Atkin L.J. said:

> The appellant [the second defendant] however contends that the plaintiffs cannot assert their title to the sum of money which was on a deposit account: 1. because it has passed through one if not two bank accounts and therefore cannot be identified as the plaintiff's money. . . . First, does it make any difference to the plaintiffs' rights that their money was paid into Farrow's Bank, and that the money representing it drawn out by Hambrouck was paid to the defendant bank on deposit? If the question be the right of the plaintiffs in equity to follow their property, I apprehend that no difficulty arises. The case of *In re Hallett's Estate* [57] makes it plain that the Court will investigate a banking account into which another person's money has been wrongfully paid, and will impute all drawings out of the account in the first instance to the wrongdoer's own moneys, leaving the plaintiff's money intact so far as it remains in the account at all. There can be no difficulty in this case in following every change of form of the money in question, whether in the hands of Hambrouck or of the appellant, and it appears to me that the plaintiffs were . . . entitled to a specific order for the return of the money in question, and, as it is now represented by the sum in Court, to payment out of Court of that sum.[58]

Notes

Hambrouck's case is noteworthy for the clear tracing through one account and into another. It must be remembered that the money would not have been recoverable had the female defendant given valuable consideration for the money, as well as receiving it in good faith. Moreover, even in the circumstances of the case, had she paid it away, even to Hambrouck, she could not have been made liable to refund it.[59]

It does not often happen that the balance on the account into which funds are " followed " is composed entirely of such funds, as

---

[57] *Supra.* [58] At pp. 332–333.

[59] *Transvaal and Delago Bay Investment Co. Ltd.* v. *Atkinson & Wife* [1944] 1 All E.R. 579.

it was in *Hambrouck's* case. Where there has been mixing with other money, the question must arise whether the money sought is still in the account, and here the rule in *Clayton's* case [60] is applied. An important exception to this application of the rule, however, was established in the *Hallett* case,[61] where it was held that one who misappropriates trust funds is presumed to draw out from his banking account first his own money and only afterwards that of the trust. On this point Jessel M.R. said in his judgment:

> Now, first upon principle, nothing can be better settled, either in our own law, or, I suppose, the law of all civilised countries, than this, that where a man does an act which may be rightfully performed, he cannot say that that act was intentionally and in fact done wrongly. . . . When we come to apply that principle to the case of a trustee who has blended trust money with his own, it seems to me perfectly plain that he cannot be heard to say that he took away the trust money when he had a right to take away his own money. . . . His money was there, and he had a right to draw it out, and why should the natural act of simply drawing out the money be attributed to anything except to his ownership of money which was at his bankers? [62]

When, however, the point is reached at which all moneys which could be withdrawn from the account without breach of trust have been allowed for, and there are still further drawings, which amount to breaches of trust, *Hallett's* case shows that the rule in *Clayton's* case must be applied to these should there be a conflict between one *cestui que trust* and another. The result is that the money first misappropriated is deemed to be withdrawn before the money misappropriated later. One *cestui que trust* may therefore find the whole of his money paid away while that of another, paid in later, is intact. This was the decision of Fry J. in the court of first instance; his judgment on the first point was overruled by the Court of Appeal in the decision dealt with above, and in view of that decision on the first point no appeal was necessary on the second.

It must always be remembered that the right to trace misappropriated money to a banking account does not necessarily involve the banker in loss if the money has already been disbursed.[63]

---

[60] *Ante*, p. 143.

[61] *Supra*.

[62] At pp. 727–728.

[63] But *cf. Aluminium Industrie Vaasen BV* v. *Romalpa Aluminium Ltd.*, *post*, p. 333, in which the principle of *Re Hallett's Estate* was applied in a manner disconcerting to bankers.

Tassell v. Cooper

(1850) 9 C.B. 509

The banker's duty is always primarily to his customer, however, and cheques must not be dishonoured merely because a third party has claimed the funds on the account

Facts

The plaintiff was an agent of Lord de l'Isle, and there passed through his account with the London and County Joint Stock Banking Co. (of which Cooper was the public officer) moneys of Lord de l'Isle as well as the private business of the plaintiff. Being dissatisfied with Tassell's work, Lord de l'Isle gave him instructions to stop acting for him, which Tassell observed, with the exception that a cheque received from a client for £180 4s. 8d. was paid into the account and collected.

Lord de l'Isle later visited the bank and asked to see Tassell's account. The manager refused to show it to him without head office sanction, so Lord de l'Isle wrote to head office and obtained permission. Having inspected the account he gave the manager a letter to the effect that all the money now standing to Tassell's credit, £128 1s. 10d., was his, and indemnifying the bank against any claim to it by Tassell. On the strength of this letter the bank dishonoured two cheques, and Tassell now brought an action against the bank (*a*) for the full balance of the account; (*b*) for dishonouring the cheques wrongfully; and (*c*) for exposing the account to a third party.

Decision

In giving judgment for the plaintiff on all three counts, Maule J. said:

. . . It seems to me that the banking company, having received the money on behalf of the plaintiff, and given him credit for it, became debtors to him for the amount; and that the circumstance that the receipt of the cheque by the plaintiff might have been blameable does not afford any answer to this action. The transaction was regular and lawful so far as the plaintiff and the bankers were concerned; it was a simple transaction of loan.[64]

Notes

The decision in *Tassell* v. *Cooper* is a useful example of the fact that the banker's primary duty is to his customer, and that third parties

[64] At p. 534.

cannot properly intervene between them without legal process. In such circumstances as those of the case the employer is not, of course, left without any remedy: he can proceed against his former employee, and apply to the court for an interim injunction against the bank to prevent them paying out any of the moneys in question until his action is decided. In such proceedings the bank can be joined as defendants; but the customer's account will not be touched without the customer's having an opportunity to put his case.

Douglass v. Lloyds Bank Ltd.

(1929) 34 Com.Cas. 263

Repayment after lapse of time

Facts

In going through the papers of her mother, lately deceased, a daughter found a deposit receipt dated May 12, 1866, issued at the Birmingham office of the defendant bank to a Mr. Fenwicke, her father, who had died in 1893. The receipt was for £6,000, with a memorandum of repayment of £2,500 indorsed upon it. No mention of the deposit was made in the will of the deceased, or in his papers. The present action was brought by the surviving executor of Mr. Fenwicke. The bank in their defence admitted that they could find no books of the Birmingham office before 1873, but contended that there was a presumption that the money had been repaid, and that in any event the plaintiff was debarred by his laches from bringing the action. The bank expressly disclaimed any intention of pleading the Statute of Limitations.

Decision

Roche J. giving judgment for the bank, decided the case on their first plea and the facts produced in evidence. He said:

> On the facts I recognise to the full the strength of the fact that the plaintiff produces this deposit receipt, but I cannot ignore what experience tells me, and the evidence in this case shows, that people lose or mislay their deposit receipts at the time when they want to get their money back, and that money is paid over, if they are respectable persons and willing to give the necessary indemnity or receipt, without production of the deposit receipt; indeed, otherwise life would be intolerable and business impossible. . . . I am satisfied, and I so find, that the practice of this bank was such that no sum like this, of £3,500, would have been treated by being carried to profit and loss account or to some reserve account, or to any of the other accounts which have been mentioned, within any such period as the short period between 1866 and 1873, or for long afterwards.[65]

Notes

This decision must not be given more than its proper weight: it was based upon the very special facts of a particular case. It is interesting, however, as a rare example of a bank successfully contesting (or indeed contesting at all) a claim against it, even though its books had been destroyed and it could not prove payment. The bank was allowed to produce its oldest surviving deposit ledgers, which showed no account in the name in question, and this was accepted as supporting the bank's claim that the deposit had been repaid. It need hardly be said that every bank keeps a strict account of " unclaimed balances," small or large, and it may be particularly noted that in the present case Lloyds Bank did not plead the Statute of Limitations [65a]; it is doubtful whether any bank would ever shelter behind the statute in such circumstances, for to do so would be, if not to admit the debt, at least not to deny it; while in any event time does not run against the customer until he has made demand for the debt owing to him.[66]

Birch and Another v. Treasury Solicitor

[1951] Ch. 298

A deposit book may be good evidence of title so as to constitute a valid donatio mortis causa

Facts

Mrs. Birch, an elderly widow, in hospital after a serious accident, was visited by her deceased husband's nephew and his wife. These were her closest friends, and she had no blood relations. On several occasions she expressed the wish that they should have the money she had on deposit in the London Trustee Savings Bank, Barclays and the Westminster Banks and the Post Office Savings Bank; and she gave them the relevant deposit books. They claimed upon her death that she had made a valid *donatio mortis causa* to them of the sums standing to her credit in the four banks.

Decision

The Court of Appeal held, *inter alia*, that in all four cases the deposit books were sufficient *indicia* of title to support the gift, notwithstanding that they did not in themselves show the whole of the conditions of the contract between the banks and the depositor,

---

65 At pp. 272, 276.

65a *Cf.* Chorley, *op. cit.* p. 28.

66 *Joachimson* v. *Swiss Bank Corporation*, *ante*, p. 1.

and notwithstanding, also, that in the case of the two joint stock banks, the rule that the book must be produced before any withdrawal was made was not always strictly observed.

In his judgment, Sir Raymond Evershed M.R. said:

In the result Mr. Buckley failed, in our judgment, to prove any such general practice as would lead to the conclusion that the contractual term as to the production of the book in either case had become a dead letter: and certainly there was no evidence of any particular arrangement with the deceased. We think accordingly that in the case of both banks the condition stated on the face of the deposit books must be taken to have remained operative, i.e., that the book was and is the essential indicia of title and that delivery of the book " amounted to transfer " of the chose in action.[67]

Notes

Donatio mortis causa is a gift made in the contemplation of and conditional upon impending death; if the donor recovers, the gift does not become effective.

Deposit receipts are less used than they were in the past, and in the clearing banks deposit books are largely superseded by statements,[67a] but neither receipts nor books have disappeared so completely as to make the *Birch* decision of purely historic interest: the National Savings Bank, for instance, still operates on the basis of deposit books.

Bank deposit books and deposit receipts do not usually contain the conditions upon which the account is maintained. It is usually a condition of payment that the book or receipt should be produced, but, as was proved in this case, the condition is not always in practice insisted upon. The decision of the Court of Appeal establishes that these facts do not invalidate the documents as evidence of title sufficient to make a good *donatio*; but it is clear from the judgment that the decision cannot be taken to mean that the documents will so serve when, for example, the deposit account is in fact worked as a current account, and the book becomes no more than a passbook.

It need hardly be emphasised that the decision does not make the deposit book or receipt a document of title giving the bearer the right to demand payment. In circumstances like those of the *Birch* case, the banks could not properly pay the balances of the accounts over to the donees, who must go to the personal representatives.

It is perhaps anomalous that the deposit book, thus lacking the attributes of a document of title, can form the substance of a *donatio*, merely because of the condition of presentation, while a passbook cannot, whatever the intention of the donor, nor indeed a cheque drawn by the deceased.

[67] At p. 313.

[67a] *Cf.* Chorley, *op. cit.* pp. 169 *et seq.*

Chapter 7

SPECIAL ACCOUNTS

Minors

R. Leslie Ltd. v. Sheill

[1914] 3 K.B. 607

Money lent to a minor is not recoverable even where he has obtained the loan through fraudulently representing himself to be of full age

Facts

The plaintiffs were a firm of moneylenders, to whom the defendant fraudulently represented that he was of full age, and who thereupon lent him £400. They brought an action against him for the amount owing on the grounds that it was obtained by fraudulent misrepresentation, and alternatively they claimed the amount as money had and received by the defendant to the use of the plaintiffs. Upon judgment being given for the plaintiffs the defendant appealed.

Decision

The Court of Appeal allowed the appeal. In the course of his judgment, Lord Sumner said:

The claim first pleaded is for the amount of principal and interest, as damages sustained because by his fraud the plaintiffs have been induced to make and act upon an unenforceable contract. So long ago as *Johnson* v. *Pye* [1] it was decided that, although an infant may be liable in tort generally, he is not answerable for a tort directly connected with a contract which, as an infant, he would be entitled to avoid. . . . As Lord Kenyon says in *Jennings* v. *Rundall*,[2] alluding to *Zouch* v. *Parsons*,[3] " this protection was to be used as a shield and not as a sword; therefore if an infant commit an assault or utter slander God forbid that he should not be answerable for it in a Court of Justice. But where an infant has made an improvident contract with a person who has been wicked enough to contract with him, such person cannot resort to a Court of law to enforce such contract." It is perhaps a pity that no exception was made where, as here, the infant's wickedness was at least equal to that of the person who innocently contracted with him, but so it is. It was thought necessary to safeguard the weakness of infants at large, even though here and there a juvenile knave slipped through. The rule is well settled . . .

---

[1] (1665) 1 Sid. 258. [2] (1799) 8 T.R. 335.
[3] (1765) 3 Burr. 1804.

Nor does the other cause of action pleaded fare any better . . . I think this would be nothing but enforcing a void contract. So far as I can find, the Court of Chancery never would have enforced any liability under circumstances like the present, any more than a Court of law would have done so, and I think that no ground can be found for the present judgment, which would be an answer to the Infants' Relief Act.[4]

Notes

The Infants Relief Act 1874, provides:

(1) All contracts, whether by specialty or by simple contract, henceforth entered into by infants for the repayment of money lent or to be lent, or for goods supplied or to be supplied (other than contracts for necessaries), and all accounts stated with infants, shall be absolutely void: Provided always, that this enactment shall not invalidate any contract into which an infant may, by any existing or future statute, or by the rules of common law or equity, enter, except such as now by law are voidable.

(2) No action shall be brought whereby to charge any person upon any promise made after full age to pay any debt contracted during infancy, or upon any ratification made after full age of any promise or contract made during infancy, whether there shall or shall not be any new consideration for such promise or ratification after full age.

It is clear that if a banker lends money to a minor, whether by overdraft or loan, such money is irrecoverable not only from the minor but also from the guarantor of such a loan.[5] The *Leslie* case underlines the danger to the banker of allowing an advance to a minor: even if he has been misled as to the minor's age, he has no relief, either in contract or in tort.[6]

Coutts & Co. v. Browne-Lecky and Others

[1947] K.B. 104

The guarantor of a minor's overdraft cannot be made liable

Facts

The first-named defendant, at all material times a minor, had an overdrawn account with the plaintiff bank, guaranteed by the other defendants. The bank sought to recover the amount of the guarantee.

---

[4] At pp. 611–612, 619.

[5] See *Coutts & Co.* v. *Browne-Lecky & others* [1947] K.B. 104, *infra.*

[6] It is to be noted that the age of majority was reduced to 18 by the Family Law Reform Act 1969.

Decision

It was held that the money could not be recovered. In his judgment, Oliver J. said:

Apart from authority, it certainly seems strange that a contract to make good a debt, default or miscarriage of another—which is the classic definition of a guarantee—could be binding where, by statute, the loan guaranteed is, in terms, made absolutely void. That, of course, is the Infants Relief Act, 1874. Looking at the matter broadly, in circumstances of that sort, how can the omission of an infant to pay that which is made void by the statute be described either as a debt or as a default or as a miscarriage? There is no debt, because the statute says so; there is no default, because the infant is entitled to omit to pay, and there is no miscarriage for the same reason. How someone can be made liable to guarantee a thing of that sort, on broad principles it is difficult to see.[7]

Notes

In view of the fact that any overdraft or loan to a minor is irrecoverable by legal proceedings, much thought has naturally been given to the question of obtaining from the minor some kind of security which will enable the lender to recover his money by indirect means. The courts have, however, refused to allow the Infants Relief Act to be circumvented in this way and have refused to enforce security provided by a minor in support of a loan. But it was commonly held until the *Browne-Lecky* case that if the security was furnished by an adult in the form of a guarantee it would be effective.

In the light of the *Browne-Lecky* decision, that opinion can no longer be held; but the position is not without difficulty. The only previous decision with any direct bearing on the problem was *Wauthier* v. *Wilson*,[8] where the minor to whom the advance had been made was joined by his father in a joint and several promissory note for the amount of the advance. In the court of first instance the father was held liable as guarantor of the advance, but the court of Appeal, while upholding the judgment against the father, did so on the grounds that he was liable as principal on the promissory note. In the *Browne-Lecky* case, Oliver J. examined the judgments in *Wauthier* v. *Wilson* and distinguished it from the facts before him on the grounds that Wilson's liability was one of indemnity rather than of guarantee; an indemnity is a distinct and separate undertaking to pay money, and the person giving it is a principal and independent debtor, not, as is a guarantor, merely a secondary debtor. This would seem to leave available to lenders the security offered by

[7] At p. 106.

[8] (1911) 27 T.L.R. 582.

adults in support of advances to minors provided it is in the form of indemnity rather than of guarantee.

The *Browne-Lecky* decision has been severely criticised, notably by Dr. E. J. Cohn.[9] Dr. Cohn pointed out, *inter alia*, that a guarantee of the kind in question is possible in the great majority of legal systems throughout the world, on the grounds that, while the protection of the minor makes it necessary to make void all loans to him, there is no such justification in avoiding guarantees given by adults. Dr. Cohn submits further that there is no justification, in general principle or in authority, for avoiding such guarantees in English law. It must be emphasised, though, that as the law stands the *Browne-Lecky* decision is within its limits authoritative.

It is implied in the headnote to the *Browne-Lecky* case that the decision is limited to cases where all parties know the facts concerning the minor's age. This limitation does not seem necessary to the decision, which is based on the invalidity of the principal transaction; it seems more likely that the invalidity would also extend to a guarantee given in circumstances like those of *R. Leslie Ltd.* v. *Sheill*,[10] where also the contract was void although the minor had misrepresented his age. If the minor in that case had made a similar misrepresentation to obtain a guarantee of the advance, it is doubtful whether the banker would be any better placed to recover against such a guarantor.

In this connection Dr. Cohn, in the article above referred to, noted that some but not all of the various systems permitting the guarantee of a minor's borrowing make the guarantor's liability dependent on his knowledge of the minority. In others even the guarantor ignorant of the minority is liable, and Dr. Cohn suggests that this is the better view.

Of course, the effect of the *Browne-Lecky* decision can be avoided by the inclusion in the form of guarantee of a clause which serves to make the guarantor liable as a principal debtor in the event of his liability as guarantor proving for any reason insufficient.[11] Such a clause is now commonly included in bank guarantee forms; but the comment of the Gilbart lecturer in 1950 is apt: "Yet I find my senses offended when banks have to amend their forms or their practice to meet a danger which arises from what may be a bad decision."[12]

---

[9] In 10 *Modern Law Review* 40.
[10] *Ante*, p. 163.
[11] *Cf. post*, p. 254.
[12] Megrah, Gilbart Lectures, 1950, *Contractual Incapacity in the Banker's Customer*, p. 7.

Joint Accounts

McEvoy v. Belfast Banking Co. Ltd.

[1935] A.C. 24

Young and Another v. Sealey

[1949] Ch. 278

Survivorship as applied to joint accounts is a presumption only, and may be rebutted

Facts of McEvoy v. Belfast Banking Co. Ltd.

In 1921 John McEvoy, who was in bad health and expecting an early death, deposited £10,000 with the respondent bank on a joint account in the names of himself and his son, then 15 years old, on the terms that either was to sign on the account, and the balance was to go to the survivor. A little later he executed his will, leaving the residue on trust for the son until he reached the age of 25, and a month after the execution of the will he died. The executors took possession of the deposit receipt for £10,000, endorsed it and withdrew the money, redepositing it in their own names. It was shown in evidence that the deceased had wrongly imagined that by opening the joint account death duties would be avoided; that in fact the executors had concealed the deposit receipt in preparing their accounts; and that the residue to be held in trust was very small, in comparison with the deposit account.

Between the death of the father and the son's twenty-fifth birthday the executors carried on the business of the father, with the son taking an increasing part in the management. Shortly before the son's twenty-first birthday, a sum of more than £2,000 was withdrawn from the deposit for the purchase of certain property by the executors, the son taking an active part in the transaction. After he came of age, but before his twenty-fifth birthday, the remaining amount on deposit was withdrawn piecemeal and credited to the executors' account, which was continually overdrawn, and concerning which the bank frequently expressed anxiety.

Some months after the son's twenty-fifth birthday he brought an action against the bank claiming that he was entitled to (*a*) the deposit account as at the time of his father's death, and (*b*) the interest thereon. He pleaded that he did not previously understand his rights in the matter. The bank denied that the son had ever been entitled to the money.

Decision

The House of Lords dismissed the son's appeal, a majority holding that the executors were entitled to receive the money and apply it in due course of administration as directed by the will. (Lord Atkin held that if the son on his majority had ratified the contract made by his father in opening the account the title would have been his, but that in fact his conduct had represented to the bank that he did not propose to ratify.)

In the course of his judgment, Lord Warrington of Clyffe said:

> . . . I think the real question is not whether the appellant would, as the effect in law of the contract, have been held entitled to be paid the money by the respondents, but what in the view of a Court of Equity would be the position between him and the executors; would he be held entitled to retain the moneys, if so paid, for his own benefit, or must he hand them over to the executors to be dealt with as part of the testator's estate? The material circumstances are these: the money deposited was that of the father alone, the son was a mere volunteer. The intention of the father as to the disposition of his estate was clearly expressed at the interview of July 19, 1921. The form of the deposit receipt in no way operated to alter this intention; it was adopted for another purpose. The money was entirely at the father's disposal during his life. The will as actually made gives effect to the expressed intention of the father and there is no evidence of any *animus donandi* except subject to the testamentary directions. The residuary personal estate, including the deposit of £2,000, but excluding the £10,000 in question, was so small that it is impossible to suppose that the testator deliberately intended to withdraw so important an item as the £10,000 from the fund to be administered by the executors and trustees until the son should attain twenty-five. Finally the illegal proceedings of the executors, so much relied on by the trial judge, were entirely irrelevant, inasmuch as the testator was not in any way implicated in them. On the whole then I am satisfied that if the matter had been brought before a Court of Equity the decision would have been in favour of the executors. . . .[13]

Facts of Young and Another v. Sealey

In 1927 Miss Jarman transferred certain balances standing to her credit at Lloyds Bank, Taunton, to a new deposit account at the same bank in the joint names of herself and her nephew, the defendant, on the terms that the signature of either was to be accepted as withdrawal authority, and that the balance was to go to the survivor. She later made similar transfers in another bank where she had funds to her credit, and also made certain investments in the names of herself and her nephew. At no time did the control of any of these moneys pass from her to the nephew, who neither added to nor drew from them. It was shown in evidence

[13] At p. 50.

that the aunt and the nephew had been on affectionate terms and that she had always displayed considerable secrecy regarding her finances. She was stated to have believed that the opening of joint accounts of the kind in question would avoid death duties.

Upon Miss Jarman's death the plaintiffs, her personal representatives, claimed that all the moneys so put in the joint names formed part of the estate.

Decision

Judgment was given for the defendant. In the course of his judgment, Romer J. said:

> Only what was left at her death was to go to the co-depositor, who was never expected to pay anything into the account and was not, so long as she was alive, to draw anything out for himself. When death should deprive her of any further use of her fortune then the benefits to her sister's issue would crystallise, but they were to remain in suspense until then and, so far as the defendant's interest in the deposit accounts was concerned, it might result in nothing at all. Such being, as I believe, Miss Jarman's intentions, it would seem at first sight to follow that the defendant has not only a legal, but also a beneficial, title to the moneys and shares which are now in issue, and none the less because Miss Jarman (as between herself and the defendant) retained control and dominion over the deposit accounts during her own lifetime.[14]

Notes

It must be noted, in connection with the cases on joint accounts, that the survivor's *legal* title to the balance on the account, when the other party to the account has died, is never in question. Thus the banker is within his rights in paying out the balance to the survivor. Dispute arises only as to the *equitable* title—*i.e.* whether the survivor is entitled to keep the money or is rather to be regarded as holding it as trustee for others who claim the beneficial interest.

The presumption is that the equitable title follows the legal title; but this presumption can be displaced by showing that such was not the intention of the parties, and most of the cases are concerned with whether there is enough evidence to displace the presumed intention of survivorship. Such difficulties normally arise only when the joint account is not, in intention, a genuine joint account at all; in all " survivorship " cases it is the intention of the person who provided the funds that is the principal issue.

Thus in *Marshal* v. *Crutwell*[15] there was a joint account in the names of husband and wife. It was shown that the husband was in

---

[14] At p. 284.
[15] (1875) L.R. 20 Eq. 328.

failing health, and further that all the money paid into the account was provided by the husband, while the wife's withdrawals were all for household goods. It was held that the presumption of survivorship was displaced by these facts and that the balance of the account at the death of the husband went not to the widow but to the executors. However, there must be clear evidence as to the ownership of the money, and in *Hirschorn* v. *Evans*,[16] Greer L.J., while dissenting from the majority view in the Court of Appeal that a garnishee order against the husband could not attach the joint account, held that in the circumstances of the case it could not do so as there was no clear evidence as to the beneficial ownership of the money in the account.

In *Jones* v. *Maynard*[17] a husband and wife had maintained a joint account fed by the husband's remuneration and investment income, the rent of a house owned by husband and wife jointly, and the wife's investment income of about £50 per annum. Periodically the surplus on the account was invested in the husband's sole name. The parties were later divorced and the wife now sought a declaration that she was beneficially entitled to half the investments so made. The husband contended that she was entitled only to such proportion as represented her own contributions to the joint account. In his judgment in favour of the wife, Vaisey J. said:

> In my view a husband's earnings or salary, when the spouses have a common purse, and pool their resources, are earnings made on behalf of both . . . the money which goes into the pool becomes joint property.[18]

The reasoning of Vaisey J. was approved by the Court of Appeal in *Rimmer* v. *Rimmer*,[19] but in *Re Bishop, deceased*,[20] Stamp J. distinguished both these cases, regarding them as having been decided on their special facts; and on the facts before him—a joint account fed by funds from both husband and wife, and used in investments, variously in the name of the husband alone, of the wife alone and of both jointly—held that there was nothing to displace the legal titles so indicated. He said:

> Where a husband and wife open a joint account at a bank on terms that cheques may be drawn on the account by either of them, then, in my judgment, in the absence of facts or circumstances which indicate that the account was intended, or was kept, for some specific or limited purpose, each spouse can draw upon it not only for the benefit of both spouses but for his or her own benefit. Each spouse, in drawing money out of the account, is to be treated as doing so with the authority of the other and,

---

16 [1938] 2 K.B. 801; *ante*, p. 53.
17 [1951] Ch. 572.
18 At p. 575.
19 [1953] 1 Q.B. 63.
20 [1965] Ch. 450.

in my judgment, if one of the spouses purchases a chattel for his own benefit, or an investment in his or her own name, that chattel or investment belongs to the person in whose name is it purchased or invested: for in such a case there is, in my judgment, no equity in the other spouse to displace the legal ownership of the one in whose name the investment is purchased.[21]

And this application of a principle enunciated as long ago as 1889, in *Re Young*,[22] was approved by Lord Upjohn in *Pettit* v. *Pettit*.[23]

It is interesting to notice that in *Young* v. *Sealey* the executors urged that the deceased had attempted to make a testamentary disposition not in conformity with the Wills Act, which was therefore invalid. Romer J., after reviewing the Irish and Canadian authorities which had been cited to him,[24] and " having regard to the disturbing effect which an acceptance of the argument might well have on titles already acquired," considered that any change in the current of authority should be left to the Court of Appeal to make.

Jackson v. White and Midland Bank Ltd.

[1967] 2 Lloyd's Rep. 68

The holders of a joint account have a joint and several right of action against the bank

Facts

The first defendant induced the plaintiff to put up £2,000 for his failing business, under a loose arrangement envisaging the creation of a partnership; and an account opened with the Midland Bank purported to be a partnership account, cheques on which were to be signed by both parties. White thereafter forged the plaintiff's signature to a number of cheques, and obtained the plaintiff's signature to others which he represented as being in payment of trade debts; in fact he used all but three of them for his own purposes. The plaintiff brought this action against the first defendant in respect of all the cheques except three, and against the bank in respect of the forged cheques.

Decision

Park J. held that the bank's agreement with the two customers was with them jointly to honour cheques jointly drawn, and an

---

[21] At p. 456. [22] (1885) 28 Ch. D. [23] [1970] A.C. 777.

[24] The point does not appear to have been raised in any previous English case.

agreement with each of them separately not to honour any cheque not drawn by him. The bank was therefore liable on the forged cheques, although it was entitled to be indemnified by the first defendant.

Notes

The nature of a bank's liability to customers on a joint account was a matter of controversy following the decision in *Brewer* v. *Westminster Bank Ltd.*[25] in 1952. Although *Jackson's* case, like *Brewer's* was only at first instance it is generally accepted that the superior courts would agree with the line taken by Park J. and it is unlikely that the contrary view will reappear.

In *Brewer's* case the plaintiff was an executor and beneficiary of her father's will, her co-executor being the managing clerk of the solicitors who had managed her father's affairs. A joint account having been opened with the defendant bank, both parties to sign, the managing clerk forged the plaintiff's signature to cheques to a total of £3,000. Upon the plaintiff bringing this action against the bank, for payment of cheques bearing only one authorised signature, the bank contended *inter alia* (*a*) that action on the joint account could be brought only by the account holders jointly, and that as one of them could not, because of his forgeries, sue the bank, the other was also debarred; and (*b*) that it is an implied term of such a contract that each customer will act honestly. McNair J. accepted the first of these arguments, but rejected the second.

The decision provoked much criticism,[26] and in a succession of cases it was either distinguished or not followed. Thus in *Baker* v. *Barclays Bank Ltd.*[27] where partnership cheques had been appropriated by one partner, and the action against the bank was for conversion, Devlin J. distinguished *Brewer's* case on the grounds that it was based on a breach of contractual duty, whereas the case before him was based on property rights. In *Weich* v. *Bank of England and Others*,[28] where the plaintiff's signature on seven Consolidated Stock warrants was forged by his co-trustee (again a matter of property rather than contract) Harman J. said:

> The point was taken in the defence that as the interest of the plaintiff and the co-trustee in the stock was a joint one she could have no better right than he had to complain. I take it that the pleader relied on *Brewer's* case which appears to have been decided on these grounds. I confess that I do not follow that decision. None of the cases in equity were cited to the judge.

---

[25] [1952] 2 All E.R. 650.
[26] *Cf.* Paget, *op. cit.* pp. 76 *et seq.*
[27] [1955] 2 All E.R. 571, *ante*, p. 114.
[28] [1955] Ch. 508.

It may be, however, that this would be a good defence at law. It is certainly, I think, no defence in equity.[29]

And in an Australian case, *Ardern* v. *Bank of New South Wales* [30] Martin J. anticipated Park J.'s view: " I consider the view put by the plaintiff is the correct one—that the undertaking of the bank not to honour cheques unless they were signed by both partners was a condition which inured for the benefit of each partner."

It is to be noted, however, that the finding on the bank's second argument in *Brewer's* case, as to the implied guarantee by each customer of the other's honesty, has not been challenged. In this connection McNair J. quoted Scrutton L.J.[31] " a term can only be implied if it is necessary in the business sense to give efficacy to the contract " and went on:

Bearing in mind that the joint account was opened by the use of the bank's own form and . . . that the number of cases where bankers sustain losses by forgery is infinitesimal in comparison with the large business they do. . . . I am unable to reach the conclusion that there is any necessity to imply such a term to give business efficacy to the contract.[32]

In view of his finding on the first argument, this view was *obiter*, but it may well be taken as good law.

PARTNERS

Alliance Bank v. Kearsley

(1871) L.R. 6 C.P. 433

A partner has no implied authority entitling him to open an account in his own name so as to bind the partnership

Facts

The defendant, William Kearsley, and his brother James were in partnership as coachbuilders, trading under the name of George Kearsley & Co. In 1864 James opened an account with the plaintiffs at Manchester, explaining that the account was a partnership account, but that as he was the only partner resident in Manchester it had better be in his name. In 1869, the account being then overdrawn, the plaintiffs sought to recover the amount of the overdraft from the defendant.

---

[29] At p. 531. [30] (1956) 7 L.D.B. 85.
[31] In *Reigate* v. *Union Manufacturing Co.* (*Ramsbottom*) [1918] 1 K.B. 592 at p. 595.
[32] [1952] 2 All E.R. 650 at p. 656.

Decision

It was held that the bank could not recover. In his judgment, Montague Smith J. said:

The partner has authority to do what is usual in the ordinary course of the business. It is established that in trade partnerships one partner may borrow money for the partnership, and will bind his co-partner by so doing. That is held to be within the implied authority of a partner because it has been found to be in the ordinary course of business necessary for the purposes of trade. But I do not think a judge can take it upon himself to assume, without evidence, that it is within the ordinary course of business for one partner to open a banking account in his own name on behalf of the partnership so as to bind his co-partners to the state of that account whatever it may be. That being so, the foundation of the implied authority entirely fails. . . . An account opened by a man in his own name is prima facie his private account, and it seems likely that such an implication of authority would give great facilities for mixing up private and partnership accounts so as to enable frauds to be committed with less chance of detection.[33]

Notes

The implied authority of a partner in a trading partnership to pledge the credit of the partnership extends only to transactions in the ordinary course of the firm's business, and when he attempts to do so outside this limit he makes only himself liable. The *Alliance Bank* case decided that the opening of an account in the partner's own name does not bind the co-partners, although it had been earlier decided, in *Beale* v. *Caddick*,[34] that one partner could effectively assent to the *transfer* of the partnership account when the business of the firm's bankers had been transferred to another bank.

Although there is no express authority in the cases it seems to follow from the fact that a partner has general authority to borrow money for the partnership business that he has power to open a banking account in the firm's name, and the importance attached by Montague Smith J. to the fact that W. Kearsley opened the Manchester account in his own name and not that of the firm supports this view. This too is the opinion of such a leading authority as Hart. In practice this important point is likely to arise only rarely, as the banker will normally obtain a mandate for the opening of an account signed by all the partners.

In *Brettel* v. *Williams* [35] the defendants were railway contractors and made a sub-contract with a firm of brick-makers. One of the partners guaranteed the payment by the brick-makers of the bills for the coal necessary to their work on the sub-contract. It was held

---

[33] At pp. 437, 438. [34] (1857) 2 H. & N. 326. [35] (1849) 4 Ex. 623.

that this guarantee was not binding on the other partners, Parke B. saying:

> To allow one partner to bind another by contracts out of the apparent scope of the partnership dealings, because they were reasonable acts towards effecting the partnership purposes, would be attended with great danger. Could one of the defendants in this case have bound the others by a contract to lease or buy lands, or a coal mine, though it might be a reasonable mode of effecting a legitimate object of the partnership business? [36]

When a debt is incurred which does in fact bind the partnership, although each of the partners is jointly liable, and judgment against the firm enables the judgment creditor to enforce it against the property of the partners individually as well as against the assets of the firm, yet if any of the partners are not sued they are freed from liability. Thus, in *Kendall* v. *Hamilton*,[37] a creditor did not discover the existence of a third partner until he had obtained judgment against two, and in the House of Lords, despite a strongly worded plea by Lord Penzance for substantial rather than formal justice, it was held by a majority of six to one that the creditor could not recover.

It must be noted that in the case of partnerships, as in all others where there is any form of joint liability, it is common banking practice to take joint and several undertakings.

Re Bourne, Bourne v. Bourne

[1906] 2 Ch. 427

Effect of a partner's death on the firm's bank account—duty of the surviving partners to realise the partnership assets, whether personalty or realty

Facts

Bourne and Grove were in partnership, and in 1901 Grove died. Bourne carried on the business in the partnership name until his own death in 1902. At the date of Grove's death the firm's account with their bankers, Berwick and Co., was £6,476 overdrawn, and some months later Bourne deposited with the bank the deeds of certain real estate forming part of the partnership assets. Between Grove's death and the deposit of the deeds Bourne had paid into the account more than £10,000 and had drawn out more than

36 At p. 630.
37 (1879) 4 A.C. 504.

£8,500. After further transactions the overdraft, at the date of Bourne's death, was £4,463. Bourne's estate proving insolvent, the question arose whether Grove's executors or the bank took priority against the proceeds of sale of the property charged.

Upon it being held that the bank took priority, Grove's executors appealed.

Decision

The Court of Appeal upheld the lower court's decision. In his judgment, Romer L.J. said:

When a partner dies and the partnership comes to an end, it is not only the right, but the duty, of the surviving partner to realise the assets for the purpose of winding up the partnership affairs, including the payment of the partnership debts. It is true that in a general sense the executors or administrators of the deceased partner may be said to have a lien upon the partnership assets in respect of his interest in the partnership on taking the partnership account, but that lien is not one which affects each particular piece of property belonging to the partnership so as to affect that property in the hands of any person dealing with the surviving partner in good faith. It is really what one may call a general lien upon the surplus assets. . . . Then the only question remaining is this: Was the debt of the bank which the surviving partner gave the charge to secure one that really to the knowledge of the bank was not a partnership debt? To my mind, on the contrary, the bank were entitled to consider it and treat it as a partnership debt. The account with them was a partnership account. It was continued under the partnership name, and apparently for the purposes of the partnership, and it appears to me impossible to say that it is not or may not be reasonable for a surviving partner to continue the partnership account for the purpose of winding up the estate.[38]

Notes

The Partnership Act 1890, s. 38, provides that surviving partners after the death of their co-partner may bind the firm and continue business as far as it is necessary to do so in winding up the business of the firm. The importance of *re Bourne* need not be emphasised: the attempt to impugn the right of the surviving partner to charge the firm's assets—the point made being that he could do this only with personal property—would, if successful, have made much more dangerous a bank's dealings with such a customer.

In *Royal Bank of Scotland* v. *Christie*[39] two surviving partners continued the partnership account after the death of a third partner, and made no arrangements to segregate from current business the amount due to the bank at the date of the death. It

[38] At pp. 431–433.

[39] (1841) 8 Cl. & Fin. 214.

was held that the deceased partner's liability in respect of the indebtedness to the bank was discharged at the point where the payings-in to the bank amounted to the total indebtedness at the time of his death; and security charged by the deceased partner to secure the borrowing of the firm was accordingly discharged, leaving the advance to that extent unsecured. It is, of course, now common practice to rule off an account which is overdrawn upon the death of a partner, or his bankruptcy or retirement.[40]

EXECUTORS

Farhall v. Farhall

(1871) 7 Ch. App. 123

Borrowing by an executor is always his personal responsibility, and, if it is unauthorised, the estate of the deceased cannot be made liable for it

Facts

Farhall was a customer of the London and County Bank, and at the time of his death was overdrawn against the security of certain real property belonging to him. His widow, the executrix, borrowed further from the bank, and charged further property of the estate as security. A decree for the administration of the estate having been made, the bank sought to prove for these advances, and by consent the whole of the security charged to them was realised. This sale left an outstanding overdraft of £987, and the bank claimed to prove for this balance owing to them. Mrs. Farhall's own affidavit showed that to a great extent her withdrawals had been misappropriated, but the bank had no knowledge of the misappropriation.

Decision

The Court of Appeal held that the bank was not entitled to prove, on the grounds that, although an executor can give a lien on a specific asset of the estate, he cannot create such a contract as will give the creditor a right to prove against the estate as a whole. In the course of his judgment Sir W. M. James L.J. said:

> . . . to say that the executrix can, by borrowing money, enable the person who has lent it to stand as a creditor upon the estate, is a position supported by no authority and no principle. The contract is with the executrix; there

[40] *Cf.* Chorley, *op. cit.* p. 196.

is no loan to the estate; there is no credit to the estate; the credit is given only to the person who borrows, though the money may be borrowed for the purposes of the estate.

It was urged for the respondents that they were, at all events, creditors to the extent to which the money was applied in payment of debts, and we were referred to *Haynes* v. *Forshaw* [41] . . . but there is nothing in that case to support the contention that, if a man lends money to an executor, who says " I am going to pay debts with it," and the debts are not paid, the lender is to stand in the same place as if the debts had been paid with the money. The bankers, no doubt, took it for granted that the executrix was going to apply the whole of the money which she borrowed from them for the purposes of the estate; but she did not do so; and I am of opinion therefore that their claim fails.[42]

Notes

The personal liability of executors and administrators is a fundamental of executorship law. Where the business of the deceased is carried on they are responsible for debts incurred even though they act ostensibly as personal representatives and even though they are authorised by the will to do so—although in the latter case they are entitled to indemnity from the estate. Similarly, in the case of unauthorised or misappropriated borrowing from a bank no contribution can be sought from the estate upon the failure of the personal representative to repay the advance.

Moreover, when there are two or more personal representatives, they have in many respects similar powers to those of partners, and can deal with the assets without binding, and without the consent of, their co-representatives. In order therefore to make all the representatives liable for loans it is necessary for all to bind themselves, and this is especially important when, at the outset of the administration, borrowing is sought to pay the death duties. The banker will normally satisfy himself as well as he can, from the will or from other available sources, that the advance is being made to the right persons; but in the event of their failure to obtain probate or letters of administration he will have no recourse against the estate beyond the extent to which such an advance has in fact been used to pay the duties due.

Just as one executor can act independently, so one can countermand another. In *Gaunt* v. *Taylor*,[43] when co-executors stopped payment of a cheque drawn by an executrix, the banker paid the money into court, and his action in doing so, and in refusing to pay the cheque, was not questioned.

A banker dealing bona fide with a personal representative may

41 (1853) 11 Hare 93.
42 At pp. 125–126.
43 (1843) 2 Hare 413.

retain any security of the estate which has been lodged with him as security for an advance. In *Berry* v. *Gibbons* [44] an executrix borrowed in her capacity as executrix against the security of a picture belonging to the estate. It was held that the fact that, unknown to the bank, an administration order had been made in respect of the estate, did not invalidate the security. The decision in this case, however, was in part based on the facts that no receiver had been appointed, and no injunction had been granted to restrain the executrix from dealing with the assets.

In the absence of express authority in the will or the unanimous approval of the creditors, a business may not be carried on by the personal representatives longer than is necessary for winding it up; and the personal representatives become personally liable if they carry it on for any longer period. Even when express authority is given in the will, a creditor who has not assented to the continuance is not bound. In *Re Elijah Murphy, deceased, Morton* v. *Marchanton* [45] the executors were given power to carry on the business, and it was carried on for two years, when the estate became insolvent. An unpaid creditor obtained judgment and a receiver was appointed; and the bank from which the estate had borrowed some £3,000 sought a declaration that they had a charge on certain property ranking prior to the creditors at the date of the death. Judgment was given for the bank in the County Palatine Court, Manchester, on the grounds that the creditor had acquiesced in the continuance of the business; had there been no such acquiescence, the authority given to the executors in the will would not have helped the bank.[46]

UNINCORPORATED ASSOCIATIONS

Bradley Egg Farm Ltd. v. Clifford and Others
[1943] 2 All E.R. 378

The officers rather than the members of unincorporated associations are normally liable for the debts and contracts of the associations

Facts

The plaintiffs, poultry farmers, contracted to have their birds tested for disease. The defendants were the executive council of the Lancashire Utility Poultry Society, and the letters in which they

---

[44] (1873) 8 Ch.App. 747. [45] (1930) 4 L.D.B. 328.

[46] *Cf.* Chorley, *op. cit.* pp. 198 *et seq.* and Paget, *op. cit.* pp. 38 *et seq.* as to the banking accounts of executors and trustees.

contracted with the plaintiffs were on paper so headed, and signed by one Gates, as Technical Manager. The society was an unincorporated one, with a large number of members, each of whom paid a subscription of 7s. 6d., and was entitled to receive the publications of the society. The rules provided that on dissolution the funds were not to be distributed amongst the members but were to be given to some institution with similar aims to those of the society. No member as such had any interest in the funds of the society.

The test contracted for was carried out by an employee of the society, and through his negligence a number of the birds died. The plaintiffs claimed damages, and upon the decision being given in their favour, the defendants appealed.

Decision

The Court of Appeal, by a majority, upheld the lower court. In the course of his judgment, on behalf of Scott L.J. and himself, Goddard L.J. said:

> The society thus has some analogy to a members' club, with this important difference, that, whereas the property of such a club belongs beneficially to the members jointly, the members of this society have no rights in the funds or property of the society at all. Its affairs are managed by a council, composed of the defendants, who are entrusted with the management and administration of its affairs. . . . In view of the objects of the society as set out in the rules, it is plain that persons must be engaged to further them, and that this appointment and the allocation of duties among them would be part of the duties of management and administration conferred on the council. Gates was appointed as technical manager and laboratory officer on April 21, 1939, at a meeting of the council. All of the defendant committee either voted for or knew and approved of his appointment. In our opinion, it is plain that Gates was employed by the council, and must be regarded as their servant. Against whom but them could he claim his salary? It was argued that if he was a servant of anyone it was of the society, that is, of every member of the society, and that, if he in the course of his duties made contracts, he made them as agent for the members of the society jointly. In our opinion, this is an impossible contention. Because members of a society, especially in a case where they have no right or interest in the funds or property of the society, entrust its affairs and management to a committee, that does not mean that they thereby give the committee authority to make contracts binding on them. Otherwise a person who pays a subscription of 7*s*. 6*d*. to this society might find himself involved in liabilities of an unknown amount. It is the defendant committee who are liable as Gates's principals, and they are his principals, not because they are members of the society, but because they are the committee entrusted with the function of directing the activities of this unincorporated body, and putting them into execution. That includes the making and performing of contracts; and the manager appointed by them becomes their agent and

servant to act on their behalf in making such contracts as they may direct and approve and appointing experts, etc.[47]

Notes

The unincorporated association, a collection of individuals bound more or less loosely and with no single legal entity, is in an anomalous position midway between that of the individual and that of the corporate body, and lacking the legal definiteness of either. In the relation of such bodies with their bankers, however, there seems to have been little difficulty in practice, and the leading case in which a bank was directly involved is still *Coutts & Co.* v. *The Irish Exhibition in London.*[48] In that case six prominent public men desired to set on foot an Irish Exhibition in London, and, before any steps had been taken to form a company for that purpose, they opened an account with the plaintiff bank, with an arranged overdraft of £10,000 against certain conditional guarantees, which later proved worthless. Two months later the exhibition was constituted a company, but, while the bank had notice of the formation of the company, no change was made in the style of the account or in the arrangements for signature. A month later, upon pressure from the plaintiff bank, securities were lodged in support of the overdraft, and three months later still the bank obtained a memorandum of charge on debts owing to the company. Upon the project failing, the bank brought an action to recover the amount of the overdraft against the company, and against the six originators of the project. For these latter defendants it was contended, *inter alia,* that throughout the transactions it was not the intention of the bank to look to them personally for the amount borrowed. The Court of Appeal held that the bank was entitled to recover from the six promoters Lindley L.J. saying:

> The ordinary relation of banker and customer must be held to have existed between Messrs. Coutts and these gentlemen, unless it could be made out that Messrs. Coutts were not to be the creditors of anybody until the exhibition was formed. But suppose, owing to some unforeseen cause, the exhibition had never been formed, was nobody to be liable to Messrs. Coutts? [49]

The effect of this decision and that in the *Bradley Egg Farm* case would seem to leave little doubt that the officers of an unincorporated association are personally liable for the debts which they incur in the name of the association. Paget contends [50] that the bank should obtain the personal undertaking of such persons as they wish to make liable; and it is clearly desirable in practice that any borrow-

[47] At pp. 380–381.
[48] (1891) 7 T.L.R. 313.
[49] At p. 314.
[50] *Op. cit.* pp. 26 *et seq.*

ing should be on the application and in the names of such persons, rather than in the name of the association alone, even though, on the authorities, it seems likely that the bank could recover against, *e.g.* the members of a committee of management even though they had not bound themselves individually and personally.

The distinction implied by Goddard L.J. between associations whose property belongs beneficially to the members and those in which the members have no rights in the property does not affect the point here discussed: the officers of the association are normally entitled to indemnity from such property, but the members as such are normally not liable personally for the acts of those officers.[51]

LIMITED COMPANIES

Introductions Ltd. v. National Provincial Bank Ltd.

[1970] Ch. 199

A company's borrowing must not be for a purpose inconsistent with the company's objects set out in the memorandum of association

Facts

Introductions Ltd. was originally founded to provide services and facilities for overseas visitors to the Festival of Britain in 1951, and it subsequently provided deck chairs in seaside resorts. In 1960 it came under new management, and embarked upon a pig breeding venture, which was a failure, the company being wound up in 1965 with liabilities of £2m., including an overdraft with the bank of £29,500. The liquidator claimed that the two debentures given by the company as security for this advance were invalid. Pig breeding not being among the objects set out in the company's memorandum was *ultra vires*, and borrowing for that purpose must be *ultra vires* also.

The bank, which had knowledge of the memorandum, contended that the borrowing was covered by a clause in it empowering the company " to borrow or raise money in such manner as the company shall think fit," while a further clause provided that " each of the preceding sub-clauses shall be construed independently of . . . any other sub-clause, and that the objects set out in each sub-clause are independent objects of the company."

[51] *Wise* v. *Perpetual Trustee Co. Ltd.* [1903] A.C. 4139.

Decision

The Court of Appeal upheld Buckley J.'s finding against the bank. Harman L.J. said:

> . . . borrowing is not an end in itself and must be for some purpose of the company; . . . you cannot convert a power into an object merely by saying so.[52]

Notes

The *ultra vires* rule, now past its centenary, was established by the House of Lords in *Ashbury Carriage Co.* v. *Riche*,[53] when it was held that the company, whose memorandum of association included only such objects as the construction of railway carriages, did not have the capacity to contract to build a railway in Belgium, notwithstanding that the shareholders approved the project. The rule provides that a company incorporated and registered under the Companies Acts can lawfully do only the acts it was formed to do, as set out in the memorandum of association in what is known as the objects clause. Activities outside this scope are said to be *ultra vires*, or beyond its powers, and any contract in which the company seeks to pursue such activities is void.

The rule has been much criticised in recent years, both the Cohen Committee and the Jenkins Committee [54] having recommended changes in it. Originally designed to protect creditors and shareholders, its frequent effect was to prejudice innocent contractors with the company, while its operation became more arbitrary as the companies legislation made it progressively easier for a company to change its memorandum. The *Introductions* case is a good example of its unfortunate operation: "The company's *ultra vires* activity was known to, and presumably endorsed by, the company's shareholders; the memorandum could have been altered with no trouble at all to cover the new activity; the bank had lent the money to a respectably constituted concern. And yet at the end of the day their contract is invalid." [55] But the law was quite clear, and what may be called the "hard line" in the matter found expression in further words of Harman L.J. in the *Introductions* case:

---

[52] At p. 210. *Cf. Thompson* v. *J. Barke & Co. (Caterers) Ltd.* [1975] S.L.T. 67, where the Court of Session held *inter alia* that the issue by the company of two cheques in repayment of a loan to a director of the company was *ultra vires*, despite a power in the memorandum to issue cheques: the nature of the transaction here was not the issue of cheques, but the repayment of a loan.

[53] (1875) L.R. 7 H.L. 653.

[54] Cmd. 6659 (1945), Cmnd. 1749 (1962). These two reports on the operation of the companies legislation were the foundation of, respectively, the 1948 and the 1967 Companies Acts.

[55] *The Banker* (March 1969), Vol. 119, p. 255.

It has always been the ambition apparently of the commercial community to stretch the objects clause of a memorandum of association, thus obtaining the advantage of limited liability with as little fetter on the activities of the company as possible. But still you cannot have an object to do every mortal thing you want, because that is to have no object at all.[56]

The position has been substantially altered by the European Communities Act 1972, which provides in section 9 (1) that:

in favour of a person dealing with a company in good faith any transaction decided on by the directors shall be deemed to be one which it is within the capacity of the company to enter into, and the power of the directors to bind the company shall be deemed to be free of any limitation under the memorandum or articles of association; and a party to a transaction so decided on shall not be bound to enquire as to the capacity of the company to enter into it or as to any such limitation on the powers of the directors, and shall be presumed to have acted in good faith unless the contrary is proved.

This provision, which is very similar to the proposals of the Jenkins Committee, is intended to bring our *ultra vires* rule nearer to the Community's attempt in 1968 to introduce uniformity on the matter into the systems of the then member States. The effect of section 9 (1) is to protect persons who do not know that a transaction is *ultra vires*. It is important to note that it does not protect persons with actual knowledge that the *ultra vires* rule is being breached, for such a person cannot be acting in good faith. How the provision may affect a bank in a situation like that of the *Introductions* case remains to be tested in court, but it seems improbable that a banker who has received a copy of the memorandum and articles (as he will normally have done on opening the account) would succeed in a claim that he was without notice of its provisions.

In *Charterbridge Corporation Ltd.* v. *Lloyds Bank Ltd.*[57] the bank successfully resisted a challenge to its security based on the *ultra vires* rule. The plaintiff company was the prospective purchaser of a property charged to the bank by a property development company. This latter company was one of a group, and its charge to the bank was in support of its guarantee of borrowing by the central company. The plaintiff company argued that the charge was void, as it had been created for purposes outside the scope of the company's business, and not for the company's benefit. But a clause in the memorandum covered the giving of guarantees and the lodgment of security in support, and Pennycuick J., finding for the bank, said:

The memorandum of a company sets out its objects and proclaims them

[56] At p. 209.

[57] [1970] Ch. 62.

to persons dealing with the company and it would be contrary to the whole function of a memorandum that objects unequivocally set out in it should be subject to some implied limitation by reference to the state of mind of the parties concerned.[58]

It is to be noted that while a company's memorandum sets the limits of its activities, the inclusion of a particular activity as one of the objects does not in itself entitle the company to any privileges associated with that activity. Thus in *United Dominions Trust Ltd.* v. *Kirkwood* [59] banking was one of the objects in the UDT memorandum, but this did not help the company to establish that they were bankers within the terms of the Moneylenders Act.

The Royal British Bank v. Turquand

(1856) 6 E. & B. 327

Freeman and Lockyer v. Buckhurst Park Properties (Mangal) Ltd.

[1964] 2 Q.B. 480

The rule in Turquand's case

Facts of the Royal British Bank v. Turquand

A company was authorised by its deed of settlement (which at that time was the equivalent of the present memorandum and articles of association) to borrow, through its directors, such sums as might be authorised by a resolution passed at a general meeting of the company. The company arranged to borrow £2,000 from the plaintiff bank, and gave the bank a bond for that amount, under seal, and signed by two directors. The bank now sued the defendant as the official manager of the company, to recover the amount advanced, and it was contended for the company that as no resolution had been passed by the shareholders in general meeting the bank could not recover.

Decision

It was held by the Court of Exchequer Chamber that, as the power to borrow money on bonds was not inconsistent with the provisions of the deed of settlement, the bank were entitled to

---

[58] At p. 69.

[59] *Ante*, p. 16.

assume that the necessary resolution had been passed by the shareholders.

In the course of his judgment, Jervis C.J. said:

We may now take for granted that the dealings with these companies are not like dealings with other partnerships, and that the parties dealing with them are bound to read the statute and the deed of settlement. But they are not bound to do more. And the party here, on reading the deed of settlement, would find, not a prohibition from borrowing, but a permission to do so on certain conditions. Finding that the authority might be made complete by a resolution, he would have a right to infer the fact of a resolution authorising that which on the face of the document appeared to be legitimately done.[60]

Facts of Freeman and Lockyer v. Buckhurst Park Properties (Mangal) Ltd.

The defendant company was formed in 1958 by Mr. Kapoor and Mr. Hoon, upon the latter's providing £40,000 to enable the former to buy the Buckhurst Park Estate. They became directors of the company, together with one nominee of each of them; and the articles of the company provided that a quorum of the company was to be four directors.

The first-named director acted throughout as managing director, to the knowledge of the other directors, but without express appointment, while for the greater part of the period in question in the case the second-named director was out of the country, so that the board was incapable of action as a board. Mr. Kapoor engaged the plaintiff firm of architects and surveyors to submit a planning application, and in this action they claimed their fees for work done.

The plaintiffs contended that Mr. Kapoor had actual authority to engage them on behalf of the company, or alternatively that he was held out by the company as having ostensible authority to do so. The defendant company argued that, in the absence of appointment generally as managing director or specifically for the purpose in question, his engagement of the plaintiff firm did not bind the company.

Decision

The Court of Appeal upheld the finding of the lower court in favour of the plaintiffs. In the course of his judgment, Diplock L.J. said:

If the foregoing analysis of the relevant law is correct, it can be summarised by stating four conditions which must be fulfilled to entitle a contractor to

[60] At p. 332.

enforce against a company a contract entered into on behalf of the company by an agent who had no actual authority to do so. It must be shown: (1) that a representation that the agent had authority to enter on behalf of the company into a contract of the kind sought to be enforced was made to the contractor; (2) that such representation was made by a person or persons who had "actual" authority to manage the business of the company either generally or in respect of those matters to which the contract relates; (3) that he (the contractor) was induced by such representation to enter into the contract, that is, that he in fact relied upon it; and (4) that under its memorandum or articles of association the company was not deprived of the capacity either to enter into a contract of the kind sought to be enforced or to delegate authority to enter into a contract of that kind to the agent.

The confusion which, I venture to think, has sometimes crept into the cases is in my view due to a failure to distinguish between these four separate conditions, and in particular to keep steadfastly in mind (a) that the only "actual" authority which is relevant is that of the persons making the representation relied on, and (b) that the memorandum and articles of association of the company are always relevant (whether they are in fact known to the contractor or not) to the questions (i) whether condition (2) is fulfilled, and (ii) whether condition (4) is fulfilled, and (but only if they are in fact known to the contractor) may be relevant (iii) as part of the representation on which the contractor relied.[61]

Notes

In earlier editions of this book the principle emerging from these cases was summarised thus:

A person dealing with a registered company should satisfy himself that the proposed transaction is not inconsistent with the memorandum and articles of association, and that the person acting for the company is not one to whom power so to deal is unlikely to have been delegated; but he need not inquire whether all the necessary steps have been taken by the company to make the matter complete and regular.

This must now be read subject to the modification of the *ultra vires* rule by the European Communities Act. As was pointed out earlier,[62] the Act may be of little avail to the banker who holds a copy of the memorandum and articles of the company, while it might even be questioned whether a banker had acted in good faith within the terms of the Act if he had failed to obtain sight of the memorandum and articles of a company whose account he held. So the development and application of the rule in particular circumstances are still of concern to bankers, at least until the question is further considered by the courts; but the notes following, unchanged

[61] At pp. 505–506.

[62] *Ante*, p. 184.

from the previous edition, must of course be read in the light of the 1972 Act.

A crucial aspect of the *ultra vires* problem is the question of delegated authority. This is of concern to bankers in their dealings with companies, especially in the drawing and indorsing of cheques and in borrowings by their company customers, for the companies' articles may well prescribe that certain formalities shall be observed which are laid down for the protection of the companies' assets. These cases are concerned with the position that arises when such formalities have not been observed.

The first decision above was the foundation of the important rule in *Turquand's* case. For many years after 1856 it was thought to be a principle of fairly simple application; for example in 1906 it was thus expressed [63]: "... where the regulations laid down by these documents, the memorandum and articles appear to have been complied with, it is not the duty of the lender to see that the apparent conformity is a real conformity." More recent decisions have tended to restrict the wide terms of the original ruling, and there has been some doubt as to the present state of the law. The judgments in the *Buckhurst Park Properties* case have gone far to resolve the confusion; of particular value is the judgment of Diplock L.J. in which he reconciled the decisions by reference to the four criteria set out above.

In *Mahony* v. *Liquidator of East Holyford Mining Co.*[64] the House of Lords applied the rule in its early, simple form. There a mining company was started and shares issued, the proceeds being paid into a banking account in the name of the East Holyford Mining Co. No meeting of shareholders was ever held, and no proper appointment of directors and secretary made. A formal notice was sent to the bank by a person signing as secretary, authorising them to pay cheques signed by two out of three named directors, and countersigned by the secretary; and a copy of the alleged resolution authorising this arrangement was enclosed. Cheques were drawn in this way, and the balance disposed of. Upon the liquidator's suing the bank it was held in the House of Lords that there was no duty on the bank to inquire whether the directors and secretary had been properly appointed. The second of Diplock L.J.'s conditions was here satisfied, he suggested, by the fact that the persons making the representation were those who, under the constitution of the company, were entitled to appoint directors and secretary. "Since they had 'actual' authority to appoint these officers, they had 'actual' authority to make representations who the officers were."

---

[63] Tillyard, *Banking and Negotiable Instruments* (2nd ed.), p. 131.
[64] (1875) L.R. 7 H.L. 869.

In a succession of cases the claim against the company has failed because the action of the agent was not of a kind that would normally be performed by a person occupying his position, so that " the conduct of the board of directors in permitting the agent to occupy that position . . . did not of itself amount to a representation that the agent had authority to enter into the contract sought to be enforced, *i.e.* condition (*a*) was not fulfilled." The following three cases all fall within this class.

In *Kreditbank Cassel G.m.b.H.* v. *Schenkers Ltd.*[65] the defendant company were forwarding agents, whose Manchester branch manager, Clarke, drew seven bills in the firm's name which were accepted by a firm in which Clarke was interested, and indorsed by him as " Manchester Manager." The bills were dishonoured by the acceptors, and the plaintiffs, who were holders in due course, sued the defendants as drawers, relying on the company's articles which empowered the directors to determine who should be entitled to " sign and make, draw, accept and indorse " bills on behalf of the company. No such authority had been given to Clarke; and the Court of Appeal held that the defendants were not liable, Atkin L.J. saying:

> ". . . Wright J. was in my view wrong, in the absence of evidence, in assuming that the manager of a branch business is a person who has ostensible authority to sign bills on behalf of his company." [66]

In *A. L. Underwood Ltd.* v. *Bank of Liverpool and Martins*,[67] it was held that a director paying into his private account cheques drawn in favour of the company could not be considered to be acting within the scope of his apparent authority, even when he was the sole director and had authority to indorse cheques for the company as " sole director." In *Alexander Stewart & Son of Dundee Ltd.* v. *Westminster Bank Ltd.*[68] in similar circumstances, Bankes L.J. said that Stewart's authority in fact could be to indorse cheques only for the benefit of the company, whereas he intended when he made the indorsements to steal the proceeds of the cheques. By section 24 of the Bills of Exchange Act 1882, the signature was wholly inoperative, and the bank could acquire no rights under it in the absence of proof that Stewart had ostensible authority to indorse cheques. There was no ostensible authority in the circumstances of the case.

It may be remarked in connection with these two cases that the receipt of cheques payable to a limited company for the credit of a private or a firm's account may well be negligence in the banker so

---

[65] [1927] 1 K.B. 826.
[66] At p. 843.
[67] [1924] 1 K.B. 775.
[68] (1926) 4 L.D.B. 40.

receiving; but in the latter case at least negligence was not relevant in view of the bank's defence that it was a holder for value. The question, which cannot be regarded as settled, whether a procuration signature becomes unauthorised merely because the signatory uses or intends to use the instrument signed unlawfully or fraudulently, is of some importance to the banker.

It is clear that no representation under condition (*a*) can be relied upon when the person dealing with the company has been put on inquiry by other circumstances. Thus in *B. Liggett (Liverpool) Ltd.* v. *Barclays Bank Ltd.*[69] it was held that, although the two directors of the company had power to appoint a third, the fact that one of those directors had expressed continuing anxiety regarding the management of the business and had insisted on signing all cheques drawn on the account was sufficient to put the bank on inquiry regarding a notice they later received, signed by the other director as chairman of the company, notifying them that his wife had been appointed as third director.

A further example of this point is to be found in *Victors Ltd. (in liquidation)* v. *Lingard*.[70] There a company had an overdraft secured by the guarantee of the directors. Later the company gave further security in the form of debentures; but one of the articles of the company provided that no director should vote on a matter in which he had a personal interest, and all the directors had by virtue of their outstanding guarantees a personal interest in the improvement of the bank's security. In an action to enforce the debentures the bank contended that although they had notice of the company's articles, and, of course, of the directors' liability under their guarantees, and so could not assume that the resolution for the issue of debentures was validly passed, yet when they received the debentures under the company's seal they were entitled to assume that the seal had been properly affixed, for the company might have sanctioned the issue in general meeting; that is, they claimed that they were entitled to rely on the *Turquand* case. But Romer J. held that the resolution creating the debentures was a nullity (although in fact because of subsequent events the company was held to be estopped from denying the validity of the debentures), and he rejected the argument of the bank on the facts of the case, holding that in fact they knew too much of the circumstances of the issue for their assumption to be justified.

[69] [1928] 1 K.B. 48. [70] [1927] 1 Ch. D. 323.

CHAPTER 8

FINANCING BY BANKERS

OVERDRAFTS

Metropolitan Police Commissioner v. Charles

[1976] 3 All E.R. 112

The issuing of a cheque without funds

Facts

The defendant had an account with the National Westminster Bank at Peckham Rye, where he had been allowed an overdraft limit of £100 and been given a cheque card. He had been instructed not to cash more than one cheque a day for £30. On one evening at a gaming club he issued all 25 cheques in a new cheque book, each for £30, and each backed by the cheque card, in exchange for chips. The bank of course had to honour the cheques, and the defendant was prosecuted under section 16 (1) of the Theft Act 1968, with having dishonestly obtained for himself a pecuniary advantage " by deliberately or recklessly representing that he was entitled and authorised to use a cheque card." He was convicted, and the Court of Appeal upheld the conviction. The basis of his appeal, which was then pursued to the House of Lords, was that the use of a cheque card does not imply any representation by the drawer as to the state of his account, or his authority to draw on that account, nor can there be any inference that any such representation induces the recipient of the cheque to accept it: he relies entirely on the bank's guarantee to pay.

Decision

The House of Lords unanimously rejected the appeal. Lord Edmund-Davies said:

The card played a vital part for (as my noble and learned friend, Lord Diplock, put it during counsel's submissions) in order to make the bank liable to the payee there must be knowledge on the payee's part that the drawer has the bank's authority to bind it, for in the absence of such knowledge the all-important contract between payee and bank is not created; and it is the representation by the drawer's production of the card that he has that authority that creates such contractual relationship and estops the bank from refusing to honour the cheque. By drawing the cheque the accused represented that it would be met, and by producing the card so that the number thereon could be endorsed on the cheque he in effect represented " I am authorised by the bank to show this to you and so create a direct contractual relationship between the bank and you that they will honour this cheque." [1]

Notes

Since early times bankers have been troubled by the misuse of cheques drawn upon them. The cheque that has been stolen and bears a forged signature is seen in such cases as *Greenwood* v. *Martins Bank Ltd.*[2] and *National Westminster Bank Ltd.* v. *Barclays Bank International Ltd.*[3] More commonly, cheques are presented for payment on accounts with insufficient funds to meet them and no pre-arrangement of overdraft facilities to cover them. Such a cheque is to be regarded as a request for a loan by way of overdraft,[4] and the banker is free to grant the overdraft or to refuse it and dishonour the cheque. But the decision which course to adopt can be a difficult one, and can have its own dangers.[5]

However, the banker in the past has relatively seldom been likely to suffer any legal wrong from such conduct by his customers. The payees of such cheques may or may not have been cheated by their issue, but they have had whatever civil action might be appropriate against the drawers. But the position has changed, on the one hand with the provision by the banks of the cheque card facility (which enables the careless or unscrupulous customer to overdraw without the bank's permission), and on the other hand by the passing of the Theft Act 1968, which has facilitated prosecutions in such cases, so that the police have been more ready to take proceedings. In the result there has been a series of reported cases in courts of appeal which are of interest, and in some cases direct concern, to practical bankers. The decision of the House of Lords in the *Charles* case is of particular significance with regard to the cheque card.

By section 15 of the Theft Act, " a person who by any deception dishonestly obtains property belonging to another, with the intention of permanently depriving the other of it," is guilty of an offence, as is, by section 16, " a person who by any deception dishonestly obtains for himself or another any pecuniary advantage." The law lords discussed, in the *Charles* case, the nature of the representation made by the person who draws a cheque. The time honoured three representations in Kenny's *Outline of Criminal Law* [6] —that the drawer has an account, that he has authority to draw for the amount of the cheque, and that the cheque is a valid order

[1] At p. 121.
[2] *Ante*, p. 66.
[3] *Ante*, p. 79.
[4] *Cf.* Chorley, *op. cit.* p. 216.
[5] See, *e.g. ante*, p. 72.
[6] 19th ed., p. 359.

for payment of that amount—they considered to be unnecessarily detailed, preferring a single representation, the equivalent of Kenny's third; in the words of Pollock B., in *R.* v. *Hazleton*,[7] quoted by Lord Edmund-Davies, " the real representation made is that the cheque will be paid."

In *Charles* a further representation was implied in the use of the cheque card, but in earlier cases under the Act the courts were concerned with unsupported cheques.

In *Director of Public Prosecutions* v. *Turner* [8] the House of Lords had to resolve conflicting decisions by the Court of Appeal on prosecutions under section 16. The section defines " pecuniary advantage " as including the reduction, evasion or deferring of a debt. In *R.* v. *Fazackerley*,[9] the Court of Appeal rejected the defence that a debt is not evaded unless the creditor has been deceived into forgiving or cancelling the debt, which does not happen when a cheque is issued without funds. But some weeks later, in *R.* v. *Turner*,[10] a differently constituted court was convinced by the apparent logic of the argument. On the appeal in the second case the House of Lords held that " debt " in the section means an obligation to pay immediately, and this obligation is evaded when a worthless cheque is given.

In *R.* v. *Greenstein* [11] the defendants had engaged in a series of " stagging " operations at a time when new issues were being heavily oversubscribed: they had applied for large quantities of shares in the hope of obtaining the smaller numbers they wanted. They sent cheques for the full amounts applied for, relying upon being able to pay into their accounts, in time to meet the cheques they had issued, the cheques they would receive for the unallotted shares. On some occasions the procedure broke down and their cheques were dishonoured on first presentation. They were charged under section 15, the deception alleged being that they had authority to draw the cheques they had issued. In most of the instances charged the application forms included a binding representation that the cheques accompanying the forms would be met on first presentation, but in three instances the forms did not include that representation, and in those three instances the cheques were in fact met on first presentation.

The jury found them guilty on all the counts alleged, including the three in which the cheques had been paid.[12] The Court of

[7] (1874) L.R. 2 C.C.R. 134. [8] [1974] A.C. 357. [9] [1973] 1 W.L.R. 632.
[10] [1973] 1 W.L.R. 653. [11] [1975] 1 W.L.R. 1353.
[12] It is extremely unlikely that in any but the exceptional circumstances of this case a prosecution would be brought in respect of cheques that were paid on presentation.

Appeal upheld the conviction: whether the defendants had been dishonest was a question of fact for the jury, and on the evidence they were entitled to conclude that, even in the three exceptional instances, the defendants had acted dishonestly in recklessly disregarding whether the " return " cheques would be available in time. As to the fact that in the three instances the application forms had contained no explicit representation (which is of course the normal position when a cheque is issued) the jury was entitled to find that the defendants had represented falsely that in the ordinary course of business there would be funds to meet the cheques,when in fact it was only as a result of their deception that in the event there were funds on the account.

These two cases, and others on the two sections,[13] did not directly involve the banks. The banks could dishonour the cheques or not as they wished. But a customer may draw a cheque for example under an open credit, which the bank has to pay. The clearing banks do not seem to have taken any such customer to court, but the National Giro raised the issue in *Halstead* v. *Patel*,[14] where the defendant drew cash from his National Giro account when there were no funds to cover the drawings, thus producing what many had thought an impossibility, an overdrawn Giro account. He was prosecuted under section 15, and while the justices dismissed the charge, on the grounds that he intended to repay the money, the Divisional Court overruled them, Lord Widgery C.J. saying that the defendant knew that there was no possibility of providing funds before the " cheque " was presented, but had merely a pious hope of covering it at some time in the future. As to the obvious difficulty in this context of the words " permanently depriving " in the section, he rested, perhaps surprisingly on a literal view of the matter saying " There can be no doubt in this case that the actual notes or coins that were handed over the counter to the respondent were leaving the control of the post office for ever."

The banks are at further risk when a credit card is used: there can be no refusal to pay a cheque so supported if the payee has observed the bank's conditions. In *R.* v. *Kovacs*,[15] when it was argued that the deception in such a case was of the payees of the cheques, not of the bank, the Court of Appeal held that section 16 requires, not that the person deceived should himself suffer any loss from the deception, but that there is a causal connection between the deception and the pecuniary advantage. The different defence in the *Charles* case—that in fact the payee had not been deceived—

---

[13] *Cf. e.g. R.* v. *Duru* [1974] 1 W.L.R. 2. [14] [1972] 1 W.L.R. 661.
[15] [1974] 1 W.L.R. 370.

was heard with some sympathy by the Court of Appeal, but they considered themselves bound by their decision in *Kovacs*; and, as one must think fortunately, the House of Lords was able to put the matter beyond doubt.

In *D.P.P.* v. *Turner* [16] Lord Reid spoke caustically of section 16: "I hope," he said "that ways can be found of drafting such provisions in a form which does not require elaborate and rarefied analysis to discover their meaning." It will have been noted that the defendants in these cases were without merit, their defences all resting on such "rarefied analysis" of the wording of the sections, although some of those defences may well be considered logically sound. But in all the cases the juries were apparently satisfied that the minds of the accused were equally guilty over the whole range of the operations, and the courts, approaching the matter as one of common sense, refused to disturb their verdicts. Few will regret that the effect of the decisions is that the issue of a cheque without funds can be a criminal offence, as can, albeit indirectly, the enforced creation of an overdraft.

COMBINATION OF ACCOUNTS

Barclays Bank Ltd. v. Okenarhe

[1966] 2 Lloyd's Rep. 87

The setting off of a credit balance against indebtedness on another account

Facts

The defendant stole a building society passbook belonging to a Mr. Crouch, and went to the Sloane Square branch of the plaintiff bank, where he claimed to be Mr. Crouch and said he wished to withdraw some £1,600 from the building society and open a deposit account at the bank. He later paid in the building society's cheque, and was allowed to withdraw almost the whole amount while it was still uncleared. On the same day he opened a current account at the plaintiffs' Battersea Park branch, and paid in the cash he had withdrawn from Sloane Square. When the building society cheque was dishonoured, payment having been stopped, the bank sought to combine the defendant's accounts.

16 [1974] A.C. 357.

Decision

Mocatta J. held that although there cannot be an overdraft on a deposit account, and therefore the payment out to the defendant was not a loan on the deposit account, yet the loan had been made and was a banking transaction; and the bank was entitled to combine the defendant's indebtedness to them at Sloane Square with their indebtedness to him at Battersea Park.

In reviewing the authorities he said:

As regards the case in which the customer has separate running current accounts at each of two branches of a bank, it is plain that the general principle is that the bank is entitled to combine the two accounts. There is clear authority for this in the case of *Garnett* v. *McKewan*.[17] The learned Barons, in giving their judgments in that case, emphasised, of course, as one would have expected, that there was no right of combination in relation to accounts maintained with a banker by one person but in two different capacities; for example, one account might be a personal account of the customer and the other might be a trust account. Further, it was made clear by Baron Bramwell that the right to combine did not arise if there was an agreement between the customer and the banker that the two accounts should be kept separate, or if such an agreement should be implied from their conduct. Furthermore, in that case the learned judges dealt with what, at first sight, might seem the apparent anomaly that the customer cannot without the specific agreement of the bank draw on account A a sum in excess of his balance on that account but which is less than the combined balance at account A and account B. That limitation on the customer's rights, in other words, the inability of the customer without specific agreement to combine two accounts, is explained as necessary to business efficacy. It would make the task of the banker impossible if every branch was expected to know the state of a customer's account at every other branch.[18]

Notes [19]

The setting off of a credit balance against an overdraft or loan of the same customer has sometimes been regarded as an example of banker's lien, but properly the two conceptions are distinct.[20]

In *Garnett* v. *McKewan* a customer drew cheques against his credit balance at one branch of a bank. At another branch he was indebted to an amount almost as great as the credit balance at the

[17] (1872) L.R. 8 Ex. 10, *infra*. See also *post*, pp. 304, 345.

[18] At p. 95.

[19] As to combination of accounts generally, *cf.* Chorley, *op. cit.* pp. 218 *et seq.* As to the notice required upon closing an account, *cf. Prosperity* v. *Lloyds Bank Ltd.*, *post*, p. 303.

[20] The distinction was discussed in *Halesowen Presswork and Assemblies Ltd.* v. *Westminster Bank Ltd. post*, p. 327; see in particular the judgment of Buckley L.J. in the Court of Appeal.

first, and the bank, without notice to him, combined the balances and dishonoured his cheques. It was held that they were entitled to do so.

Some doubt arose as to this almost unqualified right of set-off as a result of a dictum of Swift J. in *Greenhalgh & Sons* v. *Union Bank of Manchester Ltd.*,[21] in which he rejected the possibility of any set-off between two accounts. The doubts raised by this dictum were finally laid to rest when, in the *Halesowen Presswork* case,[22] Lord Kilbrandon in the House of Lords approved Lord Denning's express rejection, in the court below, of Swift L.'s view. There can no longer be any question as to the banker's right to combine accounts in appropriate circumstances.

While doubt continued, however, the banks introduced the letters of set-off which are signed by customers relying upon credit balances for borrowing on other accounts. These letters of set-off acknowledge the banker's right to combine, and are in effect no more than evidence of a right already existing; they are a useful precaution against a customer's possible protests, but do not themselves create any right.[23]

Buckingham v. *London & Midland Bank Ltd.*[24] was an example of one of the principal exceptions to the banker's right of set-off. The plaintiff had a current account, and also a loan account secured against house property. The branch manager had the property resurveyed, and decided that the advance was too high. Thereupon he told the plaintiff that his account had been closed. The plaintiff protested that he had cheques outstanding, but the manager duly combined the accounts and dishonoured the cheques. The plaintiff suing the bank for damages, the jury found that the course of dealing between bank and customer was that the customer could draw upon the current account without reference to the loan account, and was entitled to reasonable notice of the ending of this arrangement. And in *Bradford Old Bank Ltd.* v. *Sutcliffe*,[25] where also a loan account and a current account were in question, Pickford L.J. said: " If it were otherwise the company would be extremely hampered in its business, for it could never safely draw on the current account so long as the credit balance did not exceed the amount due on the loan account."

---

[21] [1924] 2 K.B. 153.

[22] *Post*, p. 327.

[23] In *Midland Bank Ltd.* v. *Reckitt* (*ante*, p. 107) the bank took a document by which Terrington charged any credit balance on one account against any borrowing on another. Lord Atkin said about this document: " How this increased their rights if the money was the customer's money, or gave them any rights if the money was client's money, it is perhaps not necessary to discuss."

[24] (1895) 12 T.L.R. 70.

[25] *Post*, p. 250.

The principle of these decisions was applied in *Re E. J. Morel (1934) Ltd.*[26] to a "frozen" current account, which Buckley J. considered could not be properly regarded as a current account at all. But in the case of a similarly frozen current account in the *Halesowen Presswork*[27] case, the House of Lords held that the bank was entitled to combine such an account with the active current account when the banker/customer relationship was ended by the winding up of the company. The same principle clearly covers any other circumstances in which the banker/customer relationship is terminated.

The *Halesowen Presswork* decision also resolved any doubt that existed as to what notice, if any, the banker must give his customer of his intention to combine accounts. In the circumstances of that case, where the accounts were combined after the winding-up order, notice could serve no useful purpose. Had the bank decided to combine when they knew that a meeting of creditors was called, notice taking immediate effect would have been the right course, subject to the duty to pay cheques drawn before the customer received that notice. On this point, Lord Cross remarked that on the one hand a period of notice would enable the customer to defeat the combination by withdrawing the credit balance, while on the other hand if he had no notice at all he might continue to pay in to his account cheques that he would have paid in to another bank if he had known the true position. It will have been observed that in *Garnett's* case no notice was given; and Paget[28] argues that "in the absence of evidence to the contrary the right to combine without notice should be insisted upon, for the necessity for combination derives from some act or omission on the part of the customer." It is true that the customer usually knows well—and often before the banker—of his act or omission that justifies combining; it is true also that the banker will often have difficulty with customers who issue cheques after receiving notice, taking care to antedate them. But Lord Cross's view, although strictly *obiter*, must carry great weight, and it seems unlikely that bankers can rely in the future on the authority of *Garnett's* case in this matter of notice.

Barclays Bank Ltd. v. *Quistclose Investments Ltd.*[29] was an interesting example of a bank being refused the right of set-off because one of the accounts was held to be impressed with a trust.[30] Quistclose provided the money for a dividend that Rolls Razor could not meet, and the cheque for this amount was placed to the credit of a separate account with the appellant bank, Rolls' bankers. Rolls went into voluntary liquidation before the dividend could be paid, and the

---

[26] *Post*, p. 339.
[27] *Post*, p. 327.
[28] *Op. cit.* p. 127.
[29] [1968] 3 W.L.R. 1097.
[30] And *cf. Re Gross*, *ante*, p. 146 and *Re Kayford Ltd.* (*In Liquidation*), *ante*, p. 148.

bank sought to combine the Rolls accounts, which, even combined, showed a substantial overdraft. But the House of Lords held that the dividend was subject to a trust in favour of the lender, and the balance on it was not available to other creditors, including, of course, the bank, which was held to have had notice of the trust.

DISCOUNT OF BILLS

Barclays Bank Ltd. v. Aschaffenberger Zellstoffwerke A.G.
[1967] 1 Lloyd's Rep. 387

The holder of a bill who sues as trustee for another can be met by any defence available against the trustee

Facts

An English company supplied the defendants, a German company, with machinery. Payment was by 18 bills of exchange drawn on the German company, which accepted them. Barclays agreed to finance the transaction, and bought the bills, paying 73 per cent. of their face value and agreeing that when the bills were met at maturity the balance of 27 per cent. would also be paid to the company. In the event the last two bills were dishonoured, the German company alleging late delivery and defective materials. The bank, as holders for value, sought and obtained summary judgment on the bills, the court not being aware of the fact that the bank had not paid the face value of the bills. The defendants appealed.

Decision

The full facts of the case now becoming apparent, the Court of Appeal held that while there was no defence in law to the claim for the full amount of the bills, a stay of execution would be granted in respect of the 27 per cent., for which the bank was trustee for its customers. Lord Denning M.R. said:

. . . we have the authority of *Thornton and Others* v. *Maynard* [31] which shows that if the holder of a bill of exchange holds it in part as trustee for someone else, then when the holder sues upon the bill, the defendant can raise against the trustee any defence or set-off which he would have available against the person who was really behind the transaction. As it is said in Chalmers on Bills of Exchange,[32] " When the holder of a bill sues as agent for another person, or when he sues wholly or in part for the benefit

[31] (1875) L.R. 10 C.P. 695.

[32] 13th ed., p. 128.

of another person, any defence or set-off available against that person is available *pro tanto* against the holder."

So it seems to me that any defence or set-off which the German company have as against Black Clawson International Ltd. is available against Barclays Bank Ltd., in so far as the proportion 26·839 per cent. is concerned; because to that extent they are trustees of Black Clawson International Ltd.

What is to be done then? In point of law on the bills of exchange themselves, there is no defence in law to the whole amount. Judgment must go for the sum claimed with interest thereon. But, on the other hand, as the German company, it now appears, claim to have this set-off (because they claim liquidated damages which would be, if available, a true set-off) for more than this 26.839 per cent., they should be at liberty to have it available to them against that part of the claim, and no more.[32a]

Notes

The decision is of interest, if seldom of direct concern, to bankers, whose financing of commerce and industry by the discounting of bills is of very long standing; in the nineteenth century bankers found the discount of bills preferable to the early forms of overdraft as a method of lending to their customers,[33] and until the First World War the bill maintained its dominance in the finance of trade generally. As already noted,[34] the inland bill has now virtually disappeared, and while the bill of exchange is still of considerable importance in international trade, it is principally as the basis of the documentary credit, which gives the banker the additional security of the goods covered. But the simple discount, as seen in this case, is still frequently undertaken, and it is not unusual for the discounting bank to provide initially only a proportion of the value of the bills, the balance being credited when the bills are met at maturity.

When a bank makes an advance by way of discount, without any recourse against the goods involved, it looks first to the acceptor for payment, and only failing that to the drawer, its customer. It is to be noted that even when, as in the present case, only a part of the value of the bills has been initially advanced, the bank becomes holder for value with a legal title to the whole amount. This legal title was not questioned in the *Aschaffenberger* case, and the judgments in the Court of Appeal were explicit that there could be no challenge to it. The relevance of the decision to the rule that a bill of exchange is normally equivalent to cash, so that any counterclaim must not be set against it, is apparent [35]; it is unfortunate that this aspect of the matter seems to have been treated rather cavalierly by the Court of Appeal, as secondary in importance to the trusteeship issue.

32a At p. 389.
33 See Holden, *History of Negotiable Instruments in English Law*, p. 297.
34 *Ante*, p. 129.
35 *Cf. ante*, pp. 125 *et seq.*

The judgments did not make it clear why the court was making an exception to a rule that they explicitly recognised. Salmon L.J. referred *inter alia* to the fact that arbitration proceedings were pending in Copenhagen, but in the *Nova (Jersey) Knit* case [36] the House of Lords refused an application for a stay of execution on the grounds of pending arbitration proceedings. The *Aschaffenberger* decision is significant in its finding on the trusteeship issue, but it would now seem to have little relevance to the cash equivalence principle.

Barclays Bank International Ltd. v. Levin Brothers (Bradford) Ltd.

[1976] 3 All E.R. 900

Section 72 (4) *of the Bills of Exchange Act* 1882 ***does not prevent judgment being given in the currency in which the bill is drawn***

Facts

The defendants bought cloth from a supplier in New York, who drew four bills of exchange on them for $23,000 each. The sellers indorsed the accepted bills to the plaintiff bank for consideration, and upon the bills being dishonoured, the defendants alleging that the cloth was defective and the sellers insolvent, the bank obtained an order for summary judgment. The master applied the rate of exchange for sight drafts applicable on each of the four dates on which the bills were due, these rates varying from $2.2725 to $2.1395. The bank appealed against the limitation to sterling.

The defendants argued that the *Miliangos* decision [37] did not cover the present case; and even if it did, section 72 (4) of the Bills of Exchange Act 1882 prevented judgment otherwise than in sterling.

The subsection provides:

> Where a bill is drawn out of but payable in the United Kingdom, and the sum payable is not expressed in the currency of the United Kingdom, the amount shall, in the absence of some express stipulation, be calculated according to the rate of exchange for sight drafts at the place of payment on the day the bill is payable.

Decision

Mocatta J. found against the defendants on both arguments. As to the first, he said:

---

[36] *Ante*, pp. 127.
[37] *Infra*.

In my view . . . the decision in the *Miliangos* case has revolutionised the position and has disposed of the once common assumption that foreign currency must be treated by our courts as if a commodity, *e.g.* a foreign cow: see *per* Lord Wilberforce in the *Miliangos* case.[38]

As to section 72 (4) he accepted the bank's argument:

. . . that the subsection can be given perfectly adequate effect if its application were limited to those cases in which the acceptor of a bill wished to exercise his option to pay at the maturity date the appropriate sum in sterling and not in the foreign currency in which the relevant bill of exchange was expressed . . . that this gave a sensible and adequate meaning to the subsection, ruling out the dates of the bill or of acceptance as relevant, and that there was no justification for applying its terms to the case where the acceptor failed to pay at the maturity date, had to be sued by the drawer or endorsee, and when judgment was given, if given in sterling, such judgment would be for money of substantially less value than the United States dollars that should have been paid at the maturity date or their equivalent in sterling at the rate of exchange ruling at that date.[39]

This interpretation, he considered, " would do substantially less injustice than the contrary construction," and he gave judgment for the bank for the total of $92,000 or the equivalent in sterling at the date of payment or enforcement of the judgment.

Notes

Until the decision of the Court of Appeal in *Schorsch Meier GmbH* v. *Hennin* [40] and that of the House of Lords in *Miliangos* v. *George Frank (Textiles) Ltd.*[41] it had been the rule that an English court could give judgment on a money claim only in sterling. The Lord's decision was given on a contract " whose proper law is that of a foreign country and where the money of account and payment is that of that country," but the reasoning on which the judgments were based proved capable of extension. In later cases it has been held that damages can be given in foreign currency in an action for breach of contract [42] or in an action in tort.[42a] The present case had its place in this development, Mocatta J. holding that, the money of account and payment being foreign, judgment in that currency was not prevented by the fact that the law of the contract was English.[43]

---

[38] At p. 911.
[39] At p. 909.
[40] [1975] 1 All E.R. 152.
[41] [1975] 3 All E.R. 801.
[42] *Kraut (Jean) A.G.* v. *Albany Fabrics* [1977] 2 All E.R. 116.
[42a] *The Despina R.*, *The Times*, June 22, 1977.
[43] *The Maratha Envoy* [1977] 1 Lloyd's Rep., 217, where Lord Denning said (at p. 225) " once it is recognised that judgment *can* be given in a foreign currency,

The importance of the *Miliangos* decision, and its application in later cases, is that payment of a debt in sterling can result, as would have been the case here, in loss to the creditor when the exchange rate has moved against him in the interval between the due date of payment of the debt and the date of judgment upon it. Mocatta J. did not accept that his ruling would result in injustice were the pound sterling to appreciate in value during that interval:

> . . . the plaintiff on either view gets the same number of dollars for which he has contracted. As stated by Lord Wilberforce, [in *Miliangos*] the creditor " has bargained for his own currency, and only his own currency. . . . The creditor has no concern with pounds sterling; for him what matters is that a Swiss franc for good or ill should remain a Swiss franc." [44]

The interest of the banker in the *Levin Brothers* case, however, lies in the decision on section 72 (4), the wording of which had seemed to allow no departure from sterling. There is interest, too, in the unexpected relevance of a provision of the 1882 Act, which has produced little litigation and was certainly not drafted in contemplation of the kind of exchange fluctuations that are familiar today.

BANKER'S COMMERCIAL CREDITS

T. D. Bailey Son & Co. v. Ross T. Smyth & Co. Ltd.

(1940) 67 Ll. L.R. 147

E. Clemens Horst Co. v. Biddell Bros.

[1912] A.C. 18

The effect of a c.i.f. contract

Facts of T. D. Bailey Son & Co. v. Ross T. Smyth & Co. Ltd.

The appellants were sellers of American corn, under a c.i.f. contract. The buyers rejected a provisional invoice on the grounds that the description of the goods did not meet the contract terms, and after arbitration and further dispute as to whether the buyer was entitled so to reject it, the case was finally argued before the House of Lords. The issues involved were too technical to be of

---

justice requires that it *should* be given in every case where the currency of the contract is a foreign currency; otherwise one side or the other will suffer unfairly by the fluctuations of the exchange."

[44] At p. 909.

interest here, but the discussion of the nature and effect of a c.i.f. contract brought an authoritative exposition from Lord Wright. In the course of it he said:

The contract in question here is of a type familiar in commerce, which is described as a c.i.f. contract. The initials indicate that the price is to include cost, insurance and freight. It is a type of contract which is more widely and more frequently in use than any other contract used for purposes of seaborne commerce. An enormous number of transactions, in value amounting to untold sums, are carried out every year under c.i.f. contracts. The essential characteristics of this contract have often been described. The seller has to ship or acquire after that shipment the contract goods, as to which if unascertained he is generally required to give a notice of appropriation. On or after shipment he has to obtain proper bills of lading and proper policies of insurance. He fulfils his contract by transferring the bills of lading and the policies to the buyer. As a general rule he does so only against payment of the price, less the freight, which the buyer has to pay. In the invoice which accompanies the tender of the documents on the "prompt," that is, the date fixed for payment, the freight is deducted for this reason. In this course of business the general property in the goods remains in the seller until he transfers the bills of lading.

These rules, which are simple enough to state in general terms, are of the utmost importance in commercial transactions. I have dwelt upon them perhaps unnecessarily because the judgment of the Court of Appeal might seem to throw doubt on one of their most essential aspects. The property which the seller retains while he or his agent or the banker to whom he has pledged the documents retains the bills of lading, is the general property, not a special property by way of security. But in general the importance of the retention of the property is not only to secure payment from the buyer but for purposes of finance. The general course of international commerce involves the practice of raising money on the documents so as to bridge the period between shipment and the time of obtaining payment against documents. These credit facilities, which are of the first importance, would be completely unsettled if the incidence of the property were made a matter of doubt. By mercantile law the bills of lading are the symbols of the goods. The general property in the goods must be in the seller if he is to be able to pledge them. The whole system of commercial credits depends on the seller's ability to give a charge on the goods and the policies of insurance. A mere unpaid seller's lien would for obvious reasons be inadequate and unsatisfactory. I need not observe that particular contracts may contain special terms or otherwise indicate a special intention which take the contract outside these rules.[45]

Facts of E. Clemens Horst Co. v. Biddell Bros.

A contract for the sale of hops to be imported into this country provided for payment at "90s. per 112 lbs. c.i.f. to London,

[45] At p. 156.

Liverpool or Hull. Terms net cash." There was no provision for payment against documents, and when the latter were in due course presented to them, with a request for payment, the buyers refused, contending that they were not bound to do so under the contract until they had been able to examine the goods.

Decision

It was held by the House of Lords that under a c.i.f. contract payment is due upon tender of documents, unless the contract expressly provides otherwise.

In the Court of Appeal,[46] which had upheld the buyers' contention, Kennedy L.J. delivered a dissenting judgment, which received the approval of the House of Lords, and may be regarded as of great authority. In it he said:

> But in truth, the duty of the purchasers to pay against the shipping documents, under such a contract as the present, does not need the application of that doctrine of the inference in mercantile contracts that each party will do what is "mercantilely reasonable," for which we have the great authority of Lord Esher. The plaintiffs' assertion of the right under a cost freight and insurance contract to withhold payment until delivery of the goods themselves, and until after an opportunity of examining them, cannot possibly be effectuated except in one of two ways. Landing and delivery can rightfully be given by the shipowner only to the holder of the bill of lading. Therefore, if the plaintiffs' contention is right, one of two things must happen. Either the seller must surrender to the purchaser the bill of lading, whereunder the delivery can be obtained, without receiving payment, which, as the bill of lading carries with it an absolute power of disposition, is, in the absence of a special agreement in the contract of sale, so unreasonable as to be absurd; or, alternatively, the vendor must himself retain the bill of lading, himself land and take delivery of the goods, and himself store the goods on quay (if the rules of the port permit), or warehouse the goods, for such time as may elapse before the purchaser has an opportunity of examining them. But this involves a manifest violation of the express terms of the contract "90*s*. per 112 lbs. cost freight and insurance." The parties have in terms agreed that for the buyer's benefit the price shall include freight and insurance, and for his benefit nothing beyond freight and insurance. But, if the plaintiffs' contention were to prevail, the vendor must be saddled with the further payment of those charges at the port of discharge which ex necessitate rei would be added to the freight and insurance premium which alone he has by the terms of the contract undertaken to defray.[47]

Notes

"General property" in an article is that which the absolute

---

[46] [1911] 1 K.B. 934.

[47] [1911] 1 K.B. 934 at pp. 958–959.

owner has in it; "special property" is here that limited ownership exercised by, for example, a bailee, where the article can be put only to a particular use. The general property in goods can be fettered in various ways, as is the case when the documents of title are pledged with a banker; but subject to the particular restriction or restrictions it remains absolute ownership, while the special property which vests in him who exercises the restriction serves that limited purpose only.[48]

W. J. Alan & Co. Ltd. v. El Nasr Export & Import Co.

[1972] 2 Q.B. 189

The nature of payment by letter of credit

Facts

The plaintiffs, coffee producers in Kenya, in 1967 entered into two contracts for the supply of coffee to the defendants, an Egyptian state trading corporation, at a price expressed in Kenya shillings, which at the time of the contracts were at parity with sterling. The letter of credit established in connection with the contracts did not conform with the terms of the contract, in particular being expressed in sterling, but the plaintiffs accepted it, and drew upon it, being paid in sterling on the date in November on which sterling was devalued. The plaintiffs now claimed additional payment to cover their Kenya shilling loss on the devaluation. The defendants contended that nothing further was owing, on the grounds either (1) that the credit, once accepted, amounted to payment of the price, or (2) that the money of account had been varied by agreement or that the sellers had waived payment in Kenya currency and accepted sterling instead.

Upon judgment being given for the plaintiffs, the defendants appealed.

Decision

The Court of Appeal allowed the appeal, holding that the plaintiffs had by their conduct waived payment in Kenya currency. Although in view of this finding the defendants' first argument was not necessary to the decision, their Lordships discussed it in their judgments. Lord Denning said:

[48] The subject of bankers' commercial credits generally, is treated in Chorley, *op. cit.* pp. 222 *et seq.* For an exhaustive treatment of the subject, the student is referred to Gutteridge and Megrah, *The Law of Bankers' Commercial Credits* (5th ed., 1976).

In my opinion a letter of credit is not to be regarded as absolute payment, unless the seller stipulates, expressly or impliedly, that it should be so. He may do it impliedly if he stipulates for the credit to be issued by a particular banker in such circumstances that it is to be inferred that the seller looks to that particular banker to the exclusion of the buyer. . . .

. . . I am of the opinion that in the ordinary way, when the contract of sale stipulates for payment to be made by confirmed irrevocable letter of credit, then, when the letter of credit is issued and accepted by the seller, it operates as conditional payment of the price. It does not operate as absolute payment. It is analogous to the case where under a contract of sale, the buyer gives a bill of exchange or a cheque for the price. It is presumed to be given, not as absolute payment, nor as collateral security, but as conditional payment. If the letter of credit is honoured by the bank when the documents are presented to it, the debt is discharged. If it is not honoured, the debt is not discharged: and the seller has a remedy in damages against both banker and buyer.[49]

Notes

The seller's rights, following on failure of the bank, for whatever reason, to pay under a letter of credit, depend upon whether the credit is regarded as absolute or conditional payment. If the payment is absolute, he will have no alternative right against the buyer, but if it is conditional (as is payment by bill of exchange or cheque) the original right against the buyer revives upon failure of payment (otherwise perhaps than by the seller's own fault) by the bank.

Curiously enough there seems to be little direct authority on the point.[50] In the present case the comments of the Court of Appeal were *obiter*, but their unanimous view that payment is normally conditional only is clearly of considerable weight, and the passages from Lord Denning's judgment quoted above are unlikely to be challenged as an accurate statement of the law.

---

[49] At pp. 210 and 212.

[50] Reference may be made to Gutteridge and Megrah, *op. cit.* pp. 34 *et seq.* for a review of the cases in which the courts here and abroad have discussed the question.

J. H. Rayner & Co. Ltd. and Others v. Hambros Bank Ltd.

(1942) 59 T.L.R. 21

Midland Bank Ltd. v. Seymour

[1955] 2 Lloyd's Rep. 147

In paying drafts drawn under a documentary credit a bank must ensure that the documents presented exactly satisfy the conditions laid down in the credit

Facts of J. H. Rayner & Co. Ltd. and others v. Hambros Bank Ltd.

A firm in Denmark established a credit with the defendant bank, their correspondents, in favour of the plaintiffs, in respect of a shipment from Madras. The credit called for, " full set straight clean bills of lading . . . Covering about 1,400 tons Coromandel groundnuts in bags at £12 2s. 6d. per ton f.o.b. . . ."

The plaintiffs later presented to the defendant bank documents which they claimed were within the terms of the credit, but which the defendants refused to accept on the grounds that the bill of lading mentioned " machine-shelled groundnut kernels," although the provisional invoice prepared by the plaintiffs in London covered " Coromandel groundnuts," as called for in the credit. The plaintiffs brought the present action alleging that the refusal to pay was wrongful and in breach of the undertaking in the terms of the credit. Evidence was called to show that in the trade there was general understanding that Coromandel groundnuts meant machine-shelled kernels. Judgment was given for the plaintiffs and the defendant bank appealed.

Decision

The Court of Appeal allowed the appeal. In his judgment, Goddard L.J. said:

> The bank, if they accept the mandate to open the credit, must do exactly what their customer requires them to do, and if the customer says: " I require a bill of lading for Coromandel groundnuts," the bank are not justified, in my judgment, in paying against a bill of lading for anything except Coromandel groundnuts. It is no answer to say: " you know perfectly well that machine-shelled groundnut kernels are the same as Coromandel groundnuts." For all the bank know, their customers may have a particular reason for wanting " Coromandel groundnuts " in the bill of lading. At any rate, that is the instruction which the customers here have given to the bank, and if the bank want to be reimbursed by the customers, they must show that they have performed their mandate.[51]

[51] At p. 24.

And MacKinnon L.J. said:

. . . it is quite impossible to suggest that a banker is to be affected with knowledge of the customs and customary terms of every one of the thousands of trades with regard to the dealings in which he may issue letters of credit. . . . It would be quite impossible for business to be carried on, and for bankers to be in any way protected in such matters, if it was said that they must be affected by knowledge of all the particular details of the way in which particular traders carry on their business.[52]

Facts of Midland Bank Ltd. v. Seymour

The defendant's business included the import of feathers from Hong Kong, and in 1952 he entered into a number of contracts with the Taiyo Trading Company, with whom he had not previously done business. Payment was to be made by means of confirmed irrevocable letters of credit, opened through the plaintiff bank. The goods shipped proved worthless, and the Hong Kong company could not thereafter be traced.

In his action against the bank the plaintiff contended, *inter alia*, that the bank had not acted in accordance with the terms of the credits. The requests for the credits had authorised payment " against delivery of the following documents . . . evidencing shipment . . . of the undermentioned goods," and while the documents taken together included all the particulars required—the description, the quantity and the price—these particulars were not all to be found in the bill of lading.

Decision

Devlin J. held that, in the absence of a clear requirement that the bill of lading should contain all the particulars of the shipment, it was sufficient that the documents taken together should do so. In his judgment he said:

. . . no principle is better established than that when a banker or anyone else is given instructions or a mandate of this sort, they must be given to him with reasonable clearness. The banker is obliged to act upon them precisely. He may act at his peril if he disobeys them or does not conform with them. In those circumstances there is a corresponding duty cast on the giver of instructions to see that he puts them in a clear form. Perhaps it is putting it too high for this purpose to say that it is a duty cast upon him. The true view of the matter, I think, is that when an agent acts upon ambiguous instructions he is not in default if he can show that he adopted what was a reasonable meaning.[53]

---

[52] At p. 23.

[53] At p. 153.

Notes

Whether refusal to honour drafts is unreasonable is a matter of fact in every case. One of the contentions of the plaintiffs in the *Rayner* case was that when it would be unreasonable for the consignee to refuse to accept the documents then it must be unreasonable also for the bank to refuse; and the decision here was a useful denial of that suggestion—the consignee may be expected to know the terms and abbreviations of his own trade, but the banker is not.

The *Seymour* case is interesting for the long judgment of Devlin J. and its detailed examination of the machinery of the documentary credit. In particular he considered the contention of the plaintiff that the fact that the bill of lading contained a " weight unknown " clause itself invalidated it under the terms of the credit. By this very common clause the carrier disclaims responsibility for the weight, quality, contents and " possibly other particulars that are asserted in the bill of lading by the shipper as a description of the goods." The plaintiff argued that " in effect by virtue of this clause the bill of lading contains no description at all," but the argument was rejected:

> ". . . I think it must be taken that what the letter of credit requires is the description in the body of the bill, whether or not it is accompanied by such a clause. If it were not so, then the bank would have to reject out of hand virtually every bill of lading that was tendered to it." [54]

There were two other findings in the *Seymour* case of importance to bankers. The plaintiff had further argued (*a*) that the bank had been wrong in accepting four of the drafts after the relevant credits had expired, even though the drafts had been negotiated in Hong Kong before the expiry dates; and (*b*) that the bank had been negligent in not passing on all the information they had received regarding the sellers. On the first point Devlin J. held that the words " available in Hong Kong " meant that the drafts could be accepted there, but not that negotiation without acceptance would meet the terms of the credit. The bank was thus at fault; but in fact the defendant was held to have later instructed the bank to accept the bills after the expiry dates. On the second point the defendants were awarded nominal damages; a bank is under a contractual duty in regard to inquiries made on behalf of its customers, and must not supply misleading information as the bank was here held to have done by not passing on the whole text of a cable received from their correspondents.

---

[54] At p. 155.

On the matter here primarily under discussion, the importance of the bank's strict adherence to the terms of the credit, perhaps the best known statement of the principle is that of Lord Sumner in *Equitable Trust Company of New York* v. *Dawson Partners Ltd.*[55]:

It is both common ground and common sense that in such a transaction the accepting bank can only claim indemnity if the conditions on which it is authorised to accept are in the matter of the accompanying documents strictly observed. There is no room for documents which are almost the same, or which will do just as well. . . . The bank's branch abroad, which knows nothing officially of the details of the transaction thus financed, cannot take it upon itself to decide what will do well enough and what will not. If it does as it is told, it is safe; if it declines to do anything else, it is safe; if it departs from the conditions laid down, it acts at its own risk.[56]

Lord Sumner's words were quoted by McNair J. in *Bank Melli Iran* v. *Barclays Bank (D.C. & O.)*.[57]

In *Scott* v. *Barclays Bank Ltd.*[58] a credit was established with the defendants in favour of the plaintiffs, payment to be against drafts accompanied by a full set of clean bills of lading, a certificate of inspection, invoice and approved insurance policy. The bank refused to honour a draft drawn under this credit, on the grounds, *inter alia*, that the documents included a certificate of insurance but no insurance policy. The Court of Appeal held that the bank was justified in their refusal to pay. Bankes L.J. pointed out in his judgment that the certificate indicated the policy issued, but did not state its terms, which could be ascertained only by reference to the actual policy, so that it was impossible to say from it whether the policy complied with the terms of the credit. It is accepted law that a policy must be tendered under a c.i.f. contract, except possibly where there is a clear trade usage permitting the tender of a certificate.

And in *Gian Singh & Co.* v. *Banque de l'Indochine*,[59] where the issuing bank was challenged on the grounds, *inter alia*, that a certificate called for by the credit was in fact forged, the Privy Council, on appeal from the Court of Appeal of Singapore, held that the paying bank had taken reasonable care to ascertain that it appeared on its face to be within the terms of the credit, and so the fact that it was a forgery did not prevent the issuing bank from recovering. " The notifying bank did as it was told; so the issuing bank is safe "—a conscious echo of Lord Sumner's words quoted above.

---

55 (1927) 27 Ll.L.Rep. 49.
56 At p. 52.
57 [1951] 2 T.L.R. 1057, *post*, p. 214.
58 [1923] 2 K.B. 1.
59 [1974] 1 W.L.R. 1234.

British Imex Industries Ltd. v. Midland Bank Ltd.

[1958] 1 Q.B. 542

But the paying banker is not entitled to call for more than is specified in the credit; and his duty to inspect documents does not extend beyond reasonable care

Facts

The defendant bank had confirmed an irrevocable credit for £23,000 in favour of the plaintiffs covering a shipment of steel bars to Jordan. Shipment took place from Antwerp under bills of lading which included among the printed clauses on the back a clause providing that the vessel would not be responsible for correct delivery in the absence of certain specified marking of the pieces and the bundles.

When sight drafts were presented under the credit the bank refused to pay them on the grounds that there was no acknowledgement on the face of the bills of lading that this clause had been complied with. The plaintiffs brought the present action on the drafts.

Decision

It was held that a credit calling for "bills of lading" without further qualification required "clean" bills of lading—*i.e.* bills containing no indication that the goods or packing were defective; that the bills in the present case were in fact clean bills, and that there was nothing in the letter of credit that called for an express acknowledgement that the clause in question had been complied with. The bank therefore had no right to insist on such an acknowledgement.

Salmon J. said:

According to [the bank's] case, it was their duty for the remuneration of £18 to read through the multifarious clauses in minute print on the back of these bills of lading, and, having observed additional clause B, to consider its legal effect and then to call for an acknowledgement that it had been complied with. I respectfully share the doubt that Scrutton L.J. expressed in *National Bank of Egypt* v. *Hannevig's Bank* [60] as to whether any such duty is cast upon the bank. I doubt whether banks are under any greater duty to their correspondents than to satisfy themselves that the correct documents are presented to them, and that the bills of lading bear no indorsement or clausing by the shipowners or shippers which could reasonably mean that there was, or might be, some defect in the goods or their packing.[61]

---

[60] (1919) 3 L.D.B. 213.

[61] At pp. 551–552.

Notes

The circumstances in which the bank sought to establish a duty wider than the court would approve were unusual. The case was heard 10 days after *Hamzeh Malas & Sons* v. *British Imex Industries Ltd.*,[62] where the plaintiffs had unsuccessfully sought an injunction to prevent the defendants from drawing under the credit. In the present case, on the same facts, Salmon J. remarked:

> If, as seems not unlikely, the bank's customers took the point that the bank was not entitled to pay on the credit, it is perhaps not at all surprising that the bank would feel obliged, for its own protection, to resist the plaintiffs' claim, so that it should be protected by an order of this court.[63]

The decision that the bank was not entitled to refuse payment supports the proposition that the duty of the paying bank to ensure conformity of the documents with the terms of the credit is not to be unreasonably widened. Scrutton L.J.'s doubt, to which Salmon J. referred, was cogently expressed:

> In some cases the obligation of a banker, under such a credit, may need very careful examination. I only say at present that to assume that for one-sixteenth per cent. of the amount he advances, a bank is bound carefully to read through all bills of lading presented to it in ridiculously minute type and full of exceptions, to read through the policies and to exercise a judgment as to whether the legal effect of the bill of lading and the policy is, on the whole, favourable to their clients, is an obligation which I should require to investigate considerably before I accepted it in that unhesitating form. . .[64]

The *National Bank of Egypt* case was decided on other grounds, so these remarks were strictly speaking *obiter dicta*, but there is little doubt that the view they embody would be generally followed by the courts.

The Privy Council decided *Commercial Banking Co. of Sydney* v. *Jalsard Pty.*[65] on similar reasoning. There the documents called for included a certificate of inspection, and when the goods proved defective the buyers brought this action against the bank on the grounds that the certificates that had been tendered were not " certificates of inspection " as that expression is used in documentary credits. The Supreme Court of New South Wales found for the buyers; the bank appealed, and the Judicial Committee allowed the appeal, holding that " certificate of inspection " could

---

[62] *Post*, p. 218.
[63] At p. 550.
[64] At p. 214.
[65] [1973] A.C. 279.

cover documents containing a variety of information if a particular method of inspection was required, it should be specified in the buyer's instructions.

Lord Diplock, delivering the judgment of the Judicial Committee, said:

> Both the issuing banker and his correspondent bank have to make quick decisions as to whether a document which has been tendered by the seller complies with the requirements of a credit at the risk of incurring liability to one or other of the parties to the transaction if the decision is wrong. Delay in deciding may in itself result in a breach of his contractual obligations to the buyer or to the seller. This is the reason for the rule that where the banker's instructions from his customer are ambiguous or unclear he commits no breach of his contract with the buyer if he has construed them in a reasonable sense, even though upon the closer consideration which can be given to questions of construction in an action in a court of law, it is possible to say that some other reasoning is to be preferred.[66]

Bank Melli Iran v. Barclays Bank (D.C. & O.)

[1951] 2 T.L.R. 1057

Undue delay may forfeit the right of the issuing bank to reject documents against which the confirming bank has paid

Facts

Bank Melli Iran, in late 1946, established an irrevocable credit for £45,000 with Barclays Bank (D.C. & O.) in favour of Eastern Development Co. in respect of the purchase by their customers Kharrazi & Co. of 100 new Chevrolet trucks, and Barclays confirmed the credit to Eastern Development. On January 17, 1947, Barclays advised Bank Melli that they had paid £40,000 against documents, and photostats of the documents reached Bank Melli on March 4. They included an invoice for trucks " in new condition," and a certificate of purchase which referred to " new, good " trucks, but did not identify them as being those invoiced. Kharrazi questioned the wording, and the query was forwarded to Barclays without comment. Barclays obtained from Eastern Development, and forwarded to Bank Melli, confirmation that the trucks were new.

The first consignment of trucks needed a further payment for carriage, and on May 14 Bank Melli agreed to an appropriate increase in the credit. The further payment by Barclays was advised

---

66 *Ibid.* at p. 286.

to them on June 15, and on that day they repudiated the first payment but said nothing on the second until July 23, when they repudiated that also, having meanwhile, *inter alia*, applied to Kharrazi for payment.

They brought the present action claiming a declaration that Barclays were not entitled to debit them in respect of either payment.

Decision

As to the first payment, MacNair J. held " without hesitation " that the documents were not in accordance with the bank's mandate and that Barclays were not entitled to pay against them. But the plaintiffs' conduct, both in having authorised an increase in the credit and in the failure to repudiate until June 15, amounted to " an overwhelming case of ratification." As to the second payment likewise, their conduct was " inconsistent with an intention to repudiate."

Notes

Article 8 of the Uniform Customs and Practice for Documentary Credits [67] provides:

> (c) If, upon receipt of the documents, the issuing bank considers that they appear on their face not to be in accordance with the terms and conditions of the credit, that bank must determine, on the basis of the documents alone, whether to claim that payment, acceptance or negotiation was not effected in accordance with the terms and conditions of the credit.
>
> (d) The issuing bank shall have a reasonable time to examine the documents and to determine as above whether to make such a claim.

The *Bank Melli* case is an example of the issuing bank's delay providing in part a defence for the confirming bank which had paid against documents not meeting the requirements of the credit. What amounts to " reasonable time " for examination of the documents must depend on the circumstances, but in practice refusal must be prompt, and it is unfortunate that MacNair J., in the case of the second payment, seemed to accept that had it not been for Bank Melli's conduct in the surrounding circumstances their defence of pressure of work in the documentary credits departments might have justified their six weeks' delay in repudiation.

---

[67] 1974 Revision. *Cf.* Chorley, *op. cit.* p. 226 as to the importance of the Uniform Customs and Practice for Documentary Credits.

This suggestion has been widely criticised,[68] and is to be contrasted with, for example, Lord Sumner's statement in *Hansson* v. *Hamel & Horley Ltd.*,[69] where he said:

> These documents have to be handled by banks, they have to be taken up or rejected promptly and without any opportunity for prolonged examination.[70]

or with the Privy Council's similar attitude in *Commercial Banking Co. of Sydney* v. *Jalsard Pty.*[71] Certainly six weeks would seem to be considerably in excess of the " reasonable time " of the Uniform Customs, while in any case unusual pressure of work would not normally be accepted as a defence for apparent inefficiency.[72]

Cape Asbestos Co. Ltd. v. Lloyds Bank Ltd.

(1921) 3 L.D.B. 314

Urquhart Lindsay & Co. v. Eastern Bank Ltd.

[1922] 1 K.B. 318

Revocable and irrevocable documentary credits

Facts of Cape Asbestos Co. Ltd. v. Lloyds Bank Ltd.

On the instructions of a Warsaw bank the defendant bank established a documentary credit in favour of the plaintiffs and advised them of its establishment. Their letter of advice ended with the words: " This is merely an advice of the opening of the above-mentioned credit, and is not a confirmation of the same." One draft was paid under the credit, and the credit was thereafter withdrawn. The bank did not advise the plaintiffs of the withdrawal and they, in the belief that it was still operative, made a further shipment, and sent to the bank the relative documents, including an invoice for an amount larger than the balance of the credit and a bill of lading made out in favour of the buyers instead of the bank. The bank would not pay against these, and in the meantime, the goods having gone forward, the buyers obtained possession of them. It was not possible to collect payment from them, and the plaintiffs claimed from the defendant bank the balance of the credit.

---

[68] *Cf.* the editor's note to the case in 6 L.D.B. 227; Paget, *op. cit.* p. 644; Gutteridge and Megrah, *op. cit.* p. 154.

[69] [1922] 2 A.C. 36.

[70] At p. 46.

[71] See the quotation from the judgment, *ante*, p. 214.

[72] *Cf. ante*, p. 109 for an unsuccessful defence on similar lines in *Ross* v. *London County and Westminster Bank Ltd.*

It was shown in evidence that the bank normally advised the beneficiaries of the cancellation of credits and that on the present occasion the official concerned had forgotten to do so.

Decision

Bailhache J. held that the bank owed no duty to advise the beneficiaries of the cancellation; and further that the irregularity in the bill of lading and in the invoice would have justified the bank's refusal to pay.

In the course of his judgment he said:

> It is to be observed that the notice that was given by the bank on the opening of the credit is of the opening of a revocable credit and not of a confirmed credit. That tells the person in whose favour the credit is opened that he may find that the credit is revoked at any time. That being the representation which is made by the bank to the person in whose favour the credit is opened, the seller in this case, are the bank under any legal obligation to him to inform him when that credit is revoked? . . . I have come to the conclusion that, however wise and however prudent, and however much in the interest of business, such a notice may be, there is no legal basis upon which I can found an obligation on the bank to give such a notice under such circumstances.[73]

Facts of Urquhart Lindsay & Co. v. Eastern Bank Ltd.

A credit was opened with the defendant bank in favour of the plaintiffs, who were manufacturers of machinery, on the terms that it was "confirmed and irrevocable." The contract in connection with which the credit had been opened contained, *inter alia*, the term that in the event of any increase in wages, cost of material or transit rates the plaintiffs' prices would be correspondingly increased.

Two drafts were drawn and paid under the credit. The buyers, finding that the plaintiffs were including in their invoices an addition to the prices already quoted, in respect of an increase in the cost of materials or wages, instructed the defendants to pay in future only so much of drafts presented as represented the original prices, the extra charges being referred to the buyers. The defendant bank advised the plaintiffs of this instruction, and then refused to meet the drafts in respect of the third shipment.

They paid these drafts later, under protest, but in the meantime the plaintiffs had issued a writ in the present action, alleging breach of contract and consequent loss of profit. The defendants at first contended (but later abandoned the point) that the letter of credit must be taken to incorporate the original contract which, in the

---

[73] At p. 315.

present case, on its true meaning, allowed increase in price only as a matter for subsequent independent adjustment.

Decision

Rowlatt J. held that the bank had committed a breach of contract. In his judgment he said:

> . . . the defendants undertook to pay the amount of invoices for machinery without qualification, the basis of this form of banking facility being that the buyer is taken for the purposes of all questions between himself and his banker or between his banker and the seller to be content to accept the invoices of the seller as correct. It seems to me that so far from the letter of credit being qualified by the contract of sale, the latter must accommodate itself to the letter of credit. The buyer having authorised his banker to undertake to pay the amount of the invoice as presented, it follows that any adjustment must be made by way of refund by the seller, and not by way of retention by the buyer.[74]

Notes

A credit is termed irrevocable when the *issuing* bank gives an unqualified undertaking to honour drafts drawn under it; it becomes confirmed only when the *advising* bank adds its own guarantee to that of the issuing bank. It is obvious that, in this sense of the words, while irrevocable credits may frequently be unconfirmed, it is rarely that a revocable credit is confirmed; the advising banker is not eager to accept a liability which the issuing banker has seen fit to avoid.

A revocable credit can be cancelled at will, as was seen in the *Cape Asbestos* case, but an irrevocable credit can be varied or withdrawn only with the consent of all parties to it. Thus in *Hamzeh Malas & Sons* v. *British Imex Industries Ltd.*,[75] where the buyers, the plaintiffs in the case, sought an injunction to restrain the defendants from drawing on an irrevocable credit established with Midland Bank, the Court of Appeal upheld Donaldson J.'s refusal. Jenkins L.J. said:

> A vendor of goods selling against a confirmed letter of credit is selling under the assurance that nothing will prevent him from receiving the price. That is no mean advantage when goods manufactured in one country are being sold in another. It is, furthermore, to be observed that vendors are often reselling goods bought from third parties. When they are doing that, and when they are being paid by confirmed letter of credit, their practice is—and I think it was followed by the defendants in this case—to finance the payments necessary to be made to their suppliers against the letter of

---

[74] At p. 323.

[75] [1958] 2 Q.B. 127 and see *ante*, p. 213.

credit. That system of financing these operations, as I see it, would break down completely if a dispute as between the vendor and the purchaser was to have the effect of "freezing," if I may use that expression, the sum in respect of which the letter of credit was opened.[76]

It is to be noted, however, that the court rejected the submission that they had no jurisdiction to interfere, Sellers L.J. saying:

I would not like it to be taken that I accept, or that the court accepts . . . that the court has no jurisdiction. There may well be cases where the court would exercise jurisdiction, as in a case where there is a fraudulent transaction.[77]

More recently, in *Discount Records Ltd.* v. *Barclays Bank Ltd. and Another*,[78] where Barclays had refused to accept instructions not to pay under an irrevocable credit, the court again refused the injunction sought by the plaintiffs. Here the plaintiffs had alleged, *inter alia*, fraud by the sellers, and while accepting that there was no English authority in support of their case, they cited an American decision, *Sztejn* v. *J. Henry Schroder Banking Corp.*[79] That decision was based on established rather than alleged fraud. Megarry J. did not reject the possibility that even alleged fraud might provide grounds for interference by the court, but the circumstances here he considered fell short of doing so. And he said:

I would be slow to interfere with bankers' irrevocable credits, and not least in the sphere of international banking, unless a sufficiently grave cause is shown; for interventions by the court that are too ready or too frequent might gravely impair the reliance which, quite properly, is placed on such credits.[80]

Pavia & Co. S.P.A. v. Thurmann-Nielsen

[1952] 2 Q.B. 84

The time within which credits must be opened

Facts

In a contract for the sale c.i.f. of shelled Brazilian groundnuts payment was to be by confirmed irrevocable credit, the contract providing that the shipping periods should be from February 1 to May 31. Despite repeated requests by the sellers for the credit to

---

[76] *Ibid.* at p. 129. *Cf.* Lord Wilberforce's comments on the bill of exchange, *ante*, p. 127.
[77] At p. 130.
[78] [1975] 1 W.L.R. 315.
[79] (1941) 31 N.V.S. 2d. 631.
[80] At p. 320.

be opened it was not in fact made available until April 22. Only a small portion of the quantity of groundnuts covered by the contract was shipped, and the sellers claimed damages for breach of contract by delay in opening the credit.

Decision

The Court of Appeal, upholding the judgment of McNair J., held that the credit should have been established on February 1. In his judgment Denning L.J. said:

In the absence of express stipulation, I think the credit must be made available to the seller at the beginning of the shipment period. The reason is because the seller is entitled, before he ships the goods, to be assured that, on shipment, he will get paid. The seller is not bound to tell the buyer the precise date when he is going to ship; and whenever he does ship the goods, he must be able to draw on the credit. He may ship on the very first day of the shipment period. If, therefore, the buyer is to fulfil his obligations he must make the credit available to the seller at the very first date when the goods may be lawfully shipped in compliance with the contract.[81]

Notes

It had been argued for the buyers that the only obligation was to establish the credit by such time as the seller was in fact ready to ship; but Somervell L.J. said on this point:

. . . the contract would be unworkable if . . . the buyer under it was under no obligation until a date, which he could not possibly know, and which there is no machinery for his finding out, namely, when the seller actually has the goods down at the port ready to put on the ship.[82]

A gloss on the *Pavia* decision was provided in *Sinason-Teicher Inter-American Grain Corporation* v. *Oilcakes and Oilseeds Trading Co. Ltd.*,[83] a case in which the contract called for a bank guarantee. Denning L.J. said with reference to the *Pavia* case:

It does not decide that the buyer can delay right up to the first date for shipment; it only decides that he must provide the letter of credit by that time at the latest. The correct view is that, if nothing is said about time in the contract, the buyer must provide the letter of credit within a reasonable time before the first date for shipment. The same applies to a bank guarantee, for it stands on a similar footing.[84]

The *Pavia* contract was c.i.f. The time in which the credit should be opened under an f.o.b. contract was the issue in *Ian Stach Ltd.* v.

[81] At p. 88.
[82] At p. 88.
[83] [1954] 1 W.L.R. 1394.
[84] At p. 1400.

Baker Bosley Ltd.,[85] the argument of the buyers being that as, under a "classic f.o.b. contract," the buyer can himself fix the date of shipment at any time within the shipping period, the time at which the credit must be opened is reasonable time before the date of shipment fixed by the buyer. Diplock J. refused to accept this argument, and held that the credit must, like the credit under a c.i.f. contract, be opened at latest by the earliest shipping date. (He doubted the extension of the *Pavia* principle in Denning L.J.'s remarks in the *Sinason-Teicher* case quoted above, and said he considered that those remarks were *obiter*.) He said:

> The alternative view . . . that the credit has to be opened a reasonable time before the actual shipping date, seems to me to lead to an uncertainty on the part of buyer and seller which I should be reluctant to import into any commercial contract.[86]

He went on to point out that such "reasonable time" might depend on circumstances known to the parties at the time of the contract, or on circumstances discovered later before instructions to ship were given, or even on circumstances as they actually were, whether known to the parties or not.

It would therefore appear that under both c.i.f. and f.o.b. contracts the rule is the same: the credit must be opened by the first possible date for shipment. But it is still perhaps open to question whether it must be a reasonable time before that date.

For performance bonds and government agencies as parties to documentary credits, see Appendix.

---

[85] [1958] 2 Q.B. 130.

[86] At p. 143.

Chapter 9

SECURITIES FOR ADVANCES

Bankers' Lien

Brandao v. Barnett

(1846) 12 Cl. & Fin. 787

The scope of bankers' lien

Facts

The plaintiff was a Portuguese merchant whose London agent, Burn, habitually purchased exchequer bills for him, received the interest upon them on his behalf, and at proper intervals exchanged them for others. Burn had an account with the defendant bankers, and there kept several tin boxes in which he lodged the plaintiff's and other such bills, and of which he held the keys. On December 1, 1836, Burn took out several bills, delivered them to the defendants and, as was his custom, asked them to get the interest upon them and to exchange them. This the defendants did, but, before Burn returned to pick up the new bills, acceptances were presented on his account in excess of the credit balance upon it, and paid. Upon Burn's failure the defendants claimed a lien on the bills in his hands. The Court of Common Pleas found for the plaintiff and the Court of Exchequer Chamber on appeal reversed this decision. The plaintiff further appealed.

Decision

The House of Lords restored the verdict for the plaintiff. In the course of his judgment Lord Campbell said:

I am of opinion that the general lien of bankers is part of the law-merchant, and is to be judicially noticed. . . . But I am humbly of opinion that, upon the facts found, there was no lien and that the judgment ought to be reversed. I do not, however, proceed upon the ground taken by the Court of Common Pleas—that these exchequer bills being the property of Brandao there was no lien as against him, although there might have been as against Burn . . .; the right acquired by a general lien is an implied pledge, and where it would arise (supposing the securities to be the property of the apparent owner), I think it equally exists if the party claiming it has acted with good faith, although the subject of that lien should turn out to be the property of a stranger. . . .

Bankers most undoubtedly have a general lien on all securities deposited with them, as bankers, by a customer, unless there be an express contract, or circumstances that show an implied contract, inconsistent with lien. . . . Now it seems to me, that, in the present case, there was an implied agreement on the part of the defendants, inconsistent with the right of lien which they claim. . . . [The bills] not only were not entered in any account between Burn and the defendants, but they were not to remain in the possession of the defendants; and the defendants, in respect of them, were employed merely to carry and hold till the deposit in the tin box could be conveniently accomplished. . . . Nor, I presume, can any weight be attached to the circumstance that the tin box . . . remained in the house of the defendants. . . . I think that the transaction is very much like the deposit of plate in locked chests at a banker's. . . . In both cases a charge might be made by the bankers if they were not otherwise remunerated for their trouble.[1]

Notes

The ordinary right of lien is a right merely to retain possession. A banker's lien is exceptional in that it carries with it the right of sale,[2] and as such approximates more closely to pledge: it is, in Lord Campbell's words, an "implied pledge." It applies, however, irrespective of the customer's knowledge of its existence: it exists by mercantile usage, and the customer is assumed to know of it.

The essential factor in deciding what property may and what may not be subject to the lien is whether or not it came to the banker's hands in the course of his business as a banker. It has sometimes been suggested that the dividing line is between items intended for collection and those deposited for safe custody, and while this is a little too broad a statement to be always accurate it does provide an approximate guide. It may be noted that in *Re United Service Co., Johnston's Claim*,[3] Sir William James considered that the securities there would have formed the subject of banker's lien. Paget[4] cites Chalmers's doubts on this point, and suggests that, possession of the certificates not being necessary for the collection of the dividends, safe custody is more likely to have been the primary purpose of the deposit—as is suggested in another connection in the notes to that case.[5]

The concept of bankers' lien was examined in the *Halesowen Pressworks* case, where, as was pointed out earlier,[6] the confusion between lien and set-off was finally resolved: set-off is a right

---

[1] At p. 805–809.

[2] Although it is considered by some that this "right of sale" arises only in the case of negotiable instruments, the most frequent objects of bankers' lien.

[3] *Post*, p. 293.

[4] *Op. cit.* p. 504.

[5] *Post*, p. 294.

[6] *Ante*, p. 198.

independent of lien. In that case also, doubt was cast on the possibility of money, in particular in the form of cheques paid in for collection, becoming subject to bankers' lien.

Earlier cases had seemed to accept the possibility without question. Thus, in *Misa* v. *Currie*,[7] where the question related to an order to pay money, Lord Hatherley said:

> A good deal of argument has arisen as to whether this document is to be treated as a bill of exchange, or whether it is to be treated simply as an authority authorising Messrs. Glyn & Co. to collect this debt due to Lizardi from Misa. . . . Supposing it to be necessary to hold it to be an authority, I do not see, regard being had to the lien which bankers have upon all documents which are placed in their hands by customers who are indebted to them in the course of their banking transactions, that it would make any important difference whether it should be held to be an authority or a bill of exchange.[8]

And in *Re Keever*[9] and in *Barclays Bank Ltd.* v. *Astley Industrial Trust Ltd.*[10] the banks were held to have obtained a lien on the cheques that had been paid in for collection. But the idea had already been questioned. Thus Paget had argued that money paid into a bank becomes the property of the bank, which thereafter owes a corresponding debt to the customer, and a debt is not a suitable subject for lien.[11]

In *Halesowen Presswork*s Buckley L.J. took the same view:

> The money or credit which the bank obtained as the result of clearing the cheque became the property of the bank, not the property of the company. No man can have a lien on his own property and consequently no lien can have arisen affecting that money or that credit. . . . It has of course long been recognised that a banker has a general lien on all securities deposited with him as a banker by a customer unless there be an express contract or circumstances that show an implied contract inconsistent with lien. . . . The term "securities" is no doubt used here in a wide sense, but does not, in my judgment, extend to the banker's own indebtedness to the customer.[12]

This passage was *obiter*, but it was expressly approved by Viscount Dilhorne in the House of Lords hearing of the same case, and on this point the earlier decisions must be viewed with considerable reserve.

It may be said that there is one clear ruling possible as to when bankers' lien does not arise. Any property which is handed to a

---

[7] (1876) 1 App.Cas. 554.
[8] At p. 567.
[9] *Ante*, p. 89, and *post*, p. 310.
[10] *Ante*, p. 88.
[11] *Law of Banking* (7th ed.), p. 485; *op. cit.* p. 504.
[12] [1971] 1 Q.B. 1, at p. 46.

banker for an express purpose cannot be subject to lien, even when the purpose itself has failed; in the old case *Lucas* v. *Dorrien*,[13] for instance, deeds were left with a banker as security for an advance. The advance was not granted, but the deeds were not picked up by the depositor; and it was later held that they could not be subject to lien in the banker's hands.[14]

PLEDGE

London Joint Stock Bank v. Simmons

[1892] A.C. 201

The pledgee of a negotiable instrument becomes the holder for value to the extent of the sum he has advanced

Facts

A firm of stockbrokers had for many years received advances from the appellant bank against various stocks, shares and bonds, these securities frequently changing. One of the partners in the firm, without the knowledge of his partner or the authority of the owner, sold certain negotiable bonds belonging to the respondent, Simmons, which the firm was holding for safe custody. The sale was in the name of the firm, as was the repurchase of the securities for the next account, but the cheque on the firm's account representing the purchase money was paid against a temporary advance by the bank against additional security including, *inter alia*, the bonds thus repurchased.

The fraudulent partner having absconded, the firm suspended payment and the bank sold the bonds to repay the advance. Simmons brought an action against the bank claiming the value of the bonds, and the Court of Appeal, upholding the lower court, considered themselves bound by authority and held the bank liable. The bank appealed.

Decision

The House of Lords allowed the appeal, and held the bank entitled to retain the value of the bonds.

In his judgment Lord Herschell said:

---

[13] (1817) 7 Taunt. 278.

[14] Fuller discussion of the topic will be found in Chorley, *op. cit.* pp. 291 *et seq.*, and in Paget, *op. cit.* pp. 498 *et seq.* Throughout this chapter, reference should be made to Holden, *Securities for Bankers' Advances.*

. . . I desire to rest my judgment upon the broad and simple ground that I find, as a matter of fact, that the bank took the bonds in good faith and for value. It is easy enough to make an elaborate presentation after the event of the speculation with which the bank managers might have occupied themselves in reference to the capacity in which the broker who offered the bonds as security for an advance held them. I think, however, they were not bound to occupy their minds with any such speculations. I apprehend that when a person whose honesty there is no reason to doubt offers negotiable security to a banker or any other person, the only consideration likely to engage his attention is, whether the security is sufficient to justify the advance required. And I do not think the law lays upon him the obligation of making any inquiry into the title of the person whom he finds in possession of them; of course, if there is anything to arouse suspicion, to lead to a doubt whether the person purporting to transfer them is justified in entering into the contemplated transaction the case would be different, the existence of such suspicion or doubt would be inconsistent with good faith. And if no inquiry were made, or if on inquiry the doubt were not removed and the suspicion dissipated, I should have no hesitation in holding that good faith was wanting in a person thus acting.[15]

Notes

The pledge with a banker of a negotiable security had been for some time before the *Simmons* case the subject of what Paget calls the " pernicious theory " that the banker was affected by constructive notice of any defect in the title of a customer whose business was that of agency, as, for example, a stockbroker. This inference had been drawn from the decision, also of the House of Lords, in *The Earl of Sheffield* v. *London Joint Stock Bank*,[16] where a money dealer had advanced large sums against securities belonging to the Earl of Sheffield, and pledged on his behalf by his agent. The money dealer in his turn pledged these and other securities with the London Joint Stock Bank as security for certain advances, and when he went into liquidation the owner of the securities and his agent brought this action against the bank to recover the stocks or their value. The Court of Appeal supported the lower court in dismissing the action, but the House of Lords reversed this decision and held that the bank were not entitled to retain the stocks.

In the *Simmons* case the *Sheffield* decision was distinguished on the point that there the bank not only might have suspected but did in fact know that the securities pledged were not the property of the pledgor. The value of the *Simmons* decision lies in the emphasis with which the theory of constructive notice is rejected where the subject of the pledge is negotiable.

The importance of negotiability in the law of pledge as it affects

---

[15] At p. 223.

[16] (1888) 13 App.Cas. 333.

bankers is considerable. It is not, strictly, necessary to have a memorandum of deposit of the instrument pledged where it is negotiable, as the deposit of it establishes prima facie the fact of the pledge.[17] Moreover, although it is desirable for the banker to have such a memorandum, to show that the securities were not left with him merely for safe custody, their negotiability makes them easily realisable, and this liquidity is of course of the greatest value in banking securities.

Sewell v. Burdick
(1884) 10 App.Cas. 74

Brandt v. Liverpool Brazil and River Plate Steam Navigation Co. Ltd.
[1924] 1 K.B. 575

A pledgee of a bill of lading does not take the general property in it unless and until he presents the bill to enforce his security

Facts of Sewell v. Burdick

Upon the shipment of certain goods to Russia, the shipper pledged the bill of lading to the appellant banker as security for a loan, and indorsed the bill to him. The goods were seized in Russia and sold to pay customs duties on them, the amount realised on the sale not covering the duties. The banker did not present his bill of lading, nor take possession of the goods.

Freight was unpaid on the consignment, and the shipowner brought the present action against the banker, contending that under the Bills of Lading Act the liability to pay the freight had passed to the banker when he became indorsee of the bill of lading. The shipowner won in the lower courts, and the banker appealed.

Decision

The House of Lords allowed the appeal, holding that the obligations under the contract pass to the indorsee only when he takes the general property in the bill of lading, and not when he takes only such special property as a pledgee takes.[18]

---

[17] Of course, in the case of quasi-negotiable documents of title, such as bills of lading, and of other forms of security, entirely lacking negotiability, the mere deposit of the documents of title without any form of charge gives a good *equitable* title to the property.

[18] As to general and special property, see *ante*, p. 205.

In his judgment, Lord Blackburn said:

No one, in ordinary language, would say that when goods are pawned, or money is raised by mortgage on an estate, the property, either in the goods or land, passes to the pledgee or mortgagee, and I cannot think that the object of the enactment was to enact that no security for a loan should be taken on the transfer of bills of lading unless the lender incurred all the liabilities of his borrower on the contract. That would greatly, and I think unnecessarily, hamper the business of advancing money on such security which the legislature has, by the Factors Acts, shown it thinks ought rather to be encouraged.[19]

Facts of Brandt v. Liverpool Brazil and River Plate Steam Navigation Co. Ltd.

A consignment of zinc ashes was sent from Buenos Aires to Liverpool. The bill of lading stated that the goods had been shipped in apparent good order, but in fact a part of the consignment had been wetted by rain before loading, and began to swell. The master of the vessel, in the interests of the safety of his ship, discharged most of the consignment to a warehouse in Buenos Aires where, after unnecessary delay, they were reconditioned and reshipped to England, arriving three months after the arrival of the first ship. In the meantime the price of zinc had fallen, and the charges involved for warehousing and for the reconditioning amounted to £748.

The bill of lading had been indorsed to pledgees who had made an advance against it to the shipper. On arrival of the cargo the pledgees paid the freight due and, under protest, the charges of £748 for which the shipowners claimed a lien on the goods. They then brought an action against the shipowners for damages for delay, and for repayment of the sum of £748.

Decision

The Court of Appeal held that as the plaintiffs had taken delivery of the goods under the bill of lading they had acquired the rights and obligations under the contract of which the bill of lading was evidence, and could uphold a claim for the delay, and for the reconditioning of the goods.

In the course of his judgment, Scrutton L.J. said:

Lord Selbourne expressed the view that if the bankers did present the bill of lading they might then be liable on the contract contained in the bill of lading. It seems to me that such a case is to be governed by the old law which existed before the passing of the Bills of Lading Act. When a holder of a bill of lading, who has some property in the goods, presents the

[19] At p. 95.

bill of lading and accepts the goods, can there be inferred a contract on each side to perform the terms of the bill of lading? The view that Greer J. has taken is that such a contract can and ought to be implied in this case, and I take the same view.[20]

Notes

The Bills of Lading Act 1855, s. 1, provides that:

Every consignee of goods named in a bill of lading, and every endorsee of a bill of lading to whom the property in the goods therein mentioned shall pass, upon or by reason of such consignment or endorsement, shall have transferred to and vested in him all rights of suit, and be subject to the same liabilities in respect of such goods as if the contract contained in the bill of lading had been made with himself.

The point decided by these two cases is that while the pledgee of a bill of lading does not, as such, acquire the rights or incur the liabilities of the original consignee, and is not, even when the bill of lading is indorsed to him when it is pledged, such an indorsee as is included within section 1 of the Act, yet when he enforces his security he does in doing so step into the shoes of the consignee. The protection given to the banker (among others) by the first decision is much diminished by the second.

Another possible danger to the pledgee of a bill of lading lies in the fact that such bills are normally issued in sets of three. This danger was exemplified in *Glyn Mills Currie & Co.* v. *East and West India Dock Co.*,[21] where the consignees indorsed to the plaintiff bank the first of such a set of bills in consideration of a loan made to them. The consignees later presented to the dock company to whom the cargo had been discharged the second bill in the series, and the dock company in good faith and without notice of the bank's claim delivered the goods to the order of the consignees. Upon the bank's action against the dock company for conversion the House of Lords held that the bank could not maintain any action. The danger can be, and now commonly is, met by the pledgee obtaining the complete set.

In *Barclays Bank Ltd.* v. *Commissioners of Customs and Excise*[22] the bank's security was unsuccessfully challenged with the argument that the bill of lading, charged to the bank after the goods had been unloaded and warehoused, was no longer at that time a document of title capable of being pledged by delivery and indorsement. But Diplock L.J., sitting as an additional judge of the Queen's Bench

---

[20] At p. 596.
[21] (1882) 7 App.Cas. 591.
[22] [1963] 1 Lloyd's Rep. 81.

Division, held that the contract evidenced by a bill of lading is not discharged by the completion of the carriage by sea alone, but continues until the shipowner actually surrenders possession. The bill of lading remains a document of title until that time.

Re David Allester Ltd.

[1922] 2 Ch. 211

Re Hamilton, Young & Co., Ex p: Carter

[1905] 2 K.B. 772

The pledgee does not necessarily cease to be pledgee because he ceases to hold the goods or the documents of title

Facts of Re David Allester Ltd.

David Allester Ltd. were wholesale seed merchants whose banking account was with Barclays Bank. They were in the habit of borrowing from the bank against the pledge of goods; and when it became necessary to sell the goods, they issued to the bank a form of trust receipt, against which the bank released the documents of title. The trust receipt read as follows:

> . . . I/we receive the above [documents or title] in trust on your account, and I/we undertake to hold the goods when received, and their proceeds when sold as your trustees. I/we further undertake to keep this transaction separate from any other and to remit you direct the entire net proceeds as realised, but not less than . . . within . . . days from this date. . . .

Upon David Allester Ltd. going into liquidation, the liquidator took out a summons to determine whether the bank was entitled to priority in respect of its claim to the proceeds of the sale of the goods. He contended that the documents were not valid against him as they had not been registered under section 93 (1) (*c*) and (*e*) of the Companies (Consolidation) Act 1908, which refer to " a mortgage or charge created or evidenced by an instrument which, if executed by an individual, would require registration as a bill of sale," and to " a mortgage or charge on any book debts of the company."

Decision

The court gave judgment in favour of the bank. Astbury J. said:

> With regard to the first point the liquidator contends, though I think without much confidence, that these letters of trust would, if executed by an individual, require registration as bills of sale. He relies on the definition

in the Bills of Sale Act 1878, s. 4, and contends that the letters of trust are "declarations of trust without transfer" within that Act, and that they are not covered by the exception "documents used in the ordinary course of business as proof of the possession or control of goods."

In my judgment these letters of trust do not fall within the bills of sale definition at all. The pledge rights of the bank were complete on the deposit of the bills of lading and other documents of title. These letters of trust are mere records of trust authorities given by the bank and accepted by the company stating the terms on which the pledgors were authorised to realise the goods on the pledgees' behalf. The bank's pledge and its rights as pledgee do not arise under these documents at all, but under the original pledge: see *Ex parte Hubbard*.[23] The bank as pledgee had a right to realise the goods in question from time to time, and it was more convenient to them, as is common practice throughout the country, to allow the realisation to be made by experts, in this case by the pledgors. They were clearly entitled to do this by handing over the bills of lading and other documents of title for realisation on their behalf without in any way affecting their pledge rights: see *North Western Bank* v. *Poynter*.[24]

If I am right about this it is unnecessary to consider the exception in the Bills of Sale Act 1878, s. 4, but if it were necessary to deal with it, it seems to me that *In re Hamilton Young & Co.*[25] is an authority for saying that these letters of trust are documents used in the ordinary course of business as proof of the possession or control of the goods in question. . . .

The second point taken by the liquidator is a more difficult one. . . . The answer however to this point is, that these letters of trust really create no mortgage or charge on book debts in any true sense of the word at all. The bank had its charge before these letters came into existence. The object of these letters of trust was not to give the bank a charge at all, but to enable the bank to realise the goods over which it had a charge in the way in which goods in similar cases have for years and years been realised in the City and elsewhere.[26]

Facts of Re Hamilton Young & Co., ex p. Carter

A mercantile firm in Manchester had periodical advances from the National Bank of India against letters of lien in the following form:

We beg to advise having drawn a cheque on you for £—, which amount please place to the debit of our loan account No. 2, as a loan on the security of goods in course of preparation for shipment to the East. As security for this advance we hold on your account and under lien to you the under-mentioned goods in the hands of . . . as per their receipt enclosed. These goods when ready will be shipped to Calcutta, and the bills of lading duly endorsed will be handed to you, and we then undertake to repay the above advance either in cash or from the proceeds of our drafts . . . to be negotiated

[23] (1886) 17 Q.B.D. 690.
[24] [1895] A.C. 56.
[25] *Infra*.
[26] At pp. 215–218.

by you and secured by the shipping documents representing the above-mentioned goods. . . .

Accompanying such letters of lien the borrowers gave the bank the receipts specified. Upon the bankruptcy of the firm the trustee in bankruptcy contended, *inter alia*, that the letters of lien were bills of sale, and that as they were not in the form set out in, nor registered as required by, the Bills of Sale Acts, they were void. Upon judgment being given for the bank, the trustee appealed.

Decision

The Court of Appeal dismissed the appeal. In his judgment, Cozens-Hardy L.J. said:

The general policy of the Bills of Sale Act, 1878, was not to interfere with ordinary business transactions. In so far as they might be hit by the general words in the definition of " bill of sale," they are taken out by the express exception. I think the letter of lien, coupled with the deposit of the bleachers' receipt, was a " document used in the ordinary course of business as proof of the control of goods " within the meaning of s. 4 of the Act of 1878. It enabled the bank to prevent the bankrupts by injunction from dealing with the goods in any manner inconsistent with the arrangement contemplated by the parties—an arrangement which would result in the handing over of bills of lading when the goods were ready for shipment to Calcutta. It thus gave the bank a " control " of the goods.[27]

Notes [28]

There is always a *prima facie* danger in parting with documents of title which are security for an advance, but the advantages of doing so are so great to a banker, who cannot in practice be also a merchant, that it has become to all intents and purposes essential for him to release the documents to his customer when sale of the goods is necessary: his advance cannot normally be repaid until the goods are sold, and the person best fitted to sell them is the merchant handling them. The trust receipt was evolved to meet this need, and the decision in *Re David Allester Ltd.* is important in that it effectively dispelled one of the attendant dangers of the practice: upon the customer's bankruptcy, the banker is as completely secured as if he had retained the documents.

A comparable decision was that of the Privy Council in *Official Assignee of Madras* v. *Mercantile Bank of India Ltd.*,[29] where the bank

---

[27] At pp. 789–790.

[28] The character and operation of trust receipts and letters of hypothecation are explained in Chorley, *op. cit.* pp. 326 *et seq.*

[29] [1935] A.C. 53.

had been in the habit of making advances against letters of hypothecation backed by railway receipts covering consignments of groundnuts. The goods were taken into possession in warehouses leased to the borrowing firm, but in doing so the bank first released the railway receipts to the firm, who arranged the unloading into the warehouse. At the time of the firm's bankruptcy goods covered by forty-six railway receipts were in transit, and the Official Assignee contended that the bank had no title to the goods, and that until they were reduced into possession in the warehouse the pledge was a pledge of the documents only. The Privy Council held that the receipts were documents of title within the terms of the Indian Contract Act of 1872, that their delivery to the bank constituted a pledge of the goods,[30] and that the pledge was effective even though the bank handed the documents back to the pledgor as trustee. Moreover, (i) even if the bank " did not get a good pledge at law by the delivery of the railway receipts, still that delivery, considered on all the facts of the case, was evidence of a good equitable charge at least as between the immediate parties, even ignoring the accompanying letters of hypothecation " and the assignee in bankruptcy must be subject to the same equity; (ii) apart from the pledge of the goods, the letter of hypothecation constituted a good equitable charge, so as to bind both lender and borrower and the assignee in bankruptcy, who could here have no better right than the insolvent firm could have had.

With regard to the second case above, *Re Hamilton, Young & Co.*, it may be remarked that it would not be safe for the banker to use a novel form of letter of hypothecation, lest it might be held to be outside the ordinary course of mercantile business, and so require registration as a bill of sale. In *R.* v. *Townshend* [31] the defendant, a fruit broker, had advances from his banker against goods consigned to him which were still at sea. He deposited as security endorsed bills of lading, but before making the advance the bank called for a letter of hypothecation. In this letter the defendant undertook to

[30] The judgment of the Privy Council, delivered by Lord Wright, included a valuable analysis of the English law of pledge, and emphasised the distinction, on the present point, between English and Indian law. In English law a pledge of documents (except a bill of lading) is not deemed to be a pledge of the goods themselves. An exception to this rule is made by s. 3 of the Factors Act, which applies only to mercantile agents: pledge of documents by such agents is deemed to be a pledge of the goods. Thus the anomaly arises that an agent can, perhaps in fraud of his principal, do what his principal cannot do—obtain an advance against documents of title without notification to the warehouseman. In practice the banks are understood not to rely on this distinction, but to obtain in all cases registrations of the goods in their own name.

[31] (1884) 15 Cox C.C. 466.

hold the goods in trust for the bankers, and to hand over the proceeds as and when received. It was held that this was a bill of sale within the terms of the Bills of Sale Acts 1878 and 1882, as being a declaration of trust without transfer. It would thus have been unenforceable for lack of registration as a bill of sale, had it not been also held that for another reason it was exempt from the necessity for registration.

The other noteworthy danger in the handling of trust receipts was seen in *Lloyds Bank Ltd.* v. *Bank of America National Trust and Savings Association.*[32] Here the plaintiff bank advanced £57,000 to Strauss & Co. Ltd. against merchandise, took a letter of hypothecation from the company, and surrendered the documents of title against trust receipts. Instead of selling the goods the company pledged the documents with the defendant bank, who advanced against them in good faith. On the company going into liquidation, Lloyds Bank claimed the value of the goods from the Bank of America. The Court of Appeal held that in the circumstances Strauss & Co. had been constituted mercantile agents within section 2 (1) of the Factors Act 1889,[33] and as such were able to make a valid pledge to the Bank of America; and judgment was accordingly given for the Bank of America.

An unusual challenge to a bank on its delivery orders was unsuccessful in *Alicia Hosiery Ltd.* v. *Brown Shipley & Co. Ltd.*[34] Cascade Stockings Ltd. had an overdraft with the defendant bank, and in 1964 they secured a further advance against a shipment of stockings from Italy, the warehousemen being instructed to hold them to the order of the bank. The plaintiff company were prospective purchasers of the stockings, and the bank, upon receiving the agreed purchase price of £11,500, issued a delivery order, but the warehouse refused to release the stockings until they received a further sum of £3,000 in respect of unpaid customs duty and purchase tax. Both Alicia Hosiery and the bank had believed that duty and tax had been paid. The plaintiffs now sought to recover the money paid to the bank on the grounds (i) that the bank was in breach of its agreement to

---

32 [1938] 2 K.B. 147.

33 This subsection provides:

Where a mercantile agent is, with the consent of the owner, in possession of goods or of the documents of title to goods, any sale, pledge, or other disposition of the goods, made by him when acting in the ordinary course of business of a mercantile agent, shall, subject to the provisions of this Act, be as valid as if he were expressly authorised by the owner of the goods to make the same; provided that the person taking under the disposition acts in good faith, and has not at the time of the disposition notice that the person making the disposition has not authority to make the same.

34 [1970] 1 Q.B. 195.

procure delivery to them and (ii) that the company having the right to immediate possession was being denied it by the bank. But Donaldson J. held that there was no contractual relationship between the plaintiffs and the bank: there were rather two contracts, between the bank and its customers, and between the customers and Alicia Hosiery. Moreover, the issue of a delivery order by the bank as pledgees (as contrasted with delivery orders issued by the sellers of goods) did not involve an undertaking by the bank that the goods would be delivered. And on the second point, while the bank was in constructive possession of the goods until the delivery order was issued, this was no longer true after the warehouse had received the order; from then onwards the warehouse held the goods to the order of the purchasers.

GUARANTEES

Hamilton v. Watson

(1845) 12 Cl. & Fin. 109

The contract of guarantee is not one uberrimae fidei

Facts

In 1835 Peter Elles obtained from his bank a loan of £750 against a bond by himself, his father and two other sureties. Upon the death of one of them in the same year, the bank pressed for payment or fresh security, but neither was forthcoming. After continuous pressure by the bank, in 1837 a new bond was signed, in which the appellant joined as surety. The appellant knew nothing of the previous history of the advance. When Elles died, insolvent, and the appellant was called upon to pay to the bank the amount of the loan he contended, *inter alia*, that he was not liable, as the full facts had not been disclosed at the time of his signing.

Decision

The House of Lords found for the respondent (the public officer of the bank). Lord Campbell said:

> Your Lordships must particularly notice what the nature of the contract is. It is a suretyship upon a cash account. Now the question is, what, upon entering into such a contract, ought to be disclosed? And I will venture to say, if your Lordships were to adopt the principles laid down, and contended for by the appellant's counsel here, that you would entirely knock up those transactions in Scotland of giving security upon a cash account, because no

bankers would rest satisfied that they had a security for the advance they made, if, as it is contended, it is essentially necessary that every thing should be disclosed by the creditor that it is material for the surety to know. If such was the rule, it would be indispensably necessary for the bankers to whom the security is to be given, to state how the account had been kept: whether the debtor was in the habit of overdrawing; whether he was punctual in his dealings; whether he performed his promises in an honourable manner; for all these things are extremely material for the surety to know. But unless question be particularly put by the surety to gain this information, I hold that it is quite unnecessary for the creditor, to whom the suretyship is to be given, to make any such disclosure; and I should think that this might be considered as the criterion whether the disclosure ought to be made voluntarily, namely, whether there is anything that might not naturally be expected to take place between the parties who are concerned in the transaction, that is, whether there be a contract between the debtor and the creditor, to the effect that his position shall be different from that which the surety might naturally expect; and, if so, the surety is to see whether that is disclosed to him. But if there be nothing which might not naturally take place between these parties, then, if the surety would guard against particular perils, he must put the question, and he must gain the information which he requires.[35]

Notes

A contract *uberrimae fidei* is one in which one of the parties is presumed to have knowledge not accessible to the other, and is bound to disclose any such knowledge which may affect the other's judgment. The most common of such contracts is that of insurance, which is voidable at the option of the insurer if any fact is withheld the withholding of which might affect his judgment, even though in the particular case it does not do so. It is clearly of the utmost importance to the banker that the guarantee should not be so regarded, as Lord Campbell made clear in his judgment here quoted.

But the fact that so early as 1845 the position as to disclosure had been so clearly laid down by Lord Campbell has not prevented a number of sureties from seeking to escape from their liability on the ground that they had not been told the material circumstances. Thus, in *National Provincial Bank of England* v. *Glanusk*,[36] Lord Glanusk had guaranteed the overdraft of his brother-in-law, who was also his agent, at the plaintiffs' Crickhowell branch. The guarantee was on the face of it for all moneys which might be owing to the plaintiffs, but the guarantor contended that there was an antecedent agreement that it should cover only the estate account, and that the bank knew, and should have informed him, that his

[35] At p. 118.

[36] [1913] 3 K.B. 335.

brother-in-law was using the overdraft for purposes not contemplated by him. It appeared that the branch manager was informed by his customer that the guarantor knew of the cheque in question, and Horridge J. held that, even had it been proved that the bank had been suspicious of the transaction, they owed no duty to communicate their suspicions to the guarantor.

In *Westminster Bank* v. *Cond* [37] the issue was even simpler. There the customer had an overdraft guaranteed by two sureties and, wishing to increase his borrowing, was told that he must first produce additional security. The defendant agreed to guarantee the account for £300, and in an interview with the branch manager inquired whether the latter considered his customer's prospects good. The manager replied that in view of his customer's salary he did not think he would have difficulty in paying off the overdraft. The defendant did not ask the manager whether there was any existing overdraft, and the manager did not volunteer the information. Upon the customer's later insolvency the defendant refused to pay under the guarantee, contending that the manager owed him a duty to disclose that there was a previous overdraft, even though he did not ask him for that particular information. Tucker J. held that there was no such duty.

Again, in *Cooper* v. *National Provincial Bank Ltd.*[38] the plaintiff contended that the bank should have told him that (*a*) the husband of the person guaranteed was an undischarged bankrupt who had (*b*) been given power to draw on the account; and (*c*) the account had been irregularly conducted in that some dozen cheques had been " stopped " by the customer. Lawrence L.J., basing his judgment on the judgment of Lord Campbell quoted above, found that there was nothing in the contract between the bank and its customer which could be regarded as unusual, and that there was therefore no duty of disclosure.

The guarantors in these cases were probably encouraged to seek to avoid their liabilities by the fact that it is not easy to define what exactly is unusual conduct, between the banker and his customer, that would require disclosure to a proposing guarantor; and every guarantor hopes, when he is called upon to pay, that there may be something in the previous history of the account which needed such disclosure. In *Royal Bank of Scotland* v. *Greenshields* [39] the law on this point was outlined in terms which are themselves clear, but which emphasise the difficulty in which the bank manager may find himself. Lord Mackenzie said:

---

[37] (1940) 46 Com.Cas. 60, *ante*, p. 145.
[38] [1945] 2 All E.R. 641.
[39] 1914 S.C. 259.

> It is well settled law that there is no obligation upon a bank agent to disclose the position of his customer's account unless he is asked a specific question which imposes that obligation upon him or unless circumstances emerge which put upon him the duty of making a full disclosure. The circumstances may be either that he volunteers a statement which is only half the truth, in which case the cautioner [guarantor] is entitled to say "I was misled; I was entitled to assume that you were disclosing the whole truth," or . . . if the intending cautioner makes a statement to the bank agent, or in his presence, which plainly shows that he is entering into a transaction in an entire misapprehension of the facts of the case, then the bank agent equally would be under an obligation, arising out of the circumstances of the case, to prevent the cautioner from being misled.[40]

In *Lloyds Bank Ltd.* v. *Harrison* [41] the customer was in difficulties and the bank had insisted that he should for six months accept only such business as would reduce his stock. The guarantor contended that this was a material and unusual fact which should have been disclosed to him when he signed the guarantee upon which this action was brought. The Court of Appeal unanimously dismissed the guarantor's appeal. In his judgment, Sargent L.J. said:

> It must be remembered that in this case, as in most cases, the surety is approached in the first instance by the principal debtor, and is brought to the bank as a person who is willing to accept a certain responsibility in connection with the banking affairs of the principal debtor. Speaking generally, I should think the bank would be wrong in disclosing, without some very special direction by the customer, the whole particulars of the state of account of that customer to the surety. . . . Then, taking the test of *Hamilton* v. *Watson*,[42] which is undoubtedly the leading case on the subject, Lord Campbell pointed out very clearly what an extraordinary and unpractical obligation would be cast upon bankers if they were to be forced to disclose to a person becoming a surety for a cash account all the circumstances of the business relations of the customer whose account was proposed to be guaranteed. Of course, in every case there must be a large number of particular circumstances which do not occur in other cases, but, . . . there is no obligation on the banker to disclose anything that might naturally take place between the parties.[43]

Paget suggests [44] that the customer, in seeking the guarantee, has given implied permission for replies to be given, when the intending guarantor asks direct questions of the bank manager, but it may well be that even here the manager should obtain his customer's express authority before answering the questions.[45]

---

[40] At p. 271.
[41] (1925) 4 L.D.B. 12.
[42] *Supra.*
[43] At p. 216.
[44] *Op. cit.* p. 601.
[45] *Cf. ante*, pp. 6 *et seq.* concerning disclosure generally. As to guarantees generally, see Chorley, *op. cit.* pp. 332 *et seq.*

Mackenzie v. Royal Bank of Canada

[1934] A.C. 468

Misrepresentation, whether innocent or otherwise, may avoid the guarantee

Facts

In 1920 the plaintiff, Mrs. Mackenzie, hypothecated to the defendant bank certain shares to the value of $10,000, as security for borrowing by Mackenzie Ltd., a company in which her husband was interested. The company later became bankrupt, and in the proceedings that followed, under Canadian bankruptcy law, the bank took over such of the company's property as had been charged to them, and the debt was thereby discharged. In the meantime, however, the bank had also taken a letter signed by the plaintiff and her husband, which referred to the proposed arrangements in bankruptcy and added: ". . . we hereby agree that your so doing shall not in any way release us from our obligation under guarantees to the bank, nor shall our personal securities be in any way affected until the amount due to the bank by Mackenzie Ltd. has been actually paid."

The company was now reconstructed, and the bank and Mackenzie required the plaintiff to guarantee the borrowing of the new company, the bank manager and Mackenzie assuring her that her shares were still bound to the bank, but that this was an opportunity of regaining them. After she had signed the guarantee and the accompanying form of hypothecation she was asked to take to a solicitor a form for him to sign, stating that he had independently advised her. This the solicitor signed, although in fact he had not so advised her.

The present action was for recovery of the shares, the plaintiff alleging that she had been induced to hypothecate them by misrepresentation. The trial judge gave judgment for her, which was reversed on appeal. She now appealed to the Privy Council.

Decision

The Privy Council allowed the appeal. Lord Atkin said:

> It may very well be that in procuring the plaintiff's signature to this document [the letter quoted above] the bank had in mind to extend their obligations so as to cover a contemplated reconstruction. If so they failed in their purpose, for it appears to their Lordships that the terms of this letter cannot be construed to give any right to the bank over securities once the debt had been discharged in the manner above mentioned. . . .

A contract of guarantee, like any other contract, is liable to be avoided if induced by material misrepresentation of an existing fact, even if made innocently. . . . The evidence conclusively establishes a misrepresentation by the bank that the plaintiff's shares were still bound to the bank with the necessary inference, whether expressed or not, and their Lordships accept the plaintiff's evidence that it was expressed, that the shares were already lost, and that the guarantee of the new company offered the only means of salving them. It does not seem to admit of doubt that such a representation made as to the plaintiff's private rights and depending upon transactions in bankruptcy, of the full nature of which she had not been informed, was a representation of fact. That it was material is beyond discussion. It consequently follows that the plaintiff was at all times, on ascertaining the true position, entitled to avoid the contract and recover her securities.[46]

Notes

The law of misrepresentation and mistake in contract (and a guarantee is merely one form of contract) is somewhat involved, and is best studied in the framework of general contract law.[47] It may be said here that a misrepresentation of fact, whether innocent or fraudulent, makes the contract voidable at the option of the person misled, while if it is fraudulent an action for damages may also lie. Mistake, if it goes to the root of the contract, may make it null *ab initio*; and the effect of misrepresentation is often, of course, extremely difficult to distinguish from that of mistake.

It is essential for the banker that the guarantee should not be vitiated either by misrepresentation or by mistake. It is not always easy for him to observe his duty to his customer and at the same time avoid any suspicion of misleading the surety, and the cases dealt with in the preceding heading show how often the surety, at any rate, considers that he has been misled.

In *Stone* v. *Compton* [48] the defendant became surety for an advance made by the plaintiff banker to a customer. The misrepresentation here was in a recital in the mortgage entered into by the debtor, which suggested that at the time of the advance the customer did not owe the bank anything, although in fact there was a considerable advance outstanding, for the clearance of which the new advance was partly designed. The mortgage deed was read in the presence of the defendant before he had bound himself, and it was held that as a result of this misrepresentation he was not liable.

---

[46] At pp. 473, 475–476.

[47] *Cf. e.g. Slater's Mercantile Law* (16th ed.), Chap. 6.

[48] (1838) 5 Bing N.C. 142.

For many years *Carlisle and Cumberland Banking Co.* v. *Bragg* [49] stood as warning of the danger of allowing the guarantee form to be taken away by the customer in order that he may obtain the signature of the surety to it. In that case the customer gave a form of guarantee to the defendant and, fraudulently representing that it was an insurance paper, obtained his signature. The customer then forged the signature of a witness and returned the form to the bank, who allowed him the advance he sought. The Court of Appeal held that the defendant had signed in complete ignorance of the nature of the transaction, and that as he owed no duty of care to the bank he was not bound as against them. This decision was expressly overruled in *Saunders* v. *Anglia Building Society*,[50] when the House of Lords redefined the scope of the principle of *non est factum*.

The effect of this important decision (often cited as *Gallie* v. *Lee*, the parties to the action in the lower courts) is that there is a heavy burden of proof on the person relying on the principle; that there must be a fundamental difference between what he signed and what he thought he signed; and, perhaps most important, that he must show that he acted carefully. Only in quite exceptional circumstances can any person of full age and understanding disavow his signature so as to prejudice the rights of an innocent third party.

In *United Dominions Trust Ltd.* v. *Western*,[51] the Court of Appeal closed a possible loophole in the *Saunders* ruling when they refused to accept the defendant's argument that signing a document in blank is of different effect from signing a completed form: this was neither good sense nor good law. If another person is authorised to complete the form the signatory takes his chance of the blanks being filled in fraudulently.[52]

It is to be noted that the overruling of the *Carlisle and Cumberland Banking Co.* decision on the particular point of the carelessness of the signatory lessens but does not remove the danger of allowing the customer to take the guarantee away for the signatory to sign, a practice that is forbidden normally by the banks.

A guarantee is a contract which is strictly construed by the courts, and it is important that its terms should be carefully observed. In *Burton* v. *Gray*,[53] for example, the plaintiff's brother had taken to his banker certain securities belonging to the plaintiff. He had shown

---

49 [1911] 1 K.B. 489.

50 [1970] 3 All E.R. 961.

51 [1976] 2 W.L.R. 64.

52 The plea of *non est factum* was rejected in the unusual circumstances of *Credit Lyonnais* v. *P. T. Barnard & Associates* [1976] 1 Lloyd's Rep. 557 where the defendants' managing director, knowing no French, accepted two bills of exchange drawn in that language in the belief that they were receipts. Mocatta J., applying the *Saunders* rule, held that the defendants had not shown that they acted carefully.

53 (1873) 8 Ch. App. 932.

the banker a letter purporting to be signed by the plaintiff and charging the securities " in consideration of your lending F. Burton the sum of £1,000 for seven days from this date." The banker allowed the brother to overdraw his account in a series of cheques which in aggregate were less than £1,000, and it was held that as no loan of £1,000 had been made, and as no term had been assigned to the overdraft that had been granted, the plaintiff was not bound, and the securities must be released.

Another rule of contract law to which particular attention has to be paid in dealing with guarantees is that relating to consideration. This is essential to the validity of the guarantee, unless it is under seal; and if a guarantee is given for an advance already granted it is essential that there should be some such consideration as an extension of time or forbearance to sue.

A case demonstrating the necessity for consideration for a guarantee not under seal, as well as, incidentally, the fact that there must be no misrepresentation, is *Provincial Bank of Ireland* v. *Donnell*.[54] Here a wife guaranteed the payment of premiums on a life policy of her husband's which was charged to the bank as security for an advance on his account. The guarantee was expressed to be in consideration for advances " heretofore made or that may hereafter be made from time to time." In fact the bank had no intention at the time of making any further advances, but the wife was not told this, nor was she informed of the state of the account. It was held that the existing debt could not form the consideration necessary to support the guarantee, that there was therefore no effective consideration, and that as a result the guarantee failed.

The banker needs to ensure that the guarantee is not weakened by any dispute as to the amount of the debt that has been guaranteed, and the guarantee normally includes a " conclusive evidence " clause, by which the guarantor agrees to accept as conclusive, in the event of demand being made, the bank's statement of the amount due. *Bache & Co. (London) Ltd.* v. *Banque Vernes et Commerciale de Paris* [55] was unusual in that there it was a bank that challenged the effectiveness of such a clause. The defendant bank had guaranteed their customers' contract with the plaintiffs, London commodity brokers, and upon being called upon to pay under the guarantee (which contained a " conclusive evidence " clause) argued (*a*) that their customers disputed the amount due, and (*b*) that in any case the clause was against public policy in purporting to oust the jurisdiction of the courts. The Court of Appeal rejected both arguments. There was no public policy objection to the clause; and

[54] [1934] N.I. 33.

[55] [1973] 2 Lloyd's Rep. 437.

if the figures proved wrong the bank's customers had an action against the brokers and the bank could claim indemnity against their customers. And Lord Denning added:

> . . . this commercial practice . . . is only acceptable because the bankers or brokers who insert them are known to be honest and reliable men of business who are most unlikely to make a mistake. Their standing is so high that their word is to be trusted. So much so that a notice of default given by a bank or a broker must be honoured. It ranks as equivalent to, if not higher than, the certificate of an artibrator or engineer in a building contract.[56]

Bank of Montreal v. Stuart and Another
[1911] A.C. 120

The effect of undue influence upon the guarantee

Facts

Mrs. Stuart was a woman of considerable private means, who, being a confirmed invalid, left the management of her affairs to her husband. He was the president of the Maritime Sulphite Company and, at first, a man of substance. The company was not successful, however, and in 1891 owed $275,000 to the Bank of Montreal. In the ten years that followed Mrs. Stuart signed guarantees of the company's account amounting to $125,000 and also assigned certain property to the bank to meet the company's indebtedness, but in 1901 the company went into liquidation.

The negotiations regarding the guarantees had been carried on by a Mr. Bruce, who was a director and secretary of the company, solicitor to the bank, and legal adviser to Stuart. He had had no communication with Mrs. Stuart until she came to his office to sign the first guarantee.

Mrs. Stuart brought this action to set aside the guarantees and assignments, alleging that her husband, under whose influence she had acted, was the agent of the bank, that she received no consideration for the guarantees and assignments, and that the bank knew that she had received no independent advice. The husband was later joined as a party, and supported his wife's allegations. In her evidence Mrs. Stuart denied that any pressure had been exerted upon her, and said that she had acted of her own free will, and

---

[56] At p. 440.

would have scorned to consult anybody in the matter. The lower court and the Court of Appeal for Ontario found for the bank, but the Supreme Court of Canada reversed this decision, and the bank now further appealed.

Decision

The Judicial Committee of the Privy Council dismissed the bank's appeal. In their judgment, delivered by Lord Macnaghten, they remarked that Mrs. Stuart's statement under cross-examination that she acted of her own free will merely showed how deep-rooted and lasting the influence of her husband was; and later said:

> [Mr. Bruce] knew that all Mr. Stuart's means were embarked in the company, and no one knew better than he that unless some one came forward and guaranteed the bank in respect of further advances his own interest and the interest of his associates as shareholders were worth nothing, and his claim as a creditor in all probability equally valueless. He and his associates other than Mr. Stuart were unwilling to risk their own moneys. Mr. Stuart had no money to risk. The game Mr. Stuart was playing was desperate. It was the throw of a gambler with money not his own. No man in his senses with any regard to the interest of Mrs. Stuart or the interest of Mr. Stuart could have advised Mrs. Stuart to act as her husband told her to do. The bank left everything to Mr. Bruce and the bank must be answerable for what he did. . . . Mr. Bruce undertook a duty towards Mrs. Stuart, but he left her in a worse position than she would have been if he had not interfered at all. His course was plain. He ought to have endeavoured to advise the wife and to place her position and the consequences of what she was doing fully and plainly before her. Probably if not certainly she would have rejected his intervention. And then he ought to have gone to the husband and insisted on the wife being separately advised, and if that was an impossibility owing to the implicit confidence which Mrs. Stuart reposed in her husband, he ought to have retired from the business altogether and told the bank why he did so.[57]

Notes

Undue influence may avoid the contract of guarantee as it may any other contract,[58] and while the bank will suffer in the failure of a guarantee in such circumstances, it will not always be in a position even to suspect the existence of the influence. In practice the most frequent examples of the danger have been found in the guarantee by wives of their husbands' accounts, but single women as well as married could usually claim with more success than men that they had been unduly influenced, and there are other circumstances which make independent advice desirable—for example, the

[57] At pp. 138–139.

[58] *Cf. Lloyds Bank Ltd.* v. *Bundy, ante*, p. 14 where undue influence is seen shading into the recognition of a special relationship between banker and customer.

guarantee by a client of a solicitor's account. For many years most of the banks had a rule that all women guarantors should be separately advised. In earlier editions of this book the rule was said to cause " some irritation to women who are themselves well versed in business," and this, for a long time before the Sex Discrimination Act 1975, had become increasingly an understatement. Now the banks seek to ensure that guarantors of either sex should understand the nature of the commitment they are entering into. The banker can take precautions only when the circumstances are known to him, but where there is any doubt the guarantor should have independent advice: for although, as was suggested in the *Stuart* judgment, such separate advice may prove in practice to be quite ineffective, the fact that it has been given makes it impossible for a guarantor later to say that she (or he) had no opportunity of realising the effect of what was being done.

In *Mackenzie* v. *Royal Bank of Canada* [59] undue influence was a second issue and, although the Privy Council decided the case on misrepresentation, there is an interesting passage in the judgment which emphasises the importance of the independent advice being given before the signing of the guarantee:

> If it had been incumbent on the bank to prove that the lady had had independent advice, their Lordships would have had the greatest difficulty in coming to the conclusion that the bank had discharged the onus. Independent advice to be of any value must be given before the transaction, for the question is as to the will of the party at the time of entering into the disputed transaction. Advice given after the event when the supposed contracting party is already bound is given under entirely different circumstances, with a different position presented to the minds both of the adviser and his client.[60]

Re Sherry, London & County Banking Company v. Terry

(1884) 25 Ch. 692

The death of the guarantor

Facts

John Sherry, who died in 1880, had guaranteed the account of his son-in-law, Edward Terry, with the Sandwich branch of the plaintiff bank. When they received notice of the guarantor's death, the bank ruled off Terry's account, then overdrawn £677 17s. 2d.,

[59] *Ante*, p. 239.
[60] At pp. 474–475.

and opened a new one, through which Terry's later transactions passed. In 1881 Terry filed a liquidation petition, and the bank sought to recover against the estate of Sherry. It was contended by the executors that breaking the account was ineffective, and that the guarantee for " all moneys which shall at any time be due " covered the whole account; but, the guarantee terminating at death, fresh advances could not be covered by it, and payments into the account, under the rule in *Clayton's* case,[61] went in reduction of the overdraft. The bank did not dispute the termination of the guarantee, but claimed that the appropriation of payments effected by the breaking of the account was a bar to the operation of the rule in *Clayton's* case.

Decision

The Court of Appeal found for the bank. In his judgment, the Earl of Selborne L.C. said:

> Then, is there an implied contract [to appropriate payments received subsequently to the termination of the guarantee towards the secured or guaranteed debt]? A surety is undoubtedly and not unjustly the object of some favour both at law and in equity, and I do not know that the rules of law and equity differ on the subject. It is an equity which enters into our system of law, that a man who makes himself liable for another person's debt is not to be prejudiced by any dealings without his consent between the secured creditor and the principal debtor. If, therefore, it could be shewn that what has been done here was done without the consent of the surety in prejudice of an implied contract in his favour, I quite agree that he ought not to suffer from it. But there being no express contract, on what ground is it to be said that there is an implied contract? I am unable to find any such contract, unless we are to hold that the mere fact of suretyship takes away from the principal debtor and the creditor those powers which they would otherwise have of appropriating payments which are not subject to any particular contract with the surety.[62]

Notes

It cannot be said with any certainty whether a guarantee is in fact determined by the death of the guarantor, but it is generally assumed that notice of the death operates as notice of determination [63] and it is for this reason that the decision in *Re Sherry* is important to the banker; had the court decided otherwise, and ruled that the breaking of the account was ineffective, he would not be able to continue business with his customer without the danger of

---

[61] *Ante*, p. 143.

[62] At pp. 703–704.

[63] *Cf.* Chorley, *op. cit.* p. 342 and Paget, *op. cit.* p. 613 for a discussion of the point.

losing the benefit of the guarantee as payments into the account were set off against the indebtedness at the date of death.

It must be noted, however, that there was no argument in *Re Sherry* on the question of the termination of the guarantee, and all three judgments were therefore based on the assumption that it had in fact terminated. It had been suggested, for the executors, that there was no difference between breaking an account during the guarantor's lifetime so as to deprive him of the benefit of subsequent payments in, and breaking it upon his death. The court distinguished the two on the assumption that the guarantee was terminated by the death, and so, in the unlikely event of its ever being decided that there is no such determination, the executors' suggestion might be made again.

In practice, of course, the point can be covered in the bank's guarantee forms by a provision that the guarantee shall be a continuing one notwithstanding the death of the guarantor, and a reservation to the bank of the right to break the account; while it is the practice of the banks to notify to the executors the existence of the liability.

In *Bradford Old Bank Ltd.* v. *Sutcliffe*,[64] it was held by Lawrence J., and not disputed on appeal, that notice of the lunacy of a guarantor determines the guarantee.

It may be added that, when the guarantee is joint and several, neither the death [65] nor the mental disorder [66] of one surety ends the continuing liability of his co-sureties. And in *Egbert* v. *National Crown Bank* [67] it was held that a joint and several guarantee which was to continue " until the undersigned . . . shall have given the bank notice in writing to make no further advances . . ." was not determined by notice by one of the guarantors alone; Lord Dunedin said that had the intention been that notice by one guarantor should determine the guarantee, " nothing would have been easier than to express such an intention by such words as ' all or any of the undersigned.' "

---

[64] *Post*, p. 250. At 3 L.D.B. 195, the case is discussed wrongly as one concerning the lunacy of the principal debtor.

[65] *Beckett* v. *Addyman* (1882) 9 Q.B.D. 783.

[66] *Bradford Old Bank Ltd.* v. *Sutcliffe, supra.*

[67] [1918] A.C. 903.

Garrard v. James

[1925] 1 Ch. 616

How far irregular borrowings can be effectively guaranteed

Facts

The plaintiff advanced to the company of which the two defendants were directors the sum of £1,500, and accepted transfers of the company's preference shares to this amount, the company agreeing that should the plaintiff so require them they would arrange for the repurchase of his shares at par, and the two defendants joining as sureties guaranteeing the performance by the company of its part of the agreement. Later the plaintiff called upon the company to implement its undertaking, but the company, failing to find a purchaser for the shares, contended that to fulfil the agreement they would have to purchase their own shares, which would be *ultra vires*. The plaintiff accordingly brought this action against the two sureties, who pleaded that their guarantee was only in the event of default by the company, and " default " meant not doing what they could legally do.

Decision

It was held that the sureties were liable. In his judgment, Lawrence J. said:

Unfortunately the company was attempting to contract in a way which, it is now admitted, was beyond its powers. It is important to observe that the company committed no statutory offence by entering into the agreement and that the transaction was not malum in se. The only result was that the agreement could not be enforced against the company. The defendants, however, as an essential part of the transaction, jointly and severally covenanted with the plaintiff (1) to guarantee the full and proper performance by the company of the covenants on its part contained in the agreement, and (2) in the event of default being made by the company under its covenants, to accept liability and to guarantee the payments to the plaintiff in such a manner, as if the covenants contained in cl. 4 of the agreement had been repeated in the covenants with the defendants. In my opinion, the true meaning of the covenant on the part of the defendants is that, if the company does not perform its obligations under the agreement, the defendants will themselves perform those obligations. The first branch of the covenant is, in my judgment, sufficient to entitle the plaintiff to succeed in this action. But I also think that the second branch applies to the facts of this case. The word " default " is a word of wide general import, and includes " failure " and " omission." It seems to me immaterial whether the failure or omission by the company to perform its obligations is attributable to its financial inability or to statutory disability, as the liability of the defendants arises, whatever may be the cause of failure. The gist of the bargain entered into by the defendants, in my opinion, was: "If you, the plaintiff, will advance this £1,500, we, the defendants, will pay you, if the company does not pay." [68]

Notes

In *Coutts & Co.* v. *Browne-Lecky* [69] it was held that the guarantee of an advance to an infant was ineffective because the advance was itself void, and there has been some doubt whether a borrowing which is *ultra vires* a limited company can be any more effectively guaranteed than a borrowing which is entirely void. It should be noted at once that either type of advance can be brought within the contract of guarantee: the guarantee form in the *Browne-Lecky* case did include a provision purporting to cover *ultra vires* borrowing by companies, and other bank guarantee forms contain clauses which very probably would have covered Coutts Bank. One clause of this kind is quoted in *Barclays Bank Ltd.* v. *Trevanion.*[70]

It may be pointed out that the effect of such clauses, whether expressly as in the example quoted or not, is to add to the secondary liability of the guarantor a primary liability more like that in the contract of indemnity; while of course the *Browne-Lecky* decision, which, as was said in the earlier reference to it,[71] has been much criticised, can anyhow be avoided by the use of a straightforward contract of indemnity.

Although the forms of guarantee, steadily growing longer, close successive stable doors after successive escapes, the law is not fundamentally altered, and the cases which caused the changes are still important. *Garrard* v. *James* is an example in the other direction, for it goes far to negative a danger which the banks have largely met in their forms. Their labour has probably saved them from difficulty, nevertheless, for this is a decision of a court of first instance, and the higher courts might take a different view of the matter.

It must be remembered that, whatever the position as to the guarantee of void or irregular borrowings, there is no difficulty regarding transactions which are *illegal* in themselves—the guarantee in such cases is quite ineffective. In *Swan* v. *Bank of Scotland,*[72] which was cited by Lawrence J. in *Garrard* v. *James*, and distinguished, the bank allowed its customer to draw unstamped documents and had thus "made itself a party to an arrangement with the customer under which he would not only commit a fraud on the revenue, but

---

[68] At pp. 622–623.
[69] *Ante*, p. 164.
[70] *Post*, p. 254.
[71] *Ante*, p. 166.
[72] (1836) 10 Bli. (N.S.) 627.

would also do acts which were not only expressly forbidden and made void by the statute, but which involved both the customer and the bank in penalties." It remains to be seen whether such a clause as the one referred to above would protect the bank even in such circumstances as these.

Bradford Old Bank v. Sutcliffe

[1918] 2 K.B. 833

Demand under a guarantee

Facts

The defendant, Frank Sutcliffe, and his brother Albert, directors of Samuel Sutcliffe & Co. Ltd., in 1894 gave a joint and several guarantee as security for the company's borrowings from its bankers. In August, 1898, the defendant became insane and the bank received formal notice of this fact in December, 1899. The company's two accounts continued as before. In 1912 the bank demanded payment of the company's indebtedness, and enforced the debentures held as part security; and in 1915 the present action was commenced against the committee in lunacy of Frank Sutcliffe. The defendants contended, *inter alia*, that the claim was now barred by the Statute of Limitations. When in the Court of first instance the decision went against them they appealed.

Decision

The Court of Appeal dismissed the appeal. On the present point Pickford L.J. said:

But another answer was given by the plaintiffs—i.e., that the cause of action did not accrue until demand by them and that no demand had been made until after the realisation of the debentures in 1912, less than six years before the beginning of the action. This seems to depend upon the construction of the document. . . . It was argued on behalf of the defendant that the words " on demand " should be neglected because the money was due, and therefore a demand was unnecessary and added nothing to the liability. This proposition is true in the case of what has been called a direct liability—for example, for money lent. There the liability exists as soon as the loan is made, and a promise to pay on demand adds nothing to it, as in the case of a promissory note for the amount payable on demand, and the words " on demand " may be neglected. It has, however, been held long ago that this doctrine does not apply to what has been called a collateral promise or collateral debt, and I think that a promise by a surety to pay the original debt is such a collateral promise or creates a collateral debt.

The only question, therefore, is whether on the construction of the guarantee the parties meant the words " on demand " to mean what they say. I cannot doubt that they did.[73]

Notes

This decision may be compared with that in *Lloyds Bank Ltd.* v. *Margolis*,[74] which turned on demand under a mortgage.

In an earlier case, *Parr's Banking Company Ltd.* v. *Yates*,[75] it was held, also by the Court of Appeal, that in a case of a guarantee that had no demand clause, in the words of Vaughan Williams L.J. " the right of action on each item of the account arose as soon as that item became due and was not paid, and the statute ran from that date in each case." The decision was criticised at the time,[76] and it might be that in similar circumstances today the matter would be viewed differently [77]; but in practice a demand clause is of course included in all bank guarantee forms.

The breaking of the account, which was in question in *Westminster Bank Ltd.* v. *Cond*,[78] was not discussed in the Court of Appeal in the present case, although one of the defences, that credits to the current account after the notice of lunacy should be considered to have paid off the indebtedness on the loan account, raised a cognate point. The court rejected the argument, Pickford L.J. saying, " The facts clearly show that the accounts must be kept distinct . . . If it were otherwise the company would be extremely hampered in its business, for it could never safely draw on the current account so long as the credit balance did not exceed the amount due on the loan account. The effect of this arrangement is that payments to the credit of the current account are appropriated to that account and cannot be taken in reduction of the loan account." [79]

Offord v. Davies and Another

(1862) 12 C.B. (N.S.) 748

In the absence of an express stipulation to the contrary in the contract, a guarantor can terminate his liability by notice

---

[73] At p. 840. [74] *Post*, p. 258.
[75] [1898] 2 Q.B. 460.
[76] *Cf.* Sir John Paget's comment at 1 L.D.B. 278.
[77] *Cf. post*, p. 259.
[78] *Ante*, pp. 145, 237.
[79] The current account was not in fact broken, and it was held in the lower court and not disputed on appeal that the small overdraft at the date of notice of lunacy was, by the rule in *Clayton's* case, paid off by the subsequent credits to the account.

Facts

The defendants guaranteed the payment of certain bills to be discounted by the plaintiff, the guarantee being expressed to be " for the space of 12 calendar months." The defendants subsequently countermanded the guarantee, but bills were discounted after the countermand and some of them were not paid; and the plaintiff claimed the amount of the unpaid bills from the defendants, contending that a guarantee in such terms could not be cancelled, but must be effective for 12 months.

Decision

It was held that there was no liability on the defendants under the guarantee. Erle C.J. said:

> This promise by itself creates no obligation. It is in effect conditioned to be binding if the plaintiff acts upon it, either to the benefit of the defendants, or to the detriment of himself. But, until the condition has been at least in part fulfilled, the defendants have the power of revoking it. In the case of a simple guarantee for a proposed loan, the right of revocation before the proposal has been acted upon did not appear to be disputed. Then, are the rights of the parties affected either by the promise being expressed to be for twelve months, or by the fact that some discounts had been made before that in question, and repaid? We think not.[80]

Notes

The effect of a contract of guarantee, like that of all other contracts, depends primarily upon its expressed terms, and the rights of the parties as to termination must be sought first in the guarantee form used. Thus some bank guarantees provide for a period of notice by the guarantor, and a bank using such a form could not, of course, contend that the guarantor could not terminate his liability by giving such notice—while it is to be noted that the termination thus effected is anyhow only for further advances; any loan already made under the guarantee is a continuing liability.

It may be added, although the point is not usually of significance to bankers, that it has been held that a guarantee is not revocable " when the consideration for it is indivisible, so to speak, and moves from the person to whom the guarantee is given once for all, as in the case of the consideration being the giving or conferring an office or employment upon any person whose integrity is guaranteed." [81] Of more importance to bankers is the decision in *Westminster Bank Ltd.* v. *Sassoon*,[82] where on a guarantee form signed in July 1924

[80] At p. 757.
[81] *Re Crace, Balfour* v. *Crace* [1902] 1 Ch. 733.
[82] (January, 1927) 48 J.I.B. 4.

were added the words: "This guarantee will expire on June 30 1925." The Court of Appeal held that in spite of these words the guarantee was a continuing one. Nevertheless, bankers should and do avoid altering or adding to the bank's standard forms.

In *Thomas* v. *Nottingham Football Club* [83] the plaintiff had guaranteed the club's overdraft with Lloyds Bank. In 1967 he gave notice to the bank to determine the guarantee, and thereafter he called upon the club to free him from his liability by paying off the advance guaranteed. Under the terms of the guarantee his liability was to arise when demand was made, and here the bank had made no demand, so the club argued that he was not entitled to the declaration he sought—that he had a right in equity to require the club to free him from his liability by paying off the overdraft. But Goff J. held that he was so entitled "it being quite unreasonable" (in the words of a judgment of 1683) "that a man should always have such a cloud hang over him."

Perry v. National Provincial Bank of England Ltd.

[1910] 1 Ch. 464

The release of the principal debtor will discharge the guarantor, unless the contract of guarantee provides otherwise

Facts

The plaintiff, who had guaranteed an advance by the defendant bank to Perry Brothers (a firm in which he was not a partner) had mortgaged certain of his property as additional security. The mortgages all contained clauses providing that the bank might without affecting their rights "vary, exchange or release any other securities held . . . and accept compositions from and make any arrangements with the debtors." Later the firm became insolvent, and a scheme was arranged to form a company to take over the business, the creditors receiving debentures in the company.

The bank applied for a share of the debenture stock, basing their claim on the amount of the indebtedness less the value of the firm's securities held. No allowance was made for the plaintiff's securities. The form of application for the stock expressly stated that such stock was issued in full settlement of the applicant's claim against Perry Brothers.

In due course, the interest on the debentures not having been paid, and the firm's securities being not expected to realise the

[83] [1972] Ch. 596.

figure at which they had been valued, the bank expressed their intention of selling the property mortgaged. Perry thereupon brought this action for a declaration that there was now nothing outstanding on the mortgages.

Decision

It was held by the Court of Appeal that Perry's property was released as to the amount of debenture stock received by the bank, but that, as to the money still owing, his property still remained liable, notwithstanding that the principal debtor was completely discharged.

In the course of his judgment, Cozens-Hardy M.R. said:

The position is this: £1,630, part of the original debt due on Perry Brothers' account, is still unpaid, and for that balance there is a security held by the bank. That gives rise to the important point which has been argued before us. It is said, " Even if that be so, still there can be no right as against the surety, because by reason of this arrangement with Perry Brothers you have released Perry Brothers, and there can be no suretyship after the release of the principal debtor." But I think the answer to that is that it is perfectly possible for a surety to contract with a creditor in the suretyship instrument that notwithstanding any composition, release, or arrangement, the surety shall remain liable although the principal does not.[84]

Notes

It must again be emphasised that the effect of a guarantee depends on the form of words in which the contract is drawn up. The decision in *Perry* v. *National Provincial Bank* depended, as far as the release of the principal debtor was concerned, entirely on the wording of the contract. *Barclays Bank Ltd.* v. *Trevanion* [85] provided an example of a form of words held not to cover the facts the bank wished to make them cover. The bank had released two of three guarantors upon their entering into an arrangement to pay a fixed sum each; the third, the defendant in the case, failed to come to terms, and was sued by the bank, under the guarantee. The contract of guarantee being joint as well as several, the release of some of the guarantors would discharge the others in the absence of a clause expressly permitting it, and the bank contended that certain clauses in their guarantee form did so permit, especially one which read:

As a separate and independent stipulation . . . I/we agree that all sums of money which may not be recoverable from the undersigned on the footing of a guarantee whether by reason of any legal limitation disability

[84] At p. 473.

[85] (1933) *The Banker* 98.

or incapacity on or of the principal or any other fact or circumstance and whether known to you or not shall nevertheless be recoverable from the undersigned as sole or principal debtor(s) in respect thereof. . . .

It was held that the bank were not protected by this form of words; and it appears that they did not appeal against the decision. It will be noticed that this clause does not refer to the co-sureties at all.

In the absence of any express clause (which in fact is now always present in bank guarantees) the effect of the release of some of several co-sureties depends upon the rights of the remaining sureties. If the guarantee is joint and several the release of some discharges the others, " the joint suretyship of the others being part of the consideration of the contract of each " [86] If on the other hand the guarantee is several only, the remaining sureties must prove an existing right of contribution which has been taken away or injuriously affected by the release of one before they will be discharged.[86]

In *National Provincial Bank of England* v. *Brackenbury* [87] it was intended that a joint and several guarantee should be signed by four guarantors, and the guarantee was so drawn. In the event only three signed, and it was held that they were not liable to the bank.

Owen v. *Tate and Another* [88] was an unusual case in which the defendants, husband and wife, had a loan from Lloyds Bank secured by a charge on a property belonging to a Miss Lightfoot. Some years after the loan was made she became concerned about the fact that her property was still mortgaged, and the plaintiff, her former employer, agreed to guarantee the advance himself in order to release the property. He did so, without the knowledge of the defendants, and deposited £350 with the bank in support of his guarantee. The defendants protested strongly but unavailingly against the change of security.

Later the advance was called in and the plaintiff's cash applied in repayment, whereupon he brought the present action claiming reimbursement from the defendants. But the Court of Appeal unanimously dismissed his appeal against the county court's dismissal of his action. A right of indemnity may arise when a man is compelled to pay money which another is bound by law to pay; not so in the case of the volunteer. Stephenson L.J. cited with approval the statement in Cheshire and Fifoot's *Law of Contract* [89]: " At common law, therefore, the volunteer, officious or benevolent,

[86] *Ward* v. *National Bank of New Zealand* (1883) 8 App. Cas. 755.
[87] (1906) 22 T.L.R. 797.
[88] [1975] 3 W.L.R. 369.
[89] 8th ed., p. 632.

has no right of action. Only if the plaintiff has paid money under restraint is he entitled to sue the defendant for restitution."

MORTGAGES

Barclays Bank Ltd. v. Beck

[1952] 2 Q.B. 47

The nature of a bank's mortgage

Facts

The defendants were overdrawn with the plaintiff bank, and in 1949 executed in the bank's favour a charge on their farm under the Agricultural Credits Act 1928. Clause 1 of the charge read:

> The farmer hereby covenants with Barclays Bank Limited (hereinafter called " the bank ") that the farmer will on demand or upon the death of the farmer without demand pay to the bank the balance of all moneys now or hereafter owing by the farmer under any account current . . . and all other moneys and liabilities now or hereafter due or to become due from the farmer to the bank in respect of any advance made or to be made by the bank to the farmer or upon any account or in any manner whatever. . . .

In 1950 the bank appointed a receiver under the charge, and the defendants, who were anxious to avoid a forced sale of their property, arranged to sell privately. Their solicitors confirmed to the bank that they had been instructed to authorise the purchaser to pay direct to the bank the sum of £4,000, part of the purchase price, against the bank's discharge of their charge. This sum was duly paid, but as a result of charges made by the receiver and other expenses there remained an outstanding overdraft of nearly £600, and it was for this sum that the present action was brought.

The defendants argued that where a higher security, such as a bond, is given for a simple contract debt, the two are merged so that only the higher security is enforceable. On this argument the debt on the banker/customer relationship of the overdraft was merged in the covenant in the charge, and, the latter having been enforced, the bank had lost its right to sue on the overdraft.

Decision

The Court of Appeal upheld the finding of Barry J. in favour of the bank. In his judgment Denning L.J. said (at p. 54):

> . . . a future debt on a running account is a debt created by parol, and it remains a simple contract debt, even though the customer has previously

given a charge to secure it, which includes a covenant under seal. The future debt on running account is not created under the deed. It may be that it would never have been created but for the deed, but that is a different thing. It only means that the deed is collateral security for its repayment.

And Somervell L.J. said (at p. 52):

The question here, as it seems to me, is whether the ordinary contractual position as between banker and customer, which would be usual in respect of advances apart from this clause, is merged in and destroyed by being replaced by what appears in clause 1. In my opinion that clause, so far from doing that, indicates that the position is the contrary.

Notes

The decision here was followed by Upjohn J. in *Lloyds Bank Ltd. v. Margolis and Others*,[90] though in that case the point at issue was decided on other grounds, the fact that the security was collateral being a subsidiary point.

The fact that the charge in the *Beck* case was executed under the Agricultural Credits Act does not affect the generality of the decision; the challenge might have been made in respect of an ordinary bank charge, and the decision would have equally applied. That decision confirms the long standing practice of the banks; it is perhaps surprising that no borrower seems to have challenged a bank on the same grounds before.

The merging of a simple contract debt into a speciality debt is seen when a debt is sued for and, judgment being given, the debt is merged in the judgment. Somervell L.J. gave the further example of a creditor giving time for payment of an existing debt, and taking a bond for it.

There, again, it is plain that the whole basis of that is that it is in substitution for the simple contract debt. It would make nonsense of the transaction if, having entered into that arrangement . . . the man the next day could sue upon the simple contract debt.[91]

But, as Denning L.J. put it, merger depends on the intention of the parties as expressed in the documents they have signed, and bank forms of charge are clear enough on the point at issue.

It is to be noted that in banking practice the word "collateral" is more often used of third-party security than in the sense in which Denning L.J. used it here.[92]

---

[90] *Post*, p. 258.
[91] At p. 51.
[92] *Cf.* Holden, *Securities for Bankers' Advances*, pp. 337 *et seq.*

Lloyds Bank Ltd. v. Margolis and Others

[1954] 1 W.L.R. 644

Demand under a mortgage

Facts

In 1936 the plaintiff bank took a mortgage on Winterslow Farm to secure the overdraft of George Lyster, its owner, the third defendant in this action. On December 19, 1938, when their customer was in process of selling the farm, the bank made demand upon him. In the years that followed the farm was sold to the first defendant, and subsequently by him to Reginald King, the second defendant, in both cases subject to the bank's mortgage; and on November 29, 1950, the bank issued a summons claiming to enforce their mortgage. The defendants claimed that the charge was no longer enforceable, being barred by the Limitation Act 1939; no advances had been made after October, 1938, more than 12 years before the date of the summons.

Decision

Upjohn J. held that time began to run from the date of the demand, not from the dates of the various advances, so that the bank were just within the statutory 12 years. In his judgment he said (at p. 649):

> . . . where there is the relationship of banker and customer and the banker permits his customer to overdraw on the terms of entering into a legal charge which provides that the money which is then due or is thereafter to become due is to be paid "on demand," that means what it says. As between the customer and the banker, who are dealing on a running account, it seems to me impossible to assume that the bank were to be entitled to sue on the deed on the very day after it was executed without making a demand and giving the customer a reasonable time to pay. It is indeed a nearly correlative case to that decided in *Joachimson* v. *Swiss Bank Corporation*,[93] where the headnote was this—
>
> "Where money is standing to the credit of a customer on current account with a banker, in the absence of a special agreement, a demand by the customer is a necessary ingredient in the cause of action against the banker for money lent."
>
> In this case the agreement has provided quite clearly what is to be done before the bank can sue. They must demand the money.

---

[93] *Ante*, p. 1.

Notes

This decision may be compared with that in *Bradford Old Bank Ltd.* v. *Sutcliffe*,[94] which turned on demand under a guarantee.

Under the Limitation Act time runs from the date at which a right of action is acquired, and the question here was whether the bank had a right of action before they made demand; if they had, then they would have lost it by the time the summons was issued. The case here was stronger in their favour than it was in the *Joachimson* case, for here, as Upjohn J. remarked, the agreement specified demand; in the current account with a credit balance it needed the *Joachimson* decision to establish the need for demand.

The demand clause is usually included in standard bank forms of charge, so that it is a largely academic question whether by analogy with *Joachimson* it might not now be held that demand by the bank is necessary in the absence of such a clause.[94a] The words of Upjohn J., quoted above, " it seems to me impossible to assume that the bank were to be entitled to sue on the deed . . . without making a demand," would be apt to cover such a situation, and would indeed be widely accepted as the justice of the matter.

In *Barclays Bank Ltd.* v. *Kiley* [95] the borrowing customer died and no personal representatives were appointed. The bank purported to make demand upon the customer six months after his death, and thereafter appointed a receiver of the rents of the property charged. The present action was on an originating summons by the bank, asking for delivery of the property, and Pennycuick J. held, *inter alia*, that the demand was good, nothing in the form of charge restricting the conditions of demand to the borrower's lifetime.

The importance of proper demand before the exercise of any rights of sale or foreclosure is emphasised by the decision in *Hunter* v. *Hunter and Others*,[96] where demand properly made was held by the House of Lords to have been waived by the taking of further security and the resumption for a year of normal working on the account. Viscount Hailsham L.C. said:

> I have felt some regret in reaching this conclusion. I have no doubt that the bank acted in perfect good faith, and that the plaintiff had full notice of what they were doing; and if he had objected at the time, the bank would undoubtedly have served a formal demand which he could not have met. But the right of sale is a very drastic remedy, and it is essential for the due protection of borrowers that the conditions of its exercise should be strictly complied with.[97]

---

[94] *Ante*, p. 250.

[94a] In so far as the banks are now lending for terms of years, care is needed to reconcile a covenant to repay on demand with the provisions of the term loan.

[95] [1961] 1 W.L.R. 1050. [96] [1936] A.C. 222. [97] At p. 247.

Cuckmere Brick Co. Ltd. v. Mutual Finance Ltd.

[1971] Ch. 949

Western Bank Ltd. v. Schindler

[1976] 2 All E.R. 393

The mortgagee's rights, and restrictions upon them

Facts of Cuckmere Brick Co. Ltd. v. Mutual Finance Ltd.

The plaintiffs borrowed £50,000 from the defendants against the mortgage of a site in Maidstone with planning permission for 100 flats. Later, with the agreement of the defendants, they obtained permission for 33 houses instead. In the event no building was put in hand for five years, and the defendants called in the advance and advertised the site for sale.

The estate agents included in the advertisement mention of the planning permission for houses, but omitted the permission for flats. The plaintiffs protested that the permission for flats should have been included, but the sale went ahead, realising £44,000. In this action the plaintiffs claimed that more would have been realised if the particulars had included the permission for flats. The defendants denied liability, and counter-claimed for the balance of the advance.

Decision

The Court of Appeal held unanimously that a mortgagee is not a trustee of the power of sale for the mortgagor, and where there is a conflict of interests he is entitled to give preference to his own over those of the mortgagor. But in exercising the power of sale he is under a duty to take reasonable care to obtain the true value of the property. The Court held further, by a majority, that the defendants here had been negligent. Salmon L.J. said:

> I accordingly conclude, both on principle and authority, that a mortgagee in exercising his power of sale does owe a duty to take reasonable precaution to obtain the true market value of the mortgaged property at the date on which he decides to sell it. No doubt in deciding whether he has fallen short of that duty, the facts must be looked at broadly, and he will not be adjudged to be in default unless he is plainly on the wrong side of the line.[98]

Facts of Western Bank Ltd. v. Schindler

The defendant had mortgaged his house on terms that no interest

[98] At pp. 968–969. *Cf.* s. 36 of the Building Societies Act 1962, requiring the exercise of reasonable care to ensure that the price obtained for a mortgaged property is the best that can be reasonably obtained.

was payable until the loan became repayable in 10 years time. By a separate agreement he also charged a life policy as collateral security. When he allowed the policy to lapse the bank claimed possession of the property, although there had been no breach of the mortgage agreement, and there could therefore be no exercise of the power of sale. The defendant argued that an implied term must be read into the mortgage that the bank could not exercise its right to possession in the absence of default in the terms of the mortgage.

Decision

The Court of Appeal rejected the defendant's argument, and found for the plaintiff. Buckley L.J. said:

> A legal mortgagee's right to possession is a common law right which is an incident of his estate in the land. It should not, in my opinion, be lightly treated as abrogated or restricted. Although it is perhaps most commonly exercised as a preliminary step to an exercise of the mortgagee's power of sale, so that the sale may be made with vacant possession, this is not its only value to the mortgagee. The mortgagee may wish to protect his property: see *ex parte Wickens*.[99] If, for instance, the mortgagor were to vacate the property, the mortgagee might wish to take possession to protect the place from vandalism. He might wish to take possession for the purpose of carrying out repairs, or to prevent waste. Where the contractual date for repayment is so unusually long delayed as it was in this case, a power of this nature to protect his security might well be regarded as of particular value to the mortgagee.[1]

Notes

In the first case Salmon L.J., while setting out clearly the duty of the mortgagee in exercising his power of sale, set out equally clearly the wide extent of that power. Once it has accrued the mortgagee can exercise it when he likes—" it matters not that the moment may be unpropitious and that by waiting a higher price could be obtained." He can properly accept the best bid at even a poorly attended auction at which the bidding is exceptionally low. " Providing none of those adverse factors is due to any fault of the mortgagee, he can do as he likes." [2] But absence of fault, on which the mortgagee's freedom of action depends in all aspects of the sale, may be difficult to establish: " the facts must be looked at broadly."

An unusual challenge to a bank's claim to possession was unsuccessful in *Lloyds Bank Ltd.* v. *Marcan and Others*.[3] There the first

---

[99] [1898] 1 Q.B. 543.
[1] At p. 396.
[2] *Cf.* the position of the receiver under a debenture, *post*, p. 330.
[3] [1973] 1 W.L.R. 1387.

defendant, in support of his guarantee of the borrowing of his horticultural business, had charged the property on which, with his wife, he carried on that business. After the bank had called in the advance and claimed possession of the property he assigned his interest in the business to his wife and granted her a 20 year lease of the property. The bank claimed that the lease was granted " with intent to defraud creditors " within section 172 of the Law of Property Act 1925, which makes any such conveyance voidable.[3a] The judges were divided as to whether " defraud " in the section is confined to actual dishonesty,[4] but they were unanimous that the bank was entitled to succeed: although the defendants' conduct had been perfectly legal it was, in the words of Russell L.J. " less than honest: it was sharp practice," The mortgagee's right to possession is independent of the power of sale, but section 36 of the Administration of Justice Act 1970, gave the court discretion to suspend an order for possession if it appears that the mortgagor can within a reasonable time make good his default. The defendant in the *Western Bank* case raised a further defence under the section, claiming that read strictly it makes the discretion dependent on default by the mortgagor, with the absurd result that a mortgagor not in default could not be so protected. As Parliament could not have intended this result, the defendant argued that the effect of the section must be to exclude altogether, except in the case of default, the common law right of possession. But Scarman and Buckley L.JJ. held that the section must be treated as giving the discretion whatever the grounds on which possession is sought, and Goff L.J., preferring the literal reading (which is supported by section 8 of the Administration of Justice Act 1973), held that on this reading the section was irrelevant in the present case, where there had been no default.

The effect of section 36 in more normal circumstances was considered in *Halifax Building Society* v. *Clark and Another*.[5] The first defendant was the mortgagor, the second his wife, whom he had deserted. When he failed to make two consecutive monthly payments the Society issued a summons for possession, and the wife sought postponement, in the hope that after her divorce proceedings she would be able, not to pay off the mortgage, but to keep up instalments. Pennycuick V.-C. held that section 36, even though it appeared in this regard not to have carried the matter further than

---

[3a] *Cf.* Langstaff, " The Cheat's Charter," 91 *Law Quarterly Review* 86, where is discussed the manner in which a mortgagor might suceed in using s. 172 to frustrate the mortgagee.

[4] *Cf. post*, p. 314 on the meaning of " fraudulent."

[5] [1973] Ch. 307.

the courts had already established, could not apply where there was no prospect of repayment of the mortgage debt.

But Parliament had intended differently, and section 8 of the 1973 Act was passed, as the Lord Chancellor said in the second reading debate, " to give effect to the true intention of Parliament " in the earlier Act.[6] In future cases on the line of the *Halifax Building Society* case the court will have discretion to postpone. But both sections use the words " within a reasonable period," and in *Royal Trust Company of Canada* v. *Markham and Another*[7] the Court of Appeal held that there must be a probability rather than a possibility that repayment can be made. Here there was merely an intention to put the house on the market at a price which the plaintiff company thought unreasonably high, and although the court might postpone possession to allow a property to be sold by the mortgagor, the circumstances here did not justify postponement.

In recent years the courts and Parliament have been concerned more directly than in the *Halifax Building Society* case with the rights of the deserted spouse (usually the wife, but the same principles apply to the husband), whose shared matrimonial home has been mortgaged by the other party to the marriage.

In *National Provincial Bank Ltd.* v. *Ainsworth*,[8] the bank had taken a charge over the house of a mortgagor who had, unknown to the bank, deserted his wife, leaving her in occupation of the house. When the bank later called in the advance and claimed possession of the house, the wife resisted their claim. The Court of Appeal held, by a majority, that the right of a deserted wife in occupation to remain in the matrimonial home was an overriding interest in land under the Land Registration Act 1925, unless inquiry had been made of her and her rights not then disclosed. The bank's right as mortgagee was on this view subject to her right to remain in occupation. Had this decision stood every mortgagee of a private house would have been in danger of finding himself in the position of the bank here, unless he made inquiries of the mortgagor's spouse. The House of Lords, however, unanimously allowed the bank's appeal: a deserted wife's rights against her husband were personal and could not operate as a clog on the legal title.

The Matrimonial Homes Act 1967 resorted part of the wife's protection which the Court of Appeal had allowed her. Under the Act the wife (or, it may be repeated, the husband) who lacks a legal title to the house is given a statutory right of occupation, which is a registrable equitable charge. In practice a prospective mortgagee,

---

[6] *Hansard*, H.L. Deb., Vol. 338, col. 397.

[7] [1975] 1 W.L.R. 1416.

[8] [1965] A.C. 1175.

finding such a charge on the register, will call for its withdrawal, or take a postponement or priority from the registering spouse.

In *Rutherford* v. *Rutherford* [9] it was held that a spouse not actually in occupation cannot register a charge under the Act, and in *Hastings and Thanet Building Society* v. *Goddard*,[10] the Court of Appeal held that it was not necessary for the wife who had registered a charge to be joined as defendant, because she was in no better position than her husband, who could only avoid possession by redeeming the mortgage, and there was no evidence that she could do so either. It is to be noted, however, that the Society conceded, and the court presumably accepted, that had the wife shown that there was any real prospect of her being able to redeem it would have been proper for her to be joined. It would seem prudent, therefore, for mortgagees finding such a charge on the register, to join the registering spouse as defendant from the outset of the action.

Harrold v. Plenty

[1901] 2 Ch. 314

The deposit of documents of title, even without a memorandum, may be a good equitable mortgage

Facts

The plaintiff made a loan of £150 to the defendant against the security of a share certificate. In the present action the plaintiff claimed an order for the transfer of the shares to himself by foreclosure. The defendant made default in appearance, and the question before the court was whether the deposit of the share certificate amounted to an equitable mortgage carrying a right to foreclosure, or whether it was a mere pledge.

Decision

It was held that the plaintiff's security was a good equitable mortgage, and that he was entitled to foreclosure.

In his judgment, Cozens-Hardy J. said:

The only material allegation in the statement of claim is that in March, 1897, the defendant deposited with Harrold the certificate of ten ordinary shares in a limited company as security for the repayment to Harrold of the sum of £150, then owing to him from the defendant, with interest thereon at the rate of £6 per cent. per annum. Now, it is plain that a

---

[9] [1970] 1 W.L.R. 1479.

[10] [1970] 1 W.L.R. 1544.

pledgee is in a very different position from an ordinary mortgagee. He has only a special property in the thing pledged. He may obtain a sale, but he cannot obtain a foreclosure. I do not think that this is properly a case of pledge. A share is a chose in action. The certificate is merely evidence of title, and whatever may be the result of the deposit of a bearer bond, such as that which Sir George Jessel dealt with in *Carter* v. *Wake*,[11] I think I cannot treat the plaintiff as a mere pledgee. The deposit of the certificate by way of security for the debt, which is admitted, seems to me to amount to an equitable mortgage, or, in other words, to an agreement to execute a transfer of the shares by way of mortgage. The result is that the plaintiff is entitled to a judgment substantially in the form which would be given if, instead of the certificate of shares, the document had been a title-deed of real estate or a policy of assurance.[12]

Notes

The essential element in mortgage by deposit of documents, unsupported by any written evidence such as is provided by the ordinary memorandum of deposit, is intention to give security: without the intention, of course, no such mortgage is created. Thus, the deposit of deeds with a banker for safe custody does not give him even a lien upon them.[13]

The simple deposit of deeds as security for an advance has been recognised as creating an equitable mortgage since *Russel* v. *Russel*.[14] At the time this decision was regarded as an unfortunate limitation on the effect of the Statute of Frauds, and Lord Eldon, who refused to apply the new rule except in the clearest cases, said in *Ex parte Haigh*,[15] " The case of *Russel* v. *Russel* is a decision much to be lamented; that a mere deposit of deeds shall be considered as evidence of an agreement to make a mortgage." The rule became established law, however, and was extended to apply to other documents: in *Spencer* v. *Clarke*,[16] for example, the deposit of a life policy was recognised as creating an equitable mortgage, and in *Harrold* v. *Plenty* the deposit of a share certificate was treated in the same way.

The distinction drawn by Cozens-Hardy J. between pledgee and mortgagee is an important one: the pledgee, as he pointed out, cannot by foreclosure obtain possession of the property pledged. In *Carter* v. *Wake*, which he mentioned in this connection, Sir George Jessel M.R., making the same distinction, based it upon the fact that the legal mortgagor executed a conveyance of the property mortgaged, and that the mortgagee's complete ownership of the property was subject only to the restraint imposed by the law in

---

[11] (1877) 4 Ch.D. 605 *infra*.
[12] At p. 316.
[13] *Ante*, p. 223.
[14] (1783) 1 Bro.C.C. 269.
[15] (1805) 11 Ves.Jr. 403.
[16] (1878) 9 Ch.D. 137, *post*, p. 288.

respect of the equity of redemption; while the equitable mortgagor was regarded as having agreed to execute a conveyance when called upon to do so. The equity of redemption being once lost, it was reasonable to regard the mortgagee's ownership as complete—hence the right of foreclosure. In pledge, of course, no such conveyance existed or could be implied, the transaction amounting only to a transfer of possession. It may be noted that since 1925 a mortgage no longer has the same implication of complete transfer of ownership, but the distinction to which it gave rise remains.

In *Carter* v. *Wake* the defendant had mortgaged certain property to the plaintiff and had also deposited with him, as security, but without memorandum, certain bonds. At the time of the action, in which the plaintiff sought foreclosure of the equity of redemption in the bonds, these were at a discount, but the plaintiff considered that if he could retain them he would recover the amount of the debt when they became due for redemption. The court held that he was not entitled to foreclosure, and he was a mere pledgee of the bonds. It is unusual for the mortgagee to have particular reason for wanting foreclosure in the case of negotiable securities, and of course he becomes in any case holder for value of the securities in question.

Northern Counties of England Fire Insurance Co. v. Whipp

(1884) 26 Ch. D. 482

A legal mortgage has preference over an equitable one

Facts

The plaintiff company employed as their manager one Crabtree, who, in January, 1878, executed a legal mortgage of property belonging to him in favour of the company to secure an advance of £4,500. The deeds were lodged with the company, who kept them in their safe. Crabtree held one of the duplicate keys to the safe and in November, 1878, having abstracted the deeds from the safe, he deposited them to secure an advance of £3,500 made to him by the defendant, Mrs. Whipp. The defendant had no knowledge of the plaintiff's legal mortgage.

The following year Crabtree was made bankrupt and a month later an order was made for winding up the plaintiff company. In 1880 the liquidator brought this action against the defendant for foreclosure; and the defendant in her counterclaim sought a declaration that the legal mortgage should be postponed to her own. Upon judgment in her favour the plaintiff company appealed.

Decision

The Court of Appeal held that the company's legal mortgage had priority. Fry L.J. quoted Lord Cairns in *Agra Bank* v. *Barry* [17]:

> It has been said in argument that investigation of title and inquiry after deeds is " the duty " of a purchaser or a mortgagee; and, no doubt, there are authorities (not involving any question of registry), which do use that language. But this, if it can properly be called a duty, is not a duty owing to the possible holder of a latent title or security. It is merely the course which a man dealing bona fide in the proper and usual manner for his own interest, ought, by himself or his solicitor, to follow, with a view to his own title and his own security. If he does not follow that course, the omission of it may be a thing requiring to be accounted for or explained. It may be evidence, if it is not explained, of a design, inconsistent with bona fide dealing, to avoid knowledge of the true state of the title. What is a sufficient explanation, must always be a question to be decided with reference to the nature and circumstances of each particular case. . . .[18]

Fry L.J. continued:

> The authorities which we have reviewed appear to us to justify the following conclusions—
>
> 1. That the Court will postpone the prior legal estate to a subsequent equitable estate: (*a*) where the owner of the legal estate has assisted in or connived at the fraud which has led to the creation of a subsequent equitable estate, without notice of the prior legal estate; of which assistance or connivance, the omission to use ordinary care in inquiry after or keeping title deeds may be, and in some cases has been, held to be sufficient evidence, where such conduct cannot otherwise be explained; (*b*) where the owner of the legal estate has constituted the mortgagor his agent with authority to raise money, and the estate thus created has by the fraud or misconduct of the agent been represented as being the first estate.
>
> But 2. That the Court will not postpone the prior legal estate to the subsequent equitable estate on the ground of any mere carelessness or want of prudence on the part of the legal owner.[19]

Notes [20]

The maxim " where the equities are equal, the law prevails," of which the *Whipp* decision is an example, has been weakened by the property legislation of 1925: in particular registration has important effects on the priority of the charges registered.

It is to be observed that in later cases, such as *Oliver* v. *Hinton*,[21]

---

[17] (1874) L.R. 7 H.L. 135.
[18] At p. 157.
[19] At p. 494.
[20] As to priorities when more than one mortgage is granted, see Holden, *Securities on Bankers' Advances*, pp. 61 *et seq.*
[21] [1899] 2 Ch. 264.

gross negligence was considered sufficient to postpone the charge of the person negligent. In that case the purchaser, through her agent, made no inquiry whatever as to the vendor's title, and only a general inquiry as to the whereabouts of the title deeds; and the earlier, equitable, mortgage was held to postpone her legal title. Conversely, in *Hudston* v. *Viney*,[22] where a bank had taken a legal mortgage of property which was already the subject of an equitable mortgage, it was contended that their failure to investigate the title was negligence sufficient to postpone their mortgage. Eve J., however, held that, although such investigation would have disclosed the prior charge, yet in the circumstances the bank had not been grossly negligent.

The change effected by the 1925 legislation can be seen in considering *Grierson* v. *National Provincial Bank of England Ltd.*,[23] where deeds of a leasehold property, deposited as security for an advance with Grant & Maddison's Bank, were later charged by legal mortgage to John Grierson, with notice of the prior equitable mortgage. The bank was not given notice of this legal mortgage, and when the mortgagor later paid off his advance to the bank they released the deeds to him. He then charged them by way of equitable mortgage to the defendant bank, who knew nothing of the legal mortgage to Grierson; nor did Grierson know of the equitable mortgage to them. Upon the death of Grierson his executors brought this action to establish their priority over the bank. It was held that the legal mortgagee had not been guilty of any misconduct, negligence or want of care that would affect his priority. It will be noticed that had these transactions occurred after 1925 Grierson, whose legal mortgage was not protected by deposit of the deeds, would have had to register his charge in the Land Charges Register.[24] Had he not done so, the bank's later equitable mortgage, without notice of the prior charge, would have taken priority.

In practice, difficulties of priority are now likely to arise only between two mortgages both of which have been originally protected by the deeds, when a fraudulent mortgagor has obtained possession of the deeds from the earlier mortgagee. If the mortgagee, either legal or equitable, who has the deeds and so has not registered his charge, allows the mortgagor to obtain possession of them, he may thereafter be postponed to a later mortgagee to whom the mortgagor has given possession of the deeds. If the earlier mortgage is equitable and the later legal, the latter will prevail in accordance with the principle mentioned above; if both are equitable, the earlier mortgagee may well be postponed by reason of his negligence.

22 [1921] 1 Ch. 98.
23 [1913] 2 Ch. 18.
24 Land Charges Act 1925, s. 13.

In *National Provincial Bank of England* v. *Jackson* [25] it was laid down that where the two competing mortgages are both equitable the Court will not apply a similar principle to that stated in *Whipp's* case—the later mortgage may take precedence on the grounds of the carelessness of the first mortgagee.[25a]

National Provincial Bank of England v. Jackson

(1886) 33 Ch. D. 1

Exceptionally the equitable mortgagee may be postponed to an earlier equitable interest other than a mortgage

Facts

One Jackson, a solicitor, was jointly entitled to certain house property with his two sisters. The property was subject to a mortgage, and the brother, giving his sisters to understand that he was arranging to repay this mortgage, obtained their signatures to conveyances to himself of their shares in the property. He then lodged the deeds with his bank to secure an advance of £2,000. In the preliminary arrangements for this advance he had told the branch manager that his sisters were making the conveyance to him in order to help him in certain business, and added that there was to be no consideration for the conveyance. In fact the deed of conveyance signed by the sisters recited certain debts alleged to be owing as the consideration. The branch manager told the bank's solicitor merely that he must investigate the title with great care, and did not repeat to him the substance of the brother's conversation.

Jackson having absconded, the property was claimed by the bank as equitable mortgagees. The sisters contended that the deeds, having been obtained by fraud, were void against them.

Decision

The Court of Appeal held that the conveyances were not void but merely voidable; but they held further that the bank having been given constructive notice of the fraud, their equity must be postponed to that of the sisters. Cotton L.J. said:

The bank had two agents, their manager and their solicitor, and cannot be in any better position by reason of one of their agents not having

[25] *Infra.*

[25a] Different priority considerations are involved where two or more banks provide funds for substantial borrowings by corporate customers, or where a bank's lending is parallel with, for example, I.C.F.C. financing. Here priority deeds normally regulate the matter.

communicated important facts to the other agent. It was the manager's duty, if he delegated to another the duty of investigating the title, to communicate to him all the facts of the case. He did not do so; but the bank must stand in the same position as if he had done so. Each deed recites a debt of £400 due from the sister, and that in consideration of a release of this debt and payment of £300 to the conveying sister, the deed was executed. This is entirely inconsistent with the story told by Jackson to the manager that nothing was to be paid to the sisters. There was great negligence therefore on the part of the bank in not making further investigation as to the inconsistency between the recitals and Jackson's statement. It follows that the bank are not entitled to say that they relied on the recitals in making the advance, so as to establish an equitable claim against the sisters.[26]

Notes

The second maxim of equity of importance to mortgagees is that where the equities are equal the first in time prevails. This, like the maxim considered above,[27] has been made of less effect by the 1925 legislation: the necessity of registration, and its absolute effect as notice, have removed many of the dangers to which the equitable mortgagee was subject. But the *Jackson* case is an example of a risk that remains unaltered; the equitable mortgagee, even when he has the deeds, may find himself postponed to a *cestui que trust*, notwithstanding that he had no notice of the latter's interest.

In *Capell* v. *Winter*[28] a trustee, whose co-trustee had died, fraudulently executed a conveyance of part of the trust property to his creditor, Melsome, during the period before the appointment of a new trustee. The conveyance purported to be in consideration of the sum of £2,000, but in fact there was no consideration, the conveyance being treated by both parties as additional security for the debt outstanding. Melsome was fully aware of the fraud committed by the trustee. Later, Melsome charged the property by way of equitable mortgage to Richard Bellis, who had no notice of the fraud. The *cestuis que trust* brought the present action against Bellis's trustee in bankruptcy. It was held that there was no contract of sale between the trustee and Melsome, and that, the equities of the beneficiaries and Bellis being otherwise equal, that of the beneficiaries must prevail by reason of its priority in time.

In *Coleman* v. *London County and Westminster Bank Ltd.*[29] 45 debentures in a private company were issued to Mrs. Coleman, who, under a family arrangement, settled them upon trust for herself for life with remainder to her three sons equally. The trustee did

---

[26] At p. 12.
[27] *Ante*, p. 267.
[28] [1907] 2 Ch. 376.
[29] [1916] 2 Ch. 353.

not register the transfer of the debentures to himself. One of the sons assigned his interest to his wife for value. Some years later the settlor obtained possession of the debentures and charged them to the defendant bank as security for an advance. The bank inspected the company's register and found the settlor registered there as the owner of the debentures; and they then gave notice of their interest to the trustee of the debenture trust deed, who was also trustee of the settlement. At this time the bank had of course no knowledge of the existence of the settlement; and the trustee merely acknowledged the notification of their interest. The trustee and the settlor later died, and the present action was by the wife, to whom 15 debentures had been assigned, and the executors of the trustee, claiming a declaration that the bank had no title to the debentures. The bank in their defence pleaded the trustee's negligence in not registering his transfer, and his non-disclosure of the existence of the settlement when he received, in his other capacity, notice of their interest.

It was held that the omission to register the transfer did not bar the trustee's title, but that, even if it did, the wife's equitable title, prior in time to the equitable title of the bank, must succeed. To reach this decision Neville J. had to distinguish two cases very nearly parallel with the present case, and his decision has been criticised [30]; but it remains an interesting example of the unpredictable dangers to which the equitable mortgagee is liable.

In *Barclays Bank Ltd.* v. *Taylor* [31] the bank had made an advance against an equitable mortgage of their customer's property, and notice of deposit of the land certificate was duly registered. Later the customer executed a legal mortgage in the bank's favour; this was not registered. Later again the defendants in this action contracted to buy the property, and registered a caution in respect of their contract. When the bank sought to register their legal mortgage the defendants claimed priority for their contract, and Goulding J. found in their favour, basing his decision on section 106 (2) of the Land Registration Act 1925, which provides that a mortgage of registered land " may, if by deed, be protected by a caution in a specially prescribed form and in no other way." This decision caused alarm in the banks, for it seemed to render ineffective a time honoured, simple and economic method of charging their customers' property. However, on appeal the decision was reversed. Russell L.J. said:

> . . . quite apart from the fact that the land certificate was in the possession of the bank, (a) failure by the bank to lodge a caution in special form was

[30] *Cf. e.g.* 3 L.D.B. 148, and Chorley, *op. cit.*, p. 183.
[31] [1974] Ch. 137.

irrelevant, (b) the Taylors' caution did not and could not confer on their equitable entitlement or interest any priority over the bank's equitable charge, (c) ordinary rules of priority between persons equitably interested in the land must apply. . . .[32]

The bank's possession of the land certificate, although not here the deciding factor, is relevant in that without it a third party cannot create a legal interest that would defeat the bank's equitable charge.

Hopkinson v. Rolt

(1861) 9 H.L. Cas. 514

The position of a mortgagee making further advances after notice of a second mortgage

Facts

The appellant was the public officer of the Commercial Bank of London. A customer of the bank, a shipbuilder named Mare, had mortgaged to them certain property as security for an advance. The respondent, Rolt, was Mare's father-in-law, who made Mare a loan against a second mortgage of the property. He knew of the bank's earlier mortgage, and the bank were notified of his second mortgage. The bank's mortgage for £20,000 was expressed to be for the " sums and sum of money which then were or was, or at any time and from time to time thereafter, should or might become due or owing." The bank continued to make advances, by discount and otherwise. On Mare's bankruptcy Rolt claimed that the bank's advances since his mortgage were postponed to his own claim.

Decision

It was held that the bank's further advances were postponed to the second mortgagee's. In his judgment, Lord Campbell L.C. said:

> Although the mortgagor has parted with the legal interest in the hereditaments mortgaged, he remains the equitable owner of all his interest not transferred beneficially to the mortgagee, and he may still deal with his property in any way consistent with the rights of the mortgagee. How is the first mortgagee injured by the second mortgage being executed, although the first mortgagee having notice of the mortgage, the second mortgagee should be preferrred to him as to subsequent advances? The first mortgagee is secure as to past advances, and he is not under any obligation to make any further advances. . . . The hardship upon bankers from this

32 At p. 147.

view of the subject at once vanishes when we consider that the security of the first mortgage is not impaired without notice of a second, and that when this notice comes, the bankers have only to consider . . . what is the credit of their customer, and whether the proposed transaction is likely to lead to profit or to loss.[33]

Notes

When a banker grants a loan on current account against a mortgage, it is normally intended that the security shall be against future as well as present advances. It was established in *Hopkinson* v. *Rolt* that if a subsequent mortgage is obtained of which he has notice it takes priority over any further advances he may make against his mortgage; and, as was settled in *Deeley* v. *Lloyds Bank Ltd.*,[34] which was itself a case of competing mortgages, the rule in *Clayton's* case operates on a current account to wipe out the overdraft at the time of notice by subsequent payments into the account, leaving further withdrawals postponed to the later mortgage.

The decision in *West* v. *Williams* [35] was a development of the rule in *Hopkinson's* case. There the mortgagees *covenanted* to make advances at certain times, and did so both before and after receiving notice of another mortgage; and it was held that even so the advances made after notice were postponed to the other mortgage, Lord Lindley M.R. saying:

> Whatever prevents the mortgagor from giving to the first mortgagee the agreed security for his further advances releases the first mortgagee from his obligation to make them.[36]

The argument that by creating a second mortgage the mortgagor weakens the security of the first mortgagee is hardly a good one, in that, had the Court not decided as it did in *West* v. *Williams*, there would be no such weakening.

How far the Law of Property Act makes the whole question academic is not clear. Section 94 of the Act provides that further advances shall have priority:

(*a*) by arrangement with later mortgagees;

(*b*) where the prior mortgagee has no notice of the subsequent mortgage (and, while registration constitutes notice, the mortgagee is not fastened with it where the prior mortgage was expressly made to secure a current account or further advances unless the later mortgage is registered at the time when the original mortgage was created or when the last search was made);

---

33 At p. 143.
34 *Ante*, p. 534.
35 [1899] 1 Ch. 132.
36 At p. 144.

(*c*) whether or not he had such notice as aforesaid, where the mortgage imposes an obligation on him to make such further advances.

The relevance of the last proviso to such circumstances as those of *West* v. *Williams* has been debated, and the reader is referred to Paget [37] for a fuller discussion of the point. Cheshire [38] considers that the Act reverses the *West* case, so that where the first mortgagee binds himself to make further advances, they will take priority. Paget disagrees, largely on the same grounds as the Master of the Rolls in the *West* case, the diminishing of the first mortgagee's security; but, it may be repeated, if in fact the law is that such further advances have priority, there is no diminishing of the security, while if the subsection in question is not intended to reverse the West decision it is not easy to see what purpose it serves.

In practice it would be only in the most exceptional circumstances that a bank mortgage would *bind* the bank to make further advances; and the normal bank advance is fully protected by the combination of proviso (*b*) and the banks' established practice of "breaking" the account on receipt of notice.

Esberger & Son Ltd. v. Capital & Counties Bank

[1913] 2 Ch. 366

Registration of charges under the Companies Acts: effective date of charges

Facts

In September 1910 Esberger & Son Ltd. deposited as security for an overdraft from the defendant bank the deeds of their property in Louth, with a covering letter from their chairman to their secretary authorising the deposit. A week later the company sealed and delivered to the bank a memorandum of the deposit of the deeds, containing an agreement to execute a mortgage when called on to do so. This document was executed in proper form, but was not dated. The overdraft continued, and in June 1911 the document was sent back to the company for two directors to initial the schedule of deposited deeds. Upon its return to the bank the branch manager filled in the date, June 14, 1911. On July 3, it was registered as a

[37] *Op. cit.*, pp. 534 *et seq.*
[38] *Modern Law of Real Property* (10th ed.), p. 711.

charge with the Registrar of Joint Stock Companies; and advances continued to be made to the company against the security of this charge.

Upon the company going into voluntary liquidation later in the same year, the liquidator appointed sought, in the present action, to recover the deeds, contending that neither the charge nor the memorandum had been registered in due time under section 93 of the Companies (Consolidation) Act 1908 (now s. 95 of the Act of 1948). The bank in their defence alleged that the original intention of the parties had been to create a temporary security for a temporary overdraft, and that when a more permanent security was sought the memorandum was perfected by the insertion of the date, under the authority of the company, the date June 14, being then the effective date of the memorandum.

Decision

It was held that the security was void against the liquidator for failure to comply with the provision of the Act. In the course of his judgment, Sargant J. said:

> The second point which is made against the bank is that the security which was actually executed on September 17, 1910, and subsequently dated June 14, 1911, was itself void by reason of non-registration. The document was registered within the proper period after the date of the creation of the charge if that date was June 14, 1911, but a long time after the expiration of the proper period if the date of creation of the charge was September 17, 1910. Now it seems to me that prima facie that point is a good one, because it is not necessarily an essential part of a deed that there should be a date to it; the date of execution can be proved aliunde. A deed that has been executed and has been delivered to a person in whose favour it is intended to operate is perfectly complete without having any date on it, and therefore the addition of the date was not material to the operation of the deed. In my opinion, from the time that the deed was in fact executed and handed to the bank, namely, September 17, 1910, the bank had a complete and valid operative charge upon the property for the amount purporting to be secured by the deed.[39]

After reviewing the contention of the bank that the date of the creation of a charge is the date upon which advances are made rather than that of execution, he went on:

> The section [section 93 of the Act of 1908] is providing for the keeping of a register, which is to shew what moneys are owing by the companies on certain securities, so that creditors may have some notion of how far the property of the company is unencumbered; and the natural date and

---

39 At p. 372.

the workable date in respect of any one particular instrument must, I think, be the date on which the instrument is executed, and not the series of dates on which various sums of money may from time to time become due.[40]

Notes

Section 95 of the Companies Act 1948 provides that mortgages and charges created by limited companies under the Companies Act must be registered with the Registrar of Companies within 21 days of their creation. The section, which replaces corresponding sections in the earlier Companies Acts, is of great importance to bankers, in that any charge not so registered is void against the liquidator or creditors of the company.[41] By section 96 of the Act it is the duty of the company to register such charges, but any interested party may effect registration, and the lender for his own protection should see that registration takes place. It is clear from the *Esberger* decision that registration must take place as soon as the charge is effected.[42]

It must be noted further that this decision establishes the date of execution as the operative date in section 95 only where there is in fact an instrument of charge. Where an equitable charge is created by the bare deposit of deeds the operative date is the date of deposit; and where deeds are deposited with the intention to create a charge later, the date of the deposit, and not the date of any later instrument, will be the operative date.[43]

Re Kent & Sussex Sawmills Ltd.

[1947] Ch. 177

Registration of charges under the Companies Acts: the distinction between sale and assignment of book debts

Facts

The company had contracted with the Ministry of Fuel and Power to supply cut logs, and the Westminster Bank agreed to allow them

---

[40] At p. 374.

[41] Including a charge created by the company to secure borrowing by a third party—*Re Wallis & Simmonds (Builders) Ltd.* [1974] 1 W.L.R. 391.

[42] See also in this connection *Re Kent & Sussex Sawmills Ltd., infra,* and *Re David Allester Ltd., ante,* p. 230.

[43] But in *Re C. L. Nye* [1971] Ch. 442 where the bank's charge was inadvertently registered out of time, the date of the charge being wrongly stated to the registrar, the Court of Appeal held, against the liquidators, that once the registrar's certificate is issued, it is, by s. 98 (2), conclusive evidence that all the requirements of the Act have been complied with.

overdraft facilities in connection with this contract, provided the company wrote to the Ministry in the following terms:

With reference to the above-mentioned contract, we hereby authorise you to remit all moneys due thereunder direct to this company's account at Westminster Bank Ltd., Crowborough, whose receipt shall be your sufficient discharge. These instructions are to be regarded as irrevocable unless the said bank should consent to their cancellation in writing, and are intended to cover any extension of the contract in excess of 30,000 tons if such should occur.

The company wrote this letter, and the Ministry accepted the instructions; and in due course, there being an extension of the contract, the bank agreed to further advances, and the company wrote a further, similar, letter to the Ministry.

Upon the company going into voluntary liquidation, the liquidator contended that the two letters of authority constituted a charge on the book debts of the company which should have been registered under section 79 of the Companies Act 1929 (now replaced by s. 95 of the Companies Act 1948), and that as they had not been so registered they were void against him. The bank claimed that they must be regarded rather as a sale to the bank of the whole of the company's interest in the moneys due under the contract.

Decision

It was held that no sale was intended, but an equitable assignment by way of security; and this not having been registered was void against the liquidator.

In his judgment, Wynn-Parry J. said:

I approach this matter more in the expectation of finding that the parties have brought into existence a document consistent with their relations of borrower and lender rather than finding that, notwithstanding the continuance of those relations, they have brought into existence a document in which their relationship is changed to that of vendor and purchaser. In my judgment, by implication an equity of redemption is to be discovered in the language of the second sentence. I can see no commercial business reason for the introduction of those words: " these instructions are to be regarded as irrevocable unless the said bank should consent to their cancellation," except on the basis that the parties deliberately contemplated that circumstances might arise in which it would become desirable that a cancellation of the instructions should be given by the bank. The existence of the previous sentence appears to me to operate strongly to lead to the conclusion that there was nothing in the nature of a sale. One is entitled to test the matter by looking at the situation in September, 1944, unembarrassed by what has happend since, and to consider what possibilities were open. Suppose that, in fact, through one source or another the company's account had become in credit with the bank, is it to be supposed that the parties ever contemplated that, notwithstanding that circumstance, it should remain entirely a matter for the bank whether it should give its consent to the cancellation of these instructions, so that, if it did not give that consent then for the rest of the period over which the contract had to be worked out, the payments still had to be paid into the company's account at the bank? . . . In my view, if the company's account had come into credit, the company would then have been entitled, on the true view of this letter, to require the bank to give the necessary instructions to the Ministry.[44]

Notes

The liquidator had argued that there was no assignment at all, basing his case on *Bell* v. *London and North-Western Railway Co.*,[45] where a railway contractor gave his bankers a letter directing the railway company to pass cheques due to him to his account with the bank. It was there held that the letter did not constitute an assignment, although it would have done so if payment had been directed to the bank and not to the customer's account with the bank: as it stood the order (in the words of Lord Romilly M.R.) " would always be revocable by the person giving it. . . ." Wynn-Parry J. distinguished this earlier decision: the case before him would have been covered by that decision had it not been for the second part of the letter, which made the order irrevocable except with the bank's permission.[46]

The charges requiring registration under section 95 of the Companies Act 1948, are as follows:

(i) A charge to secure any issue of debentures.
(ii) A charge on uncalled share capital of the company.
(iii) A charge created or evidenced by an instrument which, if executed by an individual, would require registration as a bill of sale.
(iv) A charge on land or any interest therein, but not a charge for rent issuing out of the land.
(v) A charge on book debts of the company.
(vi) A floating charge on the property of the company.
(vii) A charge on calls made but not paid.
(viii) A charge on a ship or any share in a ship.[46a]
(ix) A charge on goodwill or on patents, trade-marks, or copyright.

With the *Kent & Sussex Sawmills* case may be compared *Re David*

[44] At p. 181–182. [45] (1852) 15 Beav. 548.
[46] *Cf.* Chorley, *op. cit.* p. 269, footnote 76, where these cases, and the *Rekstin* case (*ante*, p. 53) are considered for their relevance to the legal effect of the credit transfer.
[46a] " Ship or aircraft," by Mortgaging of Aircraft Order 1972.

Allester Ltd.,[47] an example of circumstances in which it was held that no charge registrable under section 95 had been created.

William Brandt's Sons & Co. v. Dunlop Rubber Co. Ltd.
[1905] A.C. 454

The equitable assignment of choses in action

Facts

Kramrisch & Co., who were rubber merchants in Liverpool, were financed by Brandts, who were London bankers. When Kramrisch's made a purchase, Brandts provided the necessary funds, and by way of security they took delivery of the goods. When the goods were sold, they were released by Brandts, who received the purchase money direct from the purchasers. Kramrisch & Co. had entered into a similar arrangement with another firm of bankers.

Kramrisch & Co. sold certain rubber to the defendant company, and sent with the goods an invoice on which was stamped a request that the amount thereof should be sent to Brandts. There was an error in the invoice, and it was returned; the corrected invoice later sent out did not bear the instructions for remittance to Brandts. There was also sent to the defendant company a letter signed by Kramrisch & Co. requesting the Dunlop company to sign another letter, which was enclosed, promising to remit the price of the goods in question to Brandts; and this letter was signed by the defendants and sent to Brandts.

The whole correspondence was handled by the Birmingham office of Dunlops, but cheques were sent out from their London office. Only the corrected invoice was sent from Birmingham to London, and the cheque was therefore sent to the second firm of bankers, who had not in fact had anything to do with this particular transaction. When Brandts wrote to Dunlops pressing for a remittance, they were informed that the amount had been paid; and Brandts then brought the present action to recover the amount from them, claiming that the money in question had been assigned to them, and that Dunlops had notice of the assignment.

Decision

The House of Lords held that there was evidence of an equitable assignment of the debt, with notice to the defendant company, and that the plaintiffs were therefore entitled to recover the amount claimed.

---

47 [1922] 2 Ch. 211, *ante*, p. 230.

Lord Macnaghten considered it immaterial that the document did not on the face of it purport to be an assignment, and said:

> An equitable assignment does not always take that form. It may be addressed to the debtor. It may be couched in the language of command. It may be a courteous request. It may assume the form of mere permission. The language is immaterial if the meaning is plain. All that is necessary is that the debtor should be given to understand that the debt has been made over by the creditor to some third person. If the debtor ignores such a notice, he does so at his peril. If the assignment be for valuable consideration and communicated to the third person, it cannot be revoked by the creditor or safely disregarded by the debtor.[48]

Notes

A chose in action is a right which can be enforced only by legal action, and is opposed to a chose in possession. One example is the life policy, certain special features of the assignment of which are dealt with later; but the most familiar ordinary example is the simple debt. A chose in action can be (but seldom is) mortgaged, and the appropriate formal charge is by way of deed of assignment; but any expression of intention by the creditor to charge the chose in action in favour of a third party may constitute a valid equitable assignment.

Section 136 of the Law of Property Act 1925, provides that an assignment of a chose in action must be absolute, and not by way of charge only, in writing signed by the assignor, and that written notice must be given to the debtor. If these provisions are satisfied the assignment is a legal assignment; if they are not satisfied there may be a good equitable assignment according to the principles outlined by Lord Macnaghten in the passage quoted above.

There is an important distinction to be observed between an assignment of a debt and an order to pay money, such as a cheque or a bill of exchange, which by section 53 of the Bills of Exchange Act is never an assignment of the debt due to the customer.[49] The distinction was formerly of especial significance in view of the danger that an assignment in the form of written instructions might be objected to as being in effect a bill of exchange, and not properly stamped as such.[49a] In *Buck* v. *Robson* [50] Cockburn C.J. said:

> In our acceptation of the term an order for the payment of money presupposes moneys of the drawer in the hands of the party to whom the order is addressed, held on the terms of applying such moneys as directed by the order of the party entitled to them. No such obligation arises out of the

[48] At p. 462.

[49] *Cf. Schroeder* v. *Central Bank* (1876) 34 L.T. 735.

[49a] The Finance Act 1950, freed bills of exchange (including cheques) from stamp duty.

[50] (1878) 3 Q.B.D. 686.

ordinary contract of sale. If a purchaser buys goods of a manufacturer or tradesman, he undertakes to pay the price to the seller, not to a third party, who is a stranger to the contract, nor will the mere order or direction of the seller to pay to a third party impose any such obligation upon him; it is only when and because the right of the seller to the price has been transferred to the third party by an effectual assignment that the assignee becomes entitled as of right to the payment.[51]

The *Brandt* case, as well as illustrating the effect of an assignment of a chose in action, provides an illustration of the importance of notice by the assignee to the debtor. Notice, as we have seen above, is an essential element of a legal assignment of a chose in action; it is not essential to an equitable assignment, but it is always most desirable, for without it the debtor may discharge himself by paying the creditor, while priority among several assignees of otherwise equal equities is determined by the dates of notice.[52]

THE MORTGAGE OF STOCK EXCHANGE SECURITIES

Powell v. London and Provincial Bank

[1893] 2 Ch. 555

Where transfer of stock or shares is required to be by deed a blank transfer is not an effective transfer, nor will registration when it is completed make it effective

Facts

The plaintiffs were trustees of a marriage settlement, of which the previous trustees had died. The son of one of the previous trustees, one Edwards, had as his father's executor obtained possession of certain stock belonging to the trust, which had been registered in the name of his father, with no notice of the trust. The certificate for this stock he proceeded to deposit with his bankers, the defendants, as security for advances, assuring their manager that he was the absolute owner of the stock, and at the same time depositing a blank deed of transfer signed and sealed by himself. The stock was regulated by the Companies Clauses Consolidation Act 1845, by section 14 of which every transfer of stock or shares must be by deed duly stamped, section 15 providing that the deed when duly executed should be delivered to the secretary and kept by him.

The bank in due course completed the transfer and forwarded it to the secretary, who registered them as the holders of the stock. The fraudulent executor later absconded and his fraud was discovered;

---

[51] At pp. 691–692.

[52] *Dearle* v. *Hall* (1828) 3 Russ. 1.

and the new trustees of the settlement brought this action against the bank.

Decision

The Court of Appeal held that, as Edwards had given the transfer to the bank while still blank, it could not be regarded as his deed when completed, and that as a result the bank had acquired no legal title; while their equitable interest was later than that of the trustees of the settlement.

In his judgment, Bowen L.J. said:

> . . . It seems to me that the deed never was, as against the parties to this suit, the deed of the grantor. A deed, in order to be a deed, must be sealed and delivered, and although we have heard a very ingenious argument which seems to rest on the assumption that a deed can be a deed before it is delivered, I never heard of it before. The sealing and delivery are essential parts of a deed. When was this deed ever delivered as a deed? At the time of its supposed delivery it was in blank. When was it redelivered, if at all? The redelivery must be done by the grantor or by somebody who acts for him. The grantor in this case never saw the deed again. He did not himself redeliver it . . . [while] it is well-known law that an agent cannot execute a deed, or do any part of the execution which makes it a deed unless he is appointed under seal.[53]

And Kay L.J. said:

> Then as to the registration of the bank as holders of this stock. In the case of *France* v. *Clark*,[54] it was decided most distinctly by Lord Selborne that the registration where the deed itself is incomplete does not perfect the title of the transferee. . . . Therefore, in order to make out their defence that they are legal owners, the defendants must show, not merely that there was a registration, but that the deed which was registered was a perfect deed at the time it was registered. Otherwise the registration does not help their case.[55]

Notes

The practical importance of this decision hardly needs emphasising.

Where there is no need, either by statute or by the articles of the company, for the transfer of shares to be by deed, a blank transfer entitles the transferee to fill in the blanks, and operates in itself as an effective transfer.[56]

Normally the company's articles call for registration of the transfer before the legal title can pass to the transferee. The *Powell* case

---

[53] At pp. 562, 563.
[54] (1884) 26 Ch. D. 257.
[55] At pp. 566–567.
[56] *Ireland* v. *Hart* [1902] 1 Ch. 522.

establishes that where the transfer is itself inoperative (*e.g.* where it should be, and is not, by deed) registration does nothing to make the inoperative document effective.

In *Société Générale de Paris* v. *Walker* [57] the articles of the company itself required transfers to be by deed, and the fact that the transfer in question had been in blank and had not been redelivered by the transferor was one of the grounds of the decision against the bank.

A deed of transfer does not become effective to pass the legal interest to the transferee until it has been delivered to the secretary of the company, and if the secretary returns it because of any formal irregularity it is not considered to have been delivered until he has received it again corrected.[58]

Société Générale de Paris and Another v. Walker and Others

(1886) 11 A.C. 20

The articles of a company may exempt them from the duty to accept notice of equitable interests in their shares

Facts

One J. M. Walker, the holder of 100 Tramways Union Company shares, executed a blank transfer of the shares and deposited it with the share certificates with J. S. Walker as security for a loan. Later, he executed another blank transfer of the shares and sent it to the appellants, his bankers, as security for a debt for which they were pressing him. He stated to the appellants that the certificates were lost. In due course the appellants completed and stamped the transfer and sent it to the company with a request that they would " certify " it, and offering an indemnity against any claim that might arise in respect of the certificates being missing. The company declined to certify the transfer and refused to accept the indemnity. Shortly afterwards the executors of J. S. Walker, who had died, notified the company of their claim on the shares.

The bank brought an action against the executors for a declaration of their title to the shares, claiming *inter alia*, that their equitable title was superior to that of the executors in that they had given prior notice of their interest to the company.

One of the company's articles was as follows:

The company shall not be bound by or recognise any equitable, contingent, future, or partial interest in any share, or any other right in respect

---

57 *Post*, p. 283.

58 *Nanney* v. *Morgan* (1887) 37 Ch. D. 346.

of a share, except an absolute right thereto in the person from time to time registered as the holder thereof. . . .

Decision

The House of Lords held that the action could not be maintained. On the point here under discussion they held that no effective notice had in fact been given.

In the course of his judgment, the Earl of Selborne said:

I think that according to the true and proper construction of the Companies Act of 1862, and of the articles of this company, there was no obligation upon this company to accept, or to preserve any record of, notices of equitable interests or trusts, if actually given or tendered to them; and that any such notice, if given, would be absolutely inoperative to affect the company with any trust. . . .[59]

Notes

An equitable mortgagee of shares will, like any other mortgagee, be postponed to a later legal mortgagee without notice of the prior claim. The present case is a demonstration that the notice which the lending banker will always be careful to give to the company of his equitable mortgage may not be effective if the company's articles exempt them from the obligation to accept notice of equitable interests.

Even apart from such express exemptions there is some doubt as to whether section 117 of the Companies Act 1948 (replacing s. 101 of the 1929 Act), does not have the same effect in providing that no notice of a trust may be entered on the register of a company. Paget calls this suggestion " a confusion of ideas," on the grounds that notice of an equitable charge is not a notice of trust,[60] but he here regards the purpose of the notice as being only to forestall the company's own possible lien. On this point *Bradford Banking Co. Ltd.* v. *Briggs & Co. Ltd.*[61] is authority for the view that notice to the company gives the banker priority over subsequent advances granted by the company to the mortgagor; but Hart [62] suggests that the section does prevent the banker from obtaining in this way priority over subsequent private mortgagees. It is not easy to see the grounds for this distinction, but until there is a definite decision Hart's view must be given due weight.

In any case, where it is considered essential to obtain further protection, the equitable mortgagee can obtain it by service of

[59] At p. 30.
[60] *Op. cit.* p. 550.
[61] (1886) 12 App. Cas. 29.
[62] *Op. cit.* p. 986.

notice in lieu of distringas.[63] In practice this somewhat elaborate procedure is not frequently used by banks.

The Lord Mayor, etc., of Sheffield v. Barclay and Others

[1905] A.C. 392

Forged transfers of stocks or shares transferred into the name of the lender

Facts

Timbrell and Honeywill were the joint owners of certain Corporation of Sheffield stock. Timbrell applied to the defendant bankers for an advance against this stock, and in order to obtain it executed a transfer in favour of a member of the bank, forging Honeywill's name on the transfer. The bank forwarded the transfer to the registrar of the corporation, and were duly registered as owners. Upon repayment of the advance the stock was transferred to two third parties and they were in due course registered as the new owners of the stock.

Upon Timbrell's death the fraud was discovered, and Honeywill brought an action against the corporation for rectification of their register, payment of back dividends and other relief. He won this action, and as this involved the corporation in a loss of more than £11,000, they in turn brought the present action against the bank, claiming the amount of their loss on the grounds that by sending in the forged transfer for registration they had either warranted it as genuine or had by implication undertaken to indemnify the corporation against any claim that might result from registration of it. The Lord Chief Justice found against the bank, but the Court of Appeal allowed the bank's appeal. The plaintiffs further appealed.

Decision

The House of Lords allowed the appeal and restored the Lord Chief Justice's decision. In the course of his judgment the Lord Chancellor, Lord Halsbury, said:

> [The bank] have a private bargain with a customer. Upon his assurance they take a document from him as a security for a loan, which they assume to be genuine. I do not suggest that there was any negligence—perhaps business could not go on if people were suspecting forgery in every transaction—but their position was obviously very different from that of the corporation. The corporation is simply ministerial in registering a valid

[63] As to this, see Chorley, *op. cit.* p. 308.

transfer and issuing fresh certificates. They cannot refuse to register, and though for their own sake they will not and ought not to register or to issue certificates to a person who is not really the holder of the stock, yet they have no machinery, and they cannot inquire into the transaction out of which the transfer arises. The bank, on the other hand, is at liberty to lend their money or not. They can make any amount of inquiries they like. If they find that an intended borrower has a co-trustee, they may ask him or the co-trustee himself whether the co-trustee is a party to the loan, and a simple question to the co-trustee would have prevented the fraud. They take the risk of the transaction and lend the money. The security given happens to be in a form that requires registration to make it available, and the bank " demand "—as, if genuine transfers are brought, they are entitled to do —that the stock shall be registered in their name or that of their nominees, and are also entitled to have fresh certificates issued to themselves or nominees. This was done and the corporation by acting on this " demand " have incurred a considerable loss.[64]

Notes

The *Sheffield Corporation* case is an example of the principal danger to which the lending banker is liable when he advances against stocks or shares. It may be noted that in the case of a legal mortgage such a danger could be avoided by requiring the mortgagor himself to carry out the formalities of transfer, for it is only on their implied warranty of genuineness that the bank becomes liable to indemnify the company, and if the transferor himself forwards the transfer to the company there can be no warranty by the bank. The fact that the banks do not normally adopt this practice may probably be taken as evidence that the danger is not a serious one. In the case of equitable mortgage by way of blank transfer the transfer is usually registered only when the security is to be realised, and here it would anyhow often be difficult to insist upon the mortgagor completing the formalities himself.

Equitable mortgages of stocks and shares are more common than legal ones, and here there is the further danger of there being other, prior, equitable interests. The security charged may, for example, be subject to a trust.[65] In *Peat* v. *Clayton* [66] the plaintiffs were trustees of a trust under which a debtor had assigned all his property for the benefit of his creditors. Part of the property consisted of shares in a company, and the trustees, having asked the debtor for the shares and been unable to obtain them from him, gave notice to the company of the assignment. Later the debtor sold the shares through his brokers, executed a transfer and received the purchase money.

---

[64] At pp. 396–397.
[65] *Cf. National Provincial Bank of England* v. *Jackson, ante*, p. 269.
[66] [1906] 1 Ch. 659.

In spite of the notice the company registered the purchaser as owner of the shares, but later removed her name from the register and refused to issue a certificate. The brokers provided the purchaser with other shares in the company, and then claimed to have a lien on the shares they had sold. The present action was by the trustees who sought a declaration that they were entitled to the shares, and it was held that the brokers' lien could not be upon more than the interest which the debtor himself had in the shares, and that this interest was subject to the right of the plaintiffs.

THE MORTGAGE OF LIFE POLICIES

Re Wallis

[1902] 1 K.B. 719

Failure to give notice to the insurance company does not postpone the equitable mortgagee of a policy to a later incumbrancer who takes subject to the equities, or has constructive notice of the earlier mortgage

Facts

In March 1901 one Wallis deposited an assurance policy on his own life with his wife as security for a loan which she had made to him. She did not give notice of this equitable charge to the assurance company. In October 1901 a receiving order was made against Wallis on his own petition, and adjudication followed. A few days later the official receiver gave notice of the receiving order to the company. A fortnight afterwards a trustee in bankruptcy was appointed, and he claimed as against the wife to be entitled to the policy as part of the property of the bankrupt, free from incumbrances.

Decision

It was held that the wife's rights under her mortgage were not overridden by those of the trustee. In his judgment Wright J. said:

> It is singular that there is no direct authority on this point. It is plain that before the bankruptcy there was a good equitable deposit of this policy for value by the bankrupt with his wife. No doubt the general rule is that, as between several assignees or incumbrancers of a chose in action, the assignee or incumbrancer who first gives notice obtains priority. But the trustee in bankruptcy is not an incumbrancer for value. Under the bankruptcy laws he is a statutory assignee, and this policy vested in him subject to all equities existing at the date of the commencement of the bankruptcy. Therefore the

trustee could not, by giving notice to the assurance office, deprive the bankrupt's wife of her rights as an equitable mortgagee of the property. He can only have the policy on payment to the wife of what is properly due to her under her security.[67]

Notes

In *Spencer* v. *Clarke* [68] the plaintiffs lent money against a policy to one Clarke, who told them that he had left the policy at home, and would produce it the next day. He had in fact borrowed previously against it, and had deposited it with the earlier lender. The later mortgagees gave notice to the company, but it was held that this notice did not oust the claim of the first mortgagee, even though he had not given notice.

The Policies of Assurance Act 1867, s. 3, provides:

No assignment made after the passing of this Act of a policy of life assurance shall confer on the assignee therein named, . . . any right to sue for the amount of such policy . . . until a written notice of the date and purport of such assignment shall have been given to the assurance company . . .; and the date on which such notice shall be received shall regulate the priority of all claims under any assignment. . . .

Re Wallis and *Spencer* v. *Clarke* are examples of circumstances in which the normal rule, that priority is according to the time of notice, does not apply. It will be seen that, in such cases, possession of the policy is more important than notice. Thus, if a banker makes an advance against the mortgage of a policy, and does not obtain possession of it, he is fixed with constructive notice of any prior mortgage that may have been effected, and he cannot put matters right merely by giving notice to the company. If, on the other hand, his is in fact the first advance, the later bankruptcy of the insured will not affect his security, for the trustee in bankruptcy is similarly fixed with notice of his charge, even though he has omitted to give notice.

But notice to the company is effective to give priority over subsequent advances, even by an earlier mortgagor. In *Re Weniger's Policy* [69] Parker J. said:

Where a chose in action is concerned a mortgagee must give notice to the debtor for his own protection, but there is no principle establishing that subsequent incumbrancers of a policy are bound to give notice to prior incumbrancers. If the first mortgagee makes a further advance on a fresh bargain he must inquire at the office whether notice of another charge has been received, and if not he may complete his security by giving notice of it.[70]

---

[67] At p. 720.
[68] *Cf. ante*, p. 265.
[69] [1910] 2 Ch. 291.
[70] At p. 296.

Beresford v. Royal Insurance Co. Ltd.
[1938] A.C. 586

The effect of the suicide of the insured

Facts

In 1925 Major Rowlandson insured his life with the Royal Insurance Co. Ltd. for £50,000. Each of the policies contained the following clause:

If the life or any one of the lives assured (being also the assured or one of them) shall die by his own hand, whether sane or insane within one year from the commencement of the assurance, the policy shall be void as against any person claiming the amount hereby assured or any part thereof, except that it shall remain in force to the extent to which a bona fide interest for pecuniary consideration, or as a security for money . . . shall be established. . . .

In 1934 a premium became due which the assured was unable to pay, and he obtained several extensions of the time for payment. The last of these ended at 3 p.m. on August 3, and a few minutes before that hour he shot himself.

The appellant, who was the niece and the administratrix of Major Rowlandson, brought this action against the company claiming the amount of the policies. The jury found as a fact that the deceased was sane at the time of the suicide, and the court held that the plaintiff was entitled to the policy moneys. The Court of Appeal reversed the decision of the lower court on grounds of public policy and the plaintiff further appealed.

Decision

The House of Lords upheld the decision of the Court of Appeal: it was against public policy for the contract to be enforced. In his judgment, Lord Atkin said:

Anxiety is naturally aroused by the thought that this principle may be invoked so as to destroy the security given to lenders and others by policies of life insurance which are in daily use for that purpose. The question does not directly arise, and I do not think that anything said in this case can be authoritative. But I consider myself free to say that I cannot see that there is any objection to an assignee for value before the suicide enforcing a policy which contains an express promise to pay upon a sane suicide, at any rate so far as the payment is to extend to the actual interest of the assignee. It is plain that a lender may himself insure the life of the borrower against sane suicide; and the assignee of the policy is in a similar position so far as public policy is concerned. I have little doubt that after this decision the life companies will frame a clause which is unobjectionable; and they will have the support of the decision of the Court of Queen's Bench in *Moore* v. *Woolsey*,[71] where a clause protecting bona fide interests was upheld.[72]

Notes

The decision in this case was significant in establishing for the first time that a policy was unenforceable after a sane suicide even where it contained a clearly implied term that if the suicide took place more than a year after the date of the policy the insurers would pay under it.

The case was decided when suicide was a crime. Since the passing of the Suicide Act 1961 this is no longer so, but it might still be held to be against public policy to allow the personal representative of the suicide to receive the policy moneys, and it would be unsafe to assume that the Act has materially altered this aspect of the matter.

The banker is normally concerned not with the position of the personal representative, but with that of the assignee of the policy. Lord Atkin's view here quoted was expressly *obiter dictum*, but it carries great weight, and is supported by the much older decision to which he referred. The policy in *Moore* v. *Woolsey* contained a clause excluding liability in the case of persons dying " by duelling or by their own hands or by the hands of justice," but expressly exempting from the terms of the clause " any bona fide interest which may have been acquired by any other person." On grounds of strict logic it would still be open to the courts to hold even such a clause to be against public policy: in the *Beresford* case it is clear on the facts that the insured committed suicide with the definite purpose of gaining for his personal representatives the benefit of the policies which he could no longer maintain, and if in similar circumstances the insured was seeking to protect his mortgagee the inducement to suicide would be equally apparent. But the risk to the mortgagee seems remote, and the common sense of the decision in *Moore* v. *Woolsey* is unlikely to be upset by the application of logic to what is anyhow so rare an event.

It will be noted that Lord Atkin's opinion and the *Moore* v. *Woolsey* decision both concern policies with clauses protecting third party interests. And it may be worth pointing out that the whole discussion is concerned only with sane suicide: in the case of mental disorder no question of avoiding the policy arises.

While these cases illustrate the possible danger to the mortgagee of the suicide of the mortgagor, there is a further, more general, possibility that the mortgagee may find his security invalidated. All

[71] (1854) 4 E. & B. 243.

[72] At pp. 599–600.

contracts of insurance are *uberrimae fidei* (*i.e.* they have an implied condition of "utmost good faith"[73]). The validity of the policy depends on the accuracy of the representations made by the insured in his proposals to the company, and this fact, even more than the possibility of suicide, makes it impossible to value the security with perfect certainty.[74]

---

[73] *Ante*, p. 235.
[74] *Cf.* Chorley, *op. cit.* p. 316.

Chapter 10

OTHER SERVICES PERFORMED BY BANKERS

Safe Custody

Giblin v. McMullen
(1868) L.R. 2 P.C. 317

Re United Service Co., Johnston's Claim
(1870) 6 Ch. App. 212

The duty and liability of a banker who accepts valuables for safe custody

Facts of Giblin v. McMullen

For seven years the plaintiff had kept an account with the Union Bank of Australia (of which the defendant was an inspector), and had during that time lodged with the bank a box containing securities. He had kept the key of the box. The box was kept in an underground strong room, access to which could be had only through a room separated from the main office of the bank. In this room the cashier, Fletcher, sat during bank hours, and Fletcher held during the day the key to the wooden door and the two keys to the iron door separating the room from the strong room. In the strong room, with the boxes of the plaintiff and of other customers, the bank held its manager's box containing bills for discount to the value of about two million pounds, its tellers' boxes, and other property belonging to the bank. The plaintiff had on many occasions had access to his box in the strong room, and had had every opportunity of seeing the arrangements for its safe keeping.

At some time between April and July, 1864, Fletcher stole certain debentures from the plaintiff's box, and disappeared. The plaintiff sought to recover damages from the bank for their negligence in keeping his property.

Decision

The Judicial Committee of the Privy Council held that the plaintiff could not recover. In delivering their Lordships' judgment, Lord Chelmsford said:

It may be admitted not to be sufficient to exempt a gratuitous bailee from liability that he keeps goods deposited with him in the same manner as he keeps his own, though this degree of care will ordinarily repel the presumption of gross negligence. But there is no case which puts the duty of a bailee of this kind higher than this, that he is bound to take the same care of the property entrusted to him as a reasonably prudent and careful man may fairly be expected to take of his own property of the like description.[1]

Facts of Re United Service Co., Johnston's Claim

The United Service Co. were bankers, and Hudson their manager. A customer, Johnston, deposited share certificates with them, with instructions that they should receive the dividends and charge a small commission for doing so. Hudson fraudulently sold the shares and later absconded. When the theft was discovered, Johnston succeeded in recovering the shares in an action against the companies concerned and the transferees, but he was not given the costs of the action; and, the United Service Co. being now wound up, he sought to prove for his costs.

It was shown that the bank kept securities deposited for safe custody together with their own securities in a strong box in the manager's room, the manager holding the key of the box. No record was kept of such securities, for, although a book was provided for the purpose of keeping records, Hudson had given up using it, with the assent of the directors. The Master of the Rolls held that the bank were bailees for reward, and had been grossly negligent in allowing unrestricted control to be vested in their manager. The liquidator of the bank appealed.

Decision

The Court of Appeal upheld the findings of the Master of the Rolls, but on other grounds [2] gave judgment for the bank.

In the course of his judgment, Sir W. M. James L.J. said:

Under these circumstances, the Master of the Rolls was of opinion that the bankers were bailees for reward, and that there was sufficient negligence in the performance of their duty as such bailees to render them liable for the consequences of that negligence. In both these conclusions we concur. We are of opinion that this case, on the first point, is entirely distinguishable from the case of *Giblin* v. *McMullen*,[3] where a box containing documents was placed at a bank simply for the purpose of convenient deposit, and the customer alone had access to it for the purpose of placing or removing anything he pleased. In this case, although it is true that the possession of these particular documents was not essential to the collection of the moneys which the bank were authorised to collect, it appears to us that they came

---

[1] At p. 339.

[2] They held that the costs sought to be recovered were damage too remote to be allowed as recoverable.

[3] *Supra*.

into their custody in the ordinary course of their business as bankers, that they were deposited with the bank by a customer of the bank, and that such deposit was made under such circumstances as would have entitled the bank to a lien upon them for their general banking account. . . .

We are further of opinion that the negligence of the bank is proved; that leaving the securities of the customer in the way in which they were left, in the uncontrolled and unwatched power of the manager, Mr. Hudson, was a gross neglect, and is not excusable or justifiable by reason of the fact that they were equally negligent with regard to their own documents and their own securities.[4]

Notes

It has never been definitely established whether the acceptance of valuables for safe custody is a part of the business of banking, or is rather an ancillary service. In theory the difference is important, for, in the general law of bailment, a gratuitous bailee is liable only for gross negligence while a bailee for reward is liable for ordinary negligence. In practice the difference is not so important; the standard of care set by the Judicial Committee in *Giblin* v. *McMullen* is " that he must take the same care of the property entrusted to him as a reasonably prudent and careful man may fairly be expected to take of his own property of the same description," and as bankers must in their ordinary business take precautions which, reasonable in their case, would be exceptional for ordinary persons, we see that, as Hart puts it[5] " that in a banker would be gross negligence which would not be so in others."

It may be doubted whether a bank would today escape liability on the facts of *Giblin* v. *McMullen*; but the rule laid down in that case is still applicable. Similarly, it is not certain that the banker would, on the facts of the *United Service Co.* case, be regarded today as a bailee for reward, for the " small commission " was payable rather for the collection of the dividends than for the safe custody of the securities; it is an odd conclusion that the banker is a gratuitous bailee of securities calling for no such service while he is a bailee for reward of exactly similar securities belonging to the same customer if he is asked to collect the dividends. But again the question is in part irrelevant, for the negligence on the facts of the *United Service Co.* case would certainly still be held to be gross, and the banker would thus be liable whether or not he was bailee for reward.

It is to be noted that no question of negligence normally arises in connection with the surrender of such safe custody deposits to the wrong person, for here the bailee is guilty of conversion whether or not he has been negligent. In fact the principal case on this point was

[4] At p. 217.

[5] *Op. cit.* p. 687.

settled out of court, and is therefore of small value as a precedent. In *Langtry* v. *Union Bank of London*,[6] the bank surrendered the property in question against a forged order handed to them by an unauthorised person. The case, which was settled by judgment for the plaintiff by consent for £10,000, caused some alarm in banking circles and was followed by a memorandum issued by the Central Association of Bankers, in which it was said that:

> It is necessary to distinguish between cases in which valuables are by mistake delivered to the wrong person (as in Mrs. Langtry's case) and cases in which they are destroyed, lost, stolen, or fraudulently abstracted, whether by an officer of the bank or by some other person.
>
> The best legal opinion appears to be that in the former case the question of the negligence of a bailee does not arise; that the case is one of wrongful conversion of the goods, and that the bank is liable for this wrongful conversion apart from any question of negligence.

There seems to be no doubt that the banker's only safe course, if he has the least doubt as to the bona fides of the presenter of an authority of the kind in question, is to delay delivery until he can satisfy himself. In *Robarts* v. *Tucker*[7] it was said that "a refusal to deliver up the goods to the owner on the ground that the holder must have time to ascertain whether he is the owner, is no conversion."[8]

CREDIT INQUIRIES

Hedley Byrne & Co. Ltd. v. Heller & Partners Ltd.

[1964] A.C. 465

A banker may be liable for negligence in replying to a credit inquiry; but if in his reply he expressly disclaims responsibility, no action for negligence will lie

Facts

The plaintiffs, advertising agents, inquired through their bankers, the National Provincial Bank, Bishopsgate, as to the credit of their clients, Easipower Ltd., who banked with the defendant merchant

---

6 (1896) 1 L.D.B. 229.

7 *Ante*, p. 77.

8 For a fuller discussion of the law as it affects safe custody by bankers, see Chorley, *op. cit.* pp. 242 *et seq.* and Paget, *op. cit.* pp. 189 *et seq.* *Cf.* too *Brandao* v. *Barnett, ante*, p. 222; and see *Houghland* v. *R. R. Low* (*Luxury Coaches*) *Ltd.* [1962] 1 Q.B. 694, and the comment on that case in Megrah, Gilbart Lectures, 1963, p. 22.

bank. Satisfactory replies were given to two such inquiries, and the plaintiffs, relying on these replies, placed orders for advertising space in connection with which, on the subsequent liquidation of Easipower Ltd., they lost more than £17,000. They brought an action against the defendant bank alleging that the replies had been given negligently.

One of the inquiries was made, and replied to, in writing. The reply began with the words—

CONFIDENTIAL
For your private use and without responsibility
on the part of the bank or its officials.

The other inquiry was made by telephone, but it was agreed by the parties that a similar disclaimer of responsibility was accepted by the inquiring bank.

McNair J. held that the bank had in fact been negligent,[9] but he considered that, quite apart from the effect of the disclaimer, if any, he was bound by precedent to hold that a bank was not liable for damage resulting from mere statements of this kind, however negligently made. His judgment was affirmed by the Court of Appeal.

Decision

The House of Lords, after reviewing the earlier cases, held that if a person such as a banker, upon receiving a request for information or advice in circumstances that show that his skill or judgment is being relied upon, gives that information or advice without a clear disclaimer of responsibility, he accepts a legal duty to exercise proper care in doing so even though he is not under any contractual or fiduciary obligation to the inquirer, and if he is negligent an action for damages will lie.

In the circumstances of the present case the bank's disclaimer was held to be sufficient to free them from liability. Lord Devlin said:

> A man cannot be said voluntarily to be undertaking a responsibility if at the very moment when he is said to be accepting it he declares that in fact he is not.[10]

And Lord Morris said:

> They stated that they only responded to the inquiry on the basis that their reply was without responsibility. If the inquirers chose to receive and act

[9] The bank strenuously denied having been negligent, but the point was not in issue in the Court of Appeal or the House of Lords, in view of the findings of law in those courts.

[10] At p. 533.

upon the reply they cannot disregard the definite terms upon which it was given. They cannot accept a reply given with a stipulation and then reject the stipulation.[11]

Notes [12]

In the general law of negligence the *Hedley Byrne* decision is of major importance, establishing for the first time that there can be liability for financial loss resulting from negligent words (as contrasted with physical injury resulting from negligent actions) even when the parties have no contractual or fiduciary relationship.

In *Mutual Life and Citizens Assurance* v. *Evatt* [13] a majority of the Privy Council held that the *Hedley Byrne* principle did not extend to negligent advice given by one whose business did not include the giving of advice and had not held himself out as an expert. As a Privy Council decision this was not binding on the English Courts. It was criticised at the time [13a]; and in *Esso Petroleum Co. Ltd.* v. *Mardon* [13b] the Court of Appeal upheld Lawson J. in following the Privy Council minority: *Hedley Byrne* is not to be thus restricted.

In *McInerny* v. *Lloyds Bank Ltd.*,[14] a bank manager had made certain statements in a telex message to his customer, and at the customer's request had repeated the telex to the plaintiff, with whom the customer was doing business. In the plaintiff's action, based in part on an allegation of negligence in those statements, Kerr J. expressed the view that the court should be cautious in extending the *Hedley Byrne* principle to include statements made to a particular person with his interests in mind, even if they were likely to be shown to a third party.[15]

The banking interest of *Hedley Byrne* is academic to the extent that in practice the banks invariably answer credit inquiries "without responsibility." Such disclaimers were general practice for many years before 1963, and since then the banks are even less likely to answer inquiries without protecting themselves in this way.

Bankers, however, noted with interest Lord Hodson's approval of the words of Pearson L.J. in the Court of Appeal:

> Apart from authority, I am not satisfied that it would be reasonable to impose on a banker the obligation suggested, if that obligation really adds

---

[11] At p. 504.

[12] *Cf. Tournier's* case, *ante*, p. 6, for a discussion of whether a bank is entitled to answer a credit inquiry without the knowledge or consent of its customer.

[13] [1971] A.C. 793.

[13a] *Cf. The Banker* (March, 1971), vol. 121, p. 332.

[13b] [1976] Q.B. 801.

[14] [1973] 2 Lloyd's Rep. 389.

[15] The bank succeeded here and in the Court of Appeal ([1974] 1 Lloyd's Rep. 246) although the judgments in the Court of Appeal did not repeat the judge's *caveat* quoted here.

anything to the duty of giving an honest answer. It is conceded by counsel for the plaintiffs that the banker is not expected to make outside inquiries to supplement the information which he already has. Is he then expected, in business hours in the bank's time, to expend time and trouble in searching records, studying documents, weighing and comparing the favourable and unfavourable features and producing a well-balanced and well-worded report? That seems wholly unreasonable. Then, if he is not expected to do any of these things, and if he is permitted to give an impromptu answer in the words that immediately come to his mind on the basis of the facts which he happens to remember or is able to ascertain from a quick glance at the file or one of the files, the duty of care seems to add little, if anything, to the duty of honesty.[16]

Lord Hodson went on to remark that " this is to the same effect as the opinion of Cozens-Hardy M.R." in *Parsons* v. *Barclay & Co. Ltd.*[17] With respect, it seems to go further, for in that case the Master of the Rolls, having rejected the argument that before answering an inquiry the banker should make inquiries himself, still required that he answer " honestly according to his own knowledge of what he knows from the books before him, and from any other actual knowledge he has." This is rather less casual than the conduct Pearson L.J. would seem to have permitted. It need hardly be said that bankers themselves, however careful they may be to disclaim responsibility, do in practice take this aspect of their business very seriously.

There does not appear to be any reported case in which the inquirer and the object of the inquiry have their accounts with the same bank. In such a case there would be a contractual relationship between the inquirer and the bank answering the inquiry; and it is to be noted that in the *Hedley Byrne* case, Lord Pearce said of the disclaimer " I do not . . . accept that, even if the parties were already in contractual or other special relationship, the words would give no immunity to a negligent answer." This view was *obiter*, but it may well be taken as indicating the courts' probable attitude were such a case to be brought.

It would seem that a bank following current practice and giving its replies unsigned cannot be made liable even if the reply is fraudulent, *i.e.* containing a false representation made knowingly or recklessly. There is no recent reported English case on the point, but in *Hirst* v. *West Riding Banking Co. Ltd.*[18] the bank escaped liability by virtue of section 6 of the Statute of Frauds Amendment Act 1828, which provides that no action can be brought against a

[16] At pp. 512–513.
[17] *Ante*, p. 9.
[18] [1901] 2 K.B. 560.

person making a false representation regarding another person's credit unless such representation is in writing and signed [19]; the signature of the manager was held not to bind the bank. Earlier, in *Swift* v. *Jewesbury*,[20] where the manager was joined as defendant, he was held personally liable, but the bank escaped, both under the 1828 Act and because Coleridge C.J. considered that the inquiry was made to the manager personally.

More recently in *Commercial Banking Company of Sydney Ltd.* v. *R. H. Brown & Co.*[21] the Australian High Court held the bank liable for its manager's fraudulent reply to a credit inquiry, and rejected the bank's argument that, *inter alia*, the reply had been sent not to the plaintiffs but to their bankers, and had been expressed to be " confidential and for your private use." The fact that it was also " without responsibility " also failed to save the bank. But the Statute of Frauds defence was not raised, so the case, which as an Australian decision is anyhow not of binding authority in England, leaves that defence still available.

It may be regarded as unfortunate that this is so. It is improbable that a bank would resist liability in a case of what one might call gross fraud by one of its managers, but there are degrees of fraud: in the Australian case the manager had been concerned to nurse his customer through difficulties which he believed to be temporary, and it cannot be regarded as satisfactory that in such circumstances, which cannot be unique, his employers can escape liability merely because the reply to an inquiry is unsigned.

It is not without interest to note that immediately following the decision in *Swift* v. *Jewesbury*, an article in *The Economist* for February 7, 1874, strongly criticised the finding that the inquiry was addressed to the manager personally, and the " very technical " application of the 1828 Act: ". . . certainly, whatever the present law may be, few business men will question the expediency of having the law so framed that people who authorise their servants to make statements as to the credit of others in the ordinary course of their business should be held responsible for such statements." [21a]

---

[19] In the *Banbury* case (*post*, p. 301) the House of Lords held that the section applies only to fraudulent representation.

[20] (1874) L.R. 9 Q.B. 301.

[21] [1972] 2 Lloyd's Rep. 360.

[21a] *Cf. ante*, p. 74, for the dictum of Hilbery J., as to qualified privilege covering the banker's replies to inquiries.

INVESTMENT ADVICE

Woods v. Martins Bank Ltd. and Another

[1959] 1 Q.B. 55

Advice on investments may be within the scope of a bank's business

Facts

The plaintiff, a young man of no business experience, had the opportunity of investing money in a private company which banked with the Quayside, Newcastle, branch of the defendant bank. He met the manager of that branch, sought his advice, and acting upon it invested £5,000 in the company. Thereafter he himself opened an account at the same branch, and subsequently, still on the manager's advice, invested further sums in the same company, and guaranteed the account of another associated company. Throughout the period the company's account was overdrawn and the district office was pressing for reductions. The plaintiff lost more than £16,000, and brought this action against the bank and its branch manager for fraud or negligence.

Decision

Salmon J. held that the branch manager, while not fraudulent, had been grossly negligent; and after considering the bank's advertisements and booklets, rejected their defence that advice on investment was outside the scope of their business. The plaintiff was a customer of the bank from the time when the manager agreed to advise him, even though no account had then been opened.[21b]

Notes

Woods v. *Martins Bank Ltd.* was decided on its special, and unusual, facts, and more must not be read into it than those facts support. But on the point mainly in question, the bank's liability for investment advice, Salmon J. placed great weight on the bank's publicity material, and three of his four quotations therefrom offered financial advice only in general terms providing a framework in which investment advice might be thought to be included unless it were expressly excluded. The fourth contained an offer to obtain investment advice "from the best available sources"—and it is, of course, by obtaining such advice from brokers that the banks seek to avoid liability of this kind; in the present case the bank's instructions to its branch managers forbade them to give direct investment advice to customers. But the fact that the manager was acting outside the scope of his authority did not avail the bank; his purported

[21b] *Cf. ante*, p. 23.

authority was held to include the kind of advice he gave; and it seems unlikely that any bank could now escape liability for the negligent advice of its branch manager.[22] Indeed, the much wider range of services now offered by the banks through, if not by, their branch managers, has probably weakened their position as compared with 1958, notwithstanding that their direct investment services are normally provided by specialist subsidiary companies and advice on particular investments still obtained from brokers.

Until the *Woods* decision the position had been more uncertain. In *Banbury* v. *Bank of Montreal* [23] the circumstances were somewhat similar to those of the *Woods* case, the manager advising the customer to invest in a company whose account was giving the bank some trouble. When the company failed the customer brought an action against the bank, and a jury awarded him £25,000 damages, but the Court of Appeal and the House of Lords held differently, on the grounds, *inter alia*, that there was not sufficient evidence to show that advice on investments was within the scope of the bank's business, and that the branch manager had therefore no implied authority to bind the bank. But the Lords' decision on this point was by a majority of three to two, and the three did not base their finding on similar grounds. And in the *Woods* case, Salmon J. said:

> In my judgment, the limits of a banker's business cannot be laid down as a matter of law. The nature of such a business must in each case be a matter of fact and, accordingly, cannot be treated as if it were a matter of pure law. What may have been true of the Bank of Montreal in 1918 is not necessarily true of Martins Bank in 1958.[24]

It is interesting to note that, if the law is indeed as is here suggested, the standard of care required of the banker is noticeably higher in advising on investment than it is in giving a banker's reference, where he probably need be no more than "honest." [25] In the first case, of course, he owes a clear duty to his customer; in the second the fact that he is not in contractual relationship with the inquirer somewhat protects him. Should a case arise in which the inquirer and the subject of the inquiry bank with the same bank, whether or not at the same branch, this remoteness of banker and inquirer will be absent, and the higher standard of care may be enforced.[26]

---

[22] And *cf.* the different kind of liability seen in *Lloyds Bank Ltd.* v. *Bundy*, *ante*, p. 14.

[23] [1918] A.C. 626.

[24] At p. 70.

[25] *Cf. ante*, p. 297.

[26] But *cf. ante*, p. 298.

The case of *Wilson* v. *United Counties Bank Ltd.*[27] is of interest on the topic of investment advice, although the facts are so unusual that it affords little or no guidance. There the plaintiff, on leaving the country on war service, made an agreement with the defendants that their branch manager should supervise his business. The jury found that the bank had been negligent in doing this, and heavy damages were awarded; the Court of Appeal reversed this finding, but the House of Lords restored it. The decision has been criticised[28]; and the fact that such a service as that provided by the bank is quite outside the scope of ordinary banking business seems to have been ignored in the judgments.

---

[27] [1920] A.C. 102.
[28] *Cf.* Paget, *op. cit.* p. 187.

CHAPTER 11

TERMINATION OF RELATIONSHIP BETWEEN BANKER AND CUSTOMER

NOTICE

Prosperity Ltd. v. Lloyds Bank Ltd.

(1923) 39 T.L.R. 372

Termination by notice by the banker

Facts

The plaintiff company was formed in 1922 with the object of setting on foot a " snowball " insurance scheme. The scheme was explained to the manager of the Victoria Street branch of the defendant bank, who agreed to open an account in the name of the company, to receive applications from subscribers and to allot the moneys subscribed as provided in the rules of the company. The account was accordingly opened and payments received until there was a credit balance on the account of some £7,000.

The publicity which the scheme attracted was brought to the notice of the head office of the bank, and it was decided that it was undesirable for the bank to be associated with the project. A letter was sent from the head office on February 14, 1923, informing the plaintiffs that after March 14, the bank would cease to act as bankers to the company. The plaintiffs brought the present action seeking (*a*) a declaration that the bank were not entitled to close the account without reasonable notice; and (*b*) an injunction restraining the bank from closing the account.

Decision

It was held that an injunction was not an appropriate remedy in the circumstances; but that the plaintiffs were entitled to the declaration sought. In his judgment McCardie J. said:

With respect to all accounts there might be an special contract between banker and customer which bound both of them and that special contract might provide that the banking relationship should last for a given period. It might, however, provide that no notice should be given at all. If, however, there was no special contract, then, in his (his Lordship's) view, it was the law that the bank could not close an account in credit without reasonable notice. . . .

It was obvious that the question of reasonableness must depend on the special facts and circumstances of the case. An account might be a small account drawn upon only by cheques cashed by the customer for his own purposes. In that case a comparatively short notice might be all that was needed. . . . A customer might also deal with his account by sending cheques, to the knowledge of the bank, to different parts of the Continent. In that case . . . the existence of such outstanding cheques might place upon the bank a larger burden as to notice. . . . He had come to the conclusion that, having regard to the knowledge and approval in the first place of Lloyds Bank of this scheme, and having regard to their knowledge as to the far extent to which the pamphlets and forms were being sent throughout the world, one month was not an adequate notice, because it did not give the plaintiffs a sufficient opportunity of dealing with the position created by the decision of Lloyds Bank to end the account.[1]

Notes

In his judgment in *Joachimson* v. *Swiss Bank Corporation* [2] Atkin L.J. said: " It is a term of the contract that the bank will not cease to do business with the customer except upon reasonable notice." The customer can at any time close his current account without notice to the banker, but if the banker closes it without giving the customer time to make other arrangements, the subsequent dishonour of the customer's cheques may leave him liable for damage to credit.

The only question in any particular case is the length of notice required. It is seldom that an account which the banker desires to close has such extensive ramifications as those discussed in the *Prosperity* case; but while the case is an exceptional one, it serves to underline the necessity for " reasonable " notice.

Garnett v. *McKewan* [3] is an example of the banker's right to combine two accounts, and so in effect close one of them, without notice.[4] It may be remarked, however, that even in circumstances like those of that case the banker would be cautious in dishonouring a cheque on the closed account with the answer " Account closed," or " No account "; indeed it is difficult to imagine a banker today dishonouring a cheque at all in such a case.

Usually there is little difficulty in the customer's closing of his own account. Exceptional circumstances were seen in *Berry* v. *Halifax Commercial Banking Co.*[5] There a customer had an overdraft against the security of a life policy, and the mortgage provided,

---

[1] At p. 373.

[2] [1921] 3 K.B. 110; *ante*, p. 1.

[3] (1872) L.R. 8 Ex. 10; *ante*, p. 196, *post*, p. 345.

[4] Another, even more arbitrary, closing of an account is seen in *Marten* v. *Rocke, Eyton & Co.* (*ante*, p. 154), although there the unsuccessful action against the banker was brought by a third party.

[5] [1901] 1 Ch. 188.

inter alia, that the bank's statutory power of sale should be exercisable if there should be default in payment of the balance due for one month after the current account had been closed. The customer in due course wrote to the bank to inform them that there had been a meeting of creditors who had " agreed to accept all the assets I had. I gave them to understand that I was insured . . . and that you held the policy . . . as security. . . ." More than a month later the bank sold the policy; and they were held to have been justified in so doing, the letter having in effect closed the account.

MENTAL DISORDER

Re Beavan, Davies, Banks & Co. v. Beavan

[1912] 1 Ch. 196

Customer of unsound mind; bank advance for necessaries

Facts

For many years the plaintiffs, who were bankers, had had a current account in the name of J. G. Beavan. For two years before his death in 1906 the customer was of unsound mind, following a paralytic stroke, and the bank, with the approval of the other members of the family, agreed to continue his account, to be worked by his eldest son, who signed cheques " for J. G. Beavan, S. S. Beavan." The account was operated in these two years for the maintenance of the customer's household in its accustomed manner, rents being collected and credited, and necessary outgoings being debited.

Upon the death of the customer the account was overdrawn, the amount including bank charges for interest and commission. The bank claimed the amount owing to them from the four executors, and the eldest son and one of his brothers, considering that the claim should not be resisted, severed from the two other executors and did not appear.

Decision

It was held that the bank were entitled to recover from the estate, by the doctrine of subrogation, all amounts paid out by them for necessaries; but that interest and commission charges could not be so recovered. In his judgment, Neville J. said:

Now it is not disputed that the law is that a person maintaining another of unsound mind is entitled to recoupment from his estate in respect of necessary expenditure, having regard to the position in life of the person of unsound mind. Starting with that, the question is, what is the right of one who lends money to the person who is maintaining the lunatic where that money is applied in the provision of necessaries for the maintenance of the lunatic? It appears to me that no legal right arises as a result of the lending in favour of the lender, but I think an equity arises, and that that equity is to stand in the shoes of those creditors who, being creditors for necessaries supplied for the maintenance of the lunatic, have been paid out of the money advanced by the lender. That is an equity which applies in many cases, and I think that it also applies in the present case. Then it was argued that, in addition to that, there was a right on the part of the bank to recover the charges for interest and commission which, had they been dealing with a person of sound mind, they would have been entitled to charge. It does not seem to me that that contention can prevail. I think that, inasmuch as the equity which is to be applied is merely the right to stand in the shoes of the creditors who are paid off, it is impossible that in addition to that there should be a right to receive the charges which have been paid for obtaining the loan.[6]

Notes

It is to be noted that the Mental Health Act 1959 repealed the earlier statutes governing the affairs of the mentally disordered. There has been no judicial consideration of how far the " mental disorder " of the 1959 Act equates with the " lunacy " of the earlier legislation, under which the relevant cases were decided.

There have in fact been very few cases in which a question has arisen concerning the banker's relationship with a customer of unsound mind, and this may probably be taken as an indication that in practice difficulties do not often occur. It is not clear whether it is mental disorder or notice of mental disorder that does in fact end the relationship [7]; in any case, the student must seek the theory of the matter in the general law of contract, and *Re Beavan* itself is an example of the application of this law to the banker-customer relationship. It can certainly be said at least that notice of mental disorder revokes the mandate to pay the customer's cheques.

It need hardly be pointed out that no banker wishes to rest upon his right of subrogation only, and that today, in circumstances like those of *Re Beavan*, the account would be stopped pending an order of the Court of Protection. Should immediate business be necessary it would be conducted through a new account in the name of the son.

In *Scarth* v. *National Provincial Bank Ltd.*[8] the bank's customer became of unsound mind and the bank stopped his account, even

---

[6] At pp. 201–202.

[7] *Cf.* Chorley, *op. cit.* 0p. 351.

[8] (1930) 4 L.D.B. 241.

though the wife had authority to sign "*per pro*." She opened a separate account, and later, against the indemnity of herself and another, the bank transferred the balance of the husband's account to the wife's. Later the husband recovered from his disability, and claimed the balance of the account from the bank. The case was heard at York Assizes, and Humphreys J., applying the equitable principle stated by Wright J. in *Liggett's* case,[9] decided in favour of the bank on the grounds that before the balance had been transferred the wife had used a larger sum than that balance in paying the husband's debts.

There are many circumstances in which the mental disorder of the customer, or the suspicion of it, can be a matter of extreme embarrassment to the banker.[10] It may be added here that in practice the banks would not be likely to stand on their legal rights in matters of this kind, and the necessities of the dependants must often be met immediately, without any legally satisfactory arrangement being possible.

BANKRUPTCY

Ponsford, Baker & Co. v. Union of London and Smith's Bank Ltd.

[1906] 2 Ch. 444

Re Seymour

[1937] 1 Ch. 668

Termination of the relationship on the bankruptcy of the customer; position of the debtor after commission of an act of bankruptcy

Facts of Ponsford, Baker & Co. v. Union of London and Smith's Bank Ltd.

The plaintiffs were a firm of stockbrokers who had lodged with the defendant bank certain securities against an advance. In April 1906 they were declared defaulters on the Stock Exchange, and as a result the Official Assignee of the Stock Exchange had the duty of collecting their assets. In May, the plaintiffs and the Official Assignee tendered to the bank the amount due together with interest, and called for the securities, which were worth more than the loan. The bank refused to give up the securities, on the ground

---

[9] *Ante*, p. 190.

[10] *Cf.* (August, 1965) 86 J.I.B.: Smart, "No Longer Lunacy."

that in the assignment to the Official Assignee they had notice of an act of bankruptcy, and that they therefore could not release the securities to their customer until three months had elapsed without bankruptcy proceedings being instituted.

The plaintiffs sought an order that upon payment into court the bank should deliver up the securities to them.

Decision

The Court of Appeal held that the bank was entitled to refuse to surrender securities to a customer who to their knowledge had committed an act of bankruptcy, even though in certain circumstances the court might be prepared to sanction such surrender where it was desirable for the protection of the debtor's estate. In the present case there were no circumstances justifying such protective action.

Fletcher Moulton L.J., delivering the judgment of the court (himself, and Vaughan Williams and Romer L.JJ.) said:

> . . . It is necessary to examine carefully the exact legal position of a man who has committed an act of bankruptcy under the statutes at present in force. Until commission of the act of bankruptcy he was, of course, the beneficial owner of whatever assets he possessed, but by the act of bankruptcy his title to be regarded as such beneficial owner is no longer absolute, but is contingent on no bankruptcy petition being presented within three months of the date of the act of bankruptcy which leads to a receiving order being made. If such receiving order be made the whole of the assets vest in his trustee as from the date of the act of bankruptcy. He is, therefore, in the position that should such a contingency occur he is from the date of the act of bankruptcy something less than a mere trustee of his assets for the creditors in his bankruptcy. Until this state of suspense has been removed either by a receiving order or by lapse of time, he has no right to deal with those assets that were in his hands, and can give no title in them to any transferee with notice. Similarly, with regard to the debts and other choses in action which form part of his estate, he cannot collect them or give a valid discharge for them, and anyone making a payment to him with notice of the act of bankruptcy does so at his peril. But these statutory provisions have been enacted for the benefit only of the creditors of the bankrupt, and not for the benefit of his debtors. They are not intended in any way to weaken or postpone the duties of the debtors of the estate to discharge their obligations to it, nor is this period of three months from the act of bankruptcy intended to act in any wise as a moratorium to those debtors so as to give them relief or respite from payments immediately due.[11]

Facts of Re Seymour

In March 1936 a petition in bankruptcy was presented against the debtor, who had two accounts with his bank; one of these was

[11] At pp. 452–453.

at the Marble Arch branch, the other, a dormant one, at the Edgware Road branch. In May 1936 the former account was overdrawn £2 12s. 11d., and the latter £240 6s. 4d., the second overdraft being secured by the guarantee of a friend. On May 5, the debtor borrowed £300 from moneylenders, and the next day paid this sum into his account at Marble Arch. He then withdrew sufficient to pay off his Edgware Road overdraft.

On July 27, a receiving order was made against him on the petition of the previous March. The trustee claimed that his title related back to March and that the transactions of May were intended by the debtor to prefer the guarantor, the debtor knowing himself at that time to be insolvent. He therefore sought a declaration that the money formed part of the debtor's estate, and that the payment of it to the bank was void as against the trustee. The bank contended, *inter alia*, that they were protected by section 45 of the Bankruptcy Act 1914.

Decision

It was held that the bank was not liable to refund the moneys. In his judgment, Clauson J. said:

> The bank's contention that s. 45 is a protection to them seems to me to be correct and to be a complete answer to the trustee's claim. The trustee bases his claim on the provisions of the Act, which make his title to the money, with which the bankrupt paid the bank, relate back to a date antecedent to the date of the payment: the trustee, in other words, can establish his claim only by referring to and invoking the aid of the Act: but s. 45 seems to me to say in plain terms that if (as is admittedly the case here) the two conditions are complied with (i) that the payment is made before the date of the receiving order and (ii) that the payee has no notice of any act of bankruptcy, the Act is not to be invoked in support of a claim to invalidate the payment. If the trustee cannot invoke the Act, his case must, as it seems to me, fail. The section seems to me plain: the circumstances are such as to bring its protective operation into force; and the bank has, in my view, a perfectly good defence, by virtue of the section, to the claim put forward by the trustee.[12]

Notes

The Bankruptcy Act 1914, s. 48 (6), provides that moneys held by a banker on account of a bankrupt must be handed over to the trustee; but the actual date from which the banker can, and indeed must, refuse to conduct further business on the account varies with the circumstances, and is not entirely clear in the light

[12] At p. 672.

of decided cases and the provisions of sections 45 and 46 of the Act, which protect certain dealings with the bankrupt.

Section 45 provides protection of:

(*a*) Any payment by the bankrupt to any of his creditors;
(*b*) Any payment or delivery to the bankrupt;
(*c*) Any conveyance or assignment by the bankrupt for valuable consideration;
(*d*) Any contract, dealing, or transaction by or with the bankrupt for valuable consideration;

Provided that both the following conditions are complied with, namely:

(i) that the payment, delivery, conveyance, assignment, contract, dealing, or transaction, as the case may be, takes place before the date of the receiving order; and

(ii) that the person (other than the debtor) to, by, or with whom the payment, delivery, conveyance, assignment, contract, dealing, or transaction was made, executed, or entered into, has not at the time of the payment, delivery, conveyance, assignment, contract, dealing, or transaction, notice of any available act of bankruptcy committed by the bankrupt before that time.

It will be observed that in this section the date of importance to the banker is that upon which he receives notice of an act of bankruptcy; in the absence of such notice the payments specified are protected up to the time of the receiving order. It is clear that payments to the bankrupt out of the account are within (*b*); *Re Seymour* is an example of a protected transaction under (*a*).

Re Keever, A Bankrupt, Ex parte Cork v. *Midland Bank Ltd.*[13] was a case where (*d*) was relevant. The bankrupt paid in to the credit of her account a cheque for £3,000, on the day before the receiving order was made (the bank having received no notice of any available act of bankruptcy). The cheque was duly collected, the bank receiving payment on the day the receiving order was made. The trustee in bankruptcy resisted the bank's claim to set off the cheque against the overdrawn balance of the account, but Ungoed-Thomas J. held that the bank had a lien on the cheque, that the lien was a " contract dealing or transaction " within section 45, and that the overdraft was " valuable consideration " within the section, both in itself and by virtue of section 27 of the Bills of Exchange Act 1882.[14]

It is generally considered that the banker is not protected by section 45 if he pays the bankrupt's cheques to third parties, even

[13] [1967] Ch. 182. *Cf. ante*, p. 224.

[14] *Re Keever* was distinguished in *George Barker (Transport) Ltd.* v. *Eynon* [1974] 1 W.L.R. 462, where it was held that lien cannot be established over property, the possession of which is obtained after the receiving order.

if the payees are in fact creditors of the bankrupt: it would be necessary for the banker to be regarded as his customer's agent before he could be held protected in such payments. It is perhaps significant, however, that there has been no case upon the point; and in practice the banks do regard themselves as being protected in such payments where they have had no notice of an act of bankruptcy and no receiving order has been made.

The position is somewhat complicated by the wider protection given by section 46. This section provides that:

> A payment of money or delivery of property to a person subsequently adjudged bankrupt, or to a person claiming by assignment from him, shall, notwithstanding anything in this Act, be a good discharge to the person paying the money or delivering the property, if the payment or delivery is made before the actual date on which the receiving order is made and without notice of the presentation of a bankruptcy petition, and is either pursuant to the ordinary course of business or otherwise bona fide.

Here the operative date is that of notice of the presentation of a bankruptcy petition; and so notable an authority as Hart [15] considers that the payment by the banker of his customer's cheque to a third party, whether a creditor or not, is within the section as being a reduction of the bank's indebtedness to the customer, and thus in effect a payment to him. This view has not found general support; Paget,[16] for example, considers that the banker paying third-party cheques is without protection. But it is clear that payments to the bankrupt himself are protected by section 45 up to the date of notice of an act of bankruptcy, and beyond that by section 46 until notice of presentation of a bankruptcy petition.

The remarks of Russell J., delivering the judgment of the Divisional Court in *Re Dalton*,[17] are however to be noted. Speaking of section 46, and the argument that it was enacted in 1913 to deal specifically with particular hardships, to which it should now still be confined, he said:

> If it be considered a mischief that a banker be not able to meet demands from the customer for cash, it is surely no less a mischief that the banker be not able to honour cheques drawn by the customer in favour of other persons, always remembering the safeguard that for the section to operate it must be shown that the payment is made pursuant to the ordinary course of business or otherwise bona fide. (We observe that of course the payee of the cheque would not be a person claiming by assignment.) It would, in our judgment, be very strange if Parliament had enacted that a banker (with the relevant notice) must say to the customer "I cannot honour your cheques to

15 *Op. cit.* p. 409.
16 *Op. cit.* pp. 94 *et seq.*
17 [1963] Ch. 336.

tradesmen totalling £50, but here is £50 in cash for you to post or send or take to them. . . ." [18]

This dictum, the good sense of which is naturally welcome to bankers, must yet be treated with reserve; it was clearly *obiter*, the particular question not being in any way at issue in the case, and it clearly goes further than the words of the section strictly justify.[19]

Section 46 also gives protection to the banker in such circumstances as those of the *Ponsford, Baker* case, which was decided before the Act. There the customer called for release of securities, but the same considerations apply when he demands payment of his balance; before the Act the banker had to refuse either demand if he had received notice of an act of bankruptcy. Now, in the light of section 46, he may release securities or balance *to his customer or his customer's assignee* so long as he has not received notice of presentation of a bankruptcy petition and, of course, no receiving order has been made. It may be noted that Paget considers the legislation ambiguous [20]—it is certainly inconsistent—and suggests that it is still doubtful whether the circumstances of the *Ponsford, Baker* case come within section 45 or section 46. It is submitted, however, that the words " notwithstanding anything in this Act " give section 46 overriding effect where there is conflict between it and section 45.

In practice the banks refuse payment of third-party cheques immediately upon receipt of notice of an act of bankruptcy, but continue to pay their customer's own cheques out of his credit balance, and, if called upon, to release securities; only notice of the bankruptcy petition or the making of a receiving order stops the account completely. An exception to this practice occurs when the act of bankruptcy of which notice is received is an assignment of assets for the benefit of creditors generally. The assets thus assigned include any credit balance on the account, and upon notice being received by the bank all drawings on the account and all releases of securities are stopped.

It must further be noted that credits received after notice of the act of bankruptcy do not become part of the available balance upon which the bankrupt is, as outlined above, allowed to draw. Similarly, if the account is already overdrawn, such later credits are held in suspense, and not regarded as reducing the overdraft.[21]

---

18 At p. 353.

19 *Cf. post*, p. 337, where a clearing bank is noted as basing its practice on *Re Dalton*.

20 *Op. cit.* p. 102.

21 On the subject of bankruptcy generally, see Chorley, *op. cit.* pp. 352 *et seq.*

Re Simms

[1930] 2 Ch. 22

The act of bankruptcy

Facts

The debtor was in business as a builder, and upon his business increasing he wished to obtain more capital. At the time he owed his creditors £28,000, together with an amount of £6,000 which he owed to one Jameson, who was associated with him in the business. He had an overdraft with Barclays Bank of £6,500, and the bank would not agree to increase this limit. Lloyds Bank, however, agreed to advance up to £12,500, on the following terms: a private limited company was to be formed, the debtor's assets being sold to the company for £17,000, satisfied by the issue of 17,000 £1 shares and the undertaking of the company to pay the debtor's liabilities; and a debenture was to be issued to the bank as security for the advance.

These arrangements were carried through, but no notice was given to the main body of the creditors, who, when they heard of the formation of the company, began to press for payment. The more importunate of them were paid in full. There was a meeting of creditors on February 11, 1929, and on February 14, the bank put in a receiver. On February 27, there was an act of bankruptcy in the debtor's failure to comply with a notice of bankruptcy, and in due course the debtor was adjudicated bankrupt. The present action was a motion for a declaration that the sale of the debtor's assets to the company was void against the trustee.

Decision

It was held that the sale was a fraudulent transfer and itself an act of bankruptcy; and that the title of the trustee therefore related back to it, and overrode the title of the company.

In his judgment, Clauson J. said:

The result of [these] authorities appears to me to be that a transfer by a debtor of substantially the whole of his property, whether by way of charge or by way of sale, will be an act of bankruptcy, if the necessary consequence of the transfer will be to defeat or delay his creditors; and, with these authorities to guide me, I feel no difficulty in holding that the substitution, in place of a going business and substantial business assets, of (*a*) shares in a private company which has taken over the debtor's assets and liabilities together with (*b*) a right of action by the debtor against that company on its covenant to discharge his liabilities, must necessarily have the result of delaying the creditors. . . . It follows that I must hold the sale . . . to be a fraudulent transfer and an act of bankruptcy. . . .

It was, however, suggested that in some way or other the company could claim the protection of s. 45 of the Act of 1914. . . . The suggestion I think was that all the parties honestly thought that this transfer which the law holds—and they must be assumed to have known that the law would hold—to be fraudulent, was the best thing in everyone's interests. But I can rely on the authority of Cotton L.J. in *Ex parte Chaplin*[22] for the proposition that a fraudulent transaction remains a fraudulent transaction (at all events if the parties know all the facts which stamp it in law as a fraudulent transaction) whatever may be the view of the parties that it may be the best thing for the debtor, or may result in effectually paying the creditors.[23]

Notes

There are eight " acts of bankruptcy " upon which the petition in bankruptcy may be founded.[24] *Re Simms* is a useful example of one of these acts, and is also a demonstration that " fraudulent " here does not necessarily mean dishonest.

Re Douglas, Ex parte Snowball

(1872) L.R. 7 Ch. 534

What constitutes notice of an act of bankruptcy

Facts

Douglas and his son were in business as partners, and Snowball was their solicitor. In 1869 they were in debt to him and they were in other financial difficulties. The son left the country, first executing a power of attorney in favour of one Moore. In November of that year Snowball granted Moore and Douglas further help against the mortgage of the whole business. The following April the business became finally insolvent, and the son's departure from the country was held to be an act of bankruptcy. Snowball said that he had believed the reason the son gave for leaving, and that the absence was intended to be only a temporary one.

Decision

On appeal it was held (on this point) that Snowball had had notice of the act of bankruptcy. In his judgment, Mellish L.J. said:

---

[22] (1884) 26 Ch.D. 319.
[23] At pp. 34–35.
[24] As to these, see Chorley, *op. cit.* p. 361.

It appears to us that if a person is proved to know facts which constitute an act of bankruptcy, or is proved to know facts from which a Court or a jury, or any impartial person, would naturally and properly infer that an act of bankruptcy had been committed, he ought to be held to have had notice that an act of bankruptcy had been committed, and that the Court ought not to enter upon the inquiry whether he did in his own mind believe that an act of bankruptcy had been committed, or whether he did in his own mind draw the inference that the bankrupt intended to defeat and delay his creditors. A person may be proved to have had notice that an act of bankruptcy had been committed, either by proof that he had received formal notice that an act of bankruptcy had been committed, or by proof that he knew facts which were sufficient to inform him that an act of bankruptcy had been committed. If he is proved to have received a formal notice he is not allowed to escape from the effect of having had notice by saying he had not read it when he ought to have read it, or that he did not believe it when he had read it; and we think if he is proved to have known facts which were sufficient to have informed him that an act of bankruptcy had been committed, he cannot be allowed to escape from the effect of having had notice by saying that he did not draw the natural inference from the facts.[25]

Notes

We have seen earlier the importance of notice of an act of bankruptcy, in that a person who has received such notice cannot claim the protection of section 45 of the Bankruptcy Act. What constitutes constructive notice, as opposed to actual notice, must always be a matter of fact, but *Re Snowball* is an example of actual knowledge of an act which could bear an innocent interpretation being held to be notice of an act of bankruptcy.

In *Re Boocock*,[26] on the other hand, a firm had actual notice of the service upon a customer of a bankruptcy notice, which is not in itself, of course, an act of bankruptcy. They made no inquiry as to what happened thereafter, and it was held that they had not received notice of the act of bankruptcy which did, in fact, develop from the bankruptcy notice. Rowlatt J. said:

When a question arises as to whether the facts that are known are sufficient to tell the recipient of that knowledge of an act of bankruptcy, the question has to be decided on a reasonable view of the facts in the particular case. Further, it is clear that a person cannot say he has no notice of an act of bankruptcy if he has shut his eyes to information which he must have known would, if he had kept his eyes open, have informed him of an act of bankruptcy. But in this case we are asked to say that a man has notice of an act of bankruptcy merely because he has not followed up the development of the situation which was created by the service of a

---

[25] At p. 549.

[26] [1916] 1 K.B. 816.

bankruptcy notice of which he had knowledge, which bankruptcy notice without his knowledge, in fact has subsequently matured into an act of bankruptcy. There is no decided case which goes anything like as far as that.[27]

These two decisions, while not actually conflicting, present no consistent rule for the guidance of those who may have to deal with bankrupts. In practice bankers are usually wise to be more inquiring than the firm was in *Re Boocock*, and less suspicious than the decision in *Re Snowball* might suggest they should be.

The two cases may be compared with *Anglo-South American Bank* v. *Urban District Council of Withernsea*,[28] where the plaintiff bank cashed a cheque drawn by the defendants in favour of a debtor who, the defendants alleged, had to the knowledge of the bank at that time committed an act of bankruptcy. In fact the debtor had admitted to his creditors that he was insolvent, but had refused to file his petition and had said that he would carry on in business until he was stopped. Greer J. gave judgment for the bank, holding that no act of bankruptcy had been committed; to be an act of bankruptcy a statement of this kind must be an intentional statement of something done or about to be done, and must be a declaration of inability to pay each and every creditor.

Re Wigzell, Ex parte Hart
[1921] 2 K.B. 835

Payments on an account after a receiving order but before advertisement of it

Facts

Wigzell was a customer at the Stoke Newington branch of Barclays Bank. A receiving order was made against him on October 8, 1919, but on his application the County Court granted a stay of the advertisement of the order and of all proceedings thereunder, pending his appeal against the order. On November 10, the appeal was dismissed with costs.

Between the date of the order and the dismissing of the appeal against it, the debtor had paid into his account with the bank sums totalling £165 2s. 3d., and he withdrew from the account sums totalling £199 19s. 7d. The bank had no knowledge of the bankruptcy proceedings.

---

[27] At pp. 821–822.

[28] (1925) 46 J.I.B. 112.

The trustee claimed that he was entitled, as against the bank, to the sum of £165 2s. 3d., and that the bank was not entitled to deduct any of the debtor's withdrawals. The County Court and a Divisional Court held that the trustee's claim was justified, and the bank further appealed.

Decision

The Court of Appeal dismissed the appeal. In his judgment, Younger L.J. said:

It would not I think be possible in this case to accede to the argument of the appellants without in effect repealing, so far as this bankruptcy is concerned, one of the most important provisions of the Bankruptcy Act 1914. Section 45 provides that protection shall be given in respect of "(*d*) any contract, dealing, or transaction by or with the bankrupt for valuable consideration," provided, amongst other things, that the contract, dealing, or transaction takes place before the date of the receiving order. If the contention of the appellants in this case is to prevail, the result must be that every contract, dealing, or transaction by or with this bankrupt for valuable consideration is to be protected even although it takes place after the receiving order; and that because it is conceded [by counsel for the bank] that there is in relation to the transactions between the bank and this bankrupt, taking place after the date of the receiving order, no circumstance which would not equally apply to any other transaction of the bankrupt with any person other than the bank between the date of the receiving order and the date of its advertisement. The effect, therefore, as I have said, of acceding to the argument on the part of the appellants would be that, so far as this bankruptcy is concerned, this Court would in substance be ignoring that necessary condition for protection which is imposed by s. 45 of the Act.[29]

Notes

This case is a striking example of the danger to the banker that, as a result of the postponement of the advertisement of a receiving order, he may make payments on the bankrupt's account which will not be protected either by section 45 or by section 46 of the Bankruptcy Act. The bank cited a line of precedents which tended to establish that, in the words of Farwell L.J. in *Re Tyler, ex parte Official Receiver*,[30] "it would be insufferable for this court to have it said of it that it has been guilty by its officer of a dirty trick." But in *Re Wigzell* the court did not consider that the trustee's conduct had been at all at fault, especially as the postponement had naturally been sought by the debtor, not by the trustee himself.

The Bankruptcy (Amendment) Act 1926 went some way to

---

[29] At pp. 863–864.

[30] [1907] 1 K.B. 865.

remedy the position in providing that where money or property is transferred between the date of the receiving order and the date of the advertisement and the transfer is void under the principal Act as against the trustee in bankruptcy, the trustee shall not proceed against the transferor unless the court is satisfied that it is not "reasonably practicable" to recover from the transferee. It is to be remarked that this enactment would not have helped the bank in *Re Wigzell*: there the payments in question were made to the bankrupt himself, and it is obviously not "reasonably practicable" for the trustee to recover from the debtor. But the onus is now on the trustee to prove that he cannot recover otherwise than from the banker; and the banker need only prove initially that he had no notice of the receiving order (it not having yet been gazetted), his possible negligence being immaterial. In practice it seems that the danger to the banker has been substantially reduced by the amending Act.

Re Joseph Samson Lyons, Ex parte Barclays Bank Ltd. v. The Trustee

(1934) 51 T.L.R. 24

Fraudulent preference and its effect on the banker

Facts

The bankrupt had an account with Barclays Bank with an agreed overdraft of £2,000. This advance was secured by the guarantee of the bankrupt's father. It was shown in evidence that early in 1932 the bankrupt knew that he was insolvent. In August 1932 he ceased payments to his general creditors, but continued to pay into his account, with the result that by October 22, when a bankruptcy petition was presented, the overdraft had been reduced to a little over £1,300. He was adjudicated bankrupt in December, and the trustee sought a declaration that the payments in reduction of the overdraft constituted a fraudulent preference of the bank and/or the guarantor.

Clauson J. held that the facts justified the inference that the bankrupt had intended to relieve his father of his liability, and that there was therefore fraudulent preference. He made an order against the bank for the sum involved, but made no order against the guarantor. The bank appealed.

Decision

The Court of Appeal held that the facts did not justify the

inference drawn from them in the lower court, and allowed the appeal.

In his judgment Lord Hanworth M.R. said that the bankrupt's banking account was an ordinary business account into which cheques were paid, and on which cheques were drawn. Clauson J. had said that the account was operated in such a way that the only possible inference was that an effort was being made by the bankrupt to prefer his father. But was that so? The bankrupt continued to operate the account after September 12, in exactly the same way as he had done before that date, when there was admittedly no intention to prefer anyone. He paid money in and he drew money out. To deduce from that that the only explanation was that the debtor was minded to relieve his father from liability was to misread the evidence and not to look at it in its proper perspective. It overlooked the essential nature of a fraudulent preference as indicated by Lord Tomlin in *Peat* v. *Gresham Trust Ltd.*[31] as follows:

> The onus is on those who claim to avoid the transaction to establish what the debtor really intended, and that the real intention was to prefer. The onus is only discharged when the Court, upon a review of all the circumstances, is satisfied that the dominant intent to prefer was present. That may be a matter of direct evidence or of inference, but where there is not direct evidence and there is room for more than one explanation it is not enough to say there being no direct evidence the intention to prefer must be inferred.

Notes [32]

This case is of double interest to bankers. It emphasises that intent to prefer is an essential element in fraudulent preference, but it left untouched the doctrine that when a guarantor had been preferred recovery could be obtained from the bank, the guarantor escaping liability at least as far as the particular action goes—for it must be noted that the Court of Appeal reversed the decision of the lower court only on the facts of the case, not on the law involved. The bank can, of course, still sue the guarantor, but this is often not worth doing, and must always be more troublesome than the joining of the guarantor in the first proceedings.

Section 44 of the Bankruptcy Act 1914, first extended the legislation against fraudulent preference to prevent such preference of a guarantor. The section has not been consistently applied, however. In *Re G. Stanley & Co. Ltd.*,[33] Eve J. held that the section was designed to enable the liquidator to proceed against the person

[31] (1934) 50 T.L.R. 345 at p. 349.

[32] In the following notes fraudulent preference is seen in the context of winding up proceedings as well as bankruptcy.

[33] [1925] 1 Ch. 148.

actually preferred; but in *Re Lyons*, as we have seen, only the banker's liability was in question. The trustee can always be more sure of obtaining repayment from a bank than from the guarantor, and there is thus no inducement for him to bring an action against the latter; and were the bank to seek to have the guarantor joined in the action against themselves, it is probable that the court would apply the same principle as that in the *Singer* case.[34]

In *Re Conley*,[35] which established that a person charging property to secure the debt of another is a surety within the terms of section 44, the Court of Appeal touched upon, without deciding, a kindred question to that here under discussion. Sir Wilfrid Greene M.R. said:

> The judge [in the Court below] was influenced by the view which he held, that the creditor who, on receiving payment, had handed back the deposited security would be left without a remedy against the depositor. I do not think it necessary to go into this question, but it must not be taken from this that I agree with the view of the judge on this point. If, and when, it arises for decision, the question whether or not the delivery of the security to the depositor was made under a fundamental mistake of fact will have to be considered.[36]

And Luxmore J. said:

> A further point arose before FARWELL, J., and in this court with regard to the liability of the bankrupt's wife and mother, respectively, to repay any part of the moneys. . . . FARWELL, J., decided that neither of them could, on the wording of sect. 44, be held liable to repay anything paid to the bank, and in so deciding he followed the decision of CLAUSON, J., in *Re Lyons*[37] in preference to the decision of EVE, J., in *Re Stanley (G.) & Co.*[38] I find myself in complete agreement with the decision of the judge on this point, and I do not desire to add anything to it.[39]

The provisions against fraudulent preference in the Companies Acts (now s. 320 of the Act of 1948) have similar effects *vis-à-vis* the banker. In *Re M. Kushler Ltd.*[40] the guarantor and co-director of a private limited company had professional advice that the company was insolvent. Between the date of that advice and the date, a fortnight later, of the resolution for voluntary winding up, the firm's overdraft of £600 had been completely repaid, although only two trade bills had been paid in the meantime, and an important trade creditor had been pressing for payment of an account due for

[34] *Infra*.
[35] See *post*, p. 323.
[36] At p. 132.
[37] *Supra*.
[38] *Supra*.
[39] At p. 139.
[40] [1943] 2 All E.R. 22.

three months. The Court of Appeal held that on these facts fraudulent preference was established, the inference, otherwise incomplete, being completed by the pressure of the important creditor.

In *Re A. Singer & Co. (Hat Manufacturers) Ltd.*[41] the liquidator had challenged a payment to the bank as a fraudulent preference of the bank or of two guarantors. The bank alone had been made respondent to the summons, and they now sought to bring before the court the two guarantors. The Court of Appeal refused to order the liquidator to join the guarantors as parties; it was his duty merely to get in the assets, and it was not the duty of the court to vary the proceedings in order to have another question litigated.

Despite the strong representations to the Cohen Committee by the Committee of London Clearing Bankers [42] the Companies Act 1948, provided only partial protection to the banker in these circumstances. Section 321 (3) provides:

> On any application made to the Court with respect to any payment on the ground that the payment was a fraudulent preference of a surety or guarantor, the Court shall have jurisdiction to determine any questions with respect to the payment arising between the person to whom the payment was made and the surety or guarantor and to grant relief in respect thereof, notwithstanding that it is not necessary to do so for the purposes of the winding up, and for that purpose may give leave to bring in the surety or guarantor as a third party as in the case of an action for the recovery of the sum paid.

This subsection deals with the point in question in *Re Singer Ltd.*, but it does not exempt the banker from liability. In practice it is of course invariably easier and sometimes possible only to recover from the banker; but the provision does make possible the joining of the guarantor in the action, and to that extent the banker's position *vis-à-vis* the guarantor is restored. The protection of section 321 (3) may be compared with that given in other circumstances by section 4 of the Bankruptcy (Amendment) Act 1926.[43]

Section 321 (1) of the Companies Act 1948, provides as follows:

> Where, in the case of a company wound up in England, anything made or done after the commencement of this Act is void under the last foregoing section as a fraudulent preference of a person interested in property mortgaged or charged to secure the company's debt, then (without prejudice to any rights or liabilities arising apart from this provision) the person preferred shall be subject to the same liabilities, and shall have the

[41] [1943] 1 Ch. 121.
[42] Outlined in (January 1946) 67 J.I.B. 28–29.
[43] *Ante*, p. 317.

same rights, as if he had undertaken to be personally liable as surety for the debt to the extent of the charge on the property or the value of his interest, whichever is the less.

This subsection makes the third party mortgagor of property in favour of a company liable in the same way, upon a fraudulent preference, as a guarantor. It may be noted that it restores only a personal liability, as compared with the right *in rem* which has been lost upon the surrender of the security charged; but although the protection to the banker is thus not by any means complete it is, like that of section 321 (3), valuable so far as it goes.[44]

As regards bankruptcy, it is important to note that section 115 of the Companies Act 1947, one of the sections not repealed in 1948 by the consolidating Act, extends to bankruptcy law the provisions regarding the fraudulent preference of sureties and guarantors, which are now embodied in section 321.

A banker's difficulties with fraudulent preference are normally the result of a customer's attempt to ease the position of a guarantor, rather than any wish to benefit the bank directly. An unusual example of an alleged preference of the bank was *Re F.L.E. Holdings Ltd.*[45] where the company had borrowed from the bank against the deposit of deeds, which was not registered under section 95 of the Companies Act 1948. Neither the bank's manager nor the company realised that the charge was defective. The company later got into difficulties, and a second charge was arranged for one of the creditors. The bank manager, hearing of this proposal, called on the company to execute a legal charge in favour of the bank, and this was done on the day before the second charge was executed. When the company went into liquidation the liquidator claimed that the legal mortgage was a fraudulent preference of the bank, but Pennycuick J. rejected the claim: although there was no consideration for the legal mortgage, nor pressure from the bank in the sense

---

[44] *Cf.* on this point H. B. Lawson, " The Banks and the new Companies Act " (April and July 1948) 69 J.I.B. 40 and 100. He said (at p. 116): " If the fraudulent preference in respect to which the bank has to refund to the liquidator was designed as a preference of a depositor of third-party security, as is sometimes the case, the Act declares that the Bank is to have the same right against the depositor of third-party security personally . . . as the bank has against a guarantor in similar circumstances. I have good reason to know that the experts and lawyers responsible for the drafting of the Act are satisfied that in such circumstances a bank is entitled to indemnity from a guarantor on the authority of *Pritchard* v. *Hitchcock* (1843) 6 M. & G. 151, and *Petty* v. *Cooke* (1871) L.R. 6 Q.B. 790, and in order to clear up any possible doubt the Act declares that depositors of third-party security are to be treated in the same way as guarantors."

[45] [1967] 1 W.L.R. 1409.

of a threat to call in the advance, this was not conclusive as to an intent to prefer, and in the circumstances he held that there was no intention beyond that of keeping faith with the bank.

Re Conley (Trading as Caplan & Conley), Ex parte The Trustee v. Barclays Bank Ltd. Re Conley (Trading as Caplan & Conley), Ex parte The Trustee v. Lloyds Bank Ltd.

[1938] 2 All E.R. 127

The deposit of security to secure the indebtedness of a third party may, even though not accompanied by any personal undertaking by the depositor, make him a surety or guarantor within the meaning of section 44 *of the Bankruptcy Act* 1914

Facts

At various times before 1934 the bankrupt's wife and mother separately deposited various stocks and shares as collateral security for the bankrupt's advances from Barclays and Lloyds Banks. In the period immediately before November 16, 1934, the bankrupt paid in sums sufficient to put the accounts at both banks in credit, and soon afterwards the wife and the mother demanded the return of the stocks and shares deposited by them. On November 30, the business of the bankrupt was closed and he was made bankrupt; and the trustee claimed that the payments into the accounts before November 16, were a fraudulent preference of the wife and mother, and thus indirectly preferred the banks, since they reduced the advances at the expense of the other creditors. Neither the wife nor the mother had at any time become personally liable to the banks in connection with their deposit of securities, these having been made by memorandum only.

Decision

The Court of Appeal held that the depositors had been " sureties or guarantors " within the meaning of section 44 of the Bankruptcy Act 1914. In the course of his judgment, Sir Wilfrid Greene M.R. said:

> It appears to me that the assumption of personal liability is not a necessary element in suretyship. " Surety " and " security " are in origin the same, and a person who provides a pledge or security for the performance of another's obligation is, I think, making himself, by means of that

pledge or security, a surety for that other, just as much as if he pledges his personal credit. This view accords with the language used in a number of authorities. . . . In *Re Westzinthus*,[46] DENMAN, C.J., in delivering the judgment of the Court of Queen's Bench, referred to the unpaid shipper of goods for which the bill of lading had been endorsed to, and deposited with, a lender by the consignee, as having " by means of his goods become a surety." In *Perry* v. *National Provincial Bank of England*[47] a person who, without entering into any covenant to pay the debt, mortgaged his property as security for the debt of others, was referred to in all the judgments of the Court of Appeal . . . as a surety.[48]

Notes

This is a difficult case, rendered more difficult by reason that there never was any definite finding by the court of undue preference. The trustee in bankruptcy claimed that if he could prove the facts set out above there should be a finding of undue preference. The banks contended that even if he could do so his claim must fail as the expression " sureties or guarantors," in section 44 of the Bankruptcy Act 1914[49] must be construed to mean sureties or guarantors through the effect of a contract personally entered into to that effect, and not merely, as here, by the deposit of securities. The matter was brought before the court of first instance in order that this point might be decided, and for his decision the judge assumed the facts to be as given, and accepted the banks' contention. On appeal the Court of Appeal again assumed the facts as given, and reversed the judge, holding that the wife and the mother were " sureties or guarantors " within the meaning of the Act, and expressing the opinion that if the facts were as assumed the payments by the bankrupt into his accounts amounted to a fraudulent preference. The banks did not further contest the case.

This decision as to the meaning of " sureties or guarantors " is of special importance to bankers, especially coupled with the opinion that on the sort of facts here set out there would be a fraudulent preference. For on this basis the bank would have to repay to the trustee in bankruptcy the amounts paid in by the bankrupt, while it would appear that they could not recover the securities which they had returned to the sureties: an opinion to that effect was expressed by the judge of first instance, an opinion concurred in by at least one judge in the Court of Appeal.[50]

---

[46] (1833) 5 B. & Ad. 817.
[47] *Ante*, p. 253.
[48] At pp. 131–132.
[49] *Cf. ante*, p. 319.
[50] *Ante*, p. 320.

However, the position has been somewhat modified by the Companies Acts of 1947 and 1948.[51] It would now seem that, in such circumstances as those of *Re Conley*, the courts could be asked to make the preferred depositors of security parties to the action; and while, as was pointed out on p. 323, they would be only personally liable in the action—their securities, once released, are lost—still the banker is in a better position since the 1947 Act than he was before it.

Re Dutton, Massey & Co., Ex parte Manchester and Liverpool District Banking Co. Ltd.

[1924] 2 Ch. 199

A creditor wishing to prove in the bankruptcy of his debtor need give up or value only such securities as have been lodged for the particular debt for which it is sought to prove

Facts

Two of the partners of a firm deposited with the bank at which the firm's account was maintained certain of their own securities to secure the indebtedness of the firm. They also gave the bank their personal guarantees for the joint debt of the firm.

Later the firm entered into a deed of arrangement under which the firm's property was assigned to a trustee for the benefit of the creditors of the firm. The property was to be divided in proportion to the debts of the various creditors, and was to be administered in all respects in accordance with the general law of bankruptcy as though the firm had been adjudged bankrupt.

The bank sought to prove against the separate estates of the partners for their individual guarantees, and the trustee contended that they could not do so without taking into account the proceeds of the deposited securities. The trustee had already admitted the bank's claim against the partnership property in respect of the firm's overdraft.

Decision

The Court of Appeal held that, as the securities were not charged in respect of the partners' obligations under the contracts of guarantee, they need not be taken into account in the bank's proof against the partners individually.

In the course of his judgment, Sargant L.J. said:

---

[51] *Cf. ante*, pp. 321 *et seq.*

In my judgment, when the matter is looked at carefully, it seems perfectly plain that the security which was given by the two partners was not in any sense at all a security for the guarantee given by each of them, but was a guarantee simply and solely for the joint debt of the partnership. And when once that is appreciated, and also the fact that in these questions as to the administration of the joint and separate estates of partners, the partnership is to be regarded as a separate juridical entity from each of the partners individually, it seems to me to follow that there can be no obligation on the bank to give credit against the guarantee by each of the partners for a security which was given for the debt of a separate juridical entity—namely, the partnership.[52]

Notes

When a creditor seeks to prove against the estate of a bankrupt, it would obviously be inequitable to allow him to retain the benefit of any security he may hold which, if not charged, would go to augment the debtor's general estate, while at the same time proving for the full amount of his debt. The Bankruptcy Act 1914 accordingly provides:

Schedule II, r. 10. If a secured creditor realises his security, he may prove for the balance due to him, after deducting the net amount realised.

Schedule II, r. 12. If a secured creditor does not either realise or surrender his security, he shall, before ranking for dividend, state in his proof . . . the value at which he assesses it, and shall be entitled to receive a dividend only in respect of the balance due to him after deducting the value so assessed.

The present decision, of obvious importance to bankers, establishes that in the application of these rules the creditor need not bring into account securities lodged for what is properly a different debt from that sought to be proved. The bank here had only one overdraft, but in the circumstances the debt of the firm was entirely distinct from the obligations of the partners individually under their guarantees; and as there was no possibility of the bank's recovering the whole of the overdraft, no question arose as to the position if, with the separate securities, the bank had been in a position to receive more than twenty shillings in the pound. Clearly they could not do so; and the question which would arise in such a case would be between the estates of the firm and the partners respectively.

---

52 At p. 213.

WINDING UP

National Westminster Bank Ltd. v. Halesowen Presswork & Assemblies Ltd.
[1972] A.C. 785

A winding-up order terminates the banker–customer relationship and any ancillary agreements dependent on that relationship
The set-off provisions of the Bankruptcy Act 1914, *and the Companies Act* 1948, *cannot be excluded by agreement between debtor and creditor*

Facts

Early in 1968 the company had an inactive and overdrawn account with the appellant bank, the company's trading account being with Lloyds Bank. In April, 1968, the trading account was moved to the appellants, the inactive account being then frozen; and the bank agreed that the two accounts should not be combined within the following four months "in the absence of materially changed circumstances." In May a meeting of creditors was called, and on June 12 a winding up order was made. The bank then sought to combine the accounts, arguing that the agreement to keep them separate terminated at the moment when the customers' mandates were terminated. The liquidator contended, *inter alia*, (*a*) that the agreement to keep the accounts separate continued after the winding up, and (*b*) that by the agreement the bank had contracted out of section 31 of the Bankruptcy Act 1914, as applied to companies by section 317 of the Companies Act 1948.

Decision

The House of Lords held unanimously (*a*) that the agreement terminated with the ending of the banker–customer relationship, and (*b*) that the agreement did not purport to contract out of section 31. They held further, by a majority, that such contracting out is anyhow not possible: section 31 is mandatory.

Notes

The importance of this decision lies in its clarification of a number of points that had earlier been in some doubt.[53] Thus it settled that the banker has, in the absence of agreement express or implied to the contrary, a long established common law right to combine accounts of a customer; that this right is not strictly a lien; and that

[53] *Cf.* Chorley, *op. cit.* pp. 218 *et seq.*

it can be exercised without notice to the customer, again unless the contract provides otherwise.[54]

More specifically, the decision established that agreements ancillary to the banker customer relationship are terminated when the relationship is ended by a winding-up order; and that the statutory set off provisions in bankruptcy and winding-up proceedings cannot be excluded by agreement. As to the first of these two points, the importance of the decision is its reversal of the Court of Appeal's unanimous view that the agreement survived the winding up order. It is to be noted, however, that the decision depended on the wording and purpose of the agreement, designed to help keep the company solvent and so without further purpose when the winding up order was made. An agreement expressly designed to continue in force after a winding up might still be effective, though not, in view of the further finding, to exclude section 31, were any bank to enter into so unlikely an agreement.

Section 31 of the Bankruptcy Act 1914 provides for the setting off of claims between bankrupt and creditor where there have been "mutual credits, mutual debts or other mutual dealings"; and section 317 of the Companies Act 1948 extends this and other bankruptcy rules to the winding up of insolvent companies. The Lords' decision here resolved any doubt that had existed as to whether the provision was mandatory or merely permissive.

In the Court of Appeal it had been held, Buckley L.J. dissenting,[55] that section 31 did not apply, the frozen account not being within the mutual dealings of the section. The House of Lords was unanimous in reversing this finding: the dealings here were not comparable with those in other cases where a debtor had deposited money with his creditor to be applied for a special purpose. It is submitted that the same reasoning would cover a loan account, although some of the speeches based this point on the temporary nature of the separation of the current account balances.

The House of Lords resolved also the questions raised in the judgments of the Court of Appeal as to the notice required (*a*) had the bank chosen to terminate the agreement when the meeting was called (admittedly a material change of circumstances) and (*b*) when the winding up order was made. As to (*a*) it is now clear, as bankers would have wished, that notice taking immediate effect is the right course, subject to the obligation to pay cheques drawn before the customer receives the notice. In the case of (*b*) notice of any kind could serve no useful purpose.

---

[54] *Cf. ante*, pp. 198, 223.

[55] [1971] 1 Q.B. 1. *Cf. post*, p. 340, where Buckley J., as he then was, applied s. 31 in different circumstances.

It will have been appreciated that all that has been said here of section 31 applies with at least equal force to the bankruptcy proceedings in connection with which the provision originated.

Re B. Johnson & Co. (Builders) Ltd.

[1955] Ch. 634

The appointment of a receiver

Facts

The company had borrowed from Barclays Bank on the security of a debenture containing a floating charge on the company's assets. In 1947, when the company had suffered substantial losses and the borrowing stood at £29,000, the bank appointed a receiver and manager, who terminated the company's activities. In the following year a petition for the compulsory winding up of the company was presented, and a winding-up order was made. Later, a contributory issued a summons under section 333 of the Companies Act 1948, seeking to have examined the conduct of, respectively, the receiver (until the winding-up order was made) and the liquidator (after the making of the order).

Section 333 provides that in the case of a winding up such an examination may be ordered into the conduct of any " promoter, director, manager, liquidator, or officer " of the company if it appears that he has " been guilty of any misfeasance or breach of trust " in relation to the company. Here it was alleged of the receiver that he had been guilty of misfeasance in several respects, including the stopping of all building work despite being told that this would involve the company in great loss.

Decision

The Court of Appeal held (*a*) that he was not a " manager " of the company within section 333 because he was concerned, not to manage for the benefit of the company, but to realise the debenture holders' security; and (*b*) that the grounds of complaint were not within section 333 because a receiver and manager appointed by a debenture holder is under no duty to preserve the goodwill and assets of the company.

Jenkins L.J. said:

The primary duty of the receiver is to the debenture holders and not to the company. He is receiver and manager of the property of the company for the debenture holders, not manager of the company. The company is entitled to any surplus of assets remaining after the debenture debt has been discharged, and is entitled to proper accounts. But the whole purpose of the receiver and manager's appointment would obviously be stultified if the company could claim that a receiver and manager owes it any duty comparable to the duty owed to a company by its own directors or managers.[56]

Notes

The receiver appointed by a debenture holder is usually made manager also in order that he may carry on the business of the company (although it is not essential for him to be so designated if the debenture authorises him to continue the business). The *Johnson* decision was important in limiting the effect of this secondary appointment. Had the receiver been " manager " within the Companies Act there would have been no question as to his responsibility to the company as well as to the debenture holder.

The decision also established that his primary duty is to the debenture holder. Whether it is his sole responsibility is perhaps doubtful, in the light of *Re Newdigate Colliery Ltd.*[57] There it was held that it was also the receiver's duty to preserve the company's goodwill and assets, and Cozens Hardy M.R. compared the receiver's duties with those of the receiver of mortgaged property. Paget suggests that the two cases can be reconciled on the basis that in carrying out the primary duty to the debenture holder " he must bear in mind and make due allowance where he can for the interests of the company," and he goes on to point out the difference in the case of the receiver appointed by the court.[58] On this interpretation of the two cases the parallel with the position of the mortgagee realising the mortgaged property is clear.[59]

It is important that the formalities of the appointment be strictly observed. In *Windsor Refrigerator Co. Ltd.* v. *Branch Nominees Ltd.*[60] a receiver was appointed by Branch Nominees, a subsidiary of the National Provincial Bank, under a debenture conferring a power to appoint a receiver " by writing." Such appointments are normally under seal, and Branch Nominees had affixed its common seal to an undated document appointing a receiver. Some days later demand was made on the company and the day's date inserted on the document; and when payment was not forthcoming the document was handed to the named receiver. The appointment was

56 At pp. 661–662.
57 [1912] 1 Ch. 468.
58 *Op. cit.* p. 62.
59 *Cf. ante*, pp. 260 *et seq.*
60 [1961] Ch. 375.

challenged on the grounds that the deed was, in view of the circumstances of its making, invalid; but the Court of Appeal held that the document was valid as an appointment by writing, because an appointment by writing could properly be made out before it was intended to take effect.

In the more complicated circumstances of *Cripps (Pharmaceuticals) Ltd.* v. *Wickenden and Another*,[61] the *Windsor Refrigerator* decision was applied on the question of the pre-dating of the appointments, and the National Westminster Bank successfully resisted further challenges to the appointments in question, Goff J. holding, *inter alia*, that they could not be impugned on the ground that no reasonable time was given after the demand for it to be met: where a debt is payable on demand the creditor need give the debtor no more time than is needed to fetch the money. But there had been confusion over the appointments. When the initial appointments were challenged on the dating point the bank purported to make fresh appointments " to rectify this unfortunate error " (which, as was now held, was not in fact an error); and the judge's comment on the position that would have arisen had his finding been different serves as a warning of the danger of failure to observe the rules:

. . . if I had held the first appointments bad I would have had to have found the second appointments to be bad also, because no person can take advantage of his own wrong. In my judgment the bank could not appoint a receiver until it had restored the company to possession of its assets and renewed its demands. If it could not do that because it had sold the assets, then there might be a serious question whether it had forfeited its right altogether, or would be entitled to appoint a receiver after restoring the proceeds, the company having an action for damages for conversion for any loss not recouped by return of the proceeds. . . . Even if that were wrong and the second appointments were good, still the bank would be liable for damages down to [the date of the second appointments] for the first wrongful appointments, and that would include damages for loss of the opportunity to avoid the second appointments occasioned by the wrongful freezing of assets under the first.[62]

Re Yeovil Glove Co. Ltd.

[1965] Ch. 148

The effect of section 322 *of the Companies Act* 1948

Facts

In January, 1958, the company created a floating charge on its

[61] [1973] 1 W.L.R. 944.

[62] At pp. 956–957.

property and assets in favour of the National Provincial Bank, with whom it was overdrawn to the extent of nearly £70,000. The bank did not undertake to make any further advances in consideration for this charge being given.

An arrangement had earlier been made that the No. 1 account fed into the No. 3 account and the No. 4 account the exact amounts respectively of the wages paid eighteen weeks before and of the salaries paid four months before, thus providing a method by which the bank's preferential rights in a winding up in respect of money advanced for the payment of wages and salaries could be ascertained at any time.[63] All the accounts were at all times overdrawn.

In August the bank appointed a receiver, and there was no more working on the accounts. In January 1959 a petition for the compulsory winding up of the company was lodged by trade creditors, a winding-up order was made and a liquidator appointed. The liquidator claimed that the floating charge was invalid against him by virtue of section 322 of the Companies Act 1948, which provides that:

> Where a company is being wound up, a floating charge on the undertaking or property of the company created within twelve months of the commencement of the winding up shall, unless it is proved that the company immediately after the creation of the charge was solvent, be invalid, except to the amount of any cash paid to the company at the time of, or subsequently to the creation of, and in consideration for, the charge together with interest. . . .

Decision

The Court of Appeal affirmed the decision of Plowman J. that the bank could rely on the charge. Drawings from No. 1 account after January 1958 were cash paid by the bank in consideration for the charge; in accordance with the rule in *Clayton's* case [64] money credited to No. 1 account after January 1958 was to be set against the earliest advances, *i.e.* those before the charge.

In his judgment Harman L.J. said:

> The fallacy in the appellant's argument lies, in my opinion, in the theory that, because the company's payments in to the bank after the date of the charge were more or less equal to the payments out by the bank during the same period, no " new money " was provided by the bank. This is not the fact. Every such payment was in fact new money having regard to the state of the company's accounts, and it was in fact used to pay the company's creditors. That the indebtedness remained approximately at the

---

[63] *Cf. post*, p. 338.
[64] *Ante*, p. 143.

same level was due to the fact that this was the limit set by the bank to the company's overdraft.[65]

Notes

This decision is of unusual interest in that the only authority directly in point, and extensively considered in the judgments, was *Re Thomas Mortimer Ltd.*,[66] a 39-year-old decision unreported otherwise than in the *Journal of the Institute of Bankers* and *Legal Decisions affecting Bankers*. In that case the company had an overdraft of some £58,000 with the National Provincial Bank. In January 1924 a debenture of £50,000 was created in favour of the bank. Two months later the company went into liquidation, but in the meantime £40,000 had been paid into the account and £50,000 paid out. Romer J. held that section 212 of the Companies (Consolidation) Act 1908 (which was substantially re-enacted in section 322 of the 1948 Act), did not invalidate the payment.

In *Re Yeovil Glove Ltd.*, Plowman J. at first instance, and all three Lords Justices in the Court of Appeal, approved the decision of Romer J. in 1925. It may be noted that the Court of Appeal, again unanimously, refused to accept the bank's argument that, even if they disagreed with the *Mortimer* decision, they could not properly allow the appeal when the decision had stood so long, and two subsequent statutes had re-enacted the provision unaltered. Instead, after full consideration, they approved the earlier decision on its merits.

Aluminium Industrie Vaasen BV v. Romalpa Aluminium Ltd.

[1976] 2 All E.R. 552

When a supplier of goods to a company expressly reserves the property in the goods until payment for them is effected, he may, in the winding up of the company, trace the proceeds of re-sale of the goods in priority to secured creditors

Facts

The plaintiffs, Dutch manufacturers of aluminium foil, supplied foil to the defendants, an English company. The contract provided, in clause 13, that ownership of the foil would remain with the plaintiffs until the defendants had paid all sums owing to the

[65] At p. 174.

[66] (1925) 4 L.D.B. 3.

plaintiffs. It provided further that where the foil was used in the manufacture of other products, the ownership of such products was to be transferred to the plaintiffs as security for full payment. The defendants were entitled to sell such " mixed " goods on condition that, while any money was owing to the plaintiffs, the defendants would on request assign to the plaintiffs the benefit of any claim against the sub-purchasers.

When the defendants' bankers, Hume Corporation, appointed a receiver under its debenture there was an outstanding debt owing to the plaintiffs of £122,000. The plaintiffs claimed that they were entitled, in priority to all creditors, to (*a*) £35,152, representing proceeds of re-sale of foil supplied by them, and (*b*) redelivery of foil worth £50,235, still in the possession of the receiver. The second claim was admitted by the company. On the first, Mocatta J. gave judgment for the plaintiffs, and the defendants appealed.

Decision

The Court of Appeal dismissed the appeal. Roskill L.J. said:

I see no difficulty in the contractual concept that, as between the defendants and their sub-purchasers, the defendants sold as principals, but that, as between themselves and the plaintiffs, those goods which they were selling as principals within their implied authority from the plaintiffs were the plaintiffs' goods which they were selling as agents for the plaintiffs to whom they remained fully accountable.

. . . Like the learned judge, I find no difficulty in holding that the principles in *Re Hallett's Estate*,[67] to which I have already referred, are of immediate application, and I think that the plaintiffs are entitled to trace these proceeds of sale and to recover them. . . .[68]

Notes

Reservation of title, familiar on the Continent, has been possible in England since at least 1893,[69] but it has seldom been seen in practice, and its appearance in the *Romalpa* case, and its increased adoption, in part as a result of the decision in that case, has been a matter of concern to bankers.

The implications of the decision are wide ranging. The banker is concerned as a lender: the stock in trade of a company may be the only asset not encumbered by a fixed charge, and the possibility that even the stock is not wholly the property of the company must affect the banker's risk assessment. In particular, a floating charge could be of substantially less value than had seemed to be the case.

---

67 *Ante*, p. 155.
68 At p. 563.
69 *Cf.* Sale of Goods Act 1893, s. 19.

Moreover, a supplier of goods protected as the plaintiffs were here takes precedence over preferential creditors, so that advances to pay wages [70] could be similarly at risk.

There are of course other implications: for example, a receiver's work is more difficult when the company's apparent assets are in fact the property of others; and taxes as well as wages are preferential debts. These matters are not of direct banking interest, but they reinforce the concern with which accountants as well as bankers have viewed the matter.[71] " Mixed goods," which clause 13 purported also to cover, were not in issue in the case, but it does not appear from the judgments that the court would have found for the defendants if they had been. And while the court had difficulty with the wording of clause 13, it will be comparatively easy for similar clauses to avoid the complication for which translation was partly responsible in *Romalpa*. It is reasonable to assume that a well drafted clause will cover the whole area of goods supplied and not paid for, and it must be further assumed that a provision so clearly useful to suppliers will be increasingly used as it becomes more widely known.

Re T.W. Construction Ltd.

[1954] 1 W.L.R. 540

The effect of section 227 *of the Companies Act* 1948

Facts

On May 7, 1952, a petition was presented for the winding up of the company. At that date the company's account with Barclays Bank was overdrawn £803 11s. 0d. and further drawings took place thereafter. On May 21, £1,308 6s. 10d. was paid into the account by Leopold Joseph & Sons, the proceeds of a credit for machinery exported by the company. The bank had notice of the petition on May 22.

On July 31, a liquidator was appointed, and he issued a summons for an order that the payment of £1,308 6s. 10d. was void under section 227 of the Companies Act 1948, which provides that:

---

[70] As to which, see *post*, p. 338.

[71] The accountancy bodies have issued a statement of guidance to their members which recommends, *inter alia*, that there should be a note in the accounts indicating that goods are affected by reservation of title. But it seems doubtful whether any accounting practice can substantially meet the problems here discussed, while legislation may be difficult in view of the general practice in other EEC countries.

In a winding up by the Court, any disposition of the property of the company, including things in action, and any transfer of shares, or alteration in the status of the members of the company, made after the commencement of the winding up, shall, unless the Court otherwise orders, be void.

The registrar ordered the repayment by the bank of £803 11s. 0d., and the bank moved to have this order discharged.

Decision

Wynn-Parry J. held that there was no ground for distinguishing between the amount of the overdraft at the date of the petition and the amount by which the overdraft was subsequently increased. He reviewed the authorities and quoted Lord Cairns L.J. in *Re Wiltshire Iron Co. ex parte Pearson* [72]:

Section 153 [of the 1862 Act, the corresponding section to section 227 of the 1948 Act] . . . is a wholesome and necessary provision, to prevent, during the period which must elapse before a petition can be heard, the improper alienation and dissipation of the property of a company *in extremis*. But where a company actually trading, which it is in the interest of everyone to preserve, and ultimately to sell, as a going concern, is made the object of a winding-up petition, which may fail or may succeed, if it were to be supposed that transactions in the ordinary course of its current trade, bona fide entered into and completed, would be avoided . . . the presentation of a petition, groundless or well-founded, would, *ipso facto*, paralyse the trade of the company, and great injury, without any counter-balance of advantage, would be done to those interested in the assets of the company.[73]

He considered that the transaction in the present case was directly within Lord Cairns' dictum, and so allowed the bank's appeal.

Notes

The protection afforded by section 227 may be broadly compared with the protection in bankruptcy provided by section 45 of the Bankruptcy Act,[74] although as Wynn-Parry J. pointed out in the present case, section 45 leaves no discretion in the court while the protection of section 227 is discretionary.

An example of the difficulties of the matter is to be found in *D. B. Evans (Bilston) Ltd.* v. *Barclays Bank Ltd.*[75] In January, 1961, the company having got into financial difficulties, an application was made to the court for a scheme of arrangement under section 206 of the Companies Act; and on the same day a creditor presented a winding up petition. The winding up proceedings were adjourned

---

[72] (1868) 3 Ch. App. 443.
[73] At p. 446.
[74] *Ante*, pp. 307–318, *passim.*
[75] (1961) 7 L.D.B. 283.

pending the result of the application for a scheme of arrangement. The company's accounts with the defendant bank were in credit, but the bank, having regard to section 227, would not allow payments out of the account, confining activity to the collection of the company's cheques. The Court of Appeal approved an interim arrangement under which withdrawals were to be certified as necessary for carrying on the business.

In *Re Clifton Place Garage Ltd.*[76] in which the Court of Appeal exercised their discretion in favour of a receiver appointed by the debenture holders, whose payments had been challenged by the liquidator, Phillimore L.J. commented on evidence that had been given regarding banking practice when a petition for winding up is presented, and said:

> I question also whether this rigid practice of the banks in all cases is right, or whether, particularly if they were aware that the court would look with indulgence on such cases, it would not be possible, after proper enquiry, at any rate in some cases, to cash cheques for a company, even if only against current receipts on a day-to-day basis.[77]

In fact the banks' practice is not normally as rigid as was here suggested. At least one of the clearing banks is on record [78] as allowing accounts, whether in credit or debit, to continue after notice of a winding up petition "provided they are conducted in the ordinary course of business." This course of action appears to be based on just the expectation that Phillimore L.J. encouraged, that in the event of challenge by the liquidator, the court would exercise its discretion in the bank's favour. Banks that do not go as far as this may still allow withdrawals on the lines approved in the *D. B. Evans* (*Bilston*) case above; while in any event it would appear that the court will now in proper cases make an order that validates the continuance of a company's normal business activity, including the operation of its banking account, and when the bank is not prepared to take the risk that still exists in such circumstances, it can suggest that its company customer seeks such an order.

---

[76] [1970] Ch. 477. [77] At p. 494.

[78] (October, 1970) J.B.L. 253. The bank also "allows credit accounts of individuals to continue in the ordinary course of business notwithstanding that the bank has received notice of an available act of bankruptcy, relying on the decision of the court in *Re Dalton* to pay third-party cheques." As to this point, see *ante*, p. 312.

National Provincial Bank Ltd. v. Freedman and Rubens

(1934) 4 L.D.B. 444

The bank as preferential creditor for wages cheques

Facts

The defendants were receiver and debenture holder respectively of a company, N. Bach Ltd., whose account had been kept with the plaintiff bank. The company's overdraft having increased to an extent which the bank could not approve, the practice was followed, for a period of more than a year, of paying in cheques received at the time in each week at which it was desired to draw wages, the branch manager refusing to pay the wages cheque until he was satisfied that about the same amount was being paid into the credit of the company. Upon the winding up of the company the bank claimed that these payments had been in fact advances for wages, the corresponding credits to the account having been reductions of the existing indebtedness; and that by virtue of section 264 (3) of the Companies Act 1929 (now s. 319 (4) of the 1948 Act) they, the bank, were therefore entitled to stand in the shoes of the employees of the company to whom the wages had been paid, and to rank as preferential creditors to that extent in the winding up of the company. The defendants contended that no advances had been made to the company for wages, that what had happened represented the mere exchange by the bank of the cheques which the company took to them weekly, and that therefore the bank could not be preferential creditors in this connection.

Decision

It was held that the bank were entitled to the declaration they sought. In the course of his judgment, Clauson J. said:

There is a suggestion that there were conversations of a somewhat loose character, from which it can be inferred that there was an arrangement that the cheques paid in were to be used simply to provide the cash to pay the wages. What seems to me to be most important is the way in which the account was kept. The way the account was kept shows perfectly clearly that that was not the transaction at all. The transaction was that these cheques reduced the overdraft and that is the meaning of the bank account as it appears. . . . The bank manager, whatever loose language he may have used, was not going to let the overdraft be permanently increased, and accordingly it was necessary for him to take care that the wages cheque was not paid until these cheques had gone into the account. But those cheques did not provide the wages; those cheques reduced the overdraft, and the wages cheque was paid by money which was advanced by the bank for the purpose. . . . The truth of it is that danger always occurs when loose expressions used by the people whose business it is to carry on the details of business are regarded with more attention than the real settled methods of business which appear in the books kept by banks and other responsible persons.[79]

Notes

Section 319 (1) of the Companies Act 1948 provides that:

In a winding up there shall be paid in priority to all other debts:
(b) all wages or salary . . . of any clerk or servant in respect of services rendered to the company during the four months next before the relevant date and all wages . . . of any workman or labourer in respect of services so rendered.

And section 319 (4) further provides that:

Where any payment has been made (*a*) to any clerk, servant, workman or labourer in the employment of a company, on account of wages or salary; or (*b*) to any such clerk, servant, workman or labourer or, in the case of his death, to any other person in his right, on account of accrued holiday remuneration; out of money advanced by some person for that purpose, the person by whom the money was advanced shall in a winding up have a right of priority in respect of the money so advanced and paid up to the amount by which the sum in respect of which the clerk, servant, workman or labourer, or other person in his right, would have been entitled to priority in the winding up has been diminished by reason of the payment having been made.

In *Re Primrose (Builders) Ltd.*[80] the facts were almost identical with those in the *Freedman and Rubens* case, and Wynn-Parry J., following Clauson J., held that the bank were entitled to rank as preferential creditors. In the *Primrose* case the decision was expressly based upon the rule in *Clayton's* case [81]; and, of course, Clauson J.'s decision was founded upon the principle of that rule, although not expressly so. It may be repeated that the rule in *Clayton's* case raises a presumption only, and the presumption can be displaced by the facts of a particular case. That is the reason why in this case it was so strenuously argued that there was an arrangement for the bank to pay the wages out of the proceeds of the cheques paid in. In both the cases here considered the facts were held not to be sufficient to displace it.

In *Re E. J. Morel* (1934) *Ltd.*[82] the company had an overdrawn account which by arrangement with the bank had been frozen, the

[79] At p. 445.
[80] [1950] Ch. 561.
[81] *Ante*, p. 143.
[82] [1962] Ch. 21.

only workings on it being periodical credits in reduction. There were two further accounts, a No. 2 account and a wages account, the latter overdrawn but normally not in excess of the credit balance of the former. There were monthly transfers from the No. 2 account to the wages account equivalent to the withdrawals made four months previously, so that the overdraft on the wages account normally represented the previous four months' withdrawals for wages. When the company went into compulsory liquidation the bank claimed to rank as preferential creditors for the amount of the previous four months' wages, but the liquidator contended that they were preferential creditors only to the extent of the small difference between the overdraft on wages account and the credit balance on the No. 2 account. Buckley J. upheld the liquidator's argument, on the grounds (*a*) (applying the principle of *Bradford Old Bank Ltd.* v. *Sutcliffe* [83]) that a banker cannot combine a current account with an account that is not a current account, and the frozen account in this case could no longer be regarded as current; (*b*) that in the circumstances of the present case the No. 2 account and the wages account were really one account, so that the bank had not on these two accounts made any advances for wages; and (*c*) even if the first account could be combined the bank would not succeed: a debtor's credit balance must be set off primarily against such debts as rank preferentially.

The *Morel* decision has been criticised,[84] and it may certainly be questioned whether the banker should be penalised for " freezing " an account in the way the Midland Bank did in this case; it has been pointed out [85] that the decision could have other implications in the matter of ruling off accounts.

There is perhaps even more interest for bankers in the third ground of Buckley J.'s decision. This was based on section 31 of the Bankruptcy Act 1914, which is applied also to winding up proceedings by section 317 of the Companies Act 1948 [86]; but it may be noted that neither provision lays down that set-off should first take place in respect of the preferential part of the debt, section 31 providing merely that set-off should apply to any individual's various balances with the bankrupt, and that his claim should be restricted to the net balance resulting. Buckley J.'s reasoning:

> If he obtains, by set-off, payment in full (of that part of the debt) it

---

[83] *Ante*, p. 250.
[84] *Cf. e.g.* editor's comment at 7 L.D.B. 281.
[85] Ryder, 1961 J.B.L. 278, " Combination of Bank Accounts in Winding Up of Customers."
[86] *Cf. ante*, pp. 327 *et seq.*

seems reasonable that that payment in full should be treated as being in respect of that part of his debt which would rank first in priority. . . .[87]

may well concern banks in similar circumstances.[88]

The second ground of the *Morel* decision was distinguished in *Re James R. Rutherford & Sons Ltd.*,[89] where Pennycuick J. said that " the facts in that case were different from those here in an essential particular," but without specifying which particular he had in mind. In the *Rutherford* case there were two accounts, one of them being a wages account, and both being overdrawn. Transfers were made to the wages account weekly, each one being expressed to be " in repayment of the earliest advances made on (wages) account and still outstanding, utilised in payment of salaries and/or wages to persons whose salaries and/or wages since the date of such advances have exceeded £200 to the extent of that excess." On the company going into voluntary liquidation it was held that the bank was entitled to rank as a preferential creditor for the amount transferred from current to wages account as well as for the overdrawn balance of wages account, the effect of such transfers not being to repay the bank or to alter the nature of the borrowing; but, the rule in *Clayton's* case applying to credits paid in to the current account after the opening of the wages account, such credits served to reduce the indebtedness as at that date, and the amount transferred from current to wages account must be reduced accordingly.[90]

Re Rampgill Mill Ltd.[91] is of twofold interest, on the one hand as an example of the importance of the separate wages account in establishing preferential status, and on the other as a finding by the court that this status can be established without either a separate account or even a specific agreement as to the purpose of a borrowing. The circumstances were that the company had a borrowing facility for general purposes with Lloyds Bank. In order that the company might obtain cash for wages in another town open credit facilities were established with a branch of the Midland Bank, no Lloyds branch being available. Cheques were cashed under this arrangement, and debited to the company's ordinary overdrawn account. When the company went into liquidation the bank claimed that some £5,000 of the overdraft ranked as a preferential debt; but applying the rule in *Clayton's* case this was reduced to a little over £2,000. The liquidator resisted this smaller claim, on the basis

---

87 At p. 34.

88 *Cf. ante*, p. 328, where the same judge would have applied s. 31 in different circumstances.

89 [1964] 1 W.L.R. 1211.

90 *Cf.*, as to preferred creditors under s. 319, Chorley, *op. cit.* pp. 368–370.

91 [1967] Ch. 1138.

that in order to prove that an advance is entitled to preference the banker must have exercised a discretion in relation to it, and decided to make it because, as far as he knew, it was to be used for the particular purpose. But Plowman J. said that this was too rigid a test; he preferred a " benevolent construction," which gave the bank its case.

CHAPTER 12

BANKING ADMINISTRATION

Willis and Another v. Bank of England

(1835) 4 A. & E. 21

The relationship between a bank and its branches

Facts

One Norcliffe was a dealer in zinc, on whose behalf a firm of solicitors in London received a sum of £1,600. This they paid to the Bank of England, receiving in exchange four bank bills, payable to Norcliffe, at seven days' sight, and accepted by the bank at the time of issue. They duly transferred the bills to Norcliffe. Ten days later Norcliffe absconded, and thus committed an act of bankruptcy. The Bank of England was notified of this, and asked to stop the bills; but almost a month later two of these were paid at the branch of the bank at Gloucester to an agent of Norcliffe, the agent having himself no interest in the bills.

Norcliffe was subsequently declared bankrupt and the plaintiffs, as his assignees, sought to recover the amount of these two bills.

Decision

It was held that the Bank of England had been put on notice of the act of bankruptcy, and that this notice must be deemed to affect all its branches.

Lord Denman C.J., delivering the judgment of the court, said:

> The general rule of law is, that notice to the principal is notice to all his agents . . .; at any rate if there be reasonable time, as there was here, for the principal to communicate that notice to his agents, before the event which raises the question happens. . . .
>
> We have been pressed with the inconvenience of requiring every trading company to communicate to their agents everywhere whatever notices they may receive; but the argument *ab inconvenienti* is seldom entitled to much weight in deciding legal questions; and, if it were, other inconveniences of a more serious nature would obviously grow out of a different decision.[1]

Notes

To the general proposition that a bank and its branches are one legal entity (of which the *Willis* case may be regarded as a notable

[1] At p. 39.

example) there are several exceptions, based on practical expediency. In particular, notice to a head office, of, for example, a garnishee order, is not effective in less than reasonable time for it to be communicated to the branch concerned.[1a]

Countermand of payment is effective only at the branch on which the instrument to be " stopped " is drawn. In *London Provincial & South Western Bank Ltd.* v. *Buszard*[2] the defendant drew a cheque on the Oxford Street branch of the plaintiff bank, at which he had an account. The payee took it to the Victoria Street branch of the same bank, where she had an account, and was allowed to draw against it. In the meantime the defendant had stopped payment of the cheque, and in due course it was returned to the Victoria Street branch marked " Ordered not to pay." The bank brought this action as holders in due course against the drawer of the cheque, who contended that the bank had notice of the " stop," notice to one branch being notice to all; but it was held that the countermand of payment was effective only at the branch on which the cheque was drawn, and judgment was given for the bank.

In *Woodland* v. *Fear*,[3] where the payee of a cheque drawn on the Glastonbury branch of Stuckey's Bank obtained cash for it at the Bridgwater branch, and there proved to be no funds to meet it, it was held that the bank owed no duty to honour its customer's cheques except at the branch where the account was kept. So Glastonbury branch could not be regarded as having paid the cheque as the drawer's bankers, and the bank was entitled to recover the money from the payee. A further example of this rule was seen in *Clare & Co.* v. *Dresdner Bank*.[4] Here the plaintiffs had an account with the Berlin branch of the defendant bank, and, after the outbreak of war between England and Germany, sought payment of the balance of their account from the London branch of the bank. Upon this being refused they brought the present action, in which it was held that they could not demand payment except at the branch at which the account was kept.

In *Zivnostenska Banka* v. *Frankman*[5] a Prague resident became by inheritance in 1935 the owner of securities, held for safe custody by the London branch of the bank. She was advised of the position by the Prague office of the bank, with which she had an account. The action was brought by her son, as administrator of her estate, for delivery of the securities. Such delivery was forbidden by the

---

[1a] But the bank should use its utmost endeavours to locate any credit balance in the name of the judgment debtor: see S.I. 1976 No. 337 and Ord. 49, r. 2 (*c*).

[2] (1918) 35 T.L.R. 142.

[3] (1857) 7 E. & B. 519.

[4] [1915] 2 K.B. 576.

[5] [1950] A.C. 57, *post* pp. 344, 346.

current Czech exchange control regulations as the daughter was resident in this country, although it was not against English law. It was held by the House of Lords that the contract of deposit was with the Prague office, and that delivery could therefore be properly demanded only in Prague. Delivery in London could have been arranged with the consent of the Prague office, but this could not be given because of the regulations. In his judgment Lord Macdermott spoke of the "established banking practice that a customer who does business with one branch of a bank cannot, in the absence of some special provision, call as of right on another branch to complete or clear that business."

In *Rex* v. *Lovitt* [6] money deposited in a Canadian branch of the Bank of British North America was held to be subject to succession duty in the province in which the branch was situated, notwithstanding that the Head Office of the bank was in London.

But the essential unity of the bank in all its branches remains, where it is not clearly impracticable to insist upon it; *Garnett* v. *McKewan* [7] is a good example of the application of this principle.

Mackersy v. Ramsays Bonar & Co.

(1843) 9 Cl. & Fin. 818

The relationship between a bank and its agents

Facts

The appellant was a customer of the respondent banking firm. He sent to them for collection a bill of exchange for £100 drawn on a person in Calcutta. They sent it to their agents, Coutts & Co., who in their turn forwarded it to their own agents in Calcutta. In due course payment was made by the acceptor, but, the Calcutta agent going bankrupt, the money was not received by the defendant bank, who thereupon refused to credit their customer, the plaintiff.

Decision

It was held that the bank was liable to its customer. In his judgment in the House of Lords, Lord Cottenham said:

> I cannot distinguish this case from the ordinary transactions between parties having accounts between them. If I send to my bankers a bill or draft upon another banker in London, I do not expect that they will themselves go and receive the amount, and pay me the proceeds; but that

---

[6] [1912] A.C. 212.

[7] *Ante*, pp. 196, 304.

they will send a clerk in the course of the day to the clearing-house, and settle the balances, in which my bill or draft will form one item. If such clerk, instead of returning to the bankers with the balance, should abscond with it, can my bankers refuse to credit me with the amount? Certainly not.[8]

Notes

Where a bank makes agency arrangements with another bank (the bank acting as agent is generally known as the "correspondent" bank) there is normally privity of contract only between the two banks, and the fact that the bank initiating the business does so on behalf of a customer does not make the customer a party to the contract.

Thus, in *Calico Printers' Association* v. *Barclays Bank Ltd. & Anglo-Palestine Co. Ltd.*[9] the plaintiff association were in the habit of handing to Barclays Bank parcels of bills of exchange and bills of lading on one Ydlibi, of Beirut. At their request these bills were collected through the Anglo-Palestine Co. although this company was not Barclays' usual agents. If the goods were not taken up Barclays were requested to warehouse and insure them, and Barclays instructed their agents accordingly. In fact certain goods were destroyed by fire, and it was found that they had not been insured. The plaintiffs claimed against the first defendants that they had accepted a liability to insure and had been negligent in not seeing that this was effective. They claimed against the second defendants that they had been negligent in similarly failing.

It was held by Wright J. that the Palestine agents had been grossly negligent in their conduct, but that their only liability, in the absence of any privity of contract with the plaintiff, was to their principals, Barclays Bank. There had been also some degree of negligence by Barclays, but they were protected by a clause in the plaintiffs' instructions excluding liability. Upon the plaintiffs appealing only against the decision in Barclays favour, the Court of Appeal upheld the lower court.

In *Kahler* v. *Midland Bank Ltd.*,[10] which may be regarded as a complementary case to the *Zivnostenka Banka* case,[11] the plaintiff was in 1938 a customer of a bank in Prague, and arranged with them that they should hold certain of his securities on his behalf in London. Their correspondent bank in London, with which these arrangements were made, was the Midland Bank. After the shares had been virtually expropriated by the occupying power during the war, the plaintiff's title had been restored in 1946 by the Czech

---

[8] At p. 848.
[9] (1931) 36 Com. Cas. 71 and 197.
[10] [1950] A.C. 24.
[11] *Ante*, p. 344.

authorities, but as the plaintiff was no longer a Czech citizen the Czech exchange control regulations prevented him from obtaining the securities. The present action was a claim to possession as sole and unfettered beneficial owner. The House of Lords held that the Midland Bank was not a party to the contract of deposit; and, by a majority of one, that, although the plaintiff was the sole owner, yet the contract envisaged delivery in London only with authorisation from the Prague bank (which could not now be given); and that the Midland Bank could not be required to give up the securities to the plaintiff.

Barwick v. English Joint Stock Bank

(1867) L.R. 2 Ex. 259

A bank is liable for the actions of its officers in the ordinary course of banking business if those actions are within the apparent scope of their authority

Facts

The plaintiff had supplied oats on credit to J. Davis & Son, who were working under government contract. When Barwick asked for better security Davis arranged for the manager of the defendant bank, where he had his account, to write a letter undertaking to honour the firm's cheque in favour of the plaintiff on receipt of government payment for forage supplied, " in priority to any other payment except to this bank." Davis owed the bank £12,000, but the plaintiff did not know this. The government payment amounted to £2,676, but Davis's cheque for £1,227 payable to the plaintiff was dishonoured, the bank claiming the whole of the government payment in reduction of their lending. The plaintiff brought this action against the bank for false representation and for money had and received.

Decision

The Court of Exchequer Chamber held (i) that there was evidence to go to a jury that the manager knew and intended the guarantee to be unavailing and fraudulently concealed from the plaintiff the fact that would make it so; and (ii) that the bank would be liable for such fraud in their agent.

In the course of his judgment, Willes J. said:

The general rule is, that the master is answerable for every such wrong of the servant or agent as is committed in the course of the service and for the master's benefit, though no express command or privity of the master be proved. That principle is acted upon every day in running down cases. It has been applied also to direct trespass to goods, as in the case of holding the owners of ships liable for the act of masters abroad, improperly selling the cargo. It has been held applicable to actions of false imprisonment, in cases where officers of railway companies, . . . improperly imprison persons who are supposed to come within the terms of the bye-laws. . . . In all these cases it may be said, as it was said here, that the master has not authorised the act. It is true, he has not authorised the particular act, but he has put the agent in his place to do that class of acts, and he must be answerable for the manner in which the agent has conducted himself in doing the business which it was the act of his master to place him in.[12]

Notes

The act complained of must be within the estensible authority of the officer before the bank can be made liable for it. Thus in *Bank of New South Wales* v. *Owston*,[13] where the complaint was of wrongful arrest and malicious prosecution, the Judicial Committee of the Privy Council held that the act was not one for which the bank was to be held liable. Sir Montague Smith said:

> The duties of a bank manager would usually be to conduct banking business on behalf of his employers, and when he is found so acting, what is done by him in the way of ordinary banking transactions may be presumed, until the contrary is shown, to be within the scope of his authority; and his employers would be liable for his mistakes, and, under some circumstances, for his frauds, in the management of such business. But the arrest, and still less the prosecution of offenders, is not within the ordinary routine of banking business, and when the question of a manager's authority in such a case arises, it is essential to inquire carefully into his position and duties.[14]

The liability of a bank for the acts of its officers is a particular application of the principle developed from *Turquand's* case,[15] but that principle is unlikely to be explored in this context. Indeed, even the kind of question that arose in the two cases here considered is unlikely to arise in modern conditions: a bank may argue, as the bank did in *Woods* v. *Martins Bank Ltd.*,[16] that an action is outside the scope of the bank's business, but it would be reluctant to disclaim responsibility for an action by one of its officers merely on the grounds that it was outside the scope of his authority. No such claim appears to have been made in *Selangor United Rubber Estates Ltd.* v. *Cradock*.[17]

[12] At p. 265.
[13] (1879) 4 App. Cas. 270.
[14] At p. 289.
[15] *Ante*, p. 185.
[16] *Ante*, p. 299.
[17] *Ante*, p. 47.

APPENDIX

Notes on cases reported since the preparation of this edition

Consideration for a cheque

The facts of *Hasan* v. *Willson* [1] are both complicated and picturesque. Here we need note merely that the plaintiff sued the defendant on a dishonoured cheque for £50,000 on Lloyds Bank, Solihull. The cheque, payable to the plaintiff, had been obtained by fraud by one Smith, who owed the plaintiff this sum. Smith gave the defendant, by way of consideration, a cheque drawn on a company with which he said he was associated. That cheque was dishonoured on presentation, whereupon the defendant stopped payment of his cheque. When the present action was brought he pleaded, *inter alia*, that the consideration for his cheque had wholly failed.

Goff J. held that the company's cheque would have been proper consideration if Smith had been the plaintiff's agent, and that consideration had clearly failed when the cheque was dishonoured. But the plaintiff had said that Smith was not his agent, and had argued that the consideration for the cheque was Smith's debt to him. Section 21 (i) (*b*) of the Bills of Exchange Act provides that an antecedent debt can be good consideration for a bill or cheque; but his Lordship held that the antecedent debt of the sub-section has to be that of the drawer of the instrument. So on the plaintiff's argument there was no consideration, and the defendant was entitled to refuse payment.

Performance bonds

The facts of *R. D. Harbottle (Mercantile) Ltd.* v. *National Westminster Bank Ltd.*[2] and *Edward Owen Engineering Ltd.* v. *Barclays Bank International Ltd.*[3] are similar, and the two cases appear to represent the first appearance in the law reports of what Lord Denning, in the second case, called " a new creature "—the performance bond or performance guarantee, already well known to bankers.

In each case the English bank, the first defendants, at the request of their customers, the plaintiffs, had guaranteed to a bank or banks in the Middle East, joined as second defendants, a percentage of the price involved in a contract between the plaintiffs and a company banking with the Middle East bank; and this latter bank had

[1] [1977] 1 Lloyd's Rep. 431.
[2] [1977] 2 All E.R. 862.
[3] *The Times*, July 20, 1977.

guaranteed the amount to their customers. In each case the guarantee was unqualified and absolute; but in each case, after dispute between the contracting parties, the plaintiffs sought to prevent payment under the guarantee.

In both cases Kerr J. refused the plaintiffs the remedy they sought, and in the second case, the plaintiffs having appealed, the Court of Appeal upheld his ruling. Lord Denning said of the " new creature ":

> It is very like a letter of credit. It has long been settled that banks must honour letters of credit: *Hamzeh Malas & Sons* v. *British Imex Industries Ltd.*[4] If the documents are in order letters of credit have to be honoured leaving disputes between buyers and sellers to be settled in court.

The sellers here had argued that the bond had been given for their default, and that they had not been in default. That did not affect the issue:

> Banks as between one another are not concerned with relations between buyers and sellers. Banks have to honour their bond, honour their word to one another. When Barclays gave the bond to pay on demand it was virtually a promise to pay on demand in reliance upon the honour of those concerned. There was no need to inquire into the validity of the buyers' claim. Unless the banks have knowledge of fraud they must honour their bond. . . . It is only in exceptional circumstances that the courts will interfere with irrevocable obligations assumed by banks, which are the life blood of international commerce.

It is to be noted that Lord Denning appeared to assume that, as with documentary credits, knowledge of fraud might free the bank from the obligation to pay; he had earlier referred to *Sztejn* v. *J. Henry Schroder Banking Corporation*[5] and the effect of fraud under a documentary credit.

Government agencies and the documentary credit

In *Trendtex Trading Corporation* v. *Central Bank of Nigeria*[6] the plaintiffs had supplied cement to Nigeria at a time when there had been a substantial over-ordering of cement, and the government had imposed exchange control and ordered the Central Bank to refuse payment for orders not newly authorised. Payment was due to the plaintiffs under an irrevocable letter of credit, and when they brought this action the Central Bank pleaded sovereign immunity: they claimed that as a department of the Nigerian Government

---

[4] *Ante*, p. 218.
[5] *Ante*, p. 219.
[6] [1977] 1 All E.R. 881.

they were protected by the rule that no sovereign state can be sued in the English courts without its consent and against its will. Donaldson J. accepted this argument, and Trendtex appealed.

The Court of Appeal allowed the appeal on two grounds. The first was that the evidence had not satisfied them that the Central Bank was in fact a department of government, Stephenson L.J. remarking that English courts should be careful not to extend sovereign immunity to bodies not entitled to it.

The second ground for the Court's decision is of wider significance. Lord Denning said that whereas in the past governments did not indulge in commercial activities, the position now is quite different.

> Now nearly every state engages in commercial activities. It has its department of state, or it creates new legal entities, which go into the world's market places. So many countries have replaced a rule of absolute immunity by a doctrine of restrictive immunity, which gives immunity to acts of a governmental nature but not to acts of a commercial nature.

He cited as examples the United States, Belgium, Holland and West Germany, and said that England should not be left behind. Thus even if the Central Bank was indeed a department of government, it could not claim immunity.

His brethren agreed with him, although Stephenson L.J. considered that the adoption of restrictive immunity, although "consonant with justice," was properly a matter for the House of Lords or Parliament.

The decision in the *Trendtex* case is subject, as this book goes to press, to appeal to the House of Lords. In the meantime the Court of Appeal has been concerned with another case of government trading. In *C. Czarnikow Ltd.* v. *Centrala Handlu Zagranicznego Rolimpex* [7] it was the English plaintiffs who sought to establish that the defendants were an arm of government, and the foreign defendants who denied it. The plaintiffs had contracted to buy sugar beet from the defendants, the trading organisation that handled all sugar exports from Poland. The contract included a clause excusing from liability any failure resulting from *force majeure*. In the event a serious short-fall in the Polish sugar beet crop caused the government to ban all exports, and the defendants informed the plaintiffs that they could not make the delivery contracted for, citing the *force majeure* clause.

Losing their case at arbitration and before Kerr J. the plaintiffs appealed, and the Court of Appeal also found against them. The *force majeure* clause can cause difficulty when, Lord Denning said:

---

[7] *The Times*, May 31, 1977.

a government itself is a party, either by itself or by one of its departments. In such a case it can be argued that the " seller " is the government; that no " governmental intervention " is beyond the seller's control because the seller, being the government, can always exercise control over its own intervention.

But here the Court held that the defendant organisation was not an arm of government, but an independent organisation, and so was entitled to the benefit of the *force majeure* clause.

In this case also leave was given to appeal to the House of Lords.

INDEX